# Avenger
# Owners
# Workshop
# Manual

## John Fowler

**Models covered:**
All versions of Hillman/Chrysler/Talbot Avenger, Saloon and Estate;
1248, 1295, 1498 and 1598 cc

*Also covers Plymouth Cricket as marketed in USA*
*Does not fully cover Tiger models*

**ISBN 0 85010 058 6**

Printed in England (037-4K4)

**HAYNES PUBLISHING GROUP**
**SPARKFORD YEOVIL SOMERSET BA22 7JJ ENGLAND**
*distributed in the USA by*
**HAYNES PUBLICATIONS INC**
**861 LAWRENCE DRIVE**
**NEWBURY PARK**
**CALIFORNIA 91320**
**USA**

# Acknowledgements

Thanks are due to the Talbot Motor Company Ltd for the supply of technical information, and to the Champion Sparking Plug Company who supplied the illustrations showing the various spark plug conditions. Special thanks are due to all the people at Sparkford who helped in the production of this manual.

# About this manual

## Its aim

The aim of this manual is to help you get the best value from your car. It can do so in several ways. It can help you decide what work must be done (even should you choose to get it done by a garage), provide information on routine maintenance and servicing, and give a logical course of action and diagnosis when random faults occur. However, it is hoped that you will use the manual by tackling the work yourself. On simpler jobs it may even be quicker than booking the car into a garage and going there twice to leave and collect it. Perhaps most important, a lot of money can be saved by avoiding the costs the garage must charge to cover its labour and overheads.

The manual has drawings and descriptions to show the function of the various components so that their layout can be understood. Then the tasks are described and photographed in a step-by-step sequence so that even a novice can do the work.

## Its arrangement

The manual is divided into thirteen Chapters, each covering a logical sub-division of the vehicle. The Chapters are each divided into Sections, numbered with single figures, eg 5; and the Sections into paragraphs (or sub-sections) with decimal numbers following on from the Section they are in, eg 5.1, 5.2, 5.3 etc.

It is freely illustrated, especially in those parts where there is a detailed sequence of operations to be carried out. There are two forms of illustration; figures and photographs. The figures are numbered in sequence with decimal numbers, according to their position in the Chapter – eg Fig. 6.4 is the fourth drawing/illustration in Chapter 6. Photographs carry the same number (either individually or in related groups) as the Section or sub-section to which they relate.

There is an alphabetical index at the back of the manual as well as a contents list at the front. Each Chapter is also preceded by its own individual contents list.

References to the 'left' or 'right' of the vehicle are in the sense of a person in the driver's seat facing forwards.

Unless otherwise stated, nuts and bolts are removed by turning anti-clockwise, and tightened by turning clockwise.

Vehicle manufacturers continually make changes to specifications and recommendations, and these, when notified, are incorporated into our manuals at the earliest opportunity.

**Whilst every care is taken to ensure that the information in this manual is correct, no liability can be accepted by the authors or publishers for loss, damage or injury caused by any errors in, or omissions from, the information given.**

# Introduction to the Avenger

Since its announcement in the late 1960s, the Avenger has remained essentially unchanged in basic design and construction. Estate car and two-door versions have, however, been introduced, and there have been a number of detailed changes to mechanical and bodyframe components.

In late 1973 all models were equipped with larger capacity engines; the 1250 cc engine was increased to 1300 cc and the 1500 cc engine to 1600 cc. In the same year an eight-fuse electrical system was introduced which gives extra protection for the lighting circuits.

The Hillman marque name was relinquished in September 1976, at which time all new models in the Avenger range were produced under the Chrysler badge. These 1977 models were equipped with a redesigned body and interior based on the original shape, and the engines were modified to give greater economy and torque.

In 1979 the marque name was yet again changed, this time Avengers being marketed under the Talbot badge.

Perhaps one of the most significant introductions has been the use of a thermo-controlled electric cooling fan which has increased engine output, reduced engine noise, and led to a quicker warm-up period with resulting fuel economies.

The Plymouth Cricket is the North American version of the Avenger. Two models were distributed, the Cricket and the Cricket SE, the latter being a de-luxe version incorporating a more lavish body specification.

# Contents

Hillman Avenger four-door saloon

Hillman Avenger two-door saloon

Chrysler Avenger estate

Chrysler Avenger four-door saloon

# Jacking and Towing

Jacking points are built into the body stiffening members behind each front wheel arch, and in front of each rear wheel arch. Ensure correct location of the jack in the appropriate points, and raise the vehicle by turning the jack handle.

Do not under any circumstances work under the vehicle when supported only on the jack. Always use stands. If a trolley jack is employed, do not allow it to lift under the engine sump, or under the rear axle cover plate, where a serious oil leak can be caused if the plate is damaged.

The maximum towing load for the 1250/1300 models is 13 cwt (661 kg), and for the 1500/1600 models 15 cwt (762 kg). The eyes in the bumper may be used for this purpose.

A vehicle with automatic transmission may be towed, with the engine switched off and 'N' selected, up to a maximum distance of 25 miles (40 km) at speeds below 30 mph (48 kph), but first, add 2 pints (1.8 litre) of automatic transmission fluid in addition to the normal quantity. Note that if the transmission is defective, either the propeller shaft must be removed (seal off the extension housing) or the vehicle must be towed with the rear wheels raised.

# General dimensions and weights

**Kerb weights***

| | |
|---|---|
| Saloon, manual | 1900 lb (862 kg) |
| Saloon, automatic | 1950 lb (885 kg) |
| Estate, manual | 2050 lb (930 kg) |
| Estate, automatic | 2110 lb (957 kg) |

**Dimensions**

| | |
|---|---|
| Overall length, saloon | 13ft 5¼ in (409 cm) |
| Overall length, estate | 13ft 9½ in (419 cm) |
| Overall width | 5ft 2½ in (159 cm) |
| Overall height, unladen | 4ft 8 in (142 cm) |
| Ground clearance, laden | 5½ in (14 cm) |
| Turning circle | 31ft 9 in (9.7 m) |

**Roof rack load** .......... 100 lb (45 kg)

**Towing capacity**

| | |
|---|---|
| 1250/1300 engine | 13 cwt (661 kg) |
| 1500/1600 engine | 15 cwt (762 kg) |

**Vehicle loading, estate cars, including occupants****

| | |
|---|---|
| 1250 Super | 795 lb (361 kg) |
| 1250 De Luxe | 810 lb (367 kg) |
| 1500 Super, manual | 1036 lb (470 kg) |
| 1500 De Luxe, manual | 1058 lb (480 kg) |
| 1500 Super, automatic | 992 lb (450 kg) |
| 1500 De Luxe, automatic | 1014 lbs (460 kg) |

\* These are nominal, and vary with different versions
\*\* Provided that the following maximum permissible weights are not exceeded

| | Front axle weight | Rear axle weight | Gross vehicle weight |
|---|---|---|---|
| 1250/1300 | 1370 lb (621 kg) | 1620 lb (735 kg) | 2850 lb (1293 kg) |
| 1500/1600 | 1370 lb (621 kg) | 1830 lb (830 kg) | 3110 lb (1411 kg) |

# Buying spare parts
# and vehicle identification numbers

## Buying spare parts

Spare parts are available from many sources, for example: Talbot dealers, other garages and accessory shops, and motor factors. Our advice regarding spare part sources is as follows:

*Officially appointed Talbot garages* – This is the best source of parts which are peculiar to your car and are otherwise not generally available (eg complete cylinder heads, internal gearbox components, badges, interior trim etc). It is also the only place at which you should have repairs carried out if your car is still under warranty – non-Talbot components may invalidate the warranty. To be sure of obtaining the correct parts it will always be necessary to give the storeman your car's vehicle identification number, and if possible, to take the old part along for positive identification. It obviously makes good sense to go straight to the specialists on your car for this type of part for they are best equipped to supply you.

*Other garages and accessory shops* – These are often very good places to buy materials and components needed for the maintenance of your car (eg spark plugs, bulbs, fanbelts, oils and greases, filler paste etc). They also sell general accessories, usually have convenient opening hours, charge reasonable prices and can often be found not far from home.

*Motor factors* – Good factors will stock all the more important components which wear out relatively quickly (eg clutch components, pistons, valves, exhaust systems, brake cylinders/pipes/hoses/seals/shoes and pads etc). Motor factors will often provide new or reconditioned components on a part exchange basis – this can save a considerable amount of money.

## Vehicle identification numbers

Modifications are a continuous and unpublicised process carried out by the vehicle manufacturers, so accept the advice of the parts storeman when purchasing a component. Spare parts lists and manuals are compiled upon a numerical basis and individual vehicle numbers are essential to the supply of the correct component.

*The identification plate* is attached to the bonnet lock platform, and gives the serial number, service code, paint code and trim code.

*The body number* is also fixed to the bonnet lock platform.

*The engine number,* on earlier models, is to be found on the engine block next to the distributor on the camshaft tunnel. On later models, this will be found on the engine block immediately above the fuel pump.

## Series numbers

Throughout this manual references will be found to model series numbers. Until 1980, each model series was identified by number, eg Series 4 denotes 1974 models, Series 5 denotes 1975 models, etc. Starting with 1980 models, each series was identified by letter, Series A and B denoting 1980 and 1981 models respectively.

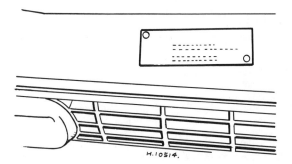

**Identification plate on bonnet lock platform**

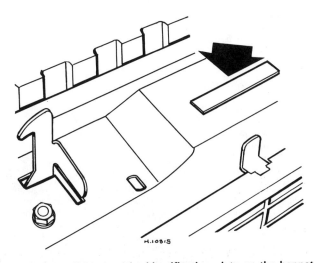

**Body number, adjacent to the identification plate on the bonnet lock platform**

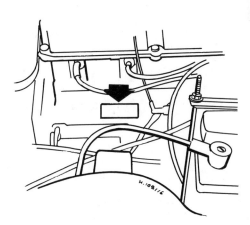

**Engine number, adjacent to the distributor on the camshaft tunnel (early models)**

# Tools and working facilities

## Introduction

A selection of good tools is a fundamental requirement for anyone contemplating the maintenance and repair of a motor vehicle. For the owner who does not possess any, their purchase will prove a considerable expense, offsetting some of the savings made by doing-it-yourself. However, provided that the tools purchased are of good quality, they will last for many years and prove an extremely worthwhile investment.

To help the average owner to decide which tools are needed to carry out the various tasks detailed in this manual, we have compiled three lists of tools under the following headings: *Maintenance and minor repair, Repair and overhaul,* and *Special.* The newcomer to practical mechanics should start off with the *Maintenance and minor repair* tool kit and confine himself to the simpler jobs around the vehicle. Then, as his confidence and experience grow, he can under-take more difficult tasks, buying extra tools as, and when, they are needed. In this way, a *Maintenance and minor repair* tool kit can be built-up into a *Repair and overhaul* tool kit over a considerable period of time without any major cash outlays. The experienced do-it-yourselfer will have a tool kit good enough for most repair and overhaul procedures and will add tools from the *Special* category when he feels the expense is justified by the amount of use these tools will be put to.

It is obviously not possible to cover the subject of tools fully here. For those who wish to learn more about tools and their use there is a book entitled *How to Choose and Use Car Tools* available from the publishers of this manual.

## Maintenance and minor repair tool kit

The tools given in this list should be considered as a minimum requirement if routine maintenance, servicing and minor repair oper-ations are to be undertaken. We recommend the purchase of combin-ation spanners (ring one end, open-ended the other); although more expensive than open-ended ones, they do give the advantages of both types of spanner.

*Combination spanners - $\frac{7}{16}$, $\frac{1}{2}$, $\frac{9}{16}$, $\frac{5}{8}$, $\frac{11}{16}$, $\frac{3}{4}$ in AF*
*Adjustable spanner - 9 inch*
*Spark plug spanner (with rubber insert)*
*Spark plug gap adjustment tool*
*Set of feeler gauges*
*Brake bleed nipple spanner*
*Screwdriver - 4 in long x $\frac{1}{4}$ in dia (flat blade)*
*Screwdriver - 4 in long x $\frac{1}{4}$ in dia (cross blade)*
*Combination pliers - 6 inch*
*Hacksaw, junior*
*Tyre pump*
*Tyre pressure gauge*
*Oil can*
*Fine emery cloth (1 sheet)*
*Wire brush (small)*
*Funnel (medium size)*

## Repair and overhaul tool kit

These tools are virtually essential for anyone undertaking any major repairs to a motor vehicle, and are additional to those given in the *Maintenance and minor repair* list. Included in this list is a comprehensive set of sockets. Although these are expensive they will be found invaluable as they are so versatile - particularly if various drives are included in the set. We recommend the $\frac{1}{2}$ in square-drive type, as this can be used with most proprietary torque spanners. If you cannot afford a socket set, even bought piecemeal, then inexpensive tubular box wrenches are a useful alternative.

The tools in this list will occasionally need to be supplemented by tools from the *Special* list.

*Sockets (or box spanners) to cover range in previous list*
*Reversible ratchet drive (for use with sockets)*
*Extension piece, 10 inch (for use with sockets)*
*Universal joint (for use with sockets)*
*Torque wrench (for use with sockets)*
*Mole wrench - 8 inch*
*Ball pein hammer*
*Soft-faced hammer, plastic or rubber*
*Screwdriver - 6 in long x $\frac{5}{16}$ in dia (flat blade)*
*Screwdriver - 2 in long x $\frac{5}{16}$ in square (flat blade)*
*Screwdriver - $1\frac{1}{2}$ in long x $\frac{1}{4}$ in dia (cross blade)*
*Screwdriver - 3 in long x $\frac{1}{8}$ in dia (electricians)*
*Pliers - electricians side cutters*
*Pliers - needle nosed*
*Pliers - circlip (internal and external)*
*Cold chisel - $\frac{1}{2}$ inch*
*Scriber*
*Scraper*
*Centre punch*
*Pin punch*
*Hacksaw*
*Valve grinding tool*
*Steel rule/straight edge*
*Allen keys*
*Selection of files*
*Wire brush (large)*
*Axle-stands*
*Jack (strong scissor or hydraulic type)*

## Special tools

The tools in this list are those which are not used regularly, are expensive to buy, or which need to be used in accordance with their manufacturers' instructions. Unless relatively difficult mechanical jobs are undertaken frequently, it will not be economic to buy many of these tools. Where this is the case, you could consider clubbing together with friends (or a motorists' club) to make a joint purchase, or borrowing the tools against a deposit from a local garage or tool hire specialist.

The following list contains only those tools and instruments freely available to the public, and not those special tools produced by the vehicle manufacturer specifically for its dealer network. You will find occasional references to these manufacturers' special tools in the text of this manual. Generally, an alternative method of doing the job without the vehicle manufacturers' special tool is given. However, sometimes, there is no alternative to using them. Where this is the case and the relevant tool cannot be bought or borrowed you will have to entrust the work to a franchised garage.

*Valve spring compressor (where applicable)*
*Piston ring compressor*
*Balljoint separator*
*Universal hub/bearing puller*
*Impact screwdriver*
*Micrometer and/or vernier gauge*
*Dial gauge*
*Stroboscopic timing light*
*Dwell angle meter/tachometer*
*Universal electrical multi-meter*
*Cylinder compression gauge*
*Lifting tackle*
*Trolley jack*
*Light with extension lead*

## Buying tools

For practically all tools, a tool dealer is the best source since he will have a very comprehensive range compared with the average garage or accessory shop. Having said that, accessory shops often offer excellent quality tools at discount prices, so it pays to shop around.

Remember, you don't have to buy the most expensive items on the shelf, but it is always advisable to steer clear of the very cheap tools. There are plenty of good tools around at reasonable prices, so ask the proprietor or manager of the shop for advice before making a purchase.

## Care and maintenance of tools

Having purchased a reasonable tool kit, it is necessary to keep the tools in a clean serviceable condition. After use, always wipe off any dirt, grease and metal particles using a clean, dry cloth, before putting the tools away. Never leave them lying around after they have been used. A simple tool rack on the garage or workshop wall, for items such as screwdrivers and pliers is a good idea. Store all normal spanners and sockets in a metal box. Any measuring instruments, gauges, meters, etc, must be carefully stored where they cannot be damaged or become rusty.

Take a little care when tools are used. Hammer heads inevitably become marked and screwdrivers lose the keen edge on their blades from time to time. A little timely attention with emery cloth or a file will soon restore items like this to a good serviceable finish.

## Working facilities

Not to be forgotten when discussing tools, is the workshop itself. If anything more than routine maintenance is to be carried out, some form of suitable working area becomes essential.

It is appreciated that many an owner mechanic is forced by circumstances to remove an engine or similar item, without the benefit of a garage or workshop. Having done this, any repairs should always be done under the cover of a roof.

Wherever possible, any dismantling should be done on a clean flat workbench or table at a suitable working height.

Any workbench needs a vice: one with a jaw opening of 4 in (100 mm) is suitable for most jobs. As mentioned previously, some clean dry storage space is also required for tools, as well as the lubricants, cleaning fluids, touch-up paints and so on which become necessary.

Another item which may be required, and which has a much more general usage, is an electric drill with a chuck capacity of at least $\frac{5}{16}$ in (8 mm). This, together with a good range of twist drills, is virtually essential for fitting accessories such as wing mirrors and reversing lights.

Last, but not least, always keep a supply of old newspapers and clean, lint-free rags available, and try to keep any working area as clean as possible.

*Spanner jaw gap comparison table*

| Jaw gap (in) | Spanner size |
|---|---|
| 0.250 | $\frac{1}{4}$ in AF |
| 0.276 | 7 mm |
| 0.313 | $\frac{5}{16}$ in AF |
| 0.315 | 8 mm |
| 0.344 | $\frac{11}{32}$ in AF; $\frac{1}{8}$ in Whitworth |
| 0.354 | 9 mm |
| 0.375 | $\frac{3}{8}$ in AF |
| 0.394 | 10 mm |
| 0.433 | 11 mm |
| 0.438 | $\frac{7}{16}$ in AF |
| 0.445 | $\frac{3}{16}$ in Whitworth; $\frac{1}{4}$ in BSF |
| 0.472 | 12 mm |
| 0.500 | $\frac{1}{2}$ in AF |
| 0.512 | 13 mm |
| 0.525 | $\frac{1}{4}$ in Whitworth; $\frac{5}{16}$ in BSF |
| 0.551 | 14 mm |
| 0.563 | $\frac{9}{16}$ in AF |
| 0.591 | 15 mm |
| 0.600 | $\frac{5}{16}$ in Whitworth; $\frac{3}{8}$ in BSF |
| 0.625 | $\frac{5}{8}$ in AF |
| 0.630 | 16 mm |
| 0.669 | 17 mm |
| 0.686 | $\frac{11}{16}$ in AF |
| 0.709 | 18 mm |
| 0.710 | $\frac{3}{8}$ in Whitworth, $\frac{7}{16}$ in BSF |
| 0.748 | 19 mm |
| 0.750 | $\frac{3}{4}$ in AF |
| 0.813 | $\frac{13}{16}$ in AF |
| 0.820 | $\frac{7}{16}$ in Whitworth; $\frac{1}{2}$ in BSF |
| 0.866 | 22 mm |
| 0.875 | $\frac{7}{8}$ in AF |
| 0.920 | $\frac{1}{2}$ in Whitworth; $\frac{9}{16}$ in BSF |
| 0.938 | $\frac{15}{16}$ in AF |
| 0.945 | 24 mm |
| 1.000 | 1 in AF |
| 1.010 | $\frac{9}{16}$ in Whitworth; $\frac{5}{8}$ in BSF |
| 1.024 | 26 mm |
| 1.063 | $1\frac{1}{16}$ in AF; 27 mm |
| 1.100 | $\frac{5}{8}$ in Whitworth; $\frac{11}{16}$ in BSF |
| 1.125 | $1\frac{1}{8}$ in AF |
| 1.181 | 30 mm |
| 1.200 | $\frac{11}{16}$ in Whitworth; $\frac{3}{4}$ in BSF |
| 1.250 | $1\frac{1}{4}$ in AF |
| 1.260 | 32 mm |
| 1.300 | $\frac{3}{4}$ in Whitworth; $\frac{7}{8}$ in BSF |
| 1.313 | $1\frac{5}{16}$ in AF |
| 1.390 | $\frac{13}{16}$ in Whitworth; $\frac{15}{16}$ in BSF |
| 1.417 | 36 mm |
| 1.438 | $1\frac{7}{16}$ in AF |
| 1.480 | $\frac{7}{8}$ in Whitworth; 1 in BSF |
| 1.500 | $1\frac{1}{2}$ in AF |
| 1.575 | 40 mm; $\frac{15}{16}$ in Whitworth |
| 1.614 | 41 mm |
| 1.625 | $1\frac{5}{8}$ in AF |
| 1.670 | 1 in Whitworth; $1\frac{1}{8}$ in BSF |
| 1.688 | $1\frac{11}{16}$ in AF |
| 1.811 | 46 mm |
| 1.813 | $1\frac{13}{16}$ in AF |
| 1.860 | $1\frac{1}{8}$ in Whitworth; $1\frac{1}{4}$ in BSF |
| 1.875 | $1\frac{7}{8}$ in AF |
| 1.969 | 50 mm |
| 2.000 | 2 in AF |
| 2.050 | $1\frac{1}{4}$ in Whitworth; $1\frac{3}{8}$ in BSF |
| 2.165 | 55 mm |
| 2.362 | 60 mm |

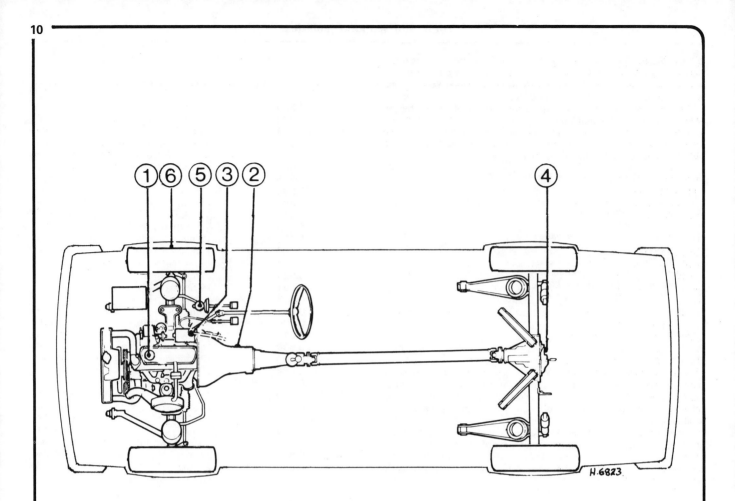

H.6823

# Recommended lubricants and fluids

| Component or system | Lubricant type or specification |
| --- | --- |
| Engine (1) | 20W/50 multigrade engine oil |
| Manual gearbox (2) | 20W/50 multigrade engine oil |
| Automatic transmission (3) | Non-Dexron type automatic transmission fluid |
| Rear axle (4) | SAE 90EP hypoid gear oil |
| Brake fluid reservoir (5) | SAE J1703 (DOT 3 and 4) hydraulic fluid |
| Front wheel bearings (6) | General purpose lithium-based grease |

Note: *The above are general recommendations only. Lubrication requirements vary from territory to territory and depend on vehicle usage. If in doubt, consult the operator's handbook supplied with the vehicle, or your nearest dealer.*

# Safety first!

Professional motor mechanics are trained in safe working procedures. However enthusiastic you may be about getting on with the job in hand, do take the time to ensure that your safety is not put at risk. A moment's lack of attention can result in an accident, as can failure to observe certain elementary precautions.

There will always be new ways of having accidents, and the following points do not pretend to be a comprehensive list of all dangers; they are intended rather to make you aware of the risks and to encourage a safety-conscious approach to all work you carry out on your vehicle.

## Essential DOs and DON'Ts

**DON'T** rely on a single jack when working underneath the vehicle. Always use reliable additional means of support, such as axle stands, securely placed under a part of the vehicle that you know will not give way.

**DON'T** attempt to loosen or tighten high-torque nuts (e.g. wheel hub nuts) while the vehicle is on a jack; it may be pulled off.

**DON'T** start the engine without first ascertaining that the transmission is in neutral (or 'Park' where applicable) and the parking brake applied.

**DON'T** suddenly remove the filler cap from a hot cooling system – cover it with a cloth and release the pressure gradually first, or you may get scalded by escaping coolant.

**DON'T** attempt to drain oil until you are sure it has cooled sufficiently to avoid scalding you.

**DON'T** grasp any part of the engine, exhaust or catalytic converter without first ascertaining that it is sufficiently cool to avoid burning you.

**DON'T** allow brake fluid or antifreeze to contact vehicle paintwork.

**DON'T** syphon toxic liquids such as fuel, brake fluid or antifreeze by mouth, or allow them to remain on your skin.

**DON'T** inhale dust – it may be injurious to health (see *Asbestos* below).

**DON'T** allow any spilt oil or grease to remain on the floor – wipe it up straight away, before someone slips on it.

**DON'T** use ill-fitting spanners or other tools which may slip and cause injury.

**DON'T** attempt to lift a heavy component which may be beyond your capability – get assistance.

**DON'T** rush to finish a job, or take unverified short cuts.

**DON'T** allow children or animals in or around an unattended vehicle.

**DO** wear eye protection when using power tools such as drill, sander, bench grinder etc, and when working under the vehicle.

**DO** use a barrier cream on your hands prior to undertaking dirty jobs – it will protect your skin from infection as well as making the dirt easier to remove afterwards; but make sure your hands aren't left slippery. Note that long-term contact with used engine oil can be a health hazard.

**DO** keep loose clothing (cuffs, tie etc) and long hair well out of the way of moving mechanical parts.

**DO** remove rings, wristwatch etc, before working on the vehicle – especially the electrical system.

**DO** ensure that any lifting tackle used has a safe working load rating adequate for the job.

**DO** keep your work area tidy – it is only too easy to fall over articles left lying around.

**DO** get someone to check periodically that all is well, when working alone on the vehicle.

**DO** carry out work in a logical sequence and check that everything is correctly assembled and tightened afterwards.

**DO** remember that your vehicle's safety affects that of yourself and others. If in doubt on any point, get specialist advice.

**IF,** in spite of following these precautions, you are unfortunate enough to injure yourself, seek medical attention as soon as possible.

## Asbestos

Certain friction, insulating, sealing, and other products – such as brake linings, brake bands, clutch linings, torque converters, gaskets, etc – contain asbestos. *Extreme care must be taken to avoid inhalation of dust from such products since it is hazardous to health.* If in doubt, assume that they *do* contain asbestos.

## Fire

Remember at all times that petrol (gasoline) is highly flammable. Never smoke, or have any kind of naked flame around, when working on the vehicle. But the risk does not end there – a spark caused by an electrical short-circuit, by two metal surfaces contacting each other, by careless use of tools, or even by static electricity built up in your body under certain conditions, can ignite petrol vapour, which in a confined space is highly explosive.

Always disconnect the battery earth (ground) terminal before working on any part of the fuel or electrical system, and never risk spilling fuel on to a hot engine or exhaust.

It is recommended that a fire extinguisher of a type suitable for fuel and electrical fires is kept handy in the garage or workplace at all times. Never try to extinguish a fuel or electrical fire with water.

## Fumes

Certain fumes are highly toxic and can quickly cause unconsciousness and even death if inhaled to any extent. Petrol (gasoline) vapour comes into this category, as do the vapours from certain solvents such as trichloroethylene. Any draining or pouring of such volatile fluids should be done in a well ventilated area.

When using cleaning fluids and solvents, read the instructions carefully. Never use materials from unmarked containers – they may give off poisonous vapours.

Never run the engine of a motor vehicle in an enclosed space such as a garage. Exhaust fumes contain carbon monoxide which is extremely poisonous; if you need to run the engine, always do so in the open air or at least have the rear of the vehicle outside the workplace.

If you are fortunate enough to have the use of an inspection pit, never drain or pour petrol, and never run the engine, while the vehicle is standing over it; the fumes, being heavier than air, will concentrate in the pit with possibly lethal results.

## The battery

Never cause a spark, or allow a naked light, near the vehicle's battery. It will normally be giving off a certain amount of hydrogen gas, which is highly explosive.

Always disconnect the battery earth (ground) terminal before working on the fuel or electrical systems.

If possible, loosen the filler plugs or cover when charging the battery from an external source. Do not charge at an excessive rate or the battery may burst.

Take care when topping up and when carrying the battery. The acid electrolyte, even when diluted, is very corrosive and should not be allowed to contact the eyes or skin.

If you ever need to prepare electrolyte yourself, always add the acid slowly to the water, and never the other way round. Protect against splashes by wearing rubber gloves and goggles.

When jump starting a car using a booster battery, for negative earth (ground) vehicles, connect the jump leads in the following sequence: First connect one jump lead between the positive (+) terminals of the two batteries. Then connect the other jump lead first to the negative (–) terminal of the booster battery, and then to a good earthing (ground) point on the vehicle to be started, at least 18 in (45 cm) from the battery if possible. Ensure that hands and jump leads are clear of any moving parts, and that the two vehicles do not touch. Disconnect the leads in the reverse order.

## Mains electricity

When using an electric power tool, inspection light etc, which works from the mains, always ensure that the appliance is correctly connected to its plug and that, where necessary, it is properly earthed (grounded). Do not use such appliances in damp conditions and, again, beware of creating a spark or applying excessive heat in the vicinity of fuel or fuel vapour.

## Ignition HT voltage

A severe electric shock can result from touching certain parts of the ignition system, such as the HT leads, when the engine is running or being cranked, particularly if components are damp or the insulation is defective. Where an electronic ignition system is fitted, the HT voltage is much higher and could prove fatal.

# Routine maintenance

Maintenance is essential for ensuring safety, and desirable for the purpose of getting the best in terms of performance and economy from your car. Over the years the need for periodic lubrication – oiling, greasing and so on – has been drastically reduced if not totally eliminated. This has unfortunately tended to lead some owners to think that because no such action is required, components either no longer exist, or will last forever. This is a serious delusion. It follows, therefore, that the largest initial element of maintenance is visual examination. This may lead to repairs or renewals.

## Every 250 miles (400 km) or weekly, whichever comes first

Check the tyre pressures
Check the tyres for wear or damage
Check the operation of the brakes
Check the operation of the handbrake on a steep incline
Check the operation of all lights, including the direction indicators and stop lights
Check that the screen wipers and washers work properly, topping up the washer reservoir if necessary
Check the level of oil in the sump
Check the level of coolant in the radiator
Check the battery electrolyte level
Check the operation of the horn

## Every 1000 miles (1500 km) or monthly, whichever comes first

Check for free play in the steering
Check the level of fluid in the brake master cylinder reservoir

## Every 5000 miles (7500 km) or six months, whichever comes first

Check all steering linkages, rods, joints and bushes for signs of wear or damage
Check the front wheel hub bearings and adjust if necessary
Check the wheel nuts for tightness
Check the steering rack unit for leaks at the points indicated in the illustration, and for security of the fixing bolts
Check the brake disc pads and drum shoes for wear. Renew if necessary
Check all brake pipes, cylinders and unions for signs of corrosion, dents or chafing. Renew as necessary
Check all brake pipe unions for leaks: do not overtighten unions
Check all suspension nuts, bolts and shackles front and rear and adjust if required
Check the suspension rubber covers and bushes for signs of deterioration
Check the oil level in the rear axle
Drain the sump and refill with correct grade oil
Fit a new oil filter
Top up the carburettor damper(s) with oil

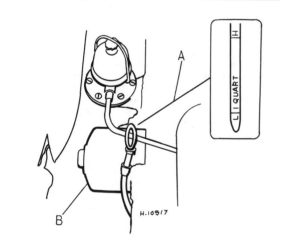

Location of engine oil level dipstick (A) and oil filter (B)

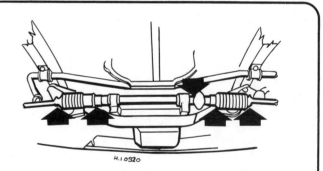

Check for leaks from the steering rack, as indicated by the arrows

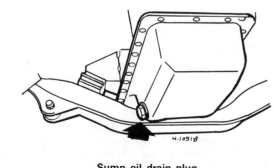

Sump oil drain plug

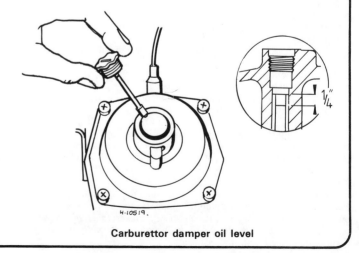

Carburettor damper oil level

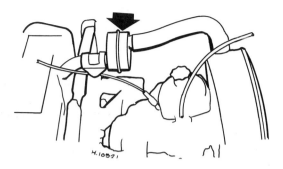

Crankcase ventilation system flame trap

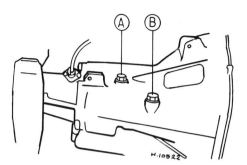

Gearbox oil filler/level plug (A) and drain plug (B)

Clean the flame trap for crankcase ventilation
Check the ignition timing
Check the valve clearances
Check the spark plug gaps. Fit new plugs if necessary
Check the distributor for cleanliness and contact breaker points gap clearance. Fit new points if necessary
Check the fanbelt tension and adjust if necessary. Examine the belt for cracks or fraying
Check and adjust the carburettor idle speed and mixture
Check the clutch release lever free play
Check the oil level in the gearbox
Clear the drain holes on the doors and heater intake box
Inspect the condition of seat belts and anchorages
Lubricate all locks, hinges and catches
Lubricate the distributor
Lubricate the dynamo bearing (where applicable)

**Every 10 000 miles (15 000 km) or twelve months, whichever comes first**

Check the underbody for rust, particularly where the rear suspension is anchored
Check the condition of the bodyframe mounting at the upper end of the front suspension units
Check the suspension dampers for leakage
Clean the fuel pump filter and sediment bowl

Clean the battery terminals and coat with petroleum jelly
Check the battery carrier for signs of acid leakage
Check headlamp alignment
Fit new windscreen wiper blades
Check the exhaust system for leaks and signs of heavy rusting
Check the handbrake pivots, pins and cable
Check the propeller shaft joints and flange bolts
Check the vehicle interior, looking for rust and water leakage
Renew or refit beading and weatherstrips as necessary
Renew the air cleaner element

**Every 15 000 miles (22 500 km) or eighteen months, whichever comes first**

Dismantle, clean and re-pack the front wheel hubs

**Every 30 000 miles (45 000 km) or three years, whichever comes first**

Renew the brake servo filter
Check the handbrake ratchet for wear
Check all rubber parts in the hydraulic system and renew if necessary

# Fault diagnosis

## Introduction

The vehicle owner who does his or her own maintenance according to the recommended schedules should not have to use this section of the manual very often. Modern component reliability is such that, provided those items subject to wear or deterioration are inspected or renewed at the specified intervals, sudden failure is comparatively rare. Faults do not usually just happen as a result of sudden failure, but develop over a period of time. Major mechanical failures in particular are usually preceded by characteristic symptoms over hundreds or even thousands of miles. Those components which do occasionally fail without warning are often small and easily carried in the vehicle.

With any fault finding, the first step is to decide where to begin investigations. Sometimes this is obvious, but on other occasions a little detective work will be necessary. The owner who makes half a dozen haphazard adjustments or replacements may be successful in curing a fault (or its symptoms), but he will be none the wiser if the fault recurs and he may well have spent more time and money than was necessary. A calm and logical approach will be found to be more satisfactory in the long run. Always take into account any warning signs or abnormalities that may have been noticed in the period preceding the fault – power loss, high or low gauge readings, unusual noises or smells, etc – and remember that failure of components such as fuses or spark plugs may only be pointers to some underlying fault.

The pages which follow here are intended to help in cases of failure to start or breakdown on the road. There is also a Fault Diagnosis Section at the end of each Chapter which should be consulted if the preliminary checks prove unfruitful. Whatever the fault, certain basic principles apply. These are as follows:

**Verify the fault.** This is simply a matter of being sure that you know what the symptoms are before starting work. This is particularly important if you are investigating a fault for someone else who may not have described it very accurately.

**Don't overlook the obvious.** For example, if the vehicle won't start, is there petrol in the tank? (Don't take anyone else's word on this particular point, and don't trust the fuel gauge either!) If an electrical fault is indicated, look for loose or broken wires before digging out the test gear.

**Cure the disease, not the symptom.** Substituting a flat battery with a fully charged one will get you off the hard shoulder, but if the underlying cause is not attended to, the new battery will go the same way. Similarly, changing oil-fouled spark plugs for a new set will get you moving again, but remember that the reason for the fouling (if it wasn't simply an incorrect grade of plug) will have to be established and corrected.

**Don't take anything for granted.** Particularly, don't forget that a 'new' component may itself be defective (especially if it's been rattling round in the boot for months), and don't leave components out of a fault diagnosis sequence just because they are new or recently fitted. When you do finally diagnose a difficult fault, you'll probably realise that all the evidence was there from the start.

## Electrical faults

Electrical faults can be more puzzling than straightforward mechanical failures, but they are no less susceptible to logical analysis if the basic principles of operation are understood. Vehicle electrical wiring exists in extremely unfavourable conditions – heat, vibration and chemical attack – and the first things to look for are loose or corroded connections and broken or chafed wires, especially where the wires pass through holes in the bodywork or are subject to vibration.

All metal-bodied vehicles in current production have one pole of the battery 'earthed', ie connected to the vehicle bodywork, and in nearly all modern vehicles it is the negative (–) terminal. The various electrical components – motors, bulb holders etc – are also connected to earth, either by means of a lead or directly by their mountings. Electric current flows through the component and then back to the battery via the bodywork. If the component mounting is loose or corroded, or if a good path back to the battery is not available, the circuit will be incomplete and malfunction will result. The engine and/or gearbox are also earthed by means of flexible metal straps to the body or subframe; if these straps are loose or missing, starter motor, generator and ignition trouble may result.

Assuming the earth return to be satisfactory, electrical faults will be due either to component malfunction or to defects in the current supply. Individual components are dealt with in Chapter 10. If supply wires are broken or cracked internally this results in an open-circuit, and the easiest way to check for this is to bypass the suspect wire temporarily with a length of wire having a crocodile clip or suitable connector at each end. Alternatively, a 12V test lamp can be used to verify the presence of supply voltage at various points along the wire and the break can be thus isolated.

If a bare portion of a live wire touches the bodywork or other earthed metal part, the electricity will take the low-resistance path thus formed back to the battery: this is known as a short-circuit. Hopefully a short-circuit will blow a fuse, but otherwise it may cause burning of the insulation (and possibly further short-circuits) or even a fire. This is why it is inadvisable to bypass persistently blowing fuses with silver foil or wire.

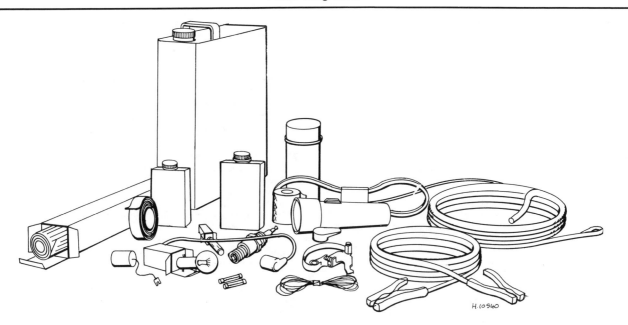

Carrying a few spares may save you a long walk

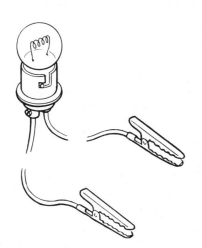

A simple test lamp is useful for investigating electrical faults

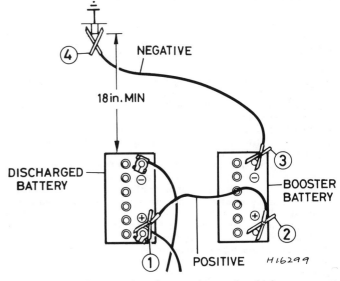

Jump start lead connections for negative earth vehicles – connect leads in order shown

## Spares and tool kit

Most vehicles are supplied only with sufficient tools for wheel changing; the *Maintenance and minor repair* tool kit detailed in *Tools and working facilities,* with the addition of a hammer, is probably sufficient for those repairs that most motorists would consider attempting at the roadside. In addition a few items which can be fitted without too much trouble in the event of a breakdown should be carried. Experience and available space will modify the list below, but the following may save having to call on professional assistance:

*Spark plugs, clean and correctly gapped*
*HT lead and plug cap – long enough to reach the plug furthest from the distributor*
*Distributor rotor, condenser and contact breaker points (as applicable)*
*Drivebelt(s) – emergency type may suffice*
*Spare fuses*
*Set of principal light bulbs*
*Tin of radiator sealer and hose bandage*
*Exhaust bandage*
*Roll of insulating tape*
*Length of soft iron wire*

*Length of electrical flex*
*Torch or inspection lamp (can double as test lamp)*
*Battery jump leads*
*Tow-rope*
*Ignition waterproofing aerosol*
*Litre of engine oil*
*Sealed can of hydraulic fluid*
*Emergency windscreen*
*'Jubilee' clips*
*Tube of filler paste*

If spare fuel is carried, a can designed for the purpose should be used to minimise risks of leakage and collision damage. A first aid kit and a warning triangle, whilst not at present compulsory in the UK, are obviously sensible items to carry in addition to the above.

When touring abroad it may be advisable to carry additional spares which, even if you cannot fit them yourself, could save having to wait while parts are obtained. The items below may be worth considering:

*Clutch and throttle cables (as applicable)*
*Cylinder head gasket*

*Dynamo or alternator brushes (as applicable)*
*Fuel pump repair kit*
*Tyre valve core*

One of the motoring organisations will be able to advise on availability of fuel etc in foreign countries.

## Engine will not start

### Engine fails to turn when starter operated
Flat battery (recharge, use jump leads, or push start)
Battery terminals loose or corroded
Battery earth to body defective
Engine earth strap loose or broken
Starter motor (or solenoid) wiring loose or broken
Automatic transmission selector in wrong position, or inhibitor switch faulty
Ignition/starter switch faulty
Major mechanical failure (seizure)
Starter or solenoid internal fault (see Chapter 10)

### Starter motor turns engine slowly
Partially discharged battery (recharge, use jump leads, or push start)
Battery terminals loose or corroded
Battery earth to body defective
Engine earth strap loose
Starter motor (or solenoid) wiring loose
Starter motor internal fault (see Chapter 10)

### Starter motor spins without turning engine
Flat battery
Starter motor pinion sticking on sleeve
Flywheel gear teeth damaged or worn
Starter motor mounting bolts loose

### Engine turns normally but fails to start
Damp or dirty HT leads and distributor cap (crank engine and check for spark)
Dirty or incorrectly gapped distributor points (if applicable)
No fuel in tank (check for delivery at carburettor)
Excessive choke (hot engine) or insufficient choke (cold engine)
Fouled or incorrectly gapped spark plugs (remove, clean and regap)
Other ignition system fault (see Chapter 4)
Other fuel system fault (see Chapter 3)
Poor compression (see Chapter 1)
Major mechanical failure (eg camshaft drive)

### Engine fires but will not run
Insufficient choke (cold engine)
Air leaks at carburettor or inlet manifold
Fuel starvation (see Chapter 3)
Ballast resistor defective, or other ignition fault (see Chapter 4)

## Engine cuts out and will not restart

### Engine cuts out suddenly – ignition fault
Loose or disconnected LT wires
Wet HT leads or distributor cap (after traversing water splash)
Coil or condenser failure (check for spark)
Other ignition fault (see Chapter 4)

### Engine misfires before cutting out – fuel fault
Fuel tank empty
Fuel pump defective or filter blocked (check for delivery)
Fuel tank filler vent blocked (suction will be evident on releasing cap)
Carburettor needle valve sticking
Carburettor jets blocked (fuel contaminated)
Other fuel system fault (see Chapter 3)

### Engine cuts out – other causes
Serious overheating
Major mechanical failure (eg camshaft drive)

## Engine overheats

### Ignition (no-charge) warning light illuminated
Slack or broken drivebelt – retension or renew (Chapter 2)

### Ignition warning light not illuminated
Coolant loss due to internal or external leakage (see Chapter 2)
Thermostat defective
Low oil level
Brakes binding
Radiator clogged externally or internally
Electric cooling fan not operating correctly (when applicable)
Engine waterways clogged
Ignition timing incorrect or automatic advance malfunctioning
Mixture too weak

**Note:** *Do not add cold water to an overheated engine or damage may result*

## Low engine oil pressure

### Gauge reads low or warning light illuminated with engine running
Oil level low or incorrect grade
Defective gauge or sender unit
Wire to sender unit earthed
Engine overheating
Oil filter clogged or bypass valve defective
Oil pressure relief valve defective
Oil pick-up strainer clogged
Oil pump worn or mountings loose
Worn main or big-end bearings

**Note:** *Low oil pressure in a high-mileage engine at tickover is not necessarily a cause for concern. Sudden pressure loss at speed is far more significant. In any event, check the gauge or warning light sender before condemning the engine.*

## Engine noises

### Pre-ignition (pinking) on acceleration
Incorrect grade of fuel
Ignition timing incorrect
Distributor faulty or worn
Worn or maladjusted carburettor
Excessive carbon build-up in engine

### Whistling or wheezing noises
Leaking vacuum hose
Leaking carburettor or manifold gasket
Blowing head gasket

### Tapping or rattling
Incorrect valve clearances
Worn valve gear
Worn timing chain
Broken piston ring (ticking noise)

### Knocking or thumping
Unintentional mechanical contact (eg fan blades)
Worn fanbelt
Peripheral component fault (generator, water pump etc)
Worn big-end bearings (regular heavy knocking, perhaps less under load)
Worn main bearings (rumbling and knocking, perhaps worsening under load)
Piston slap (most noticeable when cold)

# Chapter 1 Engine

**Contents**

**Specifications**

*1250 single carburettor models*

## Engine – general

| | |
|---|---|
| Type | 4 cylinder in-line ohv |
| Bore | 78.6 mm (3.094 in) |
| Stroke | 64.3 mm (2.53 in) |
| Capacity | 1248 cc (76.16 cu in) |
| Compression ratio | 9.2 : 1 |
| Compression pressure | 170 to 180 lbf/in$^2$ (11.95 to 12.66 kgf/cm$^2$) |
| Firing order | 1-3-4-2 |
| Location of No 1 cylinder | Front of engine next to radiator |

## Cylinder block

| | |
|---|---|
| Type | Cast iron – cylinders and water jackets integrally cast |
| Overbore sizes | 0.005 in, 0.010 in, 0.020 in, 0.030 in (max) |

## Cylinder head

| | |
|---|---|
| Type | Cast iron with vertical valves |
| Identification | None |
| Gasket identification | *SB* on gasket |
| Volume of combustion chamber | 13.7 to 16.2 cc |
| Max variation in volume between combustion chambers | $\pm$ 0.60 cc |

## Crankshaft and main bearings

| | |
|---|---|
| Bearing type | Renewable shell |
| No of bearings | 5 |
| Bearing material | Steel shell, aluminium/tin lined |
| Crankshaft endfloat | 0.002 to 0.008 in (0.05 to 0.20 mm) |
| Main journal diameter A | 2.1245 to 2.1252 in (53.962 to 53.980 mm) |
| Main journal diameter B | 2.1145 to 2.1152 in (53.708 to 53.726 mm) |
| Maximum undersize on regrind | 0.040 in (1.01 mm) |
| Crankshaft throw | 1.264 to 1.266 in (32.10 to 32.15 mm) |

## Connecting rods, big and small-end bearings

| | |
|---|---|
| Bearing type | Renewable shell |
| Bearing material | Steel shell, aluminium/tin lined |
| Connecting rod endfloat on crankpin | 0.007 to 0.012 in (0.177 to 0.304 mm) |
| Connecting rod type | H-section |
| Small-end bush bore: | |
| High grade | 0.9378 to 0.9379 in (23.820 to 23.823 mm) |
| Medium grade | 0.9377 to 0.9378 in (23.818 to 23.820 mm) |
| Low grade | 0.9376 to 0.9377 in (23.815 to 23.818 mm) |

## Gudgeon pin

| | |
|---|---|
| Type | Fully floating, retained by circlips |
| Length | 2.621 to 2.625 in (66.57 to 66.67 mm) |
| Diameter (check colour inside bore of gudgeon pin): | |
| Standard – blue | 0.9377 to 0.9378 in (23.818 to 23.820 mm) |
| High – white | 0.9376 to 0.9377 in (23.815 to 23.818 mm) |
| Medium – green | 0.9375 to 0.9376 in (23.812 to 23.815 mm) |
| Low – yellow | 0.9374 to 0.9375 in (23.810 to 23.812 mm) |
| Fit | Thumb push fit at normal working temperature (68°F or 20°C) |

## Pistons and rings

| | |
|---|---|
| Piston type | Slotted upper skirt |
| Piston material | Aluminium alloy, tin plated |
| Piston skirt clearance in bore | 0.0015 to 0.0023 in (0.038 to 0.058 mm) |
| No of rings per piston | 3-two compression and one scraper |
| Height of piston | 2.98 in (75.7 mm) |
| Piston identification | Flat crown |
| Ring gap with rings fitted in bore: | |
| Top compression rings | 0.014 to 0.018 in (0.35 to 0.45 mm) |
| 2nd and scraper rings | 0.010 to 0.014 in (0.25 to 0.35 mm) |
| Piston diameter and grades: | |
| Grade A | 3.0926 to 3.0930 in (78.550 to 78.560 mm) |
| Grade B | 3.0930 to 3.0934 in (78.560 to 78.570 mm) |
| Grade C | 3.0934 to 3.0938 in (78.570 to 78.580 mm) |
| Grade D | 3.0938 to 3.0942 in (78.580 to 78.590 mm) |
| Grade E* | 3.0942 to 3.0946 in (78.59 to 78.60 mm) |

*For service use only

| | |
|---|---|
| Maximum rebore size | + 0.030 in (0.762 mm) |

## Camshaft bearings

| | |
|---|---|
| Camshaft drive | Single row endless chain |
| Bearings | 3 renewable, aluminium/tin |
| Camshaft journal diameter: | |
| Front | 1.934 in (49.136 mm) |
| Centre | 1.747 in (45.373 mm) |
| Rear | 1.559 in (39.61 mm) |
| Camshaft clearance in bearing | 0.0013 to 0.0030 in (0.033 to 0.076 mm) |
| Camshaft endfloat | 0.004 to 0.009 in (0.101 to 0.228 mm) |
| Camshaft bearing internal diameter: | |
| Front | 1.936 to 1.937 in (49.18 to 49.21 mm) |
| Centre | 1.749 to 1.750 in (44.42 to 44.45 mm) |
| Rear | 1.561 to 1.562 in (39.66 to 39.69 mm) |

## Valves and valve springs

| | |
|---|---|
| Valve head diameter: | |
| Inlet | 1.448 in (36.78 mm) |
| Exhaust | 1.228 in (31.19 mm) |
| Valve seat angle | 45° |
| Valve to rocker arm clearances: | |
| Inlet | 0.008 in (0.20 mm) hot or cold |
| Exhaust | 0.016 in (0.40 mm) hot or cold |
| Valve stem clearance in guide: | |
| Inlet | 0.001 to 0.0025 in (0.025 to 0.063 mm) |
| Exhaust | 0.0025 to 0.0045 in (0.063 to 0.114 mm) |

Valve stem diameter standard and oversize:
    Inlet valve standard ............................................................. 0.3110 in (7.899 mm)
    Inlet valve + 0.003 in ....................................................... 0.3140 in (7.975 mm)
    Inlet valve + 0.015 in ....................................................... 0.3260 in (8.280 mm)
    Inlet valve + 0.030 in ....................................................... 0.3410 in (8.661 mm)
    Exhaust valve standard ...................................................... 0.3095 in (7.861 mm)
    Exhaust valve + 0.003 in ................................................... 0.3125 in (7.937 mm)
    Exhaust valve + 0.015 in ................................................... 0.3245 in (8.242 mm)
    Exhaust valve + 0.030 in ................................................... 0.3395 in (8.623 mm)
Exhaust valve clearance and closing position for checking timing ...... 0.100 in (2.54 mm), 25° BTDC
Valve length .............................................................................. 4.305 to 4.315 in (109.35 to 109.60 mm)
Valve springs:
    Type ................................................................................... Single coil
    Length (free) ...................................................................... 1.745 in (42.32 mm)
Valve timing:
    Inlet valve opens .............................................................. 38° BTDC
    Inlet valve closes ............................................................. 66° ABDC
    Exhaust valve opens ......................................................... 72° BBDC
    Exhaust valve closes ......................................................... 20° ATDC

## Lubrication system

Oil pump type ........................................................................... Eccentric lobe
Oil filter ..................................................................................... Full flow, renewable
Sump capacity – with filter ...................................................... 7 pints (4 litres)
Sump capacity – without filter .................................................. 6 pints (3.4 litres)
Oil pump drive .......................................................................... From skew gear on camshaft
Normal oil pressure (hot) ........................................................... 50 to 60 lbf/in$^2$ (3.5 to 4.2 kgf/cm$^2$) at 50 mph

## Torque wrench settings

|                                             | lbf ft | Nm |
|---------------------------------------------|--------|----|
| Big-end nuts                                | 29     | 39 |
| Camshaft sprocket bolt                      | 34     | 46 |
| Crankshaft pulley bolt                      | 50     | 68 |
| Cylinder head bolts                         | 60     | 81 |
| Cylinder head nuts                          | 60     | 81 |
| Cylinder head studs in cylinder block       | 14     | 19 |
| Engine mounting bracket block bolts         | 17     | 23 |
| Flywheel/driveplate securing bolts          | 40     | 54 |
| Main bearing bolts                          | 52     | 70 |
| Manifold bolts (inlet and exhaust)          | 13     | 18 |
| Manifold nuts (inlet and exhaust)           | 16     | 22 |
| Manifold studs in cylinder head             | 10     | 14 |
| Rocker pedestal mounting bolts              | 17     | 23 |
| Spark plugs                                 | 12     | 16 |

*1250 twin carburettor models*

*The engine specifications for 1250 twin carburettor models are as for the 1250 single carburettor models, except for the differences listed below*

## Engine – general
Compression pressure ............................................................................. 150 to 160 lbf/in$^2$ (10.55 to 11.25 kgf/cm$^2$)

## Cylinder head
Identification ........................................................................................... Green paint between numbers 2 and 3 spark plugs, and *S* cast on the upper face
Volume of combustion chamber ............................................................... 12.3 to 12.9 cc
Maximum variation in volume between combustion chambers ........... ± 0.3 cc
**Note**: *The 1250 twin carburettor head is a 1500 twin carburettor head fitted with 1250 single carburettor head inlet valves*

## Valves and valve springs
Valve to rocker arm clearances:
    Inlet .................................................................................... 0.010 in (0.25 mm) hot or cold
    Exhaust ............................................................................... 0.016 in (0.40 mm) hot or cold
Exhaust valve clearance and closing position for checking timing ...... 0.100 in (2.54 mm), 12° BTDC
Valve timing:
    Inlet valve opens .............................................................. 44° BTDC
    Inlet valve closes ............................................................. 78° ABDC
    Exhaust valve opens ......................................................... 69° BBDC
    Exhaust valve closes ......................................................... 23° ATDC
Valve springs:
    Type ................................................................................... Double coil
    Length (free):
        Inner .............................................................................. 1.20 in (30.48 mm)
        Outer .............................................................................. 1.51 in (38.35 mm)

| Valve head diameter: | |
|---|---|
| Inlet .................................................................................... | 1.548 to 1.552 in (39.32 to 39.42 mm) |
| Exhaust ............................................................................... | 1.336 to 1.340 in (33.93 to 34.04 mm) |
| Valve stem diameter ................................................................ | As 1250 single carburettor engine but + 0.003 in oversize on inlet and exhaust valves not used |

## 1500 single and twin carburettor models

*The engine specifications for 1500 single and twin carburettor models are as for 1250 models, except for the differences listed below*

### Engine – general

| | Single carburettor | Twin carburettor |
|---|---|---|
| Bore ............................................................................................ | 86.12 mm (3.391 in) | 86.12 mm (3.391 in) |
| Capacity ...................................................................................... | 1498 cc (91.41 cu in) | 1498 cc (91.41 cu in) |
| Compression ratios and pressures: | | |
| High compression ratio ....................................................... | 9.2 : 1 | 9.2 : 1 |
| Low compression ratio ........................................................ | 8.0 : 1 | Not applicable |
| High compression pressure .................................................. | 170 to 180 lbf/in² (11.95 to 12.66 kgf/cm²) | 150 to 160 lbf/in² (10.55 to 11.25 kgf/cm²)* |
| Low compression pressure ................................................... | 150 to 160 lbf/in² (10.55 to 11.25 kgf/cm²) | Not applicable |

**\*Note:** *Later closing of the inlet valve is responsible for the lower compression pressure in twin carburettor engines*

### Cylinder head

| | | |
|---|---|---|
| Identification ............................................................................. | None | *S* cast on top face |
| Gasket identification ................................................................. | *LB* on gasket | *LB* on gasket |

### Gudgeon pin

| | | |
|---|---|---|
| Length ........................................................................................ | 2.934 to 2.938 in (74.52 to 74.62 mm) | 2.934 to 2.938 in (74.52 to 74.62 mm) |

### Pistons and piston rings

| | | |
|---|---|---|
| Piston identification .................................................................... | Recessed crown | Recessed crown |
| Piston crown depth: | | |
| High compression ................................................................ | 0.025 to 0.035 in (0.63 to 0.88 mm) | 0.025 to 0.035 in (0.63 to 0.88 mm) |
| Low compression ................................................................. | 0.080 to 0.085 in (2.03 to 2.15 mm) | Not applicable |
| Piston skirt clearance in bore .................................................... | 0.0015 to 0.0023 in (0.038 to 0.058 mm) | 0.0025 to 0.0033 in (0.063 to 0.083 mm) |

### Piston diameter and grades

| | | |
|---|---|---|
| Grade A ...................................................................................... | 3.3887 to 3.3891 in (86.073 to 86.083 mm) | 3.3877 to 3.3881 in (86.048 to 86.058 mm) |
| Grade B ...................................................................................... | 3.3891 to 3.3895 in (86.083 to 86.093 mm) | 3.3881 to 3.3885 in (86.058 to 86.068 mm) |
| Grade C ...................................................................................... | 3.3895 to 3.3899 in (86.093 to 86.103 mm) | 3.3885 to 3.3889 in (86.068 to 86.078 mm) |
| Grade D ...................................................................................... | 3.3899 to 3.3903 in (86.103 to 86.113 mm) | 3.3889 to 3.3893 in (86.078 to 86.088 mm) |
| Grade E ...................................................................................... | 3.3903 to 3.3907 in (86.113 to 86.123 mm) | 3.3893 to 3.3897 in (86.088 to 86.098 mm) |

### Valves and valve springs

| | | |
|---|---|---|
| Valve head diameter: | | |
| Inlet ..................................................................................... | 1.448 in (36.78 mm) | 1.498 in (38.05 mm) |
| Exhaust ............................................................................... | 1.228 in (31.19 mm) | 1.228 in (31.19 mm) |
| Valve to rocker arm clearances: | | |
| Inlet ..................................................................................... | 0.008 in (0.20 mm) | 0.010 in (0.25 mm) |
| Exhaust ............................................................................... | 0.016 in (0.40 mm) | 0.016 in (0.40 mm) |
| Exhaust valve clearance and closing position for checking timing ...... | 0.100 in (2.54 mm), 22° BTDC | 0.100 in (2.54 mm), 12° BTDC |
| Valve timing: | | |
| Inlet valve opens ................................................................. | 35° BTDC | 44° BTDC |
| Inlet valve closes ................................................................ | 69° ABDC | 78° ABDC |
| Exhaust valve opens ........................................................... | 69° BBDC | 69° BBDC |
| Exhaust valve closes ................................................................ | 23° ATDC | 23° ATDC |
| Valve springs: | | |
| Type .................................................................................... | Single coil | Double coil |
| Length (free) ....................................................................... | 1.745 in (42.32 mm) | Outer 1.51 in (38.35 mm) Inner 1.20 in (30.48 mm) |

### Timing chain and gearwheels

| | | |
|---|---|---|
| Type of chain ............................................................................. | Single row | Duplex twin |
| Type of gearwheel ..................................................................... | Single track teeth | Twin track teeth |

## 1500 twin Weber 40DCOE carburettor models

*The engine specifications for this version are as for the earlier-mentioned twin carburettor models, except for the differences listed below*

### Engine – general
Compression ratio ...................................... 9.4 to 1
Compression pressure ................................ 165 to 180 lbf/in$^2$ (11.55 to 12.6 kgf/cm$^2$)

## 1300 single and twin carburettor models

*The engine specifications for 1300 single and twin carburettor models are as for 1250 models, except for the differences listed below*

| Engine – general | Single carburettor (1.50) | Twin carburettors (1.50) or single carburettor (1.75) |
| --- | --- | --- |
| Capacity | 1295 cc (79 cu in) | 1295 cc (79 cu in) |
| Bore | 3.094 in (78.6 mm) | 3.094 in (78.6 mm) |
| Stroke | 2.62 in (66.7 mm) | 2.62 in (66.7 mm) |
| Compression ratio: | | |
| High compression, up to Series 7 | 8.6 : 1 | 8.6 : 1 |
| High compression, Series 7 onwards | 8.8 : 1 | 8.8 : 1 |
| Low compression, Series 7 onwards | 7.8 : 1 | Not applicable |
| Compression pressure: | | |
| High compression | 160 to 180 lbf/in$^2$ (11 to 12.4 kgf/cm$^2$) | 150 to 170 lbf/in$^2$ (10.3 to 11.7 kgf/cm$^2$) |
| Low compression | 150 to 160 lbf/in$^2$ (10.5 to 11.2 kgf/cm$^2$) | Not applicable |

| Piston and rings | | |
| --- | --- | --- |
| Piston skirt clearance in bore | 0.0029 to 0.0037 in (0.074 to 0.094 mm) | 0.0029 to 0.0037 in (0.074 to 0.094 mm) |
| Piston identification | Recessed crown | Recessed crown |
| Ring gap (with rings fitted in standard bore): | | |
| Top compression | 0.014 to 0.019 in (0.36 to 0.48 mm) | 0.014 to 0.019 in (0.36 to 0.48 mm) |
| 2nd and scraper rings | 0.009 to 0.014 in (0.23 to 0.36 mm) | 0.019 to 0.014 in (0.23 to 0.36 mm) |
| Piston diameter and grades: | | |
| Grade A | 3.0912 to 3.0916 in (78.517 to 78.527 mm) | 3.0912 to 3.0916 in (78.517 to 78.527 mm) |
| Grade B | 3.0916 to 3.0920 in (78.527 to 78.537 mm) | 3.0916 to 3.0920 in (78.527 to 78.537 mm) |
| Grade C* | 3.0920 to 3.0924 in (78.537 to 78.547 mm) | 3.0920 to 3.0924 in (78.537 to 78.547 mm) |
| Grade D* | 3.0924 to 3.0928 in (78.547 to 78.557 mm) | 3.0924 to 3.0928 in (78.547 to 78.557 mm) |
| Grade E* | 3.0928 to 3.0932 in (78.557 to 78.567 mm) | 3.0928 to 3.0932 in (78.557 to 78.567 mm) |

*For service use only

| Valves and valve springs | | |
| --- | --- | --- |
| Valve to rocker arm clearances (hot or cold): | | |
| Inlet | 0.008 in (0.20 mm) | 0.010 in (0.25 mm) |
| Exhaust | 0.016 in (0.40 mm) | 0.016 in (0.40 mm) |
| Valve springs: | | |
| Type | Single coil | Double coil |
| Length (free) | 1.592 in (40.44 mm) | Inner 1.26 in (32.0 mm) Outer 1.592 in (40.44 mm) |
| Exhaust valve clearance and closing position for checking timing | 0.100 in (2.54 mm), 25° BTDC | 0.100 in (2.54 mm), 12° BTDC |

| Crankshaft and main bearings | | |
| --- | --- | --- |
| Connecting rod float on crankpin | 0.007 to 0.019 in (0.178 to 0.483 mm) | 0.007 to 0.019 in (0.178 to 0.483 mm) |

## 1600 single and twin carburettor models

*The engine specifications for 1600 single and twin carburettor models are as for 1500 models except for the differences listed below*

| Engine – general | Single carburettor (1.50) | Twin carburettor (1.50) or single carburettor (1.75) |
| --- | --- | --- |
| Cubic capacity | 1598 cc (97.5 cu in) | 1598 cc (97.5 cu in) |
| Bore | 3.438 in (87.33 mm) | 3.438 in (87.33 mm) |
| Stroke | 2.62 in (66.7 mm) | 2.62 in (66.7 mm) |

| | Single carburettor (150) | Twin carburettor (150) or single carburettor (175) |
|---|---|---|
| Compression ratio: | | |
| High compression, up to Series 7 | 8.6 : 1 | 8.6 : 1 |
| Low compression, up to Series 7 | 7.8 : 1 | Not applicable |
| High compression, Series 7 onwards | 8.8 : 1 | 8.8 : 1 |
| Low compression, Series 7 onwards | 7.8 : 1 | Not applicable |
| Compression pressure: | | |
| High compression | 160 to 180 lbf/ft$^2$ (11 to 12.4 kgf/cm$^2$) | 150 to 170 lbf/ft$^2$ (10.3 to 11.7 kgf/cm$^2$) |
| Low compression | 150 to 160 lbf/in$^2$ (10.5 to 11.2 kgf/cm$^2$) | Not applicable |

## Pistons and piston rings

| | Single carburettor (150) | Twin carburettor (150) or single carburettor (175) |
|---|---|---|
| Piston skirt clearance in bore | 0.0029 to 0.0037 in (0.074 to 0.094 mm) | 0.0029 to 0.0037 in (0.074 to 0.094 mm) |
| Piston identification | Recessed crown | Recessed crown |
| Ring gap with rings fitted in standard bore: | | |
| Top compression | 0.014 to 0.019 in (0.36 to 0.48 mm) | 0.014 to 0.019 in (0.36 to 0.48 mm) |
| 2nd and scraper rings | 0.010 to 0.015 in (0.25 to 0.38 mm) | 0.010 to 0.015 in (0.25 to 0.38 mm) |
| Piston diameter and grades: | | |
| Grade A | 3.4351 to 3.4355 in (87.252 to 87.262 mm) | 3.4351 to 3.4355 in (87.252 to 87.262 mm) |
| Grade B | 3.4355 to 3.4359 in (87.262 to 87.272 mm) | 3.4355 to 3.4359 in (87.262 to 87.272 mm) |
| Grade C* | 3.4359 to 3.4363 in (87.272 to 87.282 mm) | 3.4359 to 3.4363 in (87.272 to 87.282 mm) |
| Grade D* | 3.4363 to 3.4367 in (87.282 to 87.292 mm) | 3.4363 to 3.4367 in (87.282 to 87.292 mm) |
| Grade E* | 3.4367 to 3.4371 in (87.292 to 87.302 mm) | 3.4367 to 3.4371 in (87.292 to 87.302 mm) |

* For service use only

## Crankshaft and main bearings

| | Single carburettor (150) | Twin carburettor (150) or single carburettor (175) |
|---|---|---|
| Correcting rod float on crankpin | 0.007 to 0.019 in (0.178 to 0.483 mm) | 0.007 to 0.019 in (0.178 to 0.483 mm) |

## Valves and valve springs

| | Single carburettor (150) | Twin carburettor (150) or single carburettor (175) |
|---|---|---|
| Valve to rocker arm clearances (hot or cold): | | |
| Inlet | 0.008 in (0.20 mm) | 0.010 in (0.25 mm) |
| Exhaust | 0.016 in (0.40 mm) | 0.016 in (0.40 mm) |
| Valve springs: | | |
| Type | Single coil | Double coil |
| Length (free) | 1.592 in (40.44 mm) | Inner 1.26 in (32.0 mm) Outer 1.592 in (40.44 mm) |
| Exhaust valve clearance and closing position for checking timing: | | |
| Up to Series 7 | 0.100 in (2.54 mm), 19° BTDC | 0.100 in (2.54 mm), 12° BTDC |
| Series 7 onwards | 0.100 in (2.54 mm), 25° BTDC | 0.100 in (2.54 mm), 12° BTDC |
| Valve timing at normal operating temperatures up to Series 7: | | |
| Inlet valve opens | 44° BTDC | 44° BTDC |
| Inlet valve closes | 86° ABDC | 78° ABDC |
| Exhaust valve opens | 66° BBDC | 69° BBDC |
| Exhaust valve closes | 20° ATDC | 23° ATDC |
| Valve timing at normal operating temperatures, series 7 on: | | |
| Inlet valve opens | 38° BTDC | 44° BTDC |
| Inlet valve closes | 66° ABDC | 78° ABDC |
| Exhaust valve opens | 72° BBDC | 69° BBDC |
| Exhaust valve closes | 20° ATDC | 23° ATDC |

### Plymouth Cricket models
The engine specifications for Plymouth Cricket models are as for the 1500 single or twin carburettor models, except for the differences listed below

## Engine – general

| Engine types: | |
|---|---|
| 1500 single carburettor | G, H and 3 series |
| 1500 twin carburettor | H series |
| 1500 twin carburettor | 3 series |
| Bore | 3.390 in (86.12 mm) |
| Compression ratio | 8.0 : 1 |

Compression pressure:
- G, H and 3 series ............................................................... 150 to 160 lbf/in² (10.55 to 11.25 kgf/cm²)
- H and 3 series (twin carburettors) .................................... 140 to 150 lbf/in² (9.84 to 10.55 kgf/cm²)

## Pistons

Piston skirt clearance in bore (H series, twin carburettor) ...................... 0.0025 to 0.0033 in (0.063 to 0.083 mm)

## Valves

Valve clearances:
- G, H and 3 series and 3 series (twin carburettor):
  - Inlet ........................................................................ 0.008 in (0.20 mm)
  - Exhaust .................................................................. 0.016 in (0.40 mm)
- H series (twin carburettor):
  - Inlet ........................................................................ 0.010 in (0.25 mm)
  - Exhaust .................................................................. 0.016 in (0.40 mm)

Valve timing (single carb):

| | G and H series | 3 series |
|---|---|---|
| Inlet opens | 35° BTDC | 32° BTDC |
| Inlet closes | 69° ABDC | 74° ABDC |
| Exhaust opens | 69° BBDC | 44° BBDC |
| Exhaust closes | 23° ATDC | 18° ATDC |
| Valve overlap | 58° | 50° |

Exhaust valve clearance and closing position for checking valve timing ......... 0.100 in (2.54 mm), 22° BTDC / 0.100 in (2.54 mm), 17° BTDC

Valve timing (twin carb):

| | H series | 3 series |
|---|---|---|
| Inlet opens | 44° BTDC | 32° BTDC |
| Inlet closes | 78° ABDC | 74° ABDC |
| Exhaust opens | 69° BBDC | 44° BBDC |
| Exhaust closes | 23° ATDC | 18° ATDC |
| Valve overlap | 67° | 50° |

Exhaust valve clearance and closing position for checking valve timing ......... 0.100 in (2.54 mm), 12° BTDC / 0.100 (2.54 mm), 17° BTDC

## 1 General description

The engine is an in-line, four cylinder, four stroke unit of conventional design. Aluminium solid skirt pistons operate in a cast iron cylinder block, and the valves operate directly in the cast iron cylinder head. A five bearing cast iron crankshaft is used, and the H-section connecting rods are of steel with bushed small-ends and horizontally split big-ends. The chain drive camshaft runs in renewable bearing bushes. The oil pump has an in-built oil pressure relief valve, and is driven by a helical gear on the camshaft. The pump driven gear extends upwards to provide the drive, via a tonge and slot, to the distributor. The flywheel is bolted to the crankshaft, and can have a chamfer on either one, or both, sides of the ring gear to permit the use of either an inertia or pre-engaged starter motor. Vehicles with automatic transmission have a steel driving disc instead of a flywheel.

There are four basic engine sizes, the 1250, 1300, 1500 and 1600. Cylinder block identification is provided by the large letters cast on the cylinder block, as shown in Fig. 1.1:

SB signifies small bore ie 1250 and 1300 engines
LB signifies large bore ie 1500 and 1600 engines

These identifications will also be found upon the cylinder head gaskets.

The letter 'S' cast on the front of the cylinder head (see Fig. 1.1) indicates a twin carburettor high performance engine. The 1250 cylinder head is identified by an area of green paint between the No 2 and 3 spark plugs.

The differences to be found between the various units concern the following items:

(a) Pistons
(b) Cylinder bore sizes
(c) Cylinder head gaskets
(d) Distributors
(e) Air cleaner bodies
(f) Carburettors
(g) Camshaft timing wheels, chain and case
(h) Valve timing
(j) Inlet valves and seals
(k) Valve springs and caps
(l) Exhaust manifold
(m) Inlet manifold
(n) Fan

## 2 Major operations on the engine – description

The following operations can be carried out with the engine in the vehicle:

(a) Removal and refitting of the cylinder head
(b) Removal and refitting of the clutch assembly
(c) Removal and refitting of the sump
(d) Removal and refitting of the oil pump
(e) Removal and refitting of the inlet and exhaust manifolds
(f) Removal and refitting of the timing cover, seal, timing chain, wheels, and chain tensioner
(g) Removal and refitting of the camshaft
(h) Removal and refitting of the connecting rods, pistons and big-end bearings
(j) Removal and refitting of the flywheel and ring gear
(k) Removal and refitting of the engine front mountings.

2  It should be noted that for some of these operations a pit, ramps or strong stands and a jack will be needed.

3  The following operations can only be carried out with the engine removed from the vehicle:

(a) Removal and refitting of the crankshaft and main bearings
(b) Removal and refitting of the crankshaft rear oil seal

## 3 Engine removal – general

The engine complete with manual gearbox can be lifted as a unit from the engine compartment. Alternatively the engine and gearbox can be split at the front of the bellhousing, a stand or jack placed under the gearbox to provide additional support, and the engine lifted out. The easiest method is to remove the engine leaving the gearbox in place in the car. If they are removed as a unit they have to be lifted out at a very steep angle which can be difficult.

Whether or not components like the carburettor, manifolds and starter are removed first depends upon the work to be done. For example the starter can be left in place if the engine is removed in unit with the gearbox.

Note that if automatic transmission is fitted it is recommended that the engine is removed leaving the transmission in the vehicle.

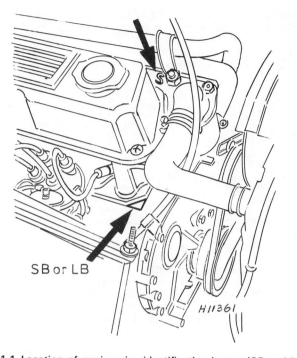

SB or LB

H11361

**Fig. 1.1 Location of engine size identification letters (SB or LB) and high performance twin carburettor engine identification letter (S) (Sec 1)**

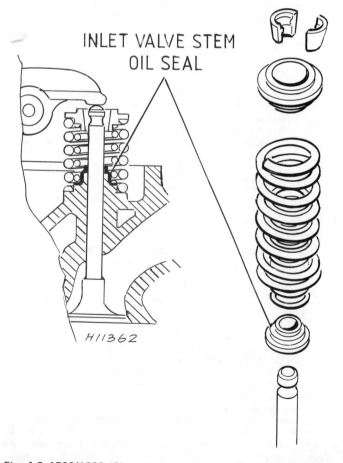

INLET VALVE STEM OIL SEAL

H11362

**Fig. 1.2 1500/1600 'S' engines – special double valve springs, larger split collets, one piece collar, and special oil seals (Sec 1)**

## 4   Engine – removal leaving gearbox in the vehicle

1    Obtain a good hoist and two strong axle stands if an inspection pit or ramps are not available. Engine removal will be much easier if you have someone to help. Before beginning work it is worth having the engine unit cleaned at a service station equipped with steam or high pressure air and water cleaning equipment. It makes the job quicker, easier and cleaner. Decide whether to jack up the car and support it on axle stands, or raise the front end on wheel ramps. If the latter, run the car up now (and chock the rear wheels) whilst you still have engine power available. Remember that with the front supported on ramps the working height and engine lifting height is increased.

2    Remove the bonnet by removing two bolts from each side.

3    Remove the radiator cap, open the drain plug on the bottom of the radiator, and the tap on the left side of the cylinder block. Check that the heater control valve is in the hot position. Do not drain the water in the place where the engine is to be removed if receptacles are not at hand to catch it. Re-use the water if it contains antifreeze. Drain the engine oil by removing the drain plug on the bottom right-hand side of the sump. Ensure that the receptacle for the oil will hold one gallon.

4    Lift the windscreen washer reservoir bag from the hooks on the battery clamp, and place it beside the battery.

5    Disconnect the battery by undoing the screw holding the earth lead terminal to the battery post. Pull off the terminal (photo).

6    Undo the clip which holds the top end of the bottom radiator hose to the water pump and pull the hose off.

7    Undo the clip which holds the top hose to the thermostat cover and pull the hose off. Disconnect the petrol feed pipe from the inlet side of the fuel pump.

8    Free the heater hoses at the bulkhead. With a $\frac{1}{2}$ in AF spanner undo the four bolts (two on each side) which hold the radiator in place (photo). Lift out the radiator with the top and bottom hoses still connected taking care not to damage the core on the fan blades.

9    Pull the two leads from the terminals at the rear of the dynamo or alternator (photo). Pull the leads from the terminal on the water temperature sender unit underneath the thermostat outlet.

10   The oil pressure warning light switch is adjacent to the oil filter. Pull the lead from the terminal (photo).

11   Disconnect the coil HT lead from the centre of the distributor cap.

12   Undo the screw which holds the choke inner cable at the carburettor(s) (photo), and free the outer cable by releasing the spring clip from the bracket.

13   Free the accelerator rod from the carburettor(s) by springing the small circlip from the groove in the end of the rod. Slide the rod out of the plastic trunnion in the throttle lever (photo).

14   Disconnect the driveshaft cable on automatic transmission models.

15   Disconnect the lead to the starter motor terminal. Remove the top starter motor bolt/nut which also carries the engine earth lead.

16   Remove the top two engine-to-bellhousing bolts.

17   Place a jack under the centre of the front crossmember, jack up the front of the car and support on two axle stands positioned under the outer ends of the crossmember. Remove the jack (photo).

18   From under the car remove the bottom starter motor bolt and withdraw the starter motor and the small flywheel splash shield. From the flywheel cover plate, bolted to the bottom portion of the front face of the bellhousing, remove the bolts and thus the plate.

19   Undo the remaining bolts which hold the manual gearbox bellhousing to the rear of the engine and place a jack under the front of the gearbox to take its weight when the engine is lifted.

20   Undo the nuts and washers which hold the exhaust downpipe to the manifold and separate. Undo the two nuts and washers from the engine mounting stud inside the crossmember, one on each side of the car.

21   If the hoist has a limited lift, remove the axle stands and lower the car to the ground. Attach the hoist to the engine. On the left side of the cylinder head are two strong heater hose support brackets, one at the front and one at the rear. These double as lifting brackets when the hose clips are removed.

22   On automatic transmission models remove the cover plate and unscrew the bolts securing the torque converter to the driveplate. These are accessible one at a time by rotating the engine. Remove the torque converter housing-to-engine bolts and support the transmission with a jack.

23   Raise the engine until the engine mounting studs clear the

4.5 Removing battery earth terminal

4.8 Removing radiator bolts

4.9 Removing distributor LT lead

4.10 Removing lead from oil pressure switch

4.12 Releasing choke inner cable

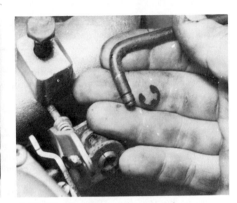
4.13 Releasing the accelerator rod

4.17 Supporting on axle stands

4.24 Lifting engine from car

crossmember, then pull the engine forward to separate it from the gearbox/transmission. On manual gearbox models pull it forward until the gearbox input shaft is clear of the clutch pressure plate. On automatic transmission models pull the engine from the transmission, making sure that the torque converter disengages from the driveplate and stays fully engaged with the transmission oil pump. The use of a cranked lever or length of wood will help during this operation.
24  Lift the engine straight up and out, rolling the car back if the hoist is fixed or pulling the engine forwards if the hoist is the trolley type (photo). During these operations, maintain and re-adjust the support underneath the gearbox/transmission as necessary. If the car is to be rolled backwards, a jack on wheels should be used, or alternatively the gearbox/transmission can usually be supported using a suitable piece of wood placed underneath it, and jammed against convenient frame or suspension items.

## 5  Engine – removal with manual gearbox

1  The engine and gearbox together have to come out at a steep angle, and removal is thus a little more difficult than removing the engine alone. Proceed as described in Section 4, paragraphs 1 to 15.
2  Remove the gear lever, as described in Chapter 6.
3  Jack up the front of the car and fit stands at each end of the front crossmember. Under the car disconnect the clutch release arm from the actuating cable by pulling off the return spring and undoing the locknut and adjuster nut from the rod which passes through the release arm.
4  Disconnect the speedometer cable from the right-hand side of the gearbox extension housing by undoing the knurled nut which holds it in place.

5   Unbolt the propeller shaft from the rear axle and withdraw it from the gearbox, catching the oil or blanking off the end, to prevent loss.

6   Place a jack under the gearbox, and remove the two $\frac{1}{2}$ in AF bolts, one at each end of the crossmember. Remove the centre bolt, and withdraw the crossmember.

7   Undo the four $\frac{7}{16}$ in AF bolts and remove the blades, fan pulley and belt. The engine can be lifted out without taking the blades off, but it is a squeeze. It is also advised that the four $\frac{1}{2}$ inch AF bolts which hold the anti-roll bar are removed to allow the bar to drop, but this is not essential and will not prevent the engine being lifted out.

8   Disconnect the leads from the side of the gearbox for the reversing lights, if fitted.

9   Undo the nuts and washers which hold the exhaust downpipe to the manifold and separate. Under the car, undo the two nuts and washers on the engine mounting studs inside the front crossmember, one on each side.

10  Position the lifting tackle to permit the engine to come out at an angle of about 45°. The front lifting bracket and the centre exhaust manifold pipe are suggested. Lift the engine up and out carefully.

## 6   Engine dismantling – general

1   Ensure that the bench is strong enough to support the engine weight, and large enough to take all the components to be removed. If the floor must be used, employ a suitable wooden or similar slab between the engine and floor.

2   Clean the complete unit with a solvent cleaner, and wash off with water. Clean all dismantled parts in petrol or paraffin, except those with oilways, where paraffin could remain and dilute lubricating oil.

3   Obtain new gaskets, but do not dispose of the old ones initially until the new ones are actually at hand, in case any replacement cannot be obtained and has to be made. Keep nuts and bolts with their respective components, or in separately labelled containers.

4   If a factory reconditioned engine is being fitted, remove the following items:

   (a)  Dynamo/alternator
   (b)  Distributor
   (c)  Thermostat and cover
   (d)  Oil filter
   (e)  Carburettor(s)
   (f)  Inlet manifold
   (g)  Exhaust manifold
   (h)  Water pump
   (j)  Fuel pump
   (k)  Engine mounting brackets
   (l)  Spark plugs

   If you are obtaining a 'short engine' or 'half-engine' comprising cylinder block, crankcase, crankshaft, pistons and connecting rods all assembled, then the cylinder head, flywheel, sump and oil pump will need removal also.

## 7   Cylinder head removal – engine out of the vehicle

1   Remove the screws (or bolts on some models) holding the rocker cover, and lift it off together with the cork sealing gasket, which may be re-used if not over-compressed or damaged.

2   Remove the carburettor(s) (Chapter 3). The inlet and exhaust manifolds may be removed but it is not essential. These are best removed as a unit. Undo the seven $\frac{3}{4}$ in AF bolts and washers, and the three $\frac{1}{2}$ in AF nuts and washers which hold the manifold to the side of the cylinder head and then lift them away.

3   Remove the HT leads, spark plugs and distributor cap. Undo the eight bolts and washers which hold the rocker pedestals to the top of the cylinder head and lift off the shaft arms and pedestals.

4   Lift out the pushrods and put them in a piece of pierced cardboard, the holes numbered one to eight, so that each rod can be identified.

5   Slacken off the ten cylinder head holding-down bolts and nuts in reverse of the tightening sequence, ie work from the outside towards the centre.

6   Lift off the cylinder head. If this proves difficult, try turning the engine over by the flywheel (with the spark plugs in position) so that compression in the cylinders can force it upwards. A few taps with a soft mallet may be needed. Under no circumstances prise the head

with a lever, as this may damage the machined surfaces.

7   If necessary, lift each tappet from the cylinder block and identify them for position.

## 8   Cylinder head removal – engine in the vehicle

1   Disconnect the battery, and drain the cooling system completely.

2   Disconnect the radiator top hose, and remove the air cleaner unit.

3   Remove the vacuum advance suction pipe, and disconnect the fuel feed pipe at the carburettor. Release the spring clip retaining the outer choke cable to the carburettor, and disconnect the accelerator rod by removing the circlip and sliding the rod from the plastic trunnion in the throttle lever.

4   Pull the lead from the terminal on the water temperature sender unit under the thermostat housing.

5   Disconnect the heater hoses at the front of the engine and free them from the spring clips on the side of the rocker cover.

6   Remove the distributor cap complete with the plug and coil leads.

7   Proceed as advised in Section 7. If the engine needs turning to assist in breaking the joint, reconnect the battery leads and give the engine a turn with the starter motor. Catch fuel from the pump in a container.

## 9   Inlet and exhaust manifolds – removal, dismantling and refitting

1   The assembled manifolds must be removed together. Remove the air cleaner(s) (see Chapter 3), and remove the exhaust flange nuts, allowing the exhaust pipe to come away.

2   Remove pipes and cables to the carburettor(s).

3   Remove three nuts and washers, and seven bolts with washers, and take off the manifolds complete with the carburettor(s).

4   Separate the inlet and exhaust manifolds, by removing the bolts joining them and parting the manifolds. Withdraw the deflector plate(s).

5   To reassemble and refit, first fit the deflector plate(s) between the manifolds and lightly bolt them together. Reassemble to the engine in reverse of the dismantling procedure, employing a new manifold joint. After tightening the manifolds to the cylinder head, finally tighten the bolts holding the two manifolds together. Retighten the manifold bolts when the engine is hot.

## 10  Rocker shaft assembly – dismantling, renovation and re-assembly

1   Remove the spring clip at each end of the shaft. If any burrs exist on the grooves where the clips have been, these should be removed with a stone to prevent damage to the rocker bores as they are withdrawn. Remove all the parts, noting their respective positions.

2   Clean the shaft and check that the oilways are all clear. Test the shaft for straightness by rolling it on a flat surface. In the unlikely event of it being bent, it must be renewed. Renew the shaft if any obvious signs of wear are present. Check the rocker arms for wear, for wear at the face which bears on the valve stem, and for wear of the adjusting screws. Wear in the bush can be checked by gripping the rocker arm tip and holding the arm on the shaft, noting if there is any lateral shake. Renew the arm if excessive play exists.

3   Check the top of the rocker arm where it bears on the valve stem for cracking or serious wear of the case hardening. Check the ball on the end of the rocker adjusting screw. Renew the screw and the pushrod if wear is uneven or the end of the ball is polished.

4   Refit all parts to the shaft in reverse order to dismantling, ensuring that the oil feed holes in the standards face towards the pushrod side. The identifying boss shown in Fig. 1.20 (inset) must face towards the rear.

## 11  Valves – removal and renovation

1   To remove the valves, compress each spring in turn with a valve spring compressor until the two halves of the split conical collets can be removed. Release the compressor and remove the spring, shroud and valve. If, when the compressor is screwed down, the valve spring

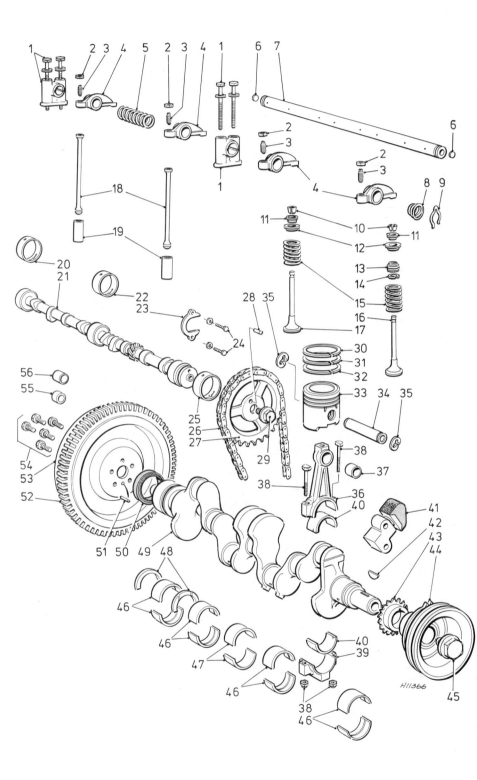

**Fig. 1.3 Engine internal parts – exploded view (Sec 6)**

1   Rocker pedestal and fixing bolts
2   Locknut
3   Adjustment screw
4   Rocker
5   Inner spring
6   Plug
7   Rocker shaft
8   Outer spring
9   Outer spring retainer
10  Valve collets
11  Inner collar
12  Valve spring cap
13  Oil seal (Inlet valve only)
14  Oil seal retainer
15  Valve spring
16  Inlet valve
17  Exhaust valve
18  Pushrod
19  Tappet
20  Rear bearing
21  Camshaft
22  Centre bearing
23  Thrust plate
24  Thrust plate fixing screws
25  Front bearing
26  Timing chain
27  Chain drivewheel
28  Chain drivewheel dowel
29  Chain wheel fixing screw
30  Top piston ring (chromium plated)
31  2nd piston ring (stepped type)
32  Oil scraper ring (slotted)
33  Piston
34  Gudgeon pin
35  Circlip
36  Connecting rod
37  Small-end bush
38  Big-end nuts and bolts
39  Connecting rod cap
40  Big-end bearing
41  Chain tensioner
42  Crankshaft chainwheel key
43  Crankshaft chainwheel
44  Pulley
45  Pulley fixing bolt
46  Main bearings 1, 2, 4, 5
47  Main bearing 3
48  Thrust washers
49  Crankshaft
50  Crankshaft rear oil seal
51  Flywheel dowel
52  Flywheel ring gear
53  Flywheel
54  Flywheel fixing bolts
55  Spigot bush – gearbox input shaft
56  Spigot bush – convertor spigot end

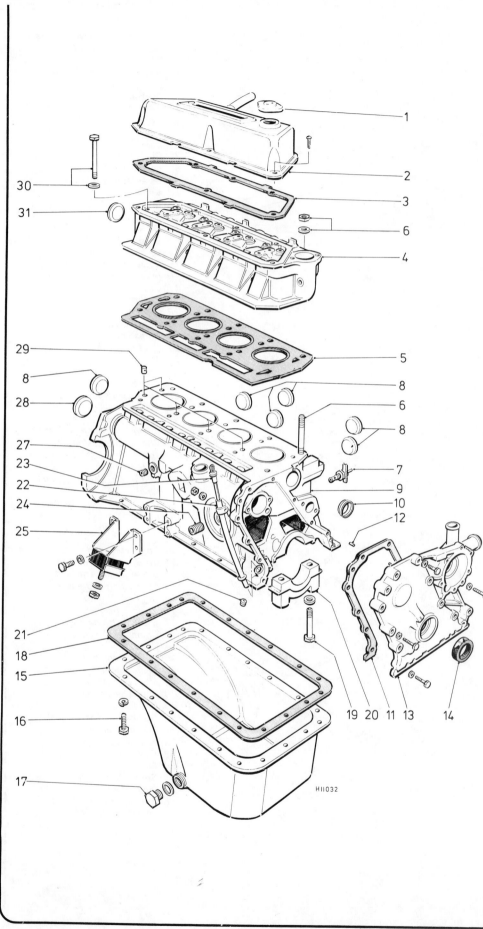

Fig. 1.4 Engine static components – exploded view (Sec 6)

1 Oil filler cap
2 Rocker cover
3 Rocker cover gasket
4 Cylinder head
5 Cylinder head gasket
6 Cylinder head stud, nut and washer
7 Cylinder block drain tap
8 Cylinder block blanking cups
9 Cylinder block
10 Front blanking cup
11 Timing cover gasket
12 Timing cover dowel
13 Timing cover
14 Oil seal
15 Sump
16 Sump screw and spring washer
17 Sump drain plug and washer
18 Sump gasket
19 Main bearing bolt and washer
20 Front main bearing cap
21 Blanking plug
22 Dipstick tube
23 Dipstick
24 Threaded sleeve – oil filter to cylinder block
25 Engine rubber mounting assembly
26 Rear main bearing side joint
27 Blanking plug
28 Camshaft rear bearing end blanking cup
29 Water jets
30 Cylinder head bolt and washer
31 Cylinder head rear end blanking cup

H11032

retaining cap refuses to free to expose the collet, do not continue to screw down on the compressor or damage may occur. Gently tap the top of the tool directly over the cap with a light hammer. This will free the cap. To avoid the compressor jumping off the cap when tapped, hold it firmly with one hand. Slide the oil control seal from each inlet valve. Drop the valves out. Scrape all carbon from them. Keep the valves in their correct sequence unless they are to be renewed. If they are to be used again, place them in a sheet of card having the holes numbered 1 to 8 to correspond with the valve positions. Keep the valve springs, washers etc in the correct order.

2    Examine the heads of the valves for pitting, splits, and burning, especially the heads of the exhaust valves. The valve seatings should be examined also. If the pitting on valve and seat is very slight, remove this by grinding them together with coarse, and then fine, valve grinding paste. Where bad pitting exists, either the seats must be recut, or in bad cases new inserts must be fitted, whilst the valve heads must either be recut or new valves must be fitted. This work should be left to a main agent or engineering works. In practice it is seldom that the seats are so worn that they require renewal. Normally, however, the valves receive the most wear, and the owner can purchase new valves and match them to the seats by grinding.

3    To grind in the valves, support the head on wooden blocks, combustion chambers uppermost. Smear a trace of coarse carborundum paste on the seat face, insert the valve in the guide, and apply a suction grinder tool to the valve head. With a semi-rotary motion, grind the valve to its seat, lifting it occasionally to redistribute the paste. When a full matt even surface finish is produced on both the seat and valve, wipe off the paste and repeat the process with fine carborundum paste, lifting and turning the valve to redistribute the paste as before. A light spring placed under the valve head will greatly ease this operation. When a smooth unbroken ring of light grey matt finish is produced on both faces, the operation is complete. Take care during this work not to allow the paste to come in contact with the valve stem and guide.

4    Scrape away all carbon from the valve head and stem, clean away every trace of grinding compound, taking great care to leave none in the ports or valve guides. Clean with a paraffin soaked rag, then with a clean rag, and finally, if an air line is available, blow all the parts clean.

## 12  Valve guides – reconditioning

1    The valve guides are machined directly in the cylinder head. If the valves become noticeably slack in the guides and if there is noticeable movement, when side pressure is exerted on the stem whilst in the guide, then the procedure is to ream out the bores and fit new valves with oversize stems. Reaming is a skilled operation and should be left to a competent engineering workshop.

e2    When valves with oversize stems are fitted, a number, to indicate the amount of oversize ie + 0.015 in or 0.030 in, is stamped on the cylinder head as shown in Fig. 1.5. If + 3 is already there, this indicates that valves with stems 0.003 in oversize were fitted during manufacture. This does not affect the oversize stems available.

## 13  Engine front mounting brackets – removal

Each bracket is held to the block by four bolts. Undo the bolts with a ring or socket spanner. The brackets may be removed if necessary, with the engine in place, The engine should be supported underneath and the bolts to the engine and frame removed. In this way the flexible mountings may also be renewed.

## 14  Sump – removal

1    The sump can be removed with the engine in or out of the car. With the engine in, raise the front of the car and support it on axle stands. Alternatively run the car over a pit or up on a pair of ramps. Disconnect the battery. Undo the oil drain plug on the right side of the sump with a 1 in AF spanner and drain the engine oil into a container with a capacity of at least 8 pints. Undo the screws round the periphery of the sump with a $\frac{7}{16}$ in AF spanner and lower the sump.

2    With the engine out, wait until the cylinder head is removed. Invert the engine, undo the screws holding the sump to the crankcase and lift

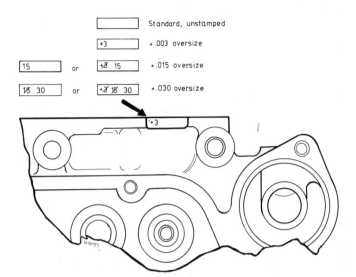

Fig. 1.5 Valve guide bore identification marks – location (Sec 12)

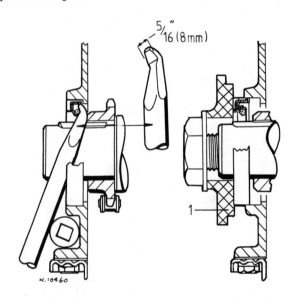

Fig. 1.6 Timing cover oil seal – removing and refitting (Sec 15)

1    Metal ring

it off. If the cylinder head is not being removed (for example if the oil pump requires attention) place the engine on its side before proceeding.

## 15  Timing cover oil seal – renewal

1    To renew the timing cover oil seal without removing the timing cover, remove the fanbelt and crankshaft pulley as described in Section 16, and extract the timing cover seal using a $\frac{1}{2}$ in (12.70 mm) diameter bar of length 20 in (508 mm), levering against a socket or similar object placed below the seal against the timing cover housing (Fig. 1.6).

2    The new oil seal can be pressed into position using the crankshaft pulley bolt and a metal ring of outside diameter 2.75 in (70 mm), inside diameter 1.5 in (38 mm), and thickness 0.625 in (16.0 mm). Polish out any defects on the crankshaft pulley sealing area before refitting it. Tighten the pulley bolt to the correct torque setting, and refit the fanbelt.

## 16 Crankshaft pulley and timing cover – removal and refitting with engine in car

1  The timing cover can be removed with the engine in the car and without removing the sump. The radiator may also be left in position if a metal fan is fitted. Where an electric fan is fitted remove it as described in Chapter 2.
2  Disconnect the battery and remove the dynamo/alternator as described in Chapter 10.
3  Drain the radiator and cylinder block, catching the water in a clean bowl if antifreeze has been added.
4  If necessary, remove the radiator as described in Chapter 2.
5  Undo the bolts and washers which hold the fan blades and pulley wheel in place and remove them with the fanbelt.
6  To remove the crankshaft pulley bolt on vehicles with manual gearboxes, engage a gear and apply the handbrake fully. Where automatic transmission is fitted, remove the starter motor and jam the torque converter ring gear with a large screwdriver or cold chisel.
7  With a socket spanner undo the crankshaft pulley bolt and pull off the pulley wheel. If it is difficult to move, place two large screwdrivers behind the wheel at 180° to each other and carefully lever it off. It is preferable to use a proper pulley extractor if available, but levers are permissible if care is taken not to damage the pulley flange.
8  Remove the Woodruff key from the crankshaft nose with pliers, and ensure that it does not become lost.
9  Undo the bolts holding the water pump, and pull it away. It is now most important that the rear of the car is jacked up, so that any water left in the block will drain out. If this is not done water can fall into the sump when the timing cover is removed. This means the sump will have to be dropped and cleaned.
10  Remove the four screws at the front of the sump under the timing cover. Undo the bolts which secure the timing cover, and if these are of different lengths insert them in their relative positions into holes in a piece of card.
11  Pull off the timing cover, tapping gently with a soft-faced hammer if necessary, as the cover can be a tight fit on two locating dowels. Take great care not to damage the sump joint. If the joint does sustain damage, the sump must be removed and the joint renewed.
12  To reassemble, coat the sump joint liberally with a non-setting jointing compound. Renew the timing cover seal if necessary. Clean off the cylinder block surface, and refit the timing cover with a new joint.
13  Refit the remaining parts in reverse order, ensuring that the oil seal surface on the crankshaft pulley is in good condition. Adjust the fanbelt and refill the cooling system.

## 17 Timing chain, sprockets and chain tensioner – removal and renovation

1  The camshaft sprockets for 1250/1300 and 1500/1600 engines are not interchangeable. The 1250/1300 sprocket can be identified by a small mark close to the centre as shown in Fig. 1.7. The 1500/1600 sprocket is plain apart from the timing marks. It should be noted that the bore in the camshaft sprocket can be either $\frac{5}{8}$ in (15.8 mm) diameter or $\frac{13}{16}$ in (20.6 mm) diameter. The $\frac{5}{8}$ in bore item is retained by a $\frac{7}{8}$ in long bolt and one washer, whilst the $\frac{13}{16}$ in bore item is retained with a 1 in long bolt and two washers.
2  To dismantle, remove the timing cover as described in Section 16.
3  Turn the engine so that the sprocket timing marks are aligned, and loosen the two bolts which hold the tensioner to the block. Hold the head of the tensioner into the body to prevent the assembly springing apart, take out the two bolts and remove the tensioner and backplate.
4  Slowly release the hold on the slipper head. Lift the head out of the body, and remove the restraint cylinder (which may have to be turned anticlockwise) and spring from the head plunger.
5  Remove the camshaft sprocket centre bolt. Remove the camshaft and crankshaft timing wheels complete with the chain, by levering them forward alternately, a little at a time, using two large screwdrivers at 180° to each other. The wheels are only a hand press fit and will probably pull off easily.
6  With both wheels off, remove the Woodruff key from the crankshaft with pliers and put it somewhere safe.
7  Examine the sprocket teeth for wear. These are shaped like an inverted 'V', and if one side is concave, the tooth is worn and the sprocket should be renewed. Renew the chain if a considerable

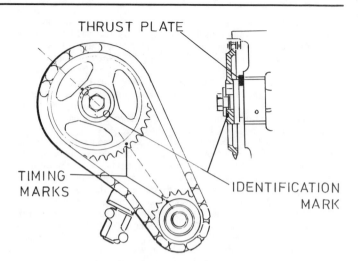

**Fig. 1.7 1250/1300 engines – correct position of the timing marks when refitting the timing chain, and location of the timing wheel identification mark (Secs 17 and 39)**

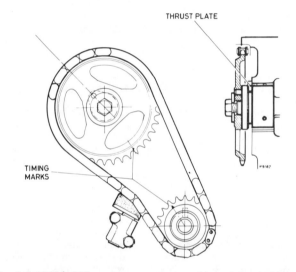

**Fig. 1.8 1500/1600 engines – correct position of the timing marks when refitting the timing chain (Secs 17 and 39)**

mileage has been covered, and always if the sprockets have been renewed. If the rubber slipper head of the tensioner is worn more than 0.05 in (1.3 mm), or if any score marks are present, renew the head. It is normal to renew the slipper head when fitting a new chain.

## 18 Timing chain, sprockets and timing case – twin carburettor models

A double-row timing chain is employed together with a wider tensioner, and a fixed rubber faced damper is fitted to the outer side of the chain. These larger items mean that a wider timing case is used.

## 19 Camshaft – removal with engine in vehicle

1  Disconnect the battery. Drain the cooling system, and remove the radiator, as described in Chapter 2. Remove the front grille. Remove the generator or alternator.
2  Remove the rocker gear, pushrods, cylinder head and tappets, as described in Section 7.
3  Remove the timing cover, sprockets and chain as described in Section 17.
4  Remove the fuel pump as described in Chapter 3. Remove the

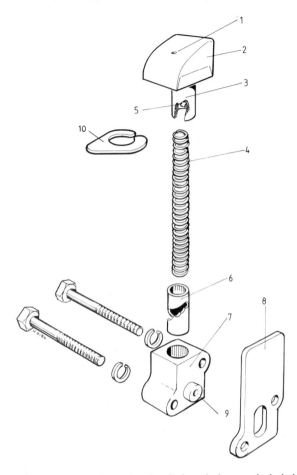

**Fig. 1.9 Automatic tensioner for the timing chain – exploded view (Sec 17)**

| | | |
|---|---|---|
| 1 | Oil feed hole to timing chain | plunger (3) |
| 2 | Slipper head | 6 Restraint cylinder |
| 3 | Slipper head plunger | 7 Chain tensioner body |
| 4 | Spring – compression type | 8 Backplate |
| 5 | Limit peg – inside | 9 Oil feed hole |
| | | 10 Cardboard packer |

sump and oil pump as described in Sections 14 and 25.

5   Remove the nuts holding the engine mountings inside the front crossmember. Place a wooden block under the front cylinder block flange, and jack up on this, thus raising the front of the engine, to allow the camshaft to be driven through the grille opening.

6   Remove the two bolts and spring washers which hold the camshaft thrust plate to the block and remove the plate. Withdraw the camshaft carefully to ensure that the cam peaks do not damage the camshaft bearings as the shaft is pulled forward.

### 20 Pistons, connecting rods and bearings – removal

1   Remove the engine if necessary then the cylinder head and sump, as described in the relevant Sections of this Chapter.

2   With the engine inverted (if removed), mark each connecting rod and cap with its cylinder number, preferably with appropriate dabs of paint. Punch or file marks may be satisfactory, but have been known to cause metal fatigue in the connecting rod. Once marked, undo the bearing cap nuts using a good quality socket spanner. Lift off each cap.

3   Turn the engine on its side and push out each piston through the top of the cylinder block, using a hammer handle to tap with if necessary. Note that if the pistons are standard there are two small letters stamped on the edge of the top face. These indicate the piston and gudgeon pin grade and also the front. Some models may be fitted with pistons which use the word 'Front' or the letter 'F'. All three forms of identification indicate the side of the piston which must be fitted

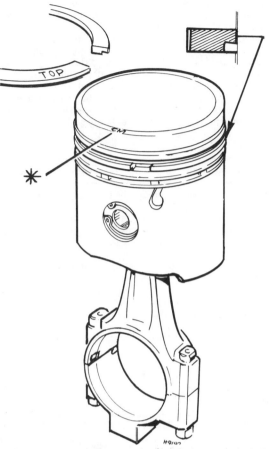

**Fig. 1.10 Front of the piston, indicated by the bore grade letter, by the word 'FRONT', or by the letter 'F' (Secs 20 and 21).**

*Inset shows correct fitting of the second compression ring. The top ring is chromium plated*

towards the front of the engine. The shell bearings in the connecting rods and caps are removed by pressing the edge opposite the notch when they will slide round and out. Keep them identified if they are to be reused.

4   Remove the gudgeon pins by cleaning the carbon from the outer ends of the gudgeon pin holes. With circlip pliers remove a circlip from one end of the hole and slide out the pin. If the pin is reluctant to move under hand pressure, heat the piston in hot water.

5   Big-end bearing failure is indicated by a pronounced knocking from the crankcase, and a small drop in the oil pressure. The general comments in Section 26, paragraphs 2 and 3 are applicable.

### 21 Piston rings – removal and refitting

1   Unless new rings are to be fitted, take care not to break them on removal. Start with the top ring, spread the ends gently, and lift it over the piston top. Remove the other rings similarly, but employ two twin feeler gauges or pieces of shim steel under the rings to prevent them from dropping into the grooves as they are removed. Label the rings to ensure that they go back in the same place.

2   When refitting the rings, first inspect and renew them in accordance with Section 29, as necessary. Ensure that the piston grooves are completely free from carbon, and if necessary clean this away. A piece of broken piston ring makes a good scraper, but care should be taken to prevent it digging into the soft surface of the piston. Ensure that the ring grooves and piston holes are clear. Fit the rings over the piston top, beginning with the bottom ring. Spread it with the fingers, gently, and employ the two feeler gauges or pieces of shim steel to assist with sliding the ring into place. Remember that the ring with the step goes in the second groove with the step towards the bottom (Fig. 1.10). The words 'TOP' and 'BOTTOM' which may be

marked on the rings indicate which way up it goes in its groove, not that the ring concerned should necessarily go in the top groove.

3   If new rings are being fitted to old bores, it is essential that the surface glaze on the cylinder walls be removed to permit the new rings to bed down properly. A wooden dummy piston, which fits closely inside the bore when wrapped with a piece of No 1 or $1\frac{1}{2}$ emery cloth, should be moved up and down the bores with a small twisting motion, until the bores are covered with a criss-crossed pattern of abrasions. Ensure that all abrasive is confined to the cylinder bores, and completely cleaned off before assembling the pistons into the cylinders. Oil the pistons, rings, and cylinder bores generously with engine oil. Space the ring gaps equally round the piston.

## 22 Flywheel and starter ring gear – removal and renovation

1   To remove the flywheel, remove the gearbox and clutch assembly (see the relevant Chapter).

2   Remove the five bolts from the centre of the flywheel. There are no washers. Using a soft-headed mallet tap the periphery of the flywheel progressively all round, gradually drawing it from the crankshaft flange and locating dowel. Do not allow it to assume a skew angle or it may join on the close fitting flange and dowel. When the flywheel is nearly off make sure it is supported so that it does not drop; it is heavy.

3   If the teeth of the ring gear are worn or if any are broken, renew the gear. Drill a hole, between two of the teeth, taking care not to damage the flywheel during this process. Protect the eyes with suitable goggles, and use a cold chisel to split the gear in the vicinity of the hole.

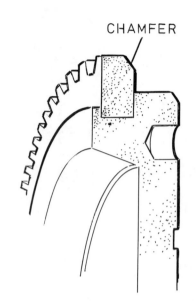

Fig. 1.11 Flywheel ring gear, with the chamfer correctly fitted towards the clutch face (Sec 22)

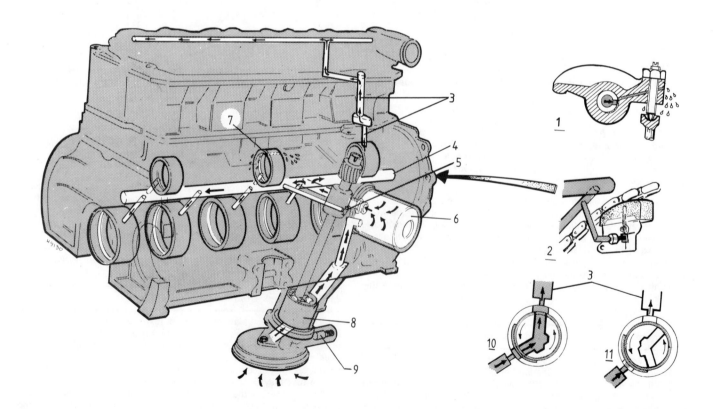

Fig. 1.12 The oil circulation system (Sec 23)

| | | |
|---|---|---|
| 1 | Oil feed from rocker shaft to pushrod cup | |
| 2 | Oil feed to timing chain automatic tensioner | |
| 3 | Oil feed to rocker shaft | |
| 4 | Oil gallery | |

5   Oil pressure warning light switch feed
6   Full flow oil filter
7   Oil feed groove in centre camshaft bearing – to adjacent cams and tappets

8   Oil pump
9   Oil pressure relief valve – in pump
10   Oil feeding through front camshaft journal from

gallery (4) to rocker shaft feed drilling (3)
11   Oil feed to rocker shaft cut off by rotation of front camshaft journal

4  Check that the mating faces of the new ring and the flywheel are clean and free from burrs. Heat the ring in an oven set at 428°F (220°C) for 30 minutes. Do not exceed the recommended temperature or the temper of the ring will be lost, causing rapid wear. Lift the heated ring from the oven with two pairs of pliers and fit it to the flywheel so that the gear teeth chamfers are towards the flywheel and clutch face side (see Fig. 1.11). If there are chamfers on both sides it can be fitted either way round. Tap the ring down on to the register, and leave it to cool naturally. The contraction of the metal on cooling will ensure the proper fit.

### 23  Engine lubrication system – general description

A forced feed system of lubrication is used, with oil circulated to all engine bearing surfaces under pressure by a pump, which draws oil from the sump. The oil is first pumped through a full-flow filter (this means that all the oil in circulation is passed through it). From the filter, oil flows into a main oil gallery cast integrally in the cylinder block. From the gallery, oil is fed via oilways in the block to the crankshaft main bearings, and then along oilways in the crankshaft to the connecting rod bearings. From the same gallery, oilways carry oil to the camshaft bearings. From the front camshaft bearing a further oilway passes oil to a gallery in the cylinder head. This gallery delivers oil through the hollow rocker shaft which contains a number of small holes to lubricate the rocker pivots. The tappets are lubricated by oil returning from the rocker gear via the pushrods, not under pressure. Once oil has passed through the bearings and out it finds its own way by gravity back to the sump. The gudgeon pins and cylinder bores are lubricated by oil thrown out from the big-end bearings.

If the filter becomes blocked, oil will continue to flow through the bypass valve, which will automatically open and allow the oil to miss out the filter element. Similarly, any blockage in oilways (resulting in greatly increased pressure) will cause the oil pressure relief valve (situated in the oil pump baseplate) to operate, returning oil direct to the sump.

The oil pressure when hot is 50 to 60 lbf/in$^2$ at 3000 rpm, this being measured after oil has passed through the filter. As the oil pressure warning light only comes on when the pressure is as low as 3 to 5 lbf/in$^2$, it is most important that the filter element is regularly changed and the oil changed at the recommended intervals. Should the warning light come on when the engine is running at any speed above idling, stop at once and investigate, or serious damage may result.

The crankcase is ventilated to prevent pressure building up from the action of the pistons, and to ensure that oil, and sometimes fuel vapour, is carried away. The fumes travel via a short tube from the left of the rocker cover to a flame trap, which in turn is connected by oil resistant rubber hose to the air cleaner. The fumes are drawn through the air cleaner and burnt with the fuel air mixture during normal combustion.

### 24  Oil filter – removal and refitting

1  The throw-away filter screws on a sleeve on the lower front right side of the block. The sleeve, which is threaded, feeds directly to the main oil gallery.
2  To remove the filter, turn it anticlockwise off the sleeve. If it cannot be removed by hand (the sealing ring tends to stick to the joint face) use a 1 in AF spanner or an oil filter wrench.
3  Clean the joint face on the block, smear grease or oil on the sealing ring and screw it into place until it just touches the cylinder block. Turn the filter two thirds of a turn further. Do not overtighten; use hand pressure only. Top up the sump to compensate for the oil lost from the filter (approximately 1 pint), run the engine and check for leaks.

### 25  Oil pump – removal, examination and renovation

1  Unclip and remove the distributor cap. Turn the engine so that the rotor arm would be pointing to the segment in the cap carrying the lead to No. 4 cylinder. Ensure that the timing cover TDC mark is in line with the mark on the crankshaft pulley.
2  Remove the distributor (Chapter 4) and the sump (Section 14).

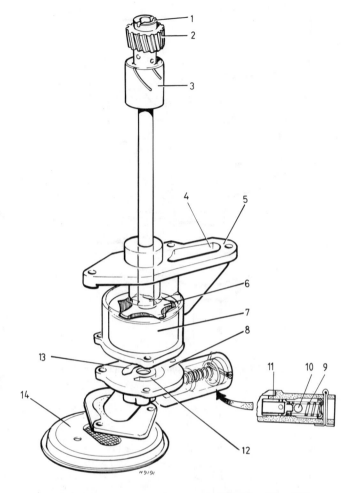

Fig. 1.13 Oil pump and pressure relief valve (Sec 25)

1  Distributor offset drive slot
2  Oil pump driven gear
3  Three oil grooves feeding oil to gear (2)
4  Oil feed channel to cylinder block oil gallery
5  Oil pump body
6  Four lobe rotor and pump shaft
7  Five lobe driven rotor
8  Oil pump base
9  Oil pressure relief valve spring
10  Oil pressure relief valve discharge hole – shown in this position for illustration only.
11  Oil pressure relief valve piston
12  Oil outlet port to oil pressure relief valve
13  Oil inlet port from oil pump intake filter
14  Oil pump intake gauze filter

3  Undo the three bolts which retain the oil pump. Withdraw the oil pump.
4  To check if the pump is serviceable, check if there is any slackness in the spindle bushes. Next, remove the bottom cover, held by three screws, and allow the outer rotor ring to fall out under its own weight. Do not drop it as it may crack. Clean all oil from the mating faces of the rotors and pump, and refit the outer ring ensuring that the chamfered end is towards the gear end of the pump. With a feeler gauge and straight edge check the clearance between the end faces of the inner and outer rotor rings and the pump body (see Fig. 1.14). The permissible gap is between 0.001 in (0.025 mm) and 0.003 in (0.075 mm). Check with a feeler gauge the side clearance between the top of the inner and outer lobes as shown in 'A' in Fig. 1.15. The permissible gap is between 0.001 in (0.025 mm) and 0.006 in (0.15 mm). Check the clearance between the inside of the pump body and the outside of the outer rotor as shown at 'B' in Fig. 1.15. The permissible gap is between 0.005 in (0.125 mm) and 0.008 in (0.20 mm). If any

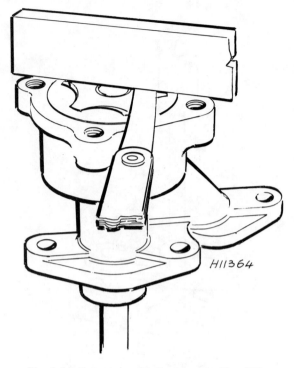

**Fig. 1.14 Rotor-to-endplate clearance (Sec 25)**

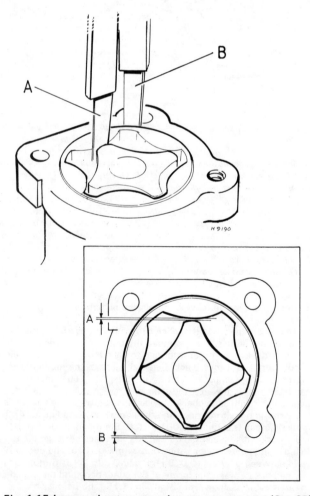

**Fig. 1.15 Inner and outer rotor clearances – see text (Sec 25)**

measurements are outside the permitted clearances, fit a replacement pump.

5   To clean the relief valve and spring, remove the spring clip (inset, Fig. 1.13), and thus the ball and spring. Do not stretch or compress the spring. Refit using a new split pin.

### 26 Crankshaft and main bearings – removal, examination and renovation

1   With the engine removed from the car, remove the sump, oil pump, timing chain, sprockets and flywheel or driveplate. If the cylinder head is also removed, the engine can be inverted onto the head face.

2   Remove the connecting rod bearing caps. Remove the two cap bolts from each of the five main bearing caps, and lift away each cap noting its position. The bearing shells will probably come off with the caps, and can be removed by pushing them round from the end opposite the notch.

3   Lift the crankshaft out. Put it somewhere safe where it cannot fall. Remove the shell bearings from the inner housings, and recover the thrust washers from the rear main bearing. Also recover the crankshaft rear oil seal.

4   Examine the crankpins and main bearing journals for scoring and scratching. If they appear satisfactory they must still be properly measured to ensure that they have not worn to an oval shape, and this should be done by a motor engineering works. If the shaft is worn in any of the ways outlined, it should be reground professionally.

5   Main bearing failure is normally accompanied by vibration which can be quite severe at high speeds, and by a significant drop in oil pressure. The surface of the bearings themselves should be matt grey in colour with no sign of pitting or scoring. Replacement shell bearings are supplied in thicknesses dependent on the degree of regrinding that the crankshaft requires, this being carried out in multiples of 0.010 in, and the bearing shells are supplied as 0.010 in undersize and so on. The engineering works regrinding the crankshaft will normally supply the correct shells with the reground crank. If the crank is found to be in good order, it is felt always to be worth renewing the bearing shells as a matter of course.

### 27 Crankshaft spigot bearing – removal and refitting

1   This bearing is located in the end of the crankshaft, at the flywheel end (see Fig. 1.3). Early models were fitted with a plain sintered bush, later models with a needle roller bearing. If the early type requires renewal, fit a needle roller type as a replacement.

2   This plain bearing can be removed by filling it with high viscosity grease, inserting a close fitting steel rod, and giving the end a sharp blow to force the bearing out by hydraulic action. Removal and fitting of the needle roller bearing calls for the use of a special tool, and a main agent should be consulted. Ensure that the seal end of this type of bearing enters last, thus causing the lubricant to be retained.

3   On automatic transmission models a steel spigot bearing is used, its purpose being to centralise the torque converter.

### 28 Cylinder bores – examination and renovation

1   In some cases prior indication of worn cylinders and pistons will have been given by blue smoke from the exhaust, in conjunction with heavy oil consumption. After dismantling, examine the bores for a step at the top, and for scoring.

2   Cylinder wear may be overcome by fitting new piston rings, by special oil control ring sets, or by reboring. To avoid wasting time and money, and because of the equipment required to accurately measure the wear in the cylinder, it is advised that a specialist motor engineer be consulted.

3   If the cylinders have already been bored to their maximum, liners can be fitted. This situation will not often arise, however.

### 29 Pistons and rings – examination and renovation

1   Examine the pistons for signs of damage to the crown and to the top edge. If any rings have broken there could be damage to the grooves, and the piston must then be renewed. Deep scores in the

piston walls also call for renewal. If the cylinders are being rebored new oversize pistons and rings will be needed. If the cylinders do not need reboring and the pistons are in good condition, only the rings need be checked.

2    To check an existing ring, place it in the cylinder and press down to near the bottom of the stroke, using an inverted piston to keep the ring square. Measure the gap with a feeler gauge and compare with the Specifications. If the gap is too large, renew the ring.

3    Check the ring side clearance in the piston groove, and compare with the Specifications (Fig. 1.16). If the gap is too big, new pistons and rings will be required if genuine 'official' spares are used. However, independent producers of pistons and rings can normally provide the rings separately. If new standard pistons and rings are being used it will be necessary to have the ridge grooved away from the top of each cylinder bore. If special oil control rings are being obtained from an independent supplier, ridge removal will not be necessary as the top rings will be stepped to give the necessary clearance. If the top ring of a new set is not stepped, it will hit the ridge made by the old ring and break. If new pistons are obtained the rings will be included and it must be emphasised that the top ring must be stepped if the piston is fitted to a bore which has not been either rebored or de-ridged.

4    Check the ring gaps in the bores as described in paragraph 2. Any gaps which are too small should be increased by filing one end of the ring with a fine file. Be careful not to break the ring as they are brittle, expensive and sometimes difficult to obtain individually. Do not allow the gap to remain below the minimum figure given in the Specifications, or the gap may close under operating temperatures and the ring break. The groove side clearance of new rings in old pistons should be within the specified tolerances. If it is not enough, the rings can stick in the piston grooves causing loss of compression and possibly breakage.

## 30 Camshaft and camshaft bearings – examination and renovation

1    Remove the camshaft, and examine the bearings for wear. If wear exists, take the block to a specialist motor engineer, who will have the tools necessary for this work. However, it should be noted that camshaft bearing renewal is not commonly necessary.

2    Examine the camshaft for wear on the bearing journals or cam profiles, and renew if necessary. If the skew gear is worn, the camshaft will also have to be renewed. Examine the camshaft thrust plate, which also locates the shaft. If this is scored or otherwise worn, renew it.

## 31 Tappets – examination and renovation

Examine the tappets, particularly the surface which operates on the camshaft. Indentations or cracks on this face indicate serious wear and the tappets should be renewed. Remove all traces of sludge. It is unlikely that the sides will prove worn, but if they are very loose and can be rocked, renew them. Tappet wear is not common, and any present is likely to occur only at high mileages.

## 32 Connecting rods – examination and renovation

Check the mating faces of the big-end caps and connecting rods to see if they have been filed in a mistaken attempt to take up wear. If so, they must be renewed. Check the rods visually for any sign of twisting, and if in any doubt about them have them examined by a main agent on the special jig available for this purpose.

## 33 Decarbonisation – general

1    Remove with a wire brush and blunt scraper all carbon deposits from the combustion spaces and ports on the cylinder head. Clean all carbon from the valve guides. Scrape the head surface clean with a suitable scraper, and wash the head clean.

2    Check the head face for flatness by placing a good quality steel rule or other straight object across it. If this gives rise to doubts, have the face checked, and if necessary machined, by a motor engineering works. Note, however, that no more than 0.005 in (0.127 mm) should be removed, or rough running will occur.

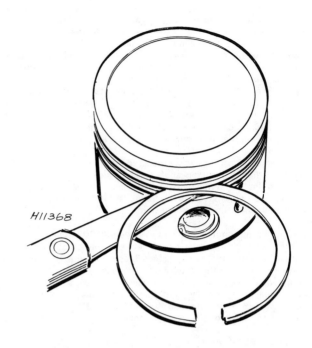

H11368

**Fig. 1.16 Piston to piston ring vertical clearance (Sec 29)**

3    Clean the pistons and top of the cylinder bores. If the pistons are in the block it is essential that care is taken to ensure that no carbon gets into the bores. This can scratch the cylinder walls or cause damage to the piston and rings. To prevent this, turn the crankshaft so that two pistons are at the top of their bores. Seal the other two bores with rag or paper and masking tape. The waterways should also be covered with pieces of tape to prevent carbon entering the cooling system and damaging the water pump. Carefully clear away all loose carbon, and rotate the crankshaft to bring the outer two pistons to the top. Proceed as before.

4    Remove the carbon ring around the top of each cylinder bore, ensuring first that rag is inserted in the bore to collect the pieces of carbon.

## 34 Valve springs and valve stem oil seals

1    If the engine has covered a high mileage, it is false economy not to fit new valve springs. Old springs can break, allowing the valve to drop, with very serious results. On low mileage engines stand the springs on a flat surface and renew the complete set if any are less than the specified length.

2    The inlet valves are fitted with oil seals round their stems. These must be renewed when the cylinder head is overhauled or the valves removed (see Fig. 1.18). Push new seals into position on the valve guide after the valve has been fitted. Ensure the correct seal is used and that the clip is in place. Those for standard valves, or for valves with stems 0.003 in (0.076 mm) oversize have plain exteriors. Seals for valve stems 0.015 in (0.381 mm) or 0.030 in (0.762 mm) oversize have '15' or '30' on their top face.

## 35 Engine reassembly – general

Everything must be spotlessly clean, the oilways clear, locking washers and spring washers must be fitted where indicated and all bearing and other working surfaces lubricated during assembly. Renew any bolts or studs where the threads are damaged. Where possible use new spring washers. Have available all normal tools, a supply of clean rag, an oil can filled with engine oil, (a detergent bottle cleaned out, will do) new spring washers, a set of new gaskets, and a torque wrench. The sequence given for rebuilding the engine was found satisfactory, but is not necessarily the only correct one.

## 36 Crankshaft and main bearings – refitting

1 Stand the engine upside down on clean paper. Ensure that the crankcase is clean and the oilways clear. Use compressed air or non-fluffy pipe cleaners to clear them. Clean the protective grease from the new main bearing shells by immersing them in hot water.
2 Fit the five upper halves of the shells in place after wiping their locations in the crankcase clean. Ensure the lugs on the backs lie in the recesses in the block. Oil generously (photo). Note that the centre main bearing shell has a plain surface whilst all the others are grooved.
3 After ensuring that the crankshaft oilways are clean, lower it into place (photo).
4 Two semicircular thrust washers, located either side of the cylinder block half of the crankshaft rear bearing, are used to control the endfloat. Fit the semicircular thrust washer to the front of the journal with the two grooves facing forwards. Fit the rear semicircular thrust washer with the grooves towards the rear of the crankshaft (photo).
5 The crankshaft endfloat should be between 0.002 in and 0.008 in and is measured with a feeler gauge between the thrust face of the rear thrust washer and the crankshaft flange with the shaft pushed rearwards. Fit oversize thrust washers if necessary (photo).
6 Fit the lower shell bearings in the main bearing caps, ensuring that the right shell goes into the right cap if old shells are being used. Ensure that the plain bearing is in the middle (No 3) cap. Ensure that the tags on the back of the bearings enter the notches in the caps (photo).
7 Oil the crankshaft main bearing journals generously. Note that the underside of the main bearing caps carries a cast number from 1 to 5. This ensures that the caps are refitted in their correct locations with No 1 cap at the front of the engine. To ensure that the bearing caps are fitted the right way round, check that the tag on the back of the bearing in the block is adjacent to the tag on the back of the bearing in the cap. Fit all the bearing caps in place except the rear one. Fit new seals to the sides of this, and smear suitable jointing compound over the seals (photo). Fit the rear cap but do not fully tighten it until the rear seal is in place.
8 Tighten the main bearing cap bolts to the torque figure given in the Specifications. After securing each cap turn the crankshaft, and if it tightens up, remove and check the bearing and cap tightened last.
9 Check there are no imperfections on the oil seal journal at the rear of the crankshaft, and smear the circular seal and crankshaft seal face with grease. Carefully fit the oil seal with its flat face outwards, tapping it gently into place with a soft-faced hammer until fully home (photo).
10 Tighten the rear main bearing cap bolts and washers to the correct torque wrench setting.

## 37 Pistons and connecting rods – refitting

1 Turn the engine onto its left-hand side. Wipe the connecting rod half of the big-end bearing cap and the underside of the shell bearing clean. Fit the bearing in position with its locating tongue engaged with the corresponding groove in the connecting rod.
2 Wipe the connecting rod bearing cap and shell and fit the shell in the same way. Note that the locating tongues must be adjacent when the cap is fitted later (photo).
3 The pistons, complete with connecting rods, are fitted to their bores from above. As each piston is inserted, ensure that it is the correct assembly for that particular bore, that the connecting rod is the right way round, and that the front of the piston is towards the front of the engine. The caps should have been marked with centre punch dots during dismantling to assist with identification. With a wad of clean rag wipe the cylinder bores clean. Position the piston rings so the gaps are spread evenly round the piston. Check that the front of the piston (which may be marked 'FRONT', 'F', or with 2 letters such as 'LA' or 'CM') is to the front of the rod and cylinder bore, and slide a piston into the bore as far as the oil control ring.
4 It is then necessary to compress the piston rings in a clamp, but if this is not available, the rings can be compressed with the aid of a $3\frac{1}{2}$ in diameter jubilee clip (photo).
5 Holding the clamp or jubilee clip firmly against the block face (this is very important) gently tap the piston into the cylinder bore with the wooden handle of a hammer (photo).
6 Generously lubricate the crankpin journals with engine oil, and

turn the crankshaft so that the crankpin is in the most advantageous position to the connecting rod to be drawn onto it.
7 Fit the connecting rod caps making certain that the correct cap goes on the correct rod and that they are the right way round (photo). Tighten the big-end nuts to the specified torque, and upon tightening each set, rotate the shaft to ensure all is well. It if locks up, remove the last big-end cap tightened down and examine for faults or incorrect fitting.

## 38 Camshaft – refitting

1 Wipe the camshaft bearing journals and cams clean and oil them generously. Insert the camshaft into the crankcase gently (photo), until the camshaft thrust plate can be positioned (photo).
2 Check the endfloat of the shaft, employing a feeler gauge between the thrust plate and the inside of the camshaft gearwheel boss. Fit an oversize location/thrust plate if necessary, the specified endfloat being 0.004 in to 0.009 in. Fit the two bolts and washers which hold the thrust plate in position and tighten down firmly.
3 If the engine is in the vehicle, reverse the procedures given in Section 19.

## 39 Timing chain, sprockets, and chain tensioner – refitting

1 Turn the crankshaft so that Nos 1 and 4 cylinders are at TDC and turn the camshaft so the dowel is at 11 o'clock (see Figs. 1.7 and 1.8). Slip the chain over the gearwheels.
2 Position the camshaft gearwheel so that it will fit correctly onto its dowel, and then disengage the crankshaft gearwheel from the chain and rotate it until the timing dots are exactly opposite one another (Figs. 1.7 and 1.8). Re-engage the crankshaft gearwheel with the chain (photo).
3 If the gearwheels can now be refitted on the camshaft and crankshaft (a Woodruff key locates in the crankshaft gearwheel) and the timing marks are still adjacent and in line with the gearwheel centres, fit and tighten the camshaft wheel securing bolt and washer. If the shafts are still not in quite the right position, turn the camshaft slightly and try again. When tightening down the camshaft gearwheel securing bolt, the crankshaft can be prevented from turning by a sturdy screwdriver placed as shown between two flywheel bolts (photo).
4 To refit the chain tensioner (Fig. 1.9) release the tensioner from its locked down position by pressing the slipper head firmly against the tensioner body and, with the head held in this position bolt the tensioner in place on the front of the block (photo).
5 Release the slipper head, so that it can move out to tension the chain. Ensure it has moved out and is not in its locked down position (photo).

## 40 Timing cover and seal – refitting with engine out of vehicle

1 To renew the oil seal in the timing cover position two blocks of wood under the outside of the cover as close to the bore of the seal as possible. Drive out the old seal from inside the cover with a screwdriver (photo). Ensure that the old seal is driven out squarely so as not to damage the seal housing.
2 Turn the cover the other way up, so that the outside is facing upwards. Re-site the wooden blocks underneath it. Fit a new seal, so that the circular coiled spring is towards the inside of the cover (photo). With a soft-faced hammer, or a hammer and a block of wood, carefully tap the seal into the housing, finishing off with a small block of wood until the seal is below the level of the housing, and if fully home (photo).
3 Position a new timing cover gasket, using one or two dabs of jointing compound to retain it in place (photo). Offer up the timing cover to the engine. Note that it may be a little difficult to get the cover on as the dowels are a tight fit.
4 Refit the bolts and washers which hold the cover in place noting the correct positions of the longer bolts through the water pump (see Chapter 2, Section 8).

## 41 Oil pump – refitting

Refit the oil pump with No 4 cylinder at TDC on its firing stroke

36.2 Oiling the main bearing shells

36.3 Positioning the crankshaft

36.4 Positioning a thrust washer

36.5 Measuring the crankshaft endfloat

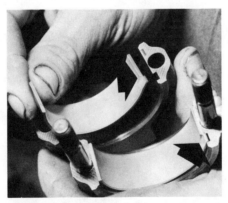

36.6 Fitting a main bearing shell to a cap

36.7 Fitting a seal to the main bearing cap

36.9 Fitting the crankshaft rear seal

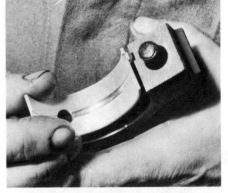

37.2 Fitting the big-end shells

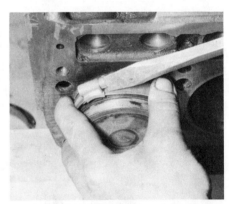

37.4 Compressing the piston rings using a jubilee clip

37.5 Tapping a piston into a cylinder

37.7 Fitting a big-end cap

38.1a Inserting the camshaft in the block

38.1b Positioning the camshaft thrust plate

39.2 Fitting the timing chain assembly

39.3 Holding the crankshaft to prevent rotation

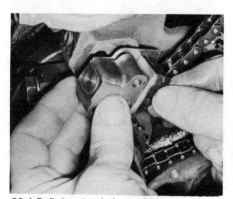
39.4 Refitting the chain tensioner

39.5 Check the tensioner operation

40.1 Driving out the timing cover seal

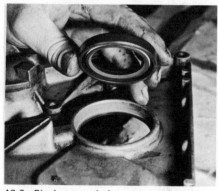
40.2a Placing new timing cover seal on the cover

40.2b Tapping a new timing cover seal into place

40.3 Positioning a new timing cover gasket

(the lobes on the camshaft for No 4 cylinder should be horizontal). No gasket or jointing compound should be used. As the skew gear on the oil pump driveshaft engages with the gear on the camshaft it must turn to the position shown (photo). It is essential that the slot in the oil pump gear takes up this position, or the distributor timing will be wrong. Tighten the three nuts and washers holding the pump in place.

## 42 Sump – refitting

1   Place the sump gasket into position (photo). Squirt oil over the timing chain, crankshaft and into the bores, and lower the sump into place.
2   Refit all the setscrews and washers and tighten the sump down evenly (photo).

## 43 Crankshaft pulley and flywheel – refitting

1   Ensure that the crankshaft pulley is free from damage and is smooth and polished where it runs in the seal. Defects in this area will cause rapid oil seal wear. Refit the pulley (photo). Fit the pulley retaining bolt and washer but do not fully tighten.
2   Ensure that the flange on the crankshaft which accepts the flywheel or driveplate, and the flywheel or driveplate itself, are clean. Offer the flywheel or driveplate up to the crankshaft, noting the locating dowel and the corresponding hole in the flywheel or driveplate (photo).
3   Refit the bolts and tighten them evenly in rotation so that it goes on squarely. Screw in two of the clutch cover or driveplate bolts as shown (photo) and place a strong screwdriver between them and the bench to prevent the engine turning when the bolts are tightened to the specified torque.

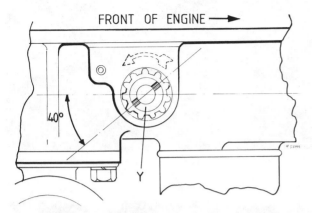

Fig. 1.17 Correct position of
the slots in the oil pump
drive gear when pump is
fully in position (Sec 41)
Y – Larger segment

FRONT OF ENGINE →

41.1 Position of the oil pump skew gear after
correct fitting

42.1 Positioning the sump gasket

42.2 Securing the sump

43.1 Refitting the crankshaft pulley

43.2 Offering up the flywheel

43.3 Fitting the flywheel securing bolts

43.4 Tightening the crankshaft pulley bolt

4   With the screwdriver still in place to prevent the crankshaft turning tighten the crankshaft pulley bolt to the specified torque (photo).

## 44 Tappets and accessories – refitting

1   Turn the engine over so it stands on its sump. Wipe the tappets clean, oil them, and return them to the same bores from which they were removed. The open ends face upwards (photo).
2   Pull the old rubber seal from the distributor housing. Fit a new one to the seal groove on the distributor (photo).
3   Turn the distributor drive shaft so that the driving tonge engages with the slot in the top of the oil pump drive gear (see Fig. 1.17). Insert the distributor, and fit and tighten the securing bolt and washer (photo).
4   Fit the fuel pump to the cylinder block, employing a new gasket. Insert and tighten the two securing bolts and washers (photo). Note

that if the pump is being refitted with the engine in the car, it is difficult to get at the right-hand bolt without removing the oil filter and the oil pressure sender. The oil pressure sender unit fits in a tapped hole between the oil filter and the fuel pump. Screw the unit into place (photo).
5   Press the base of the dipstick tube into place in its hole in the side of the crankcase (photo). The tube is held at its upper end by a clip which locates over the left-hand timing cover bolt. Insert the bolt through the clip and tighten the nut and washer (photo).
6   The dynamo/alternator is held at three points. It swivels at the two inner points on the block, and the drivebelt is adjusted by the slot in the adjuster strap which is fixed to the remaining attachment point (photo). Insert and partially tighten the three bolts, nuts and washers. Do not tighten fully at this stage as the drivebelt has still to be fitted and adjusted.
7   Fit the fan blades when fitted (metal four-bladed type shown), and the fan pulley, to the flange on the shaft on the front of the water pump

44.1 Fitting the tappets

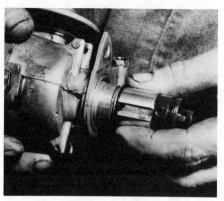
44.2 Fitting a distributor oil seal

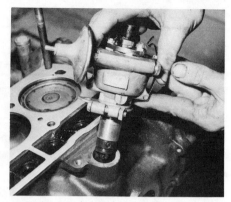
44.3 Inserting the distributor

44.4a Securing the fuel pump

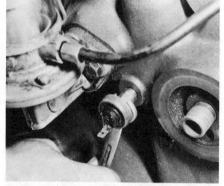
44.4b Fitting the oil pressure sender unit

44.5a Fitting the dipstick tube

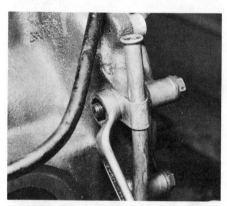
44.5b Securing the dipstick tube

44.6 Refitting the dynamo

44.7 Offering up the fan blades and pulley

44.8 Refitting the fanbelt

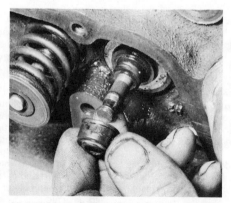
45.1 Refitting an inlet valve oil seal

45.2 Positioning a collar and a cap

(photo). Line up the fixing holes in the blades, pulley and flange, and fit and tighten the bolts and washers which hold the pulley and blades in place.

8    Fit the fanbelt and adjust it to give $\frac{5}{8}$ in (16 mm) movement on its longest run. Tighten the dynamo/alternator fixing bolts/nuts (photo).

### 45 Cylinder head – reassembly and refitting

1    Ensure that the cylinder head and valves are completely clean. Fit any reconditioned valves to their original positions. Oil the valve stems before fitting, and once in position, fit new oil seals on the inlet valves (photo).

2    Note that the coils at one end of the springs are closer than at the other. Fit the springs, close coil end first, and follow by placing the collar and cap over the valve stems (photo).

3    Place the screw head of the spring compressor on the valve head

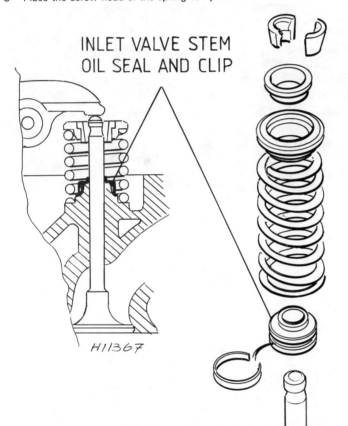

INLET VALVE STEM
OIL SEAL AND CLIP

H11367

**Fig. 1.18 Inlet valve oil seal and retaining clip (Sec 45)**

and the other end over the cap and valve stem. Screw up the clamp until the spring is compressed past the groove on the valve stem (photo).

4    Place the two halves of the split collar (collets) into the valve stem groove, narrow ends towards the cylinder head.

5    Release the clamp slowly and carefully making certain that the collets are not dislodged. The top semicircular edges of the collets should now be in line with each other (photo).

6    Examine the mating surfaces of the head and block. Remove any defects with a fine file. Place the gasket in position on the block. It will only fit one way.

7    With a mole wrench screw in the two studs, one at either end of the left side of the block (photo).

8    Lubricate the cylinder bores, and lower the assembled cylinder head into place (photo).

9    Refit all the cylinder head bolts, washers and nuts (for the two studs), and with a torque wrench tighten them down $\frac{1}{4}$ to $\frac{1}{2}$ a turn at a time to the specified torque wrench setting, in the order shown in Fig. 1.19. This procedure is to keep the tightening stresses even over the whole head, and to prevent distortion.

10    Lubricate the tappets, and fit the pushrods, mushroom shaped ends first, into the position they were in originally (photo).

11    Fit the rocker shaft assembly, ensuring that the ball ends on the rocker arms fit squarely in the cups on the top of the pushrods (photo).

12    Tighten the rocker shaft pedestal bolts to the specified torque figures. Note that the pedestal with the vertical rocker shaft oil hole must be at the front of the engine.

13    If the engine is in the vehicle, reverse the procedure given in Section 8.

### 46 Valve clearances – adjustment

1    The adjustment must be made with the engine either hot or cold, never half warm. First remove the rocker cover and gasket.

2    Turn the crankshaft so that No 1 cylinder is at TDC on its compression stroke.

3    Slacken the locknuts on No 1 cylinder rocker arms (photo). Place a feeler gauge of the correct size (see Specifications) between the rocker arm pad and valve stem and turn the adjusting screw until the feeler is firm but not tight (photo). Hold the screw to prevent it turning, and tighten the locknut. After adjusting both rocker clearances on No 1 cylinder turn the crankshaft a half turn at a time in order to adjust the valves on Nos 3, 4 and 2 cylinders in that order (see Fig. 1.20).

4    Refit the rocker cover and gasket.

### 47 Engine – final reassembly

1    Lubricate sparingly with grease the spigot bearing in the crankshaft flange.

2    Refit the clutch (see Chapter 5), and fit the gearbox bellhousing to the rear of the engine on manual models (photo). Insert and tighten the nuts, bolts and washers which hold the bellhousing to the engine. Check that the earth strap is on the top starter motor bolt (photo).

3    Slide the starter motor into place complete with protective shield. Tighten the two nuts and washers which secure the motor (photo).

45.3 Compressing a valve spring

45.5 Refitting the collets

45.7 Refitting the end studs on the cylinder block

45.8 Lowering the assembled cylinder head into place

Fig. 1.19 Cylinder head nut and bolt tightening sequence, working from No 1 to No 10 (Sec 45)

45.10 Fitting the pushrods

45.11 Fitting the rocker shaft assembly

46.3a Slackening the rocker shaft locknuts (No 4 cylinder shown)

46.3b Adjusting the valve clearance screw (No 4 cylinder shown)

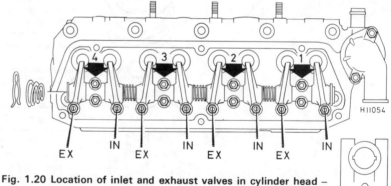

Fig. 1.20 Location of inlet and exhaust valves in cylinder head – inset shows correct positioning of rocker pedestals, with boss to rear (Secs 45 and 46)

47.2a Offering up the gearbox bellhousing

47.2b Securing the gearbox bellhousing

47.3 Refitting the starter motor

4   Fit the flywheel splashguard in place at the bottom front of the bellhousing, and tighten the securing bolts (photo).
5   Position a new gasket on the exhaust/inlet manifold mating face of the cylinder head (photo).
6   Fit the inlet and exhaust manifolds to the cylinder head and secure (photo).
7   Fit a new oil filter.
8   Refit the rocker cover using a new gasket. Secure the cover in place with the six screws or bolts (photo).

## 48 Engine – refitting in the vehicle

1   This is generally speaking a straightforward reversal of the removal sequence. If the engine and gearbox have been removed together it is best to refit them together. This will mean fitting the gearbox assembly to the engine on the bench and makes the mating of the items easier.
2   When the unit is being put back into the car, watch every inch of the way to ensure that no pipes or wires become caught or damaged. If the unit will not go where it should, look and see why. Do not force anything. As soon as the engine is relocated on its forward mounting, support it at the rear until the gearbox is secured by placing a block of wood behind the cylinder head.
3   If the engine is separated from the gearbox smear a little grease on the tip of the gearbox input shaft. On automatic transmission models make sure that the torque converter is fully engaged with the oil pump.
4   Always fit new oil and air cleaner elements after an overhaul.
5   The bonnet will need two pairs of hands when refitting. Fix the bracket bolts and nuts just tight enough to hold it and then close the bonnet to ensure it is correctly lined up. Tighten the bolts.
6   The following check list should ensure that the engine starts safely and with the minimum of delay:

(a)   Fuel lines to pump and carburettor connected and tightened
(b)   Water hoses connected and clipped
(c)   Radiator and engine drain taps closed
(d)   Water system replenished
(e)   Sump drain plug fitted and tight
(f)   Oil in engine
(g)   Oil in gearbox and level plug tight
(h)   LT wires connected to distributor and coil
(i)   Spark plugs tight
(j)   Tappet clearances set correctly
(k)   HT leads connected securely to distributor, spark plugs and coil
(l)   Rotor arm refitted in distributor and pushed fully home
(m)   Choke and throttle linkages connected
(n)   Braided earthing cable, engine to frame reconnected
(o)   Starter motor lead connected

47.4 Fitting the flywheel splash guard

47.5 Positioning a new manifold gasket

47.6 Offering up the manifold assembly

47.8 Refitting the rocker cover

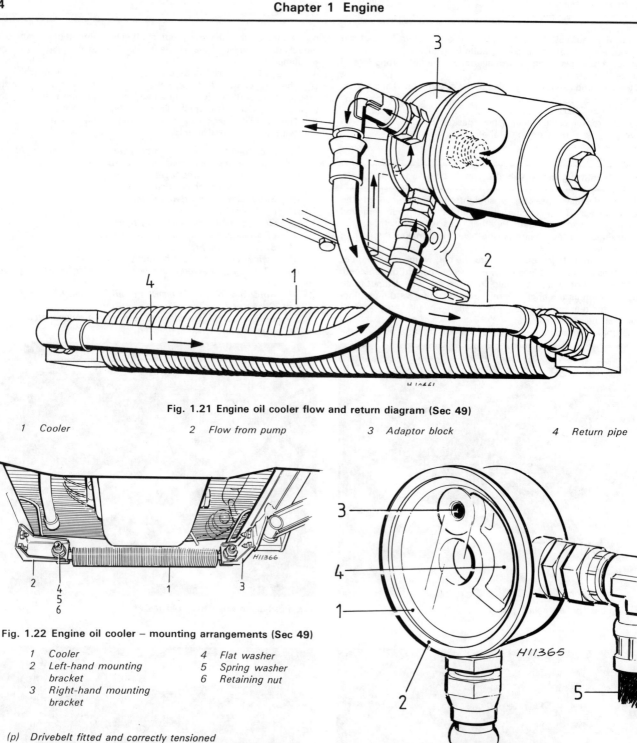

**Fig. 1.21 Engine oil cooler flow and return diagram (Sec 49)**

| | | | |
|---|---|---|---|
| *1 Cooler* | *2 Flow from pump* | *3 Adaptor block* | *4 Return pipe* |

**Fig. 1.22 Engine oil cooler – mounting arrangements (Sec 49)**

| | | | |
|---|---|---|---|
| *1* | *Cooler* | *4* | *Flat washer* |
| *2* | *Left-hand mounting bracket* | *5* | *Spring washer* |
| *3* | *Right-hand mounting bracket* | *6* | *Retaining nut* |

*(p) Drivebelt fitted and correctly tensioned*
*(q) Dynamo/alternator leads connected*
*(r) Battery charged and leads connected to clean terminal*

7   After 500 miles the cylinder head nuts and bolts should be retightened to the specified torque, and the valve clearances adjusted with the engine hot.

## 49 Oil cooler – installation

1   An engine oil cooler is an optional extra on certain models, and may be fitted into the oil feed circuit by installing an adaptor plate and union beneath the existing oil filter.
2   The oil cooler element is mounted on brackets attached to the front suspension drag strut mounting bolts. Ensure that the longer bracket is fitted to the left-hand side of the car. Details are clearly

**Fig. 1.23 Engine oil cooler adaptor block (Sec 49)**

| | | | |
|---|---|---|---|
| *1* | *Rubber sealing ring* | *5* | *Flexible hose – pump to oil cooler* |
| *2* | *Adaptor block, cylinder block side* | *6* | *Flexible hose – oil cooler to filter* |
| *3* | *Bypass valve* | | |
| *4* | *Oil receipt compartment* | | |

shown in Fig. 1.22.

3    Remove the oil filter and the threaded connection from the cylinder block.

4    Refer to Fig. 1.23 and ensure that the sealing ring (1) is in place on the adaptor block (2).

5    Place the adaptor block on the cylinder block in the old filter position, sealing ring against the engine.

6    Put the lockwasher under the hexagon of the union, put the union through the adaptor block and partially tighten, leaving the unions

facing downwards.

7    Fit the flexible hoses and tighten their unions. Tighten the adaptor block union to the correct torque figure. Secure the locking tabs on the washer.

8    Refit or renew the oil filter, tightening by hand only. Add 1½ pints (0.85 litres) of oil to the engine to compensate for the oil cooler capacity.

9    Check the security of all union nuts, run the engine, and inspect for oil leaks.

## 50  Fault diagnosis – engine

| Symptom | Reason(s) |
| --- | --- |
| Engine refuses to turn when starter switch is operated | Discharged or defective battery<br>Dirty or loose battery leads or connections<br>Defective solenoid, starter switch or leads<br>Loose or broken starter motor leads<br>Starter motor faulty ot jammed<br>Earthing strap broken or faulty |
| Engine spins, but does not start | Ignition components wet or damp<br>Spark plug insulators dirty<br>Distributor cap defective<br>Low tension lead broken<br>Dirty contact points<br>Condenser faulty<br>Ignition coil faulty<br>No fuel in tank, or fuel not reaching carburettor<br>Fuel pump faulty<br>Too much fuel, swamping spark plugs<br>Engine timing incorrect<br>Vapour lock in fuel system (in hot conditions) |
| Engine stops and will not re-start | Ignition failure<br>Fuel pump failure<br>No fuel in tank<br>Water in fuel system |
| Engine lacks power | Defective or burnt valves<br>Incorrect engine or ignition timing<br>Incorrect valve clearances<br>Blown cylinder head gasket<br>Leaking carburettor gasket(s)<br>Incorrect mixture adjustment<br>Ignition faults<br>Blocked air intake, or dirty filter<br>Ignition automatic advance faulty<br>Cylinder/piston wear |
| Excessive oil consumption | Defective inlet valve stem oil seals<br>Worn pistons and bores<br>Blocked engine breather<br>Oil leaks |
| Engine noisy | Incorrect valve clearances<br>Worn timing chain<br>Worn distributor drive<br>Worn engine bearings<br>Defective water pump bearing |

# Chapter 2 Cooling system

*For modifications, and information applicable to later models, see Supplement at end of manual*

## Contents

## Specifications

| | |
|---|---|
| **System type** | Pressurised with centrifugal pump and fan |
| **Coolant capacity** | 13 pints (7.33 litres) including heater |
| **Radiator cap opening pressure** | 9 lbf/in² (0.63 kgf/cm²) |

**Thermostat (bypass closing type)**

| | |
|---|---|
| Nominal opening temperature | 82°C (180°F) |
| Bypass port closed | 95°C (203°F) |

**Thermostat (non-bypass closing type)**

| | |
|---|---|
| Nominal opening temperature | 88°C (190°F) |
| Nominal opening temperature – air conditioning fitted | 82°C (180°F) |

**Torque wrench settings**

| | lbf ft | Nm |
|---|---|---|
| Viscous fan centre bolt | 12 | 16 |

## 1 General description

The cooling system comprises the radiator, top and bottom water hoses, water pump, cylinder head and block water jackets, radiator cap with pressure relief valve, and flow and return heater hoses (see Fig. 2.1). The thermostat is located in a recess at the front of the cylinder head. Cold water in the bottom of the radiator circulates up through the lower hose to the pump where the pump impeller pushes the water round the cylinder block and head and through cast-in passages to cool the cylinder bores, combustion surfaces and valve seats. When sufficient heat has been absorbed by the water and the engine has reached working temperature, the water moves from the cylinder head past the now open thermostat through the top hose, and into the radiator header tank. It then travels down the radiator tubes where it is rapidly cooled by the in-rush of air when the vehicle is in forward motion. A fan, either mounted on the water pump pulley or electrically driven, assists cooling. The water reaches the bottom of the radiator and the cycle is repeated.

When the engine is cold the thermostat remains closed until the coolant reaches a pre-determined temperature (see Specifications). This assists rapid warming-up. Water temperature is measured by an electro-sensitive capsule located immediately below the thermostat housing. Connection between the capsule and the facia gauge is by a single cable and Lucar type connector. The cooling system also provides the heat for the heater. The heater matrix is fed directly with water from the hottest part of the engine – the cylinder head – returning through a connection on the water pump housing.

## 2 Routine maintenance

1 The coolant level should be checked weekly, or more often in conditions of high mileage or exceptionally high temperatures. Coolant loss should not normally occur in a pressurised system. Lowering of the water level must be investigated. Top up with soft clean water and when the system contains an antifreeze mixture use topping up mixture in similar proportions to the existing coolant.

2 Check the fanbelt tension (see Section 9) at least every 5000 miles and examine hoses and connections for leaks or deterioration. Ensure that the two system drain taps are securely off. The radiator tap of white plastic is located at the base of the unit (Fig. 2.2) and the cylinder block tap (Fig. 2.3) is on the left of the engine behind the generator (or alternator).

## 3 Cooling system – draining and refilling

1 Should the system be left empty both the cylinder block and radiator must be drained as with a partly drained system corrosion of the water pump impeller seal face may occur with subsequent early failure of the seal and bearing.

2 Place the car on a level surface. Have ready a container with a capacity of two gallons which will slide beneath the radiator and sump.

3 Move the heater control on the facia to 'HOT' and remove the radiator cap. If hot, unscrew the cap very slowly, first covering it with a cloth to prevent scalding when the pressure is released.

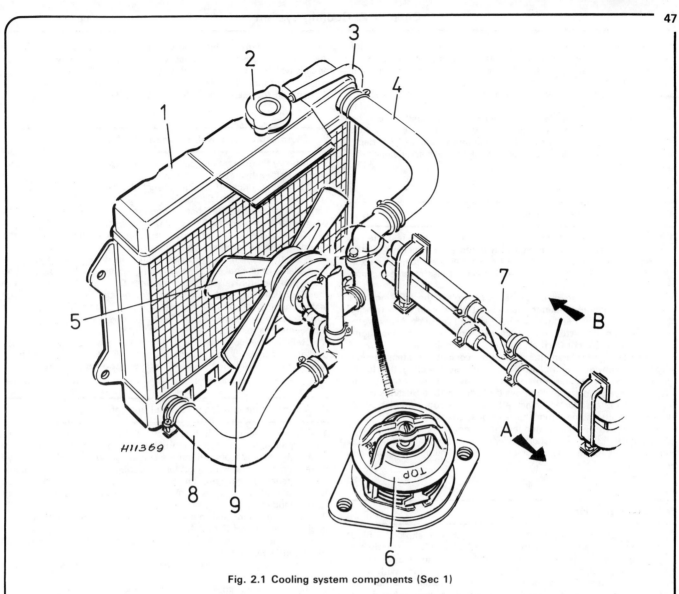

**Fig. 2.1 Cooling system components (Sec 1)**

| | | | |
|---|---|---|---|
| 1 | Radiator | 4 | Radiator top hose |
| 2 | Pressure filler cap | 5 | Fan blades |
| 3 | Overflow tube | 6 | Thermostat |

| | | | |
|---|---|---|---|
| 7 | Heater hose bypass | A | Heater flow hose |
| 8 | Radiator bottom hose | B | Heater return hose |
| 9 | Fanbelt | | |

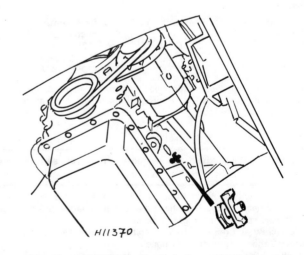

**Fig. 2.2 Radiator drain tap (Sec 1)**

**Fig. 2.3 Cylinder block drain tap (Sec 1)**

4    Unscrew the drain tap at the base of the radiator. When coolant ceases to flow into the receptacle, repeat the operation by unscrewing the cylinder block tap on the left of the engine. Retain the coolant if it contains antifreeze.
5    To fill the system, place the heater control to the 'HOT' position, screw in the radiator drain tap, finger tight only, and close the cylinder block tap. Pour coolant slowly into the radiator so that air can be expelled through the thermostat pin hole without being trapped in a waterway. Fill to the correct level, 1 in below the radiator filler neck, and refit the filler cap. Run the engine, check for leaks and recheck the coolant level.

## 4    Cooling system – flushing

1    The radiator and waterways can, after a time, become restricted or blocked with scale or sediment which reduces the efficiency of the cooling system. If this occurs or if the coolant appears rusty or dark in colour the system should be flushed. In severe cases reverse flushing may be required.
2    To flush the system, place the heater controls to the 'HOT' position and unscrew fully the radiator and cylinder block drain taps. Remove the radiator filler cap and place a hose in the filler neck. Allow water to run through the system until it emerges from both drain taps quite clear in colour. Do not flush a hot engine with cold water.
3    In severe cases of contamination of the coolant or system, reverse flush by removing the radiator cap and disconnecting the lower radiator hose at the radiator outlet. Remove the top hose at the radiator connection end and remove the radiator. (See Sections 6 and 16). Invert the radiator and place a hose in the bottom outlet. Flush until clear water comes from the radiator top tank.
4    To flush the engine water jackets, remove the thermostat and place a hose in the thermostat location until clear water runs from the water pump inlet. Cleaning by chemical compounds is not recommended.

## 5    Antifreeze solution

1    Before cold weather arrives, the cooling system should be filled with an antifreeze solution, conforming to BS 3152. Modern antifreeze of good quality also prevents corrosion and rusting, and may be left in the system to advantage all year round. Drain and refill with fresh solution each year. Before adding antifreeze, check all hose connections and the tightness of the cylinder head bolts, as such solutions are searching.
2    The quantity of antifreeze which provides various levels of protection is given below, expressed as a percentage of system capacity:

| Antifreeze volume | Protection to | Safe pump circulation |
|---|---|---|
| 25% | -26°C (-15°F) | -12°C (10°F) |
| 30% | -33°C (-28°F) | -16°C (3°F) |
| 35% | -39°C (-38°F) | -20°C (-4°F) |

Where the cooling system contains an antifreeze solution, top up with a solution made up in similar proportions to the original, to avoid dilution.

## 6    Radiator (belt driven fan system) – removal, servicing and refitting

1    Drain the cooling system as described in Section 3.
2    Disconnect the top hose from the radiator header tank pipe, and the bottom hose from the outlet pipe.
3    Unscrew and remove the four bolts which secure the radiator to the front engine compartment panel.
4    Lift out the radiator, taking care not to damage the cooling fins. Do not allow antifreeze solution to drop onto the bodywork, or damage may result.
5    Radiator repairs are best left to a specialist, although minor leaks may be tackled with a proprietary repairing compound. Clean flies and

dirt from the matrix by brushing with a soft brush or by hosing. Flush the radiator as described in Section 4. Examine and renew any hoses or clips which have deteriorated, and check the drain tap and its rubber washer, renewing if suspect.
6    Refit in reverse order. Refill the system and check for leaks.

## 7    Thermostat – removal, testing and refitting

1    A faulty thermostat can cause overheating, slow engine warm up, and also affect heater performance.
2    To remove, drain off coolant through the radiator tap until the level is below the thermostat housing joint face. An indication that the correct level has been reached is when the cooling tubes are exposed when viewed through the filler cap. Unscrew and remove the two bolts (4) (see Fig. 2.4) and withdraw the cover sufficiently to permit the thermostat to be removed from its seat.
3    Test the thermostat by suspending it in water. Heat the water, then allow it to cool, and whilst doing so check the opening and closing temperatures using a thermometer. Compare the readings with the Specifications, and renew if faulty or stuck. Operation is not instantaneous and sufficient time must be allowed for movement during testing. Never refit a faulty unit – leave it out until a replacement is available.
4    Refit in reverse order. Clean the housing faces and use a new gasket with jointing compound. The word 'TOP', on the thermostat face, must be visible from above. Refill the cooling system.

## 8    Water pump and fan – removal and refitting

1    The water pump comprises an impeller which is a press fit on the pump spindle, a light alloy pump body, a pressure balanced seal and a fan hub which is a press fit on the bearing spindle (see Fig. 2.5). The water pump bearing is greased for life during assembly annd requires no maintenance. Leakage from the drain hole (7) will indicate the need for a replacement unit, as dismantling or servicing the pump is not recommended.
2    The pump is located in a housing which is an integral part of the engine timing cover (Fig. 2.4).
3    To remove the pump, drain the radiator and cylinder block as described in Section 3.
4    Slacken the generator or alternator mounting bolts as described in Section 9.
5    If a six-bladed fan is fitted, remove the radiator. Remove the fan securing screws and withdraw the fan blades and pulley together with the belt.
6    Remove the five bolts which hold the water pump to the timing case. The two longer bolts are located in the lower holes. Lift the pump from the timing case. It is located in position by two dowels and may be tight, but do not hammer the body or prise the flange. Remove the gasket.
7    Refit in reverse order, ensuring that the mating flanges are clean and free from burrs. It is essential to use a new gasket to provide the correct clearance between the pump impeller and the timing cover face.

## 9    Fanbelt – adjustment, removal and refitting

1    Fanbelt tension is important. If it is overtightened, the bearings in the water pump and dynamo or alternator may wear prematurely. If slack it will slip, causing overheating and a discharged battery through low dynamo or alternator output. The fanbelt is correctly tensioned when a total movement of $\frac{5}{8}$ in (16 mm) can be obtained at the middle of the longest run. Always adjust with the engine cold. Slacken the bolts which secure the generator (Fig. 2.6) and move it until the correct belt tension is obtained. Retighten the securing bolts. Do not overtighten.
2    To renew a fanbelt, always slacken the alternator or dynamo mountings and push the alternator or dynamo as far towards the engine as possible. It will then be found quite easy to slip the belt over the pulley rim. Never attempt to prise a belt over a pulley rim without first having slackened the alternator or dynamo mountings.

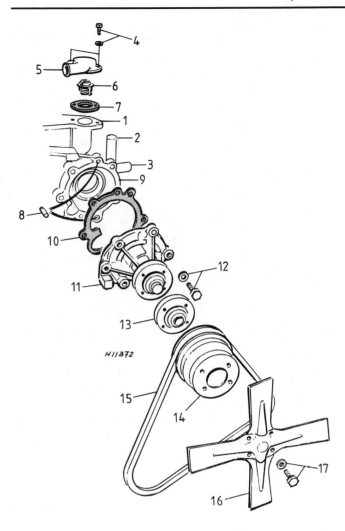

**Fig. 2.4 Water pump and thermostat – exploded view (Sec 7)**

| | |
|---|---|
| 1 Cylinder head | 9 Timing case |
| 2 Heater return hose connection | 10 Pump to timing case gasket |
| 3 Radiator bottom hose connection | 11 Water pump body |
| 4 Thermostat housing bolts | 12 Pump securing bolts |
| 5 Thermostat housing | 13 Fan pulley hub |
| 6 Thermostat | 14 Fan pulley |
| 7 Thermostat housing to cylinder head gasket | 15 Fan belt |
| 8 Locating dowels – pump to timing case | 16 Fan (4-blade metal type) |
| | 17 Fan assembly securing bolts |

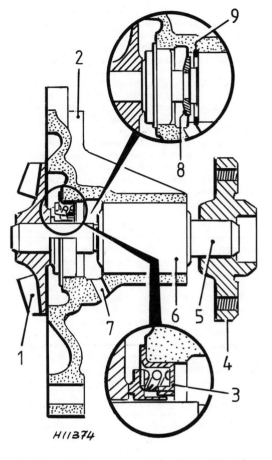

**Fig. 2.5 Water pump – sectional view (Sec 8)**

| | |
|---|---|
| 1 Impeller | 7 Drain hole |
| 2 Pump body | 8 Thrower |
| 3 Seal | 9 Circlip |
| 4 Fan blade hub | (Items 8 and 9 not fitted |
| 5 & 6 Combined pump spindle and bearing | to early model pumps) |

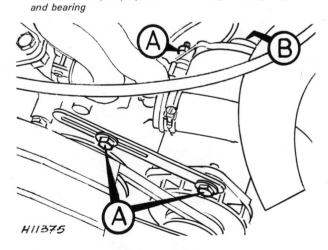

**Fig. 2.6 Dynamo mounting and lubrication arrangement (Sec 9)**

| | |
|---|---|
| A Mounting bolts | B Lubrication hole |

### 10 Water temperature gauge

1 Correct operation of the water temperature gauge is very important in preventing engine overheating. The gauge is electrically operated, and consists of a transmitter unit screwed in the front of the cylinder head, transmitting through a Lucar connector and cable to the dial on the instrument panel. The instrument only operates when the ignition is on.

2 Where the gauge reads high or low intermittently or not at all, check the cable between the transmitter unit and the gauge. Disconnect the Lucar connector from the transmitter unit and switch on the ignition, when the gauge should read 'cold'. Now earth the cable to the engine block, when the gauge needle should indicate 'hot'. This test proves the gauge to be functional and the fault must therefore lie in

the transmitter unit. If the fuel gauge shows signs of malfunction at the same time as the water temperature gauge, a fault in the voltage stabilizer may be the cause.

## 11 Holset viscous fan drive unit

1   On certain models, this unit is fitted between the water pump
pulley and the fan blades. It operates in a similar manner to a torque
converter and slipping clutch, the drive being transmitted through a
fluid film. The unit incorporates limited torque output, the maximum
speed being governed to 3500 rpm, and this has the effect of reducing
fan noise and power absorption. The unit is maintenance-free and, if a
fault develops or damage is sustained, it must be replaced by a
complete new unit.
2   To remove the unit, remove the radiator and then the centre bolt
which secures the drive unit to the water pump pulley flange.
3   Withdraw the fan complete with drive unit.
4   Remove the bolts which secure the fan to the drive unit and
separate the two components. Renew the drive unit as an assembly if
necessary.
5   Refit in reverse order.

## 12 Electric cooling fan assembly – general description

Certain models are fitted with an electric cooling fan instead of a
belt-driven fanblade assembly fitted to the water pump, the advantages compared to the normal arrangement being a quicker warm-up
period and a reduction in engine power absorption by the fan. The
motor and fan unit is mounted on a bracket behind the radiator, and
a bi-metallic thermal switch, located in the radiator bottom tank,
controls the motor, which maintains the coolant at its most efficient
temperature. The electrical circuit consists of the motor, thermal
switch, and switch relay.

## 13 Electric cooling fan assembly – removal and refitting

1   Disconnect the battery negative terminal, and separate the plug
and socket connector on the motor supply lead.
2   Remove the two motor support bracket bolts and withdraw the
assembly from beneath the car. The fan blade can be removed from

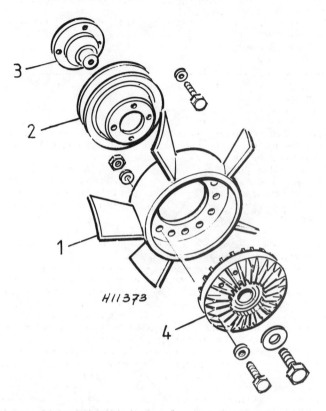

**Fig. 2.7 Holset viscous fan unit – exploded view (Sec 11)**

| 1 Plastic type fan blades | 3 Hub |
| 2 Pulley | 4 Drive unit |

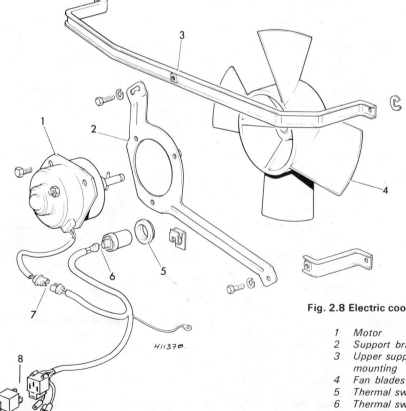

**Fig. 2.8 Electric cooling fan system (Sec 11)**

1   Motor
2   Support bracket
3   Upper support bracket to radiator
     mounting
4   Fan blades
5   Thermal switch seal
6   Thermal switch plug connector
7   Motor supply lead connector
8   Relay unit

the motor driveshaft by extracting the C-clip and withdrawing the fan from the engagement pin.

3    Remove the three motor securing bolts and separate the motor from the bracket.

4    Refit in reverse order.

## 14  Electric cooling fan thermal switch – removal, inspection and refitting

1    Disconnect the battery negative terminal. Drain the cooling system. Pull the wiring plug away from the thermal switch socket, prise the retaining clip away, and withdraw the switch from the radiator bottom tank.

2    Check the thermal switch seal in the radiator for signs of deterioration and, if necessary, renew by extracting it with a suitable lever, being careful not to damage the radiator. When inserting a new seal, dip it in soapy water solution to assist the lip of the seal to seat properly in the radiator bottom tank.

## 15  Electric cooling fan system – testing

1    If the system develops a fault and becomes inoperative, check the two fuses which independently supply the thermal switch and motor via the relay unit. Ensure that the fuses are making good contact with their terminals and, using a 12 volt test lamp and leads, check that current is reaching the fuse terminals with the ignition switched on.

2    On early models the thermal switch and motor are in series with each other, whereas on later models they are in parallel. On both arrangements, check that current is reaching the switch by removing the plug and connecting the test lamp to each terminal in turn. *Keep hands and clothing clear of the fan blades during testing.* If there is no current at either switch plug terminal a fault is indicated in the relay

unit, but should current be reaching one terminal of the switch plug proceed as follows:

(a)  *On early model cars connect a wire between both switch plug terminals and check that current is reaching the motor. The thermal switch is faulty if the motor is now operative.*

(b)  *On later model cars check that the switch earth lead is making good contact with the body frame, connect a wire between both switch plug terminals, and check that current is reaching the motor. The thermal switch is faulty if the motor is now operative.*

3    Check the supply to the motor, by switching on the ignition and bridging the pins at '6' (Fig. 2.8). Separate the motor supply lead (7) and connect a test lamp between the socket and earth. If the lamp does not light the black/green harness wire is faulty. If the lamp lights connect the test leads between the socket and pin on (7). If the lamp lights the motor is faulty, whereas if it remains unlit the black earth wire of the harness is faulty.

## 16  Radiator (electric fan system) – removal and refitting

1    Disconnect the battery negative terminal, and disconnect the electrical harness from the thermal switch and fan motor.

2    Drain the cooling system, and disconnect the top and bottom hoses from the radiator.

3    Remove the two lower radiator retaining bolts.

4    Remove the two upper radiator retaining bolts, and withdraw the radiator whilst supporting the cooling fan assembly. Ensure that the radiator fins and the fan blades are not damaged. If the radiator is to be renewed, disconnect the fan assembly and remove the thermal switch by prising the clip to one side.

5    Refit in reverse order, ensuring that the thermal switch retaining clip is seated correctly on the switch body.

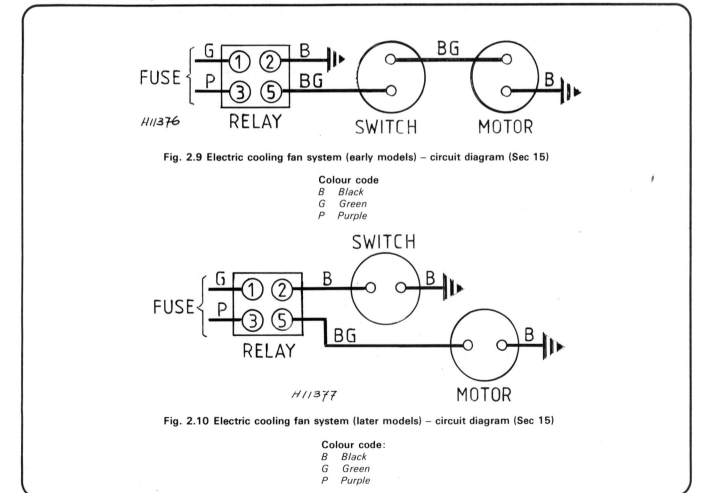

Fig. 2.9 Electric cooling fan system (early models) – circuit diagram (Sec 15)

Colour code
B    Black
G    Green
P    Purple

Fig. 2.10 Electric cooling fan system (later models) – circuit diagram (Sec 15)

Colour code:
B    Black
G    Green
P    Purple

## 17 Fault diagnosis – cooling system

**Symptom    Reason(s)**

| Symptom | Reason(s) |
|---|---|
| Overheating | Low coolant level |
| | Slack fanbelt |
| | Thermostat not operating |
| | Radiator pressure cap faulty or of wrong type |
| | Defective water pump |
| | Cylinder head gasket blowing |
| | Radiator core clogged |
| | Radiator blocked |
| | Binding brakes |
| | Bottom hose or tank frozen |
| | Ignition timing incorrect |
| | Carburettor setting incorrect |
| | Exhaust partially blocked |
| | Oil level too low |
| | Cracked or porous cylinder head or wall |
| | Faulty thermal switch |
| Engine running too cool | Defective thermostat |
| | Wrong thermostat |
| | Missing thermostat |
| | Faulty thermal switch |
| Loss of coolant | Leaking radiator or hoses |
| | Cylinder head gasket leaking |
| | Leaking cylinder block core plugs |
| | Faulty radiator filler cap or wrong type fitted |
| | Loose clips on water hoses |
| | Cracked or porous cylinder head or wall |

# Chapter 3 Fuel, exhaust and emission control systems

*For modifications, and information applicable to later models, see Supplement at end of manual*

## Contents

## Specifications

### Fuel pump

| | |
|---|---|
| Make and type .............................................................................. | AC mechanical |
| Delivery pressure (fuel pump with glass filter bowl) ................... | 2.75 to 4.25 lbf/in$^2$ (0.19 to 0.29 kgf/cm$^2$) |
| Delivery pressure (fuel pump with metal dome) .......................... | 3.5 to 5 lbf/in$^2$ (0.25 to 0.35 kgf/cm$^2$) |

### Fuel tank capacity ..........................................................................  10 Imp gal, 11.6 US gal (45.5 litres)

### Carburettor types

**Note:** *Carburettors identified as Zenith models are identical to Stromberg models of the same type designation*

| | |
|---|---|
| Stromberg CDS ........................................................................... | Manual choke and adjustable jet |
| Stromberg CD3 ........................................................................... | Manual choke and adjustable metering needle |
| SU HS4C ..................................................................................... | Manual choke and adjustable jet |
| Stromberg CDSE ......................................................................... | Manual choke and non-adjustable metering needle |
| Stromberg CDSET ....................................................................... | Automatic choke: Adjustable or non-adjustable metering jet* |
| Stromberg CDSEV ....................................................................... | Manual choke: Adjustable or non-adjustable metering needle: Float chamber vent control system |

* *Adjustable metering needle fitted from introduction of exhaust gas recirculation system*

## Carburettor applications

### Stromberg 150CDS

| | Slow running rpm | | Needle | Piston spring | Fast idle gap |
|---|---|---|---|---|---|
| | Manual | Automatic | | | |
| **Pre-4 series models** | | | | | |
| 1250 single carburettors .............. | 700/750 | N/A | 5BB or 6AL | Red | SA cam 0.040 to 0.050 in (1.02 to 1.27 mm) M cam 0.030 to 0.040 in (0.76 to 1.02 mm) |
| 1500 single carburettor ................ | 700/750 | 600 (D selected) | 6AG or 6AK | Red | SA cam 0.04 to 0.05 in (1.02 to 1.27 mm) M cam 0.03 to 0.04 in (0.76 to 1.02 mm) |
| 1500 twin carb (HC) ...................... | 950/1050 | 600/650 (D selected) | 6BE | Blue | 0.040 to 0.050 in (1.02 to 1.27 mm) |

### Stromberg 150CD3

| | Slow running rpm | | Needle | Piston spring | Fast idle gap |
|---|---|---|---|---|---|
| | Manual | Automatic | | | |
| **Pre-4 series models** | | | | | |
| 1250 single carb ........................... | 700/750 | N/A | B5CJ | Red | 0.025 to 0.030 in (0.64 to 0.76 mm) |
| 1250 twin carb ............................. | 1100 | N/A | B5CU** | Not fitted | 0.025 to 0.035 in (0.64 to 0.89 mm) |
| 1500 single carb (HC) .................. | 800 | 600 in 'N' | B6BJ | Red | 0.025 to 0.030 in (0.64 to 0.76 mm) |
| 1500 single carb (LC) ................... | 800 | 600 in 'N' | B6BJ | Red | 0.025 to 0.030 in (0.64 to 0.76 mm) |
| 1500 twin carb (HC) ...................... | 950/1000 | 950/1000 in 'N' | B5CD | Blue | 0.025 to 0.035 in (0.64 to 0.89 mm) |

*** superseded by BSDP*

| | Slow running rpm | | Needle | Piston spring | Fast idle gap |
|---|---|---|---|---|---|
| **4 series models** | | | | | |
| 1600 single carb (HC and LC) ..... | 770/830 | N/A | B5DK | Blue | 0.027 in (0.69 mm) |
| 1300 and 1600 twin carb ........... | 870/930 | N/A | B5DM | Plain | 0.025 in (0.64 mm) |
| **5 series models** | | | | | |
| 1300 single carb (HC and LC) ..... | 770/830 | N/A | B5DS | Blue | 0.027 in (0.69 mm) |
| 1600 single carb (HC and LC) ..... | 770/830 | N/A | B5DQ | Red | 0.037 in (0.94 mm) |
| 1300 and 1600 twin carb ........... | 870/930 | N/A | B5DM | None | 0.025 in (0.64 mm) |
| **6 series models** | | | | | |
| 1300 HC and LC) ......................... | 770/830 | N/A | B5DS | Blue | 0.027 in (0.69 mm) |
| 1300 (HC 15.01 engine) .............. | 770/830 | N/A | B5DK | Blue | 0.025 to 0.035 in (0.64 to 0.89 mm) |
| 1300 (LC) .................................... | 770/830 | N/A | B5DK | Blue | 0.025 to 0.035 in (0.64 to 0.89 mm) |
| 1600 (HC and LC) ........................ | 770/830 | 770/830 in 'N' | B5DQ | Red | 0.037 in (0.94 mm) |
| 1600 (HC) (type S3800) ............... | 770/830 | 770/830 in 'N' | B5DV | Blue | 0.025 to 0.035 in (0.64 to 0.89 mm) |
| **7 series models** | | | | | |
| 1300 (HC) .................................... | 770/830 | N/A | B4DU | Blue | 0.025 to 0.035 in (0.64 to 0.89 mm) |
| 1300 (LC) .................................... | 770/830 | N/A | B5DK | Blue | 0.025 to 0.035 in (0.64 to 0.89 mm) |
| 1600 (HC) .................................... | 770/830 | 770/830 in 'N' | B5EE | Blue | 0.025 to 0.035 in (0.64 to 0.89 mm) |
| 1600 (LC) .................................... | 770/830 | 770/830 in 'N' | B5DK | Blue | 0.025 to 0.035 in (0.64 to 0.89 mm) |

### Stromberg 175CD3

| | Slow running rpm | | Needle | Piston spring | Fast idle gap |
|---|---|---|---|---|---|
| | Manual | Automatic | | | |
| **6 series models** | | | | | |
| 1300 (HC) .................................... | 870/930 | N/A | B1EB | None | 0.025 to 0.035 in (0.64 to 0.89 mm) |
| 1600 (HC) .................................... | 870/930 | 870/930 in 'N' | B1EC | None | 0.025 to 0.035 in (0.64 to 0.89 mm) |
| **7 series models** | | | | | |
| 1300 (HC) .................................... | 870/930 | N/A | B1EB | None | 0.025 to 0.035 in (0.64 to 0.89 mm) |
| 1600 (HC) .................................... | 870/930 | 870/930 in 'N' | B1EC | None | 0.025 to 0.035 in (0.64 to 0.89 mm) |

### Stromberg CDSE

| | Slow running rpm | | Needle | Piston spring | Fast idle gap |
|---|---|---|---|---|---|
| | Manual | Automatic | | | |
| 1500 single carb (LC) .................. | 770/830 | 600/630 in 'D' | B5BD | Red | 0.025 to 0.035 in (0.64 to 0.89 mm) |

### Stromberg CDSET

| | Slow running rpm | | Needle | Piston spring | Fast idle gap |
|---|---|---|---|---|---|
| | Manual | Automatic | | | |
| 1500 single carb (LC) .................. | 770/830 | 600/660 in 'D' | B6BD | Red | N/A (Automatic choke) |
| With exhaust gas recirculation system (EGR) ................................. | 770/830 | 600/660 in 'D' | B5DC | Red | N/A (Automatic choke) |

### Stromberg CDSEV

| | Slow running rpm | | Needle | Piston spring | Fast idle gap |
|---|---|---|---|---|---|
| | Manual | Automatic | | | |
| 1500 twin carb (LC) ..................... | 750/1000 | 700/760 in 'D' | B5CC | Blue | 0.025 to 0.035 in (0.64 to 0.89 mm) |
| With exhaust gas recirculation system (EGR) ................................. | 950/1000 | 700/760 in 'D' | B5DD | Not fitted | 0.025 to 0.035 in (0.64 to 0.89 mm) |

| *SU HS4C* | Slow running rpm | | Needle | Piston spring | Fast idle speed |
|---|---|---|---|---|---|
| | Manual | Automatic | | | |
| **4 series models** | | | | | |
| 1300 single carb (HC) .................. | 770/830 | N/A | ABR | Yellow | 1800 rpm |
| **5 series models** | | | | | |
| 1300 single carb (HC) .................. | 770/830 | N/A | ACA | Red | 1250 rpm |
| **6 series models** | | | | | |
| 1300 (HC) ........................................ | 770/830 | N/A | ACA | Red | 1250 rpm |
| **7 series models** | | | | | |
| 1300 (HC) ........................................ | 770/830 | N/A | ADL | Red | 1250 rpm |
| 1600 (HC) ........................................ | 770/830 | 770/830 in 'N' | ADK | Green | 1250 rpm |

| *Weber 40 DCOE Type 70 (front) and Type 71 (rear)* | **1500 cc** | **1600 cc** |
|---|---|---|
| Main jet ......................................................................................... | 110 | 110 |
| Idle jet .......................................................................................... | 45F 11 | 45F 11 |
| Pump jet ....................................................................................... | 35 | 35 |
| Starting jet ................................................................................... | 100F 5 | 100F 5 |
| Air correction jet ......................................................................... | 240 | 240 |
| Needle valve ................................................................................. | 1.50 mm | 1.50 mm |
| Float weight ................................................................................. | 26 gm | 26 gm |
| Slow running speed ..................................................................... | 950/1050 rpm | 950/1050 rpm |

| **Torque wrench settings** | **lbf ft** | **Nm** |
|---|---|---|
| Carburettor to manifold (except Weber) ...................................... | 8 | 10.8 |
| Fuel pump to cylinder block ........................................................ | 10 | 13.6 |

*Note: HC – High Compression; LC – Low Compression*
*With all the above carburettors, if an air-conditioning system is installed, the idling speed must be set with the compressor operating.*

## 1  General description

The fuel system has a rear mounted fuel tank from which fuel is drawn by a camshaft operated pump mounted on the right of the crankcase. Fuel is pumped to either single or twin carburettors according to the vehicle specification. Crankcase emission of fumes is controlled on all vehicles. In certain territories an evaporative emission control system is fitted to prevent the discharge of fuel vapour into the atmosphere. An air filter of the disposable paper element type is fitted to the carburettor intake(s).

**Note**: *Carburettors identified as Zenith models are identical to Stromberg models of the same type designation. All procedures described for Stromberg carburettors therefore apply to Zenith models.*

## 2  Routine maintenance

1  Every 10 000 miles (16 000 km) clean the fuel pump. Unscrew the crimped nut on the top cover and move aside the clip. Lift away the cover and pull the gauze filter from the neck of the pump. Wash the filter in fuel and clean out the sediment chamber. Refit the filter, glass cover and clip, making sure that the sealing gasket is in good condition and seating properly. Tighten the cover nut. Check the security of inlet and outlet fuel line unions. Later models are equipped with a canister type fuel pump. Access to the gauze filter is gained by removing the cover screw and cover.
2  Every 5000 miles top up the carburettor damper with engine oil. Unscrew the damper and top up to within $\frac{1}{4}$ in (6 mm) of the upper end of the bore in which the damper operates. A low oil level may cause a flat spot or poor acceleration.
3  At the proper intervals, renew the air cleaner element and clean the crankcase ventilation flame trap, as described in the relevant Sections. Reposition the air filter intake as appropriate, turning the tube so that the W (Winter) or S (Summer) marks are in line with the arrow on the filter casing (Fig. 3.1).

## 3  Fuel pump – removal and refitting

1  Disconnect the fuel pipes by unscrewing the two unions on the pump. Plug the inlet fuel line from the tank. Remove the two nuts which secure the pump to the cylinder block and lift it away, noting carefully the number of gaskets used between the pump and block mating faces.

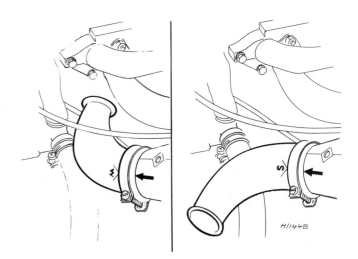

Fig. 3.1 Air intake – summer and winter positions (Sec 2)

3  To refit the pump, refit the exact number of gaskets as removed, unplug the fuel feed pipe and reconnect both unions.

## 4  Fuel pump (early type) – dismantling, examination and re-assembly

1  Clean the pump exterior, and mark across the two housing flange edges as a guide to refitting.
2  Refer to Fig. 3.2, and remove the six securing screws.
3  Separate the two halves of the main casting. Turn the diaphragm and pullrod assembly through an angle of 90° and disconnect it from its slot in the link. Remove the diaphragm spring. Do not attempt to separate the permanent assembly of diaphragm and pullrod.
4  Hold the rocker arm in a vice fitted with jaw protectors and tap the face of the body mounting flange with a soft-faced mallet until the two retainers are dislodged. Remove the rocker arm, link, spring and washers.
5  The valves are a press fit into the valve body and are staked in position. They should not be removed unless renewal is essential as

**Fig. 3.2 Fuel pump – exploded view (Sec 4)**

| | |
|---|---|
| 1 Cover | 11 Body – lower |
| 2 Joint | 12 Joint |
| 3 Gauze | 13 Link |
| 4 Body – upper | 14 Packing washers |
| 5 Gaskets | 15 Rocker arm |
| 6 Valve – outlet | 16 Return spring |
| 7 Valve – inlet | 17 Retainer |
| 8 Diaphragm | 18 Pivot pin |
| 9 Rod | 19 Screw |
| 10 Diaphragm spring | 20 Clip |

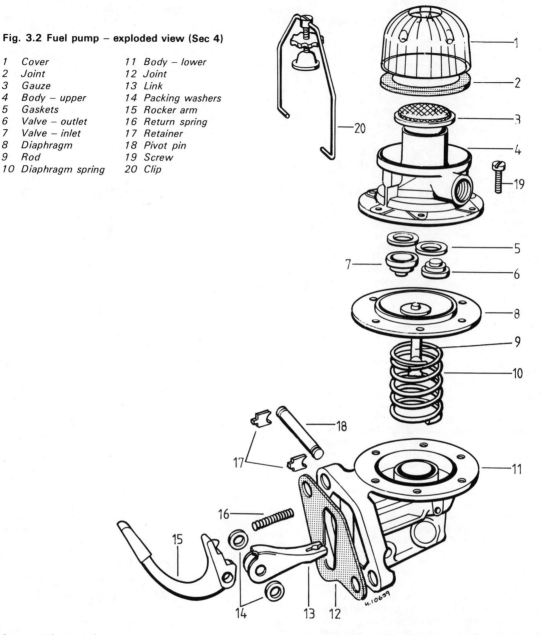

levering them out destroys them.

6    Clean all parts in paraffin. The diaphragm and pullrod assembly should be renewed if hard or cracked. Check all components for wear, particularly the rocker arm pin hole, link slot and their contact faces. Renew as necessary. The valve assemblies must be renewed as complete units as they cannot be disturbed. Check the diaphragm spring and in the event of deterioration renew with a spring having similar colour identification. Renew all gaskets and joints. Where new valves have to be fitted, fit new gaskets in the bottom of the valve seat bores.

7    Ensure that the new valves are assembled in the valve body (Fig. 3.3) as illustrated, or they will not operate. Press them into the pump body using a piece of ¾ in (0.19 mm) outside diameter tubing. Stake the pump body around each valve in about six equidistant places using a suitable punch.

8    See Fig. 3.2 and assemble the link, rocker arm and packing washers onto the pivot pin. Place the assembly into the lower half of the main body. Add the return spring, ensuring correct seating.

9    Tap new retainers in the pump body until they press hard against the rocker arm pin. Stake over to secure.

10   Position the diaphragm spring in the pump body. Place the diaphragm assembly rod downwards over the spring. Press downwards on the diaphragm and turn the assembly clockwise so that the

slots in the pullrod engage the fork in the link. Move the assembly a quarter turn clockwise to place the pullrod in its working position in the link and to ensure diaphragm and body hole alignment. When first inserting the diaphragm assembly into the body the locating tab should be in the position shown by the solid line (A) in Fig. 3.4. After rotating a quarter of a turn the tab should take up the position indicated by the broken line (B) in the diagram.

11   Push the rocker arm inwards until the diaphragm is level with the pump body flange and then position the top half of the pump body so that the original flange edge mating marks are in alignment. Install the flange securing screws and tighten. Unscrew each screw one turn and before retightening, depress the rocker arm and hold it at the limit of its stroke. Correctly fitted, the diaphragm edges should be flush with the edges of the two clamping flanges.

12   Test the pump by placing a finger over the inlet port and working the rocker arm several times. Remove the finger, and a distinct suction noise should be heard. Place a finger over the outlet port, depress the rocker arm to its fullest extent and, holding it in this position, immerse the pump in paraffin. Watch for air bubbles indicating leakages at the flanges. Disconnect the fuel pipe at the carburettor whilst slowly rotating the engine, when a series of well defined spurts of petrol should indicate correct operation of the pump.

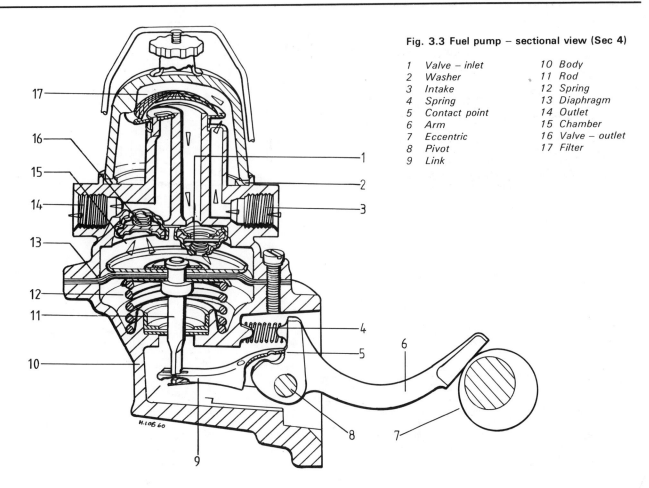

**Fig. 3.3 Fuel pump – sectional view (Sec 4)**

| | | | |
|---|---|---|---|
| 1 | Valve – inlet | 10 | Body |
| 2 | Washer | 11 | Rod |
| 3 | Intake | 12 | Spring |
| 4 | Spring | 13 | Diaphragm |
| 5 | Contact point | 14 | Outlet |
| 6 | Arm | 15 | Chamber |
| 7 | Eccentric | 16 | Valve – outlet |
| 8 | Pivot | 17 | Filter |
| 9 | Link | | |

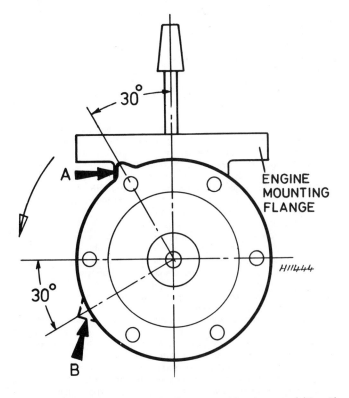

**Fig. 3.4 Fuel pump – correct diaphragm position (see text) (Sec 4)**

## 5 Air cleaner (Stromberg single carburettor) – maintenance

1   At the recommended intervals, the air filter element should be renewed.

2   At the recommended intervals, the interior of the air filter case should be cleaned, the paper element air pressure cleaned or knocked gently to remove adhering particles, and the element refitted in a different position.

3   Remove the two through-bolts (see Fig. 3.5) which secure the air filter to the carburettor flange, release the rubber tubing which connects the filter casing to the flame trap, and separate the air filter cover from the casing by removing the four retaining screws noting their relative position to the casing.

4   Clean the interior of the casing and service the element as already detailed.

5   Reassemble in reverse order. Ensure that the two rubber sealing rings are in good condition and correctly positioned before locating the filter element and lid. Adjust the intake to the Winter (W) or Summer (S) positions as required.

## 6 Air cleaner (Stromberg twin carburettors) – maintenance

1   Clean or renew the air filter element at the recommended intervals. Remove the screw in the centre of the top cover, and lift off the cover and element, noting the rubber joint rings above and below the element.

2   Remove dust from the cover, the base, and also the element if it is not being renewed.

3   Refit in reverse order, noting the locating slot and peg in the cover and base.

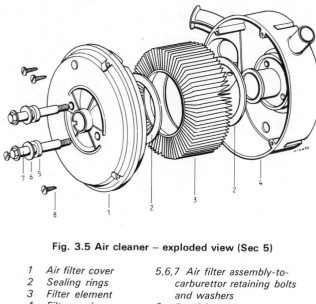

**Fig. 3.5 Air cleaner – exploded view (Sec 5)**

1  Air filter cover
2  Sealing rings
3  Filter element
4  Filter casing

5,6,7  Air filter assembly-to-
        carburettor retaining bolts
        and washers
8  Retaining screws

## 7  Air cleaner and airbox (Weber 40 DCOE) – maintenance

1  Airbox removal necessitates removing the rearmost of the two studs which hold it to the backplate. Use pliers between the airbox and the backplate, after removing the capnuts and fibre washers.
2  To renew the element, remove the trunking from the air cleaner after loosening the clip.
3  Place the wheels on full right lock, undo the two nuts holding the air cleaner to the panel, remove the spring washers and reinforcement plate, and lift out the air cleaner.
4  Slacken the wing nut on the air cleaner, tap with a mallet to break the joint, remove the wing nut and washer, and separate the parts.
5  Clean the air cleaner case interior. Check the condition of the rubber seals, and refit them.
6  Fit the new element and reassemble all parts. Reclip the trunking to the air cleaner.

## 8  Air cleaner (SU HS4C) – maintenance

1  To renew the element, remove the breather hose from the air cleaner body. Remove the two bolts securing the body to the carburettor, and lift the assembly away complete with the gaskets and separator plate.
2  Remove the four screws securing the cover to the main body, remove the cover, and remove the filter element and the two sealing rings.
3  Wipe the body and cover clean, and refit the new element followed by all other parts in reverse order.

## 9  Air cleaner (air temperature controlled type) – general description and servicing

1  The system is designed to provide an initial rapid warm up. The advantages are the ease of tuning which results, and the fact that the choke can be employed less, resulting in both the reduction of exhaust pollution and greater fuel economy. The system consists of an exhaust manifold stove to provide hot air, a thermal sensor which senses the carburettor air flow temperature, and a diaphragm motor controlling the position of the intake tube flap valve.
2  To remove the air cleaner, refer to Fig. 3.7 and disconnect pipes (1) and (2), remove the two through-bolts, and withdraw the air cleaner whilst sliding off the metal tube.
3  To renew the element, remove the air cleaner. Remove the single

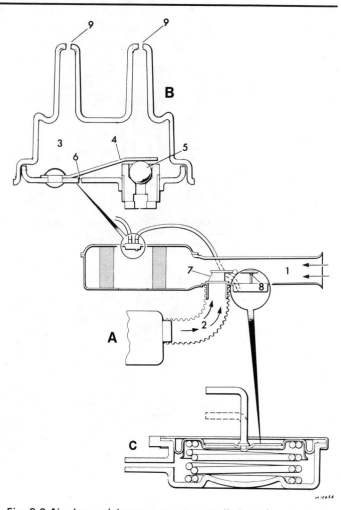

**Fig. 3.6 Air cleaner (air temperature controlled type) – schematic diagram (Sec 9)**

A  Exhaust manifold stove
   motor
1  Air cleaner intake
2  Heated air tube
3  Vacuum chamber
4  Bi-metallic strip
5  Vacuum relief valve

B  Thermal sensor
C  Diaphragm
6  Air admission hole
7  Dual flap valve
8  Diaphragm motor pivot
9  Vacuum restrictor holes

cover screw, ease off the cover, remove the old element and clean the body and cover. Prevent dirt from entering the sensor holes. Fit the new element, check that the sealing rings are in place, and refit the remaining parts in reverse order to dismantling.
4  If the system becomes defective, the air intake will automatically remain open. Symptoms of faulty operation are difficulty in obtaining a smooth idle together with very weak mixture indications, and a flat spot and tendency to stall when moving off. To check for faults, remove the stove-to-air intake pipe and press on the hot air valve to check for smooth movement. Renew any defective pipes.
5  If all is in order, remove the air cleaner assembly and disconnect the tube from the sensor to the motor, at the sensor end. Check the motor by applying vacuum using the connection on the manifold; with the engine running the valve should fully open. If the tube is clamped the valve open position should be maintained. If a motor defect exists, the cleaner body must be renewed.
6  To test the sensor, remove the air cleaner cover and ensure that the air temperature is not above 20°C (68°F). Check the restrictor holes and vents to ensure that they are clear, if necessary using light suction only, not probes or air pressure. Reconnect the sensor to motor tube, apply vacuum to the sensor and check for operation of the motor. If inoperative, renew the sensor by supporting the air cleaner cover and prising the sensor clip away. Refit with a new sensor, seal and clip. Refit all parts.

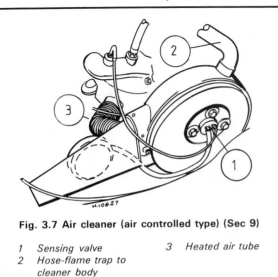

**Fig. 3.7 Air cleaner (air controlled type) (Sec 9)**

1  Sensing valve
2  Hose-flame trap to cleaner body

3  Heated air tube

## 10 Carburettors (Stromberg 150CDS) – general description

This is a constant depression type of carburettor with a separate starter assembly. The design permits use of a variable choke and a needle which moves in a single jet to provide a fuel/air mixture to meet all conditions of engine operation. Sectional and external views of the

carburettor and its starter assembly are shown in Figs. 3.8, 3.9 and 3.10. The float is made from a synthetic material and cannot be punctured. When the engine is not operating the air valve piston rests on the carburettor body. When the choke control is operated the fast idle cam rotates and opens the throttle and operates the starter assembly disc valve to meter extra fuel for cold starting and running. Immediately the engine fires the air valve piston is lifted by air pressure to a position dependent upon throttle opening. At idling speed the air valve piston is lifted by air pressure. The jet to needle annulus area is then set by the jet adjuster so that in conjunction with the slow running setting, correct idling is obtained. Above idling speed the needle and piston are raised by air pressure acting on the underside of the diaphragm. Above the diaphragm there exists a lower pressure (partial inlet manifold vacuum). Operating the throttle raises and lowers it to give the necessary fuel/air ratio and constant air speed over the jet orifice to ensure good fuel atomisation. The hydraulic damper prevents sudden rising of the air valve piston during acceleration when temporary mixture enrichment is required. The flexible diaphragm provides an air seal and locates the air piston. Fuel flow to the float chamber is controlled by needle valve closed by float when fuel rises to the correct level. The float chamber is vented to the inside of the air filter mounting flange and fuel from it reaches the jet through drillings.

Cold starting requires an initial rich mixture, together with a means of progressively weakening the mixture and a throttle opening mechanism for fast idling. The starter assembly provides these conditions and is situated behind the fast idle cam (Fig. 3.9). The disc valve controls the extra fuel needed for cold starting. The fuel is fed through channel (8) from the float chamber through the disc valve metering holes through channel (7) and into the throttle body between the air

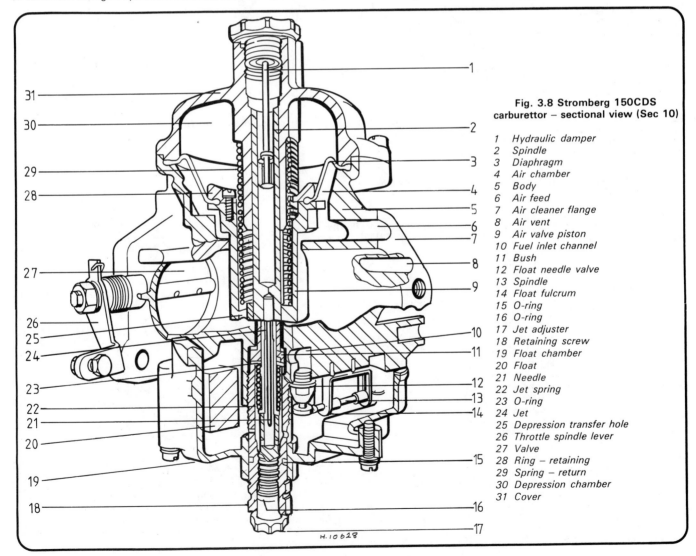

**Fig. 3.8 Stromberg 150CDS carburettor – sectional view (Sec 10)**

1   Hydraulic damper
2   Spindle
3   Diaphragm
4   Air chamber
5   Body
6   Air feed
7   Air cleaner flange
8   Air vent
9   Air valve piston
10  Fuel inlet channel
11  Bush
12  Float needle valve
13  Spindle
14  Float fulcrum
15  O-ring
16  O-ring
17  Jet adjuster
18  Retaining screw
19  Float chamber
20  Float
21  Needle
22  Jet spring
23  O-ring
24  Jet
25  Depression transfer hole
26  Throttle spindle lever
27  Valve
28  Ring – retaining
29  Spring – return
30  Depression chamber
31  Cover

H.10628

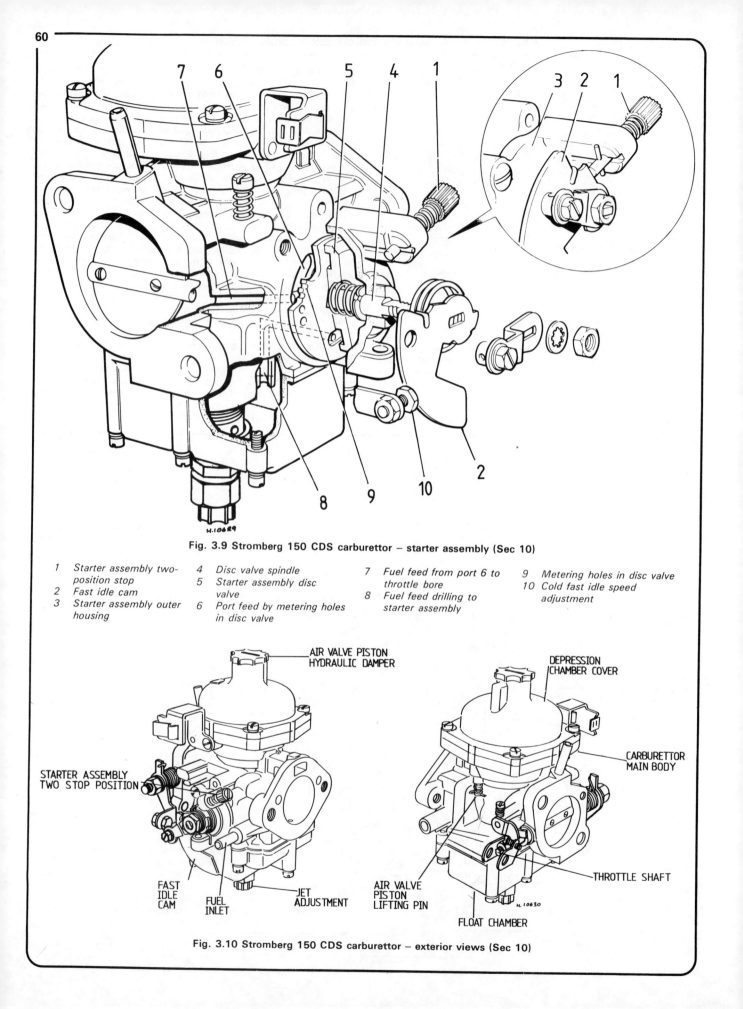

Fig. 3.9 Stromberg 150 CDS carburettor – starter assembly (Sec 10)

1 Starter assembly two-position stop
2 Fast idle cam
3 Starter assembly outer housing
4 Disc valve spindle
5 Starter assembly disc valve
6 Port feed by metering holes in disc valve
7 Fuel feed from port 6 to throttle bore
8 Fuel feed drilling to starter assembly
9 Metering holes in disc valve
10 Cold fast idle speed adjustment

AIR VALVE PISTON HYDRAULIC DAMPER

DEPRESSION CHAMBER COVER

STARTER ASSEMBLY TWO STOP POSITION

CARBURETTOR MAIN BODY

FAST IDLE CAM

FUEL INLET

JET ADJUSTMENT

AIR VALVE PISTON LIFTING PIN

THROTTLE SHAFT

FLOAT CHAMBER

Fig. 3.10 Stromberg 150 CDS carburettor – exterior views (Sec 10)

valve piston and throttle valve. When the engine starts the air valve piston rises sufficiently to provide the air needed for engine operation. The two position stop is provided to permit all, or some, of the disc valve metering holes to be used, depending on ambient temperatures. For normal conditions the position of the stop shown in Fig. 3.9 is correct. Below -23°C (-10°F) use the alternative stop position. As the choke is pushed home the number of holes metering fuel through the disc valve decreases until finally the disc valve is blanked off and no fuel passes to the throttle bore.

There is no separate idling circuit. The fuel/air mixture and quantity depends upon the throttle opening set by the slow running adjustment screw (A) (Fig. 3.12).

Part and full throttle driving causes the air valve piston to rise and fall by action of the throttle. This in turn controls the metering of fuel by varying the annular discharge as the differing profile of the needle passes up and down in the jet orifice. When the air flow under the air valve piston reaches a certain speed, according to the position of the carburettor butterfly valve, a depression is caused above the diaphragm to cause the air valve piston to lift and float on air pressure. The position of the air valve piston is dependent upon the throttle opening and the consequent air flow and depression above the diaphragm. The air valve piston movement is also controlled slightly by the compression return spring (Fig. 3.8). Sudden acceleration with an attendant inrush of air could cause a weakening of the mixture but this is overcome by the provision of the hydraulic damper piston (1) which restricts the upward movement of the air valve piston. Downward motion of this component is not so restricted.

## 11 Carburettor (Stromberg 150CDS) – removal and refitting

1    Remove the air cleaner, and disconnect the fuel pipe, the choke cable, and the throttle cable.
2    Pull off the vacuum pipe, remove the flange securing nuts, and lift off the carburettor.
3    Refit in reverse order, adjusting the choke cable and idling as necessary.

## 12 Carburettor (Stromberg 150CDS) – dismantling and re-assembly

1    To renew the diaphragm, remove the depression chamber cover and screws and lift out the air valve piston complete with diaphragm (Fig. 3.11) and retaining ring. Remove the retaining ring screws and ring. Fit a new diaphragm, taking care to ensure that the locating tag engages with the cut-out in the flange.
2    Complete dismantling and cleaning can be carried out after removing the carburettor from the engine. Unscrew and remove the six screws holding the float chamber to the body and remove the float chamber by drawing it carefully down the jet bushing retaining screw. The O-ring seal may make removal difficult but on no account use levers. Remove the jet adjusting screw (17), the hydraulic damper and depression chamber cover. Lift out the air valve piston, needle and diaphragm assembly.
3    Using a tyre pump blow air into the fuel feed hole to the starter assembly (Fig. 3.9) and at the same time move the starter assembly over the whole range of movement with its travel stop in the fully raised (extreme cold) position. Clean the component parts in fuel or paraffin.
4    Reassemble in reverse order, and adjust as described in Section 13.

## 13 Carburettor (Stromberg 150CDS) – adjustment and tuning

1    Slow running adjustment affects the whole carburettor operating range and must be carefully carried out. Remove the air valve piston damper, insert a thin screwdriver or rod into the damper bore and, applying firm downward pressure, turn the jet adjustment screw (Fig. 3.8) in a clockwise direction until the jet just touches the air valve piston. The adjustment screw becomes tight to turn when this occurs. Slacken the adjustment screw two complete turns (anti-clockwise), fill the damper bore with oil (see 'Routine Maintenance') and refit the piston.
2    Start the engine and attain normal operating temperature. Adjust

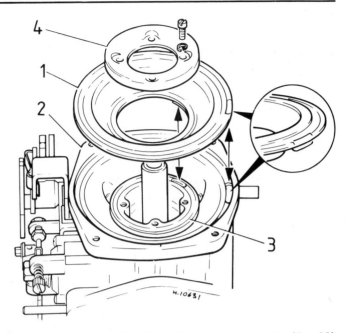

**Fig. 3.11 Diaphragm location – Stromberg carburettor (Sec 12)**

| | |
|---|---|
| 1    *Diaphragm* | 3    *Air valve piston* |
| 2    *Body* | 4    *Retaining ring* |

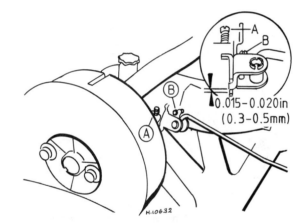

**Fig. 3.12 Slow running and throttle linkage screws – Stromberg carburettor (Sec 13)**

| | |
|---|---|
| A    *Slow running adjustment screw* | B    *Throttle linkage adjustment screw* |

the slow running speed adjustment screw (A) (Fig. 3.12) to obtain correct idling, if necessary varying the jet adjustment screw not more than half a turn to improve idling. Clockwise rotation weakens the mixture, anti-clockwise rotation enriches the mixture. If the jet cannot be adjusted within these limits, check the position of the needle in the air valve piston. It should be level with the lower face of the air valve piston.
3    To adjust the throttle linkage, move screw (B) (Fig. 3.12) to give the indicated clearance. Ensure that the choke cable pinch bolt allied to the fast idle cam (Fig. 3.9) is only tightened when the choke control knob is withdrawn about $\frac{1}{8}$ in (3 mm) from the panel. This will ensure that the cam rests against its stop when the choke is not in use. Check that the outer cable clip does not restrict release of the cam.
4    The fast idle speed ensures that the engine runs at a suitable speed when the engine fires with the choke withdrawn. Refer to Fig. 3.13 and adjust the clearance between the cam and the adjuster screws in accordance with the Specification relating to cam type. Make sure that the cam is home against its stop, the choke control

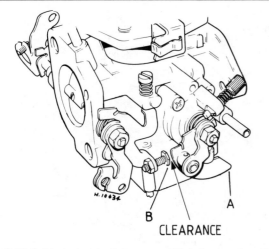

Fig. 3.13 Cold start cam clearance – Stromberg carburettor
(Sec 13)

A    Fast idle cam          B    Adjuster screw

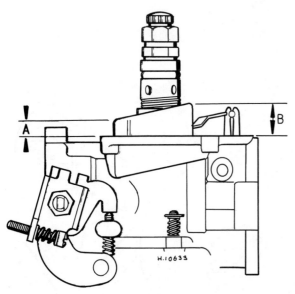

Fig. 3.14 Float setting dimensions – Stromberg carburettor
(Sec 13)

A = 9 mm                    B = 16 mm

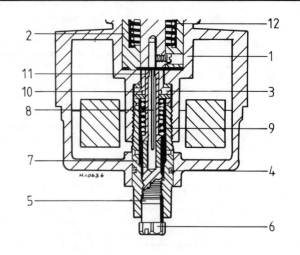

Fig. 3.15 Stromberg carburettor – detail parts involved in jet
centralising procedure (Sec 13)

| | | | |
|---|---|---|---|
| 1 | Body | 7 | Screw |
| 2 | Piston air valve | 8 | Needle |
| 3 | Bush | 9 | Jet spring |
| 4 | O-ring | 10 | O-ring |
| 5 | O-ring | 11 | Jet |
| 6 | Jet adjuster | 12 | Depression chamber |

trunnion. Hold the accelerator pedal down onto a piece of $\frac{1}{2}$ in (12 mm) thick wood placed beneath it. With the throttle butterfly valve fully open, tighten the trunnion nut. Release the pedal and check at the carburettor that with the pedal depressed to within $\frac{1}{2}$ in (12 mm) of the floor, the linkage is fully back against its stop.

Fig. 3.16 Exploded view of Stromberg 150 CDS carburettor
(Sec 13)

| | | | |
|---|---|---|---|
| 1 | Damper | 34 | Spindle |
| 2 | Screw and washer | 35 | Disc |
| 3 | Cover | 36 | Screw |
| 4 | Screw and washer | 37 | Gasket |
| 5 | Retaining ring | 38 | Float chamber |
| 6 | Diaphragm | 39 | Washer |
| 7 | Piston | 40 | Screw and washer (short) |
| 8 | Needle | 41 | Screw and washer (long) |
| 9 | Slow running screw and | 42 | Float |
| | spring | 43 | Fulcrum |
| 10 | Body | 44 | Valve and seat |
| 11 | Bracket | 45 | Washer |
| 12 | Clip | 46 | Retaining clip |
| 13 | Screw | 47 | Spring |
| 14 | Cover | 48 | Lifting pin |
| 15 | Spring | 49 | Locking screw |
| 16 | Retaining pin | 50 | Jet adjuster |
| 17 | Stop | 51 | O-ring |
| 18 | Screw | 52 | O-ring |
| 19 | Spring | 53 | Bush |
| 20 | Cam | 54 | Jet |
| 21 | Lever assembly | 55 | Spring |
| 22 | Washer | 56 | Washer |
| 23 | Nut | 57 | O-ring |
| 24 | Screw | 58 | Bush |
| 25 | Nut | 59 | Washer |
| 26 | Washer (shakeproof) | 60 | Spring |
| 27 | Washer (plain) | 61 | Lever |
| 28 | Screw and nut | 62 | Bush |
| 29 | Lever | 63 | Lever |
| 30 | Spring | 64 | Nut |
| 31 | Spring retainer | 65 | Screw and spring (throttle |
| 32 | Spring | | adjustment) |
| 33 | Valve | | |

knob is fully depressed and that the slow running speed is correctly set before carrying out this adjustment.
5    In cases of flooding, or of high fuel consumption, the float level may need adjustment. Remove the float chamber, invert it, and set the high and low float levels in accordance with Fig. 3.14. To adjust, carefully bend the float arm extension or place an extra washer under the float needle valve assembly (Fig. 3.8).
6    The face of the lower shoulder on the needle (Fig. 3.16) should be flush with the lower face of the air valve piston. Adjust by loosening the locking setscrew and resetting the needle. The air valve piston should fall freely in the carburettor body if raised and allowed to fall. If the piston sticks or the jet has been removed, the jet must be centralised. Check that the needle is correctly positioned in the air valve piston. Referring to Fig. 3.15, loosen off screw (7) half a turn. Screw up the jet adjustment screw until the jet is level with the bridge face on which the piston rests. Give the retaining screw (7) a sharp tap with a spanner on one of its hexagon sides to centralise the jet. The air valve piston should now fall freely. Tighten the jet screw (7).
7    To adjust the accelerator with reference to full throttle position, slacken the trunnion nut (Fig. 3.17) located on the lower engine bulkhead under the bonnet so that the operating rod can slide in the

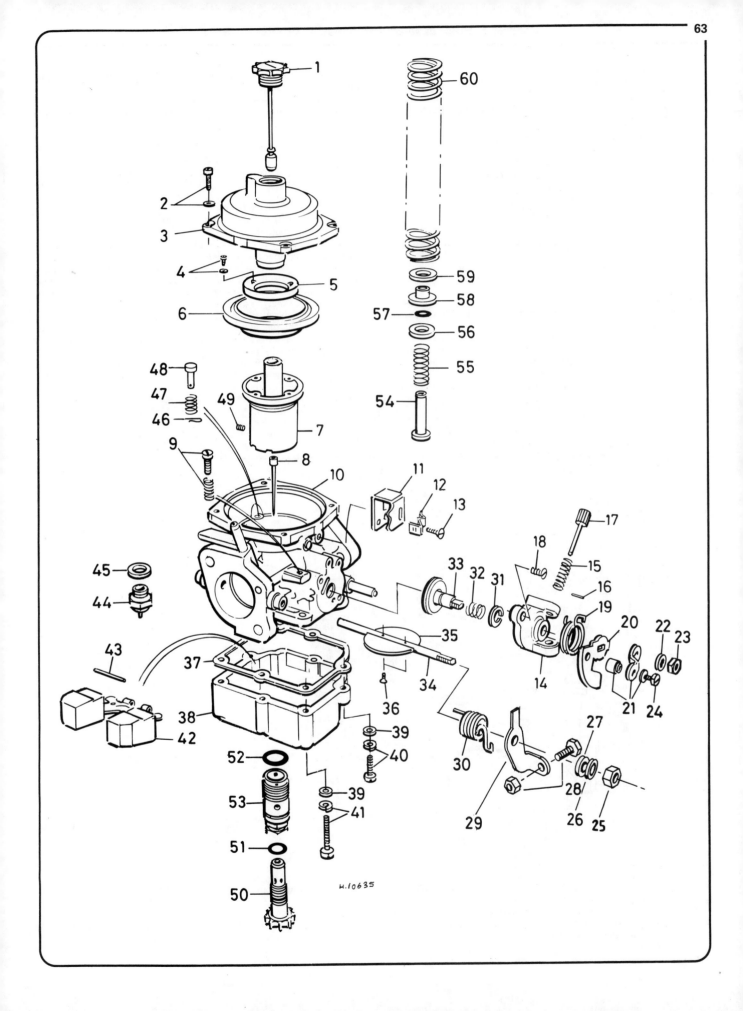

H.10635

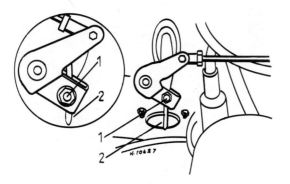

**Fig. 3.17 Accelerator connections – single carburettor (Sec 13)**

1    Trunnion nut          2    Link rod

## 14 Twin carburettor installation (Stromberg 150CDS) – removal and refitting

1    Remove the flame trap connections at the rocker cover and airbox, remove the air cleaner cover and element, and disconnect the vacuum advance pipe.
2    Disconnect the accelerator and choke cables at the carburettors.
3    Disconnect the airbox-to-air cleaner hose at the airbox, and the fuel feed pipe. Remove the four nuts, and lift of the carburettors complete with the air box.
4    Refit in reverse order. Dismantling of the individual carburettors is as described in Section 12, for the single carburettor installation.

## 15 Twin carburettor installation (Stromberg 150CDS) – adjustment and tuning

1    Adjust slow running by turning the adjustment screws (Fig. 3.18) by equal amounts.
2    Synchronise the carburettors after checking spark plugs, points and valve clearances, and with the engine at operating temperature (not overheated under a closed bonnet).
3    Remove the air cleaner and both hydraulic dampers. Remove both depression chamber covers and lift out the air valve pistons and return springs.
4    Remove both needles from the air valve pistons, check their type against Specifications, and refit as described for single carburettors in Section 13, paragraph 6.
5    Refit the air valve pistons, return springs and depression chamber covers ensuring that the diaphragms are correctly located (Fig. 3.11).
6    Hold each air valve piston down in turn, and screw up the jet adjuster (Fig. 3.18) until it makes contact with the piston. Check that each air valve piston falls freely. If not, centralise the jets as described in Section 13. Refill the damper bores with oil and then screw each jet adjuster down exactly 2½ turns.
7    Unscrew the fast idle speed adjustment screw until it is well clear of the cam on the front carburettor, and slacken the most accessible clamping bolt on the throttle couplings. Screw back the slow running screws until well clear of the throttle levers, then rotate each screw until a 0.002 in feeler is just gripped between them and the levers, with the throttle butterflies in the closed position. Now rotate each screw clockwise by two turns. Tighten the clamp bolt.
8    Start and run the engine until it regains normal operating temperature. If needed, adjust the jet adjusters not more than half a turn each way and readjust each slow running screw to improve overall idling.

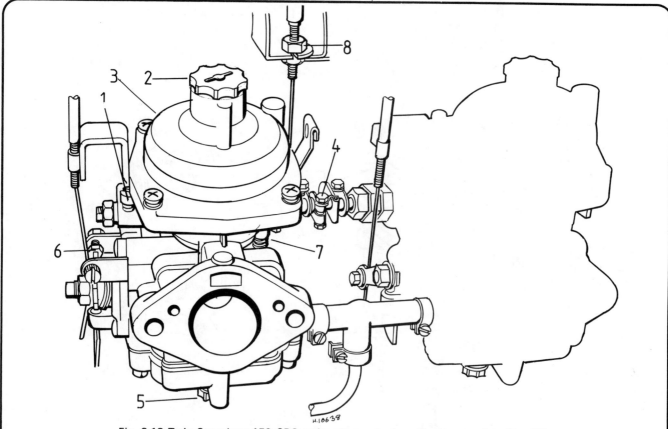

**Fig. 3.18 Twin Stromberg 150 CDS carburettors – tuning adjustment points (Sec 15)**

| | | |
|---|---|---|
| 1  Slow running speed adjustment screw | 3  Depression chamber cover | 5  Jet adjuster | 7  Air valve piston lifting pin |
| 2  Air valve piston hydraulic damper | 4  Coupling clamping bolt | 6  Fast idle speed adjustment screw | 8  Throttle cable adjustment |

## 16 Carburettor (Stromberg CDSE) – general description

1    This carburettor is employed on certain vehicles to obtain very low emission levels of noxious gases. It has a fixed non-adjustable jet as shown in Fig. 3.20 and a spring-loaded needle which operates with the rise and fall of the air valve piston. A throttle bypass valve (Fig. 3.19) temperature controlled valve and slow running mixture air control screw are incorporated. The throttle bypass valve permits mixture to pass the closed throttle butterfly during overrun conditions. It is operated by inlet manifold vacuum. The temperature controlled valve weakens the idling and light load mixture when the carburettor is hot.

2    Servicing and adjustments to this carburettor are described in Sections 31 and 32.

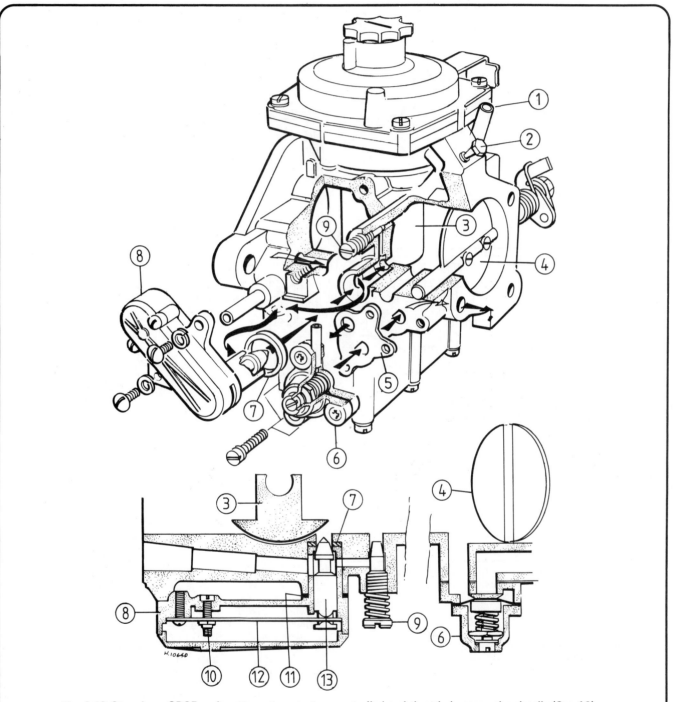

**Fig. 3.19 Stromberg CDSE carburettor – temperature controlled and throttle bypass valve details (Sec 16)**

| | | |
|---|---|---|
| 1 | Vacuum advance connection | 5 | Gasket (bypass valve to carburettor body) | 9 | Slow running (idle) air adjustment screw – limited range | 11 | Rubber joint ring |
| 2 | Blanking plug – do not remove | 6 | Throttle bypass valve | | | 12 | Bi-metal spring |
| 3 | Air valve piston | 7 | Rubber joint ring | 10 | Adjustment for temperature controlled valve spring | 13 | Valve operated by bi-metal spring |
| 4 | Throttle | 8 | Temperature controlled valve | | | | |

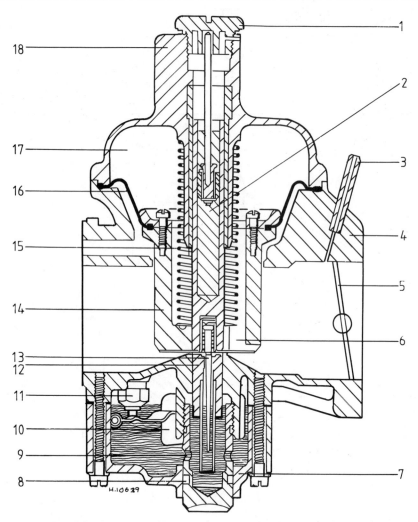

**Fig. 3.20 Stromberg CDSE carburettor – sectional view (Sec 16)**

| | | |
|---|---|---|
| 1 | Air valve piston damper assembly | |
| 2 | Piston damper reservoir | |
| 3 | Vacuum advance connection | |
| 4 | Carburettor body | |
| 5 | Throttle | |

6   Depression feed holes to 17
7   Float chamber
8   O-ring
9   Fuel feed holes to jet

10   Twin float
11   Float needle valve seat
12   Metering jet and feed tube
13   Metering needle
14   Air valve piston

15   Air valve piston return spring
16   Diaphragm
17   Depression chamber
18   Depression chamber cover

## 17 Carburettor (Stromberg CDSET) – general description

This carburettor is similar to the CDSE carburettor described in Section 16, except that it has an automatic choke system heated by water from the engine. General servicing and adjustment details are as described in Sections 31 and 32.

## 18 Carburettor (Stromberg CDSET) – automatic choke

1   To adjust, set the slow running screw (Fig. 3.24) until the engine idles at the specified rpm – at normal operating temperature, or the cold start fast idle speed will be incorrect.

2   The plunger to fast idle cam clearance is set up during production and will only require resetting if it has been altered. To do this, adjust the fast idle screw and locknut until there is a clearance of between 0.043 and 0.053 in (1.0922 and 1.3462 mm) between the end of the plunger and the cam. Ensure that the cam is in the 'HOT' idling position. The setting of the bi-metal coil spring is correct when the positioning marks are in alignment. Adjust if necessary by loosening screws (27 and 28) (Fig. 3.23). Do not overtighten the screws when refitting them.

3   Removal of the cold starting device is carried out by draining the cooling system and removing the water jacket cover. Dismantling will be made clear by Fig. 3.23. Do not attempt to remove the nylon fast idle plunger or its brass housing.

4   Wash all components in paraffin and air dry. Renew all O-rings and rubber seals.

5   Reassemble in reverse, ensuring that the aluminium washer is located below the retaining bolt head. Refill the cooling system and bleed air from the system by slackening one of the hose clips on the starting device water jacket and prising off the end of the hose.

6   Unsatisfactory operation of the automatic cold starting device will give rise to bad starting or excessive fuel consumption. If malfunction is suspected, carry out the following check. Switch off the engine when at normal operating temperature and allow it to cool completely, preferably overnight. Have an assistant depress the accelerator pedal fully once only and then release it. At the same time listen to the operation of the cold start device, when a faint click should be heard indicating that the mechanism has moved to its cold start position. Operate the engine starter switch when the engine should fire immediately and run at a fast idle. As the engine warms up, the idling speed should reduce when the accelerator pedal is depressed. Switch off the engine before it has warmed up and remove the plug (7). Look into the screw hole while an assistant starts and then stops the engine.

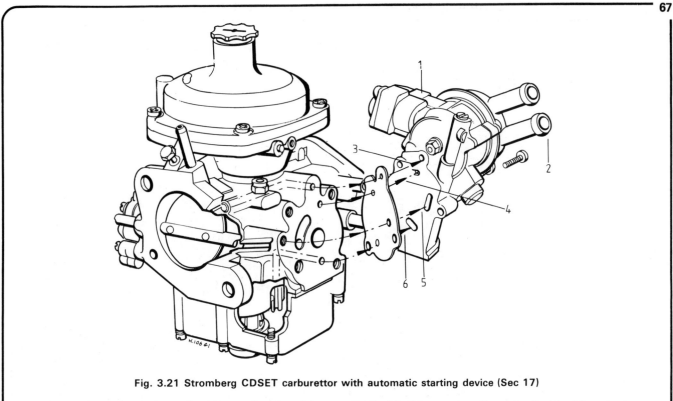

**Fig. 3.21 Stromberg CDSET carburettor with automatic starting device (Sec 17)**

1  Automatic starting device
2  Cooling system connections

3  Vacuum feed from inlet manifold
4  Air inlet from intake side of carburettor

5  Fuel feed from automatic starting device to air valve side of throttle

6  Fuel feed from float chamber to automatic starting device metering jet

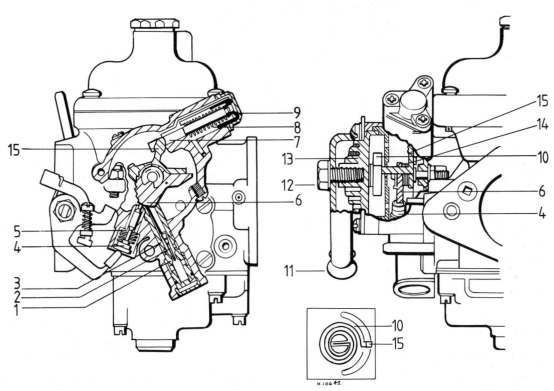

**Fig. 3.22 Stromberg CDSET carburettor – sectional view of automatic starting device (Sec 17)**

1  Metering jet
2  Fuel metering needle
3  O-ring seal
4  Fast idle plunger

5  Plunger return spring
6  Fast idle cam
7  Vacuum kick piston rod
8  Vacuum kick piston return

9  Vacuum kick piston
10  Bi-metal temperature sensitive coil spring
11  Water jacket

12  Water jacket retaining bolt
13  Heat mass
14  Coil torsion spring
15  Connecting lever

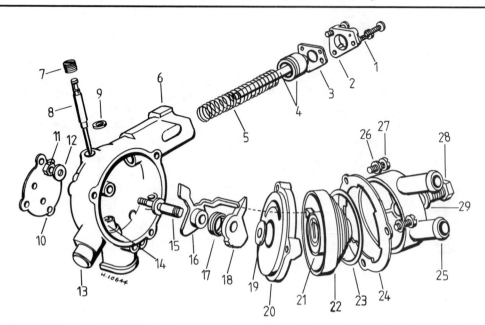

**Fig. 3.23 Stromberg CDSET carburettor – exploded view of automatic starting device (Sec 18)**

| | | | |
|---|---|---|---|
| 1 | Retaining screw | 7 | Plug |
| 2 | Vacuum kick piston cylinder cover | 8 | Fuel metering needle |
| 3 | Gasket | 9 | O-ring seal |
| 4 | Vacuum kick piston and piston rod | 10 | Gasket |
| 5 | Vacuum kick piston return spring | 11 | Nut |
| | | 12 | Shakeproof washer |
| 6 | Automatic starting device body | 13 | Fast idle plunger and peg |
| | | 14 | Needle jet orifice |

| | | | |
|---|---|---|---|
| 15 | Spindle | 22 | Heat mass |
| 16 | Lever | 23 | Rubber sealing ring |
| 17 | Spring | 24 | Retaining ring |
| 18 | Fast idle cam | 25 | Water jacket cover |
| 19 | C-washer | 26 | Spring washers |
| 20 | Heat insulator | 27 | Retaining screws |
| 21 | Bi-metal temperature sensitive coil spring | 28 | Retaining bolt |
| | | 29 | Aluminium sealing washer |

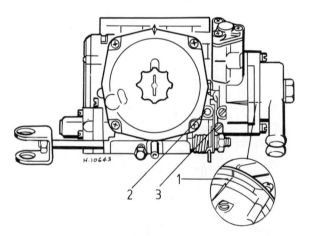

**Fig. 3.24 Stromberg CDSET carburettor – automatic starting device (Sec 18)**

| | | |
|---|---|---|
| 1 | Automatic starter setting marks | |
| 2 | Fast idle screw | |
| 3 | Slow running screw | |

Immediately the engine starts, the vacuum kick piston and rod should move quickly to mask part of the hole and return equally quickly when the engine is switched off. This test proves that the vacuum kick piston is not sticking. If the unit still fails to perform correctly, the fault must lie in a broken or distorted component.

## 19 Carburettor (Stromberg CDSEV) – general description

This carburettor is installed as part of a twin carburettor unit where full emission control is employed. The carburettor differs from the CDSE carburettor in the following points:

(a) The carburettor has a float chamber vent valve operated from the throttle spindle lever
(b) The rear carburettor only is fitted with a throttle bypass valve
(c) No control valve, distributor retard capsule or external connecting pipes are fitted as is the case with single carburettor emission control systems

## 20 Carburettor (Stromberg CDSEV) – servicing and adjustment

1   At 5000 mile intervals a check should be made of valve clearances, spark plug gaps, distributor points gap, idling speed and quality, and idle spark timing. At 25 000 miles an additional servicing item is specified, in that dismantling should take place to permit the fitting of items supplied in the manufacturer's red emission pack. Dismantling details are as given in Sections 12 and 13, for the Stromberg 150CDS carburettor. Synchronisation of the carburettors is carried out as described in Section 15, for 150CDS twin carburettor installations, and adjustments are as described in Sections 31 and 32.

2   The bypass valve on the rear carburettor is preset during production and will not normally require adjustment. However if its operation is suspect, place the transmission in neutral and open the throttle slowly until the engine reaches 3500 rpm. Release the throttle and check the time taken for the engine to slow to 1500 rpm. A tachometer and a stop watch will be needed. If the time taken exceeds 3.5 seconds, the bypass valve is opening too far (probably indicated by lack of engine braking on the road) and the unit should be renewed. As a temporary measure, dismantle the valve and drive out the brass sealing disc (Fig. 3.25). Reassemble the valve and turn the adjusting screw clockwise to reduce the deceleration time, not more than $\frac{1}{4}$ of a turn at a time. When adjustment is complete refit the sealing disc.

3   If the valve is not opening enough, the fact will not be noticeable on the road. The only effect is an adverse one on the overrun exhaust emission, only detectable by sophisticated equipment and in practice rarely found. However, a rough check can be made using the stop watch and noting the time taken to decelerate from 3550 to 1500 rpm. If this is less than 2.8 seconds then the bypass valve should be

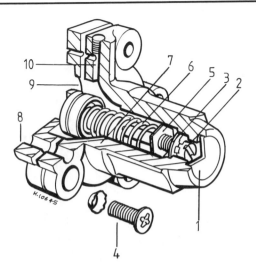

Fig. 3.25 Stromberg CDSEV carburettor twin installation – cutaway drawing of rear carburettor by-pass valve (Sec 20)

| | | | |
|---|---|---|---|
| 1 | Brass disc | 6 | Diaphragm return spring |
| 2 | Adjustment screw | 7 | Upper body |
| 3 | O-ring | 8 | Lower body |
| 4 | Body securing screws | 9 | Diaphragm/valve assembly |
| 5 | Spring adjusting nut | 10 | Vacuum feed passage |

renewed or, as a temporary measure, adjusted as previously described. It must be emphasised that, when set in production, atmospheric pressure, carburettor mixture strength and the tightness of the engine are all taken into account. The temporary adjustment outlined should, therefore, be looked upon as only a short-term measure.

## 21 Carburettor (Stromberg 150CD3) – general description

This unit differs from the CDS type by having a fixed metering jet, but an adjustable metering needle which is adjusted internally by means of a special tool. Operation, dismantling, cleaning and re-assembly are similar to the CDS, and reference should be made to the relevant Section.

## 22 Carburettor (Stromberg 150CD3) – adjustment

1   Run the engine to normal operating temperature (on the road) and raise the bonnet on stopping to prevent excessive heat build up. Adjust the slow running speed as specified by turning the adjustment screw (Fig. 3.26).

2   Where adjustment of the mixture is required, a special tool must be obtained from a Stromberg/Zenith agent. This comprises an inner member similar to an Allen key which engages with the metering needle adjustment screw, and an outer tubular member which incorporates a peg to engage with the air valve piston damper bore slot. During adjustment, the inner member is turned while the outer is held quite still to prevent the rubber diaphragm twisting. Before adjusting the needle, check that the basic setting of the needle is correct. Unscrew and pull out the air valve piston damper (Fig. 3.27). Remove the carburettor top cover and withdraw the air valve

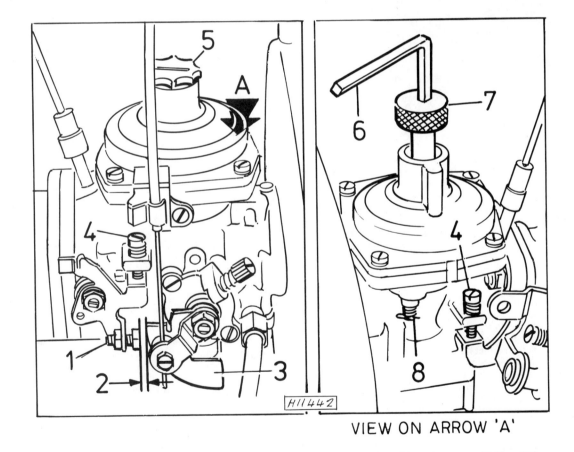

VIEW ON ARROW 'A'

Fig. 3.26 Stromberg 150CD3 adjustment screws (note alternative positions for screw 4) (Sec 22)

| | | | | | | | |
|---|---|---|---|---|---|---|---|
| 1 | Fast idle screw | 3 | Fast idle cam | 5 | Air valve piston damper | 7 | Adjustment tool for metering needle |
| 2 | Fast idle screw to cam gap | 4 | Slow running adjustment screw (alternative positions) | 6 | Adjustment tool for metering needle | 8 | Air valve piston lifting pin |

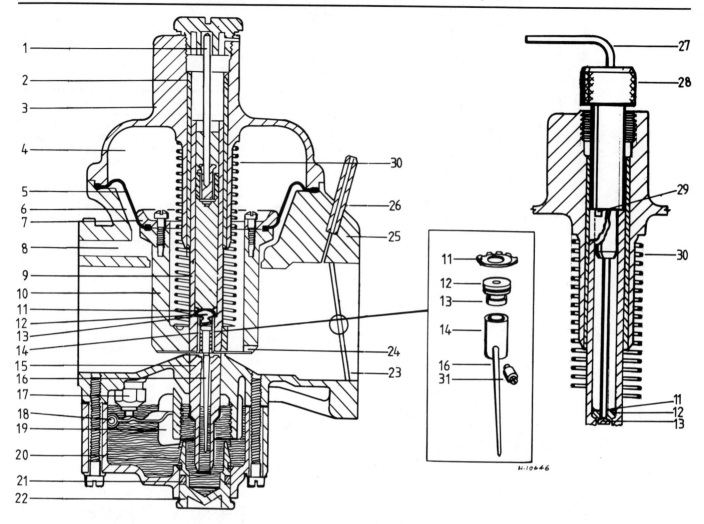

**Fig. 3.27 Stromberg 150CD3 carburettor — sectional view showing adjustment tool in use (Sec 22)**

1  Air valve piston hydraulic damper
2  Sleeve
3  Cover
4  Depression chamber
5  Flexible diaphragm
6  Air space
7  Diaphragm retaining ring
8  Air passage
9  Air valve piston guide spindle
10  Air valve piston
11  Metering needle adjustment retainer
12  O-ring seal
13  Metering needle adjustment screw
14  Metering needle holder and bias spring
15  Fixed metering jet
16  Metering needle
17  Fuel inlet needle valve
18  Float pivot
19  Float
20  Float chamber
21  O-ring seal
22  Plug
23  Throttle valve
24  Depression feed hole
25  Carburettor body
26  Vacuum (distributor) advance connection
27  Inner component of adjustment tool
28  Outer component of adjustment tool
29  Locating peg
30  Air valve piston return spring
31  Metering needle spring-loaded locating screw

piston/rubber diaphragm assembly. Invert the assembly and using a straight edge, check that the shoulder of the metering needle or its Delrin washer (if fitted) is flush with the air valve piston lower face. If not, engage the inner member of the adjusting tool and rotate the metering needle until the correct basic setting is obtained. Refit the air valve piston/diaphragm ensuring that the alignment lug on the periphery of the diaphragm locates correctly in the recess in the carburettor body. Refit the top cover and check that the piston rises and falls freely by depressing the lifting pin. If it sticks loosen the cover screws, gently tap the cover, then retighten the screws. If it still sticks, lift the cover and rotate it through 90° at a time and test in each new position until the piston rises and falls freely.

3  To adjust the mixture, insert both components of the tool into the damper orifice, ensuring that the outer member engages securely with the piston bore slot. If the carburettor is being adjusted without having checked the setting of the needle, then the bore will contain oil. This will make it difficult to insert the tool, and even pressure will have to be exerted on the outer member until the oil is ejected through the channels provided in the tool.

4  To enrich the mixture, rotate the inner member of the tool in a clockwise direction and to weaken it, rotate anti-clockwise. Do not rotate the inner member of the tool more than one turn in either direction from the basic setting position or the needle will become disengaged from its holder. Should this happen, remove the piston/diaphragm assembly and re-engage the needle with its holder by supporting the lower face of the needle, exerting pressure on the holder with the tool, and turning it at the same time.

5  The mixture can be adjusted by rotating the tool with the engine running but downward pressure on the tool will close the air valve piston and stall the engine. It will therefore be more satisfactory if the tool is rotated not more than $\frac{1}{8}$th of a turn at a time and removed, before starting the engine and checking the effect of the needle adjustment.

6  When the best position of the needle for even running is found, it may be necessary to readjust the slow running speed screw. Note that where needle adjustment is carried out with the engine running and it stalls, rev the engine on restarting to clear the inlet manifold before checking the idling.

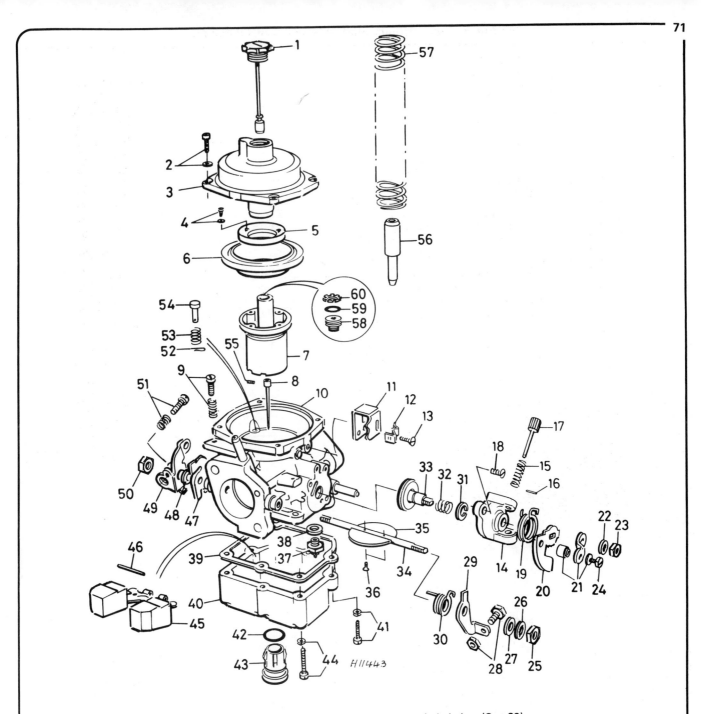

**Fig. 3.28 Stromberg 150CD3 carburettor – exploded view (Sec 22)**

| | | | |
|---|---|---|---|
| 1 Damper | 18 Screw | 33 Disc valve | 47 Lever |
| 2 Cover screw | 19 Spring | 34 Throttle valve spindle | 48 Bush |
| 3 Cover | 20 Cam | 35 Throttle valve plate | 49 Lever |
| 4 Diaphragm ring screw | 21 Lever | 36 Retaining screws | 50 Nut |
| 5 Diaphragm retaining ring | 22 Washer | 37 Fuel inlet valve | 51 Throttle spindle free |
| 6 Diaphragm | 23 Nut | 38 Washer | movement screw |
| 7 Air valve piston | 24 Screw | 39 Gasket | 52 Spring clip |
| 8 Metering needle | 25 Nut | 40 Float chamber | 53 Coil spring |
| 9 Slow running screw | 26 Lockwasher | 41 Retaining screw and | 54 Lifting pin |
| 10 Body | 27 Washer | lockwasher | 55 Metering needle screw |
| 11 Bracket | 28 Fast idle screw and | 42 O-ring | 56 Metering jet |
| 12 Clip | locknut | 43 Plug | 57 Spring |
| 13 Screw | 29 Lever | 44 Retaining screw and | 58 Metering needle adjustment |
| 14 Cover | 30 Spring | lockwasher | screw |
| 15 Spring | 31 Circlip | 45 Float | 59 O-ring |
| 16 Retaining pin | 32 Coil spring | 46 Float pivot | 60 Retainer |
| 17 Stop | | | |

7    Other carburettor adjustments for choke control, starter assembly travel stop, float level and fast idle speed are carried out as for the CDS type carburettor.

## 23 Twin carburettor installation (Stromberg 150CD3) – synchronisation

1    Where twin carburettors of this type are fitted, check the basic setting of each metering needle as described in Section 22.
2    Unscrew the fast idle speed adjustment screw (Fig. 3.26) until well clear of the cam on the front carburettor.
3    Slacken the more accessible clamp bolt on the couplings between the carburettors. Check that the accelerator cable is not holding the throttle open. Slacken off both slow running adjustment screws until their ends are clear of the levers. Then screw each one in again until a 0.002 feeler gauge (or piece of paper) is lightly held between the screw ends and the levers. Remove the gauge, and rotate each screw clockwise a further two turns, thus opening each throttle an equal amount. Tighten the coupling clamp bolt.
5    With the engine at operating temperature, check the mixture as described in the previous Section, adjusting each carburettor if necessary with the special tool by equal amounts. Check for synchronisation by listening at the same spot on each carburettor with a length of tube until each carburettor gives an equivalent 'hiss'. Check that the mixture strength of the two carburettors is equal, using a suitable mixture indicating device if available.
6    Reset the fast idle gap in accordance with that specified in Specifications Section and refill both damper bores with the correct viscosity oil.

## 24 Carburettor (SU HS4C) – general description

This carburettor is of the automatically expanding choke type. The degree of throttle opening and the prevailing road load determine the position of a choke controlling piston and taper needle metering jet. A feature is the cold start choke which moves the jet downwards and, due to the tapered profile of the piston needle, provides an enriched mixture.

## 25 Carburettor (SU HS4C) – adjustment

1    Run the engine until it reaches the normal operating temperature, refer to Fig. 3.29, and adjust screw (2) to give the specified idle speed.
2    Check the mixture strength by raising the piston lifting pin approximately $\frac{1}{32}$ in (0.8 mm) while the engine is idling. If the engine speed increases appreciably, the mixture is too rich. If it stalls immediately, the mixture is too weak.
3    To adjust the mixture strength, turn the jet adjusting screw clockwise to enrich or anti-clockwise to weaken. The mixture is correct when, by raising the lifting pin $\frac{1}{32}$ in (0.8 mm) the engine speed remains constant or increases a minimal amount. Alteration of the mixture strength may mean that the idle speed will need readjusting.
4    To adjust the choke cable, ensure that there is a minimum of $\frac{1}{16}$ in (1.5 mm) free-play at the inner cable with the fast idle cam against its stop. Pull out the choke knob until the linkage is just about to move the metering jet, start the engine, and check that its fast idle speed is as given in the Specifications. The fast idle screw (Fig. 3.29) should be turned as necessary and the locknut finally tightened. Release the choke knob and switch off the engine.

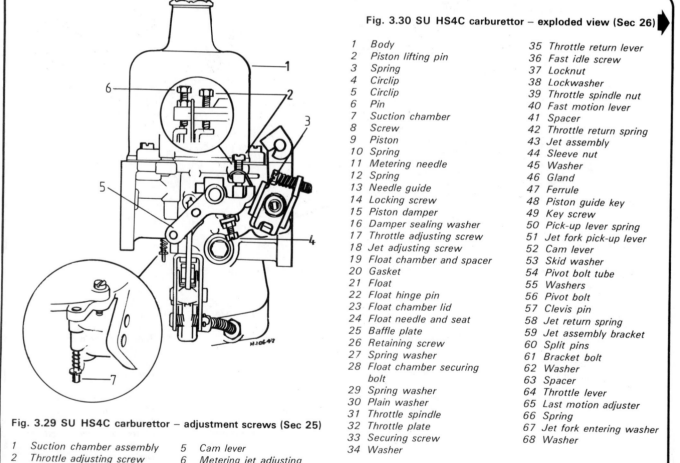

**Fig. 3.30 SU HS4C carburettor – exploded view (Sec 26)**

| | | | |
|---|---|---|---|
| 1 | Body | 35 | Throttle return lever |
| 2 | Piston lifting pin | 36 | Fast idle screw |
| 3 | Spring | 37 | Locknut |
| 4 | Circlip | 38 | Lockwasher |
| 5 | Circlip | 39 | Throttle spindle nut |
| 6 | Pin | 40 | Fast motion lever |
| 7 | Suction chamber | 41 | Spacer |
| 8 | Screw | 42 | Throttle return spring |
| 9 | Piston | 43 | Jet assembly |
| 10 | Spring | 44 | Sleeve nut |
| 11 | Metering needle | 45 | Washer |
| 12 | Spring | 46 | Gland |
| 13 | Needle guide | 47 | Ferrule |
| 14 | Locking screw | 48 | Piston guide key |
| 15 | Piston damper | 49 | Key screw |
| 16 | Damper sealing washer | 50 | Pick-up lever spring |
| 17 | Throttle adjusting screw | 51 | Jet fork pick-up lever |
| 18 | Jet adjusting screw | 52 | Cam lever |
| 19 | Float chamber and spacer | 53 | Skid washer |
| 20 | Gasket | 54 | Pivot bolt tube |
| 21 | Float | 55 | Washers |
| 22 | Float hinge pin | 56 | Pivot bolt |
| 23 | Float chamber lid | 57 | Clevis pin |
| 24 | Float needle and seat | 58 | Jet return spring |
| 25 | Baffle plate | 59 | Jet assembly bracket |
| 26 | Retaining screw | 60 | Split pins |
| 27 | Spring washer | 61 | Bracket bolt |
| 28 | Float chamber securing bolt | 62 | Washer |
| 29 | Spring washer | 63 | Spacer |
| 30 | Plain washer | 64 | Throttle lever |
| 31 | Throttle spindle | 65 | Last motion adjuster |
| 32 | Throttle plate | 66 | Spring |
| 33 | Securing screw | 67 | Jet fork entering washer |
| 34 | Washer | 68 | Washer |

**Fig. 3.29 SU HS4C carburettor – adjustment screws (Sec 25)**

| | | | |
|---|---|---|---|
| 1 | Suction chamber assembly | 5 | Cam lever |
| 2 | Throttle adjusting screw | 6 | Metering jet adjusting screw |
| 3 | Throttle movement adjusting screw | 7 | Piston lifting pin |
| 4 | Fast idle adjusting screw | | |

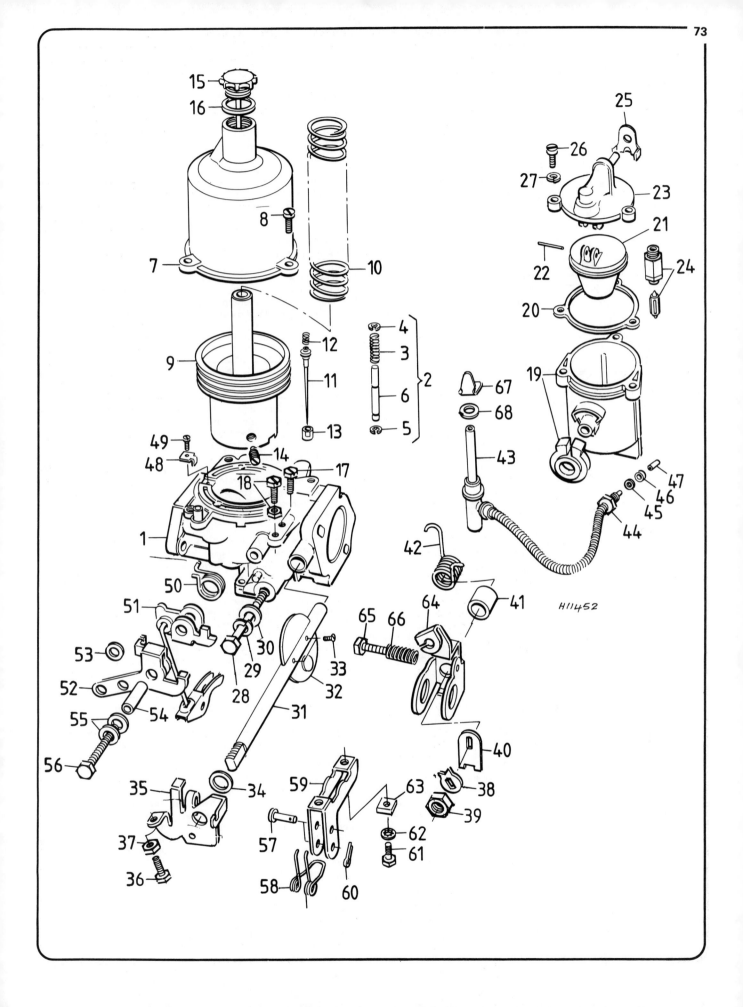

H11452

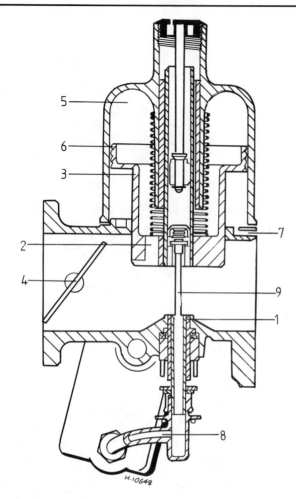

H.10648

**Fig. 3.31 SU HS4C carburettor – sectional view (Sec 26)**

| | | | |
|---|---|---|---|
| 1 | Metering jet | 6 | Piston suction disc |
| 2 | Bypass drillings | 7 | Vent |
| 3 | Piston valve | 8 | Nylon fuel tube |
| 4 | Throttle plate | 9 | Fuel metering needle |
| 5 | Vacuum chamber | | |

## 26 Carburettor (SU HS4C) – removal, dismantling, servicing and refitting

1    Removal and refitting is as described in Section 11.
2    Removal of the suction chamber, piston assembly and float chamber lid can be carried out with the carburettor in-situ. If complete dismantling is required, it will be necessary to remove the carburettor from the engine inlet manifold and air cleaner.
3    To dismantle, clean the carburettor exterior with petrol or paraffin and remove the piston damper (Fig. 3.30).
4    Mark the suction chamber in relation to the carburettor body, and remove the retaining screws. Withdraw the chamber vertically.
5    Remove the spring and piston and empty the oil from the piston shaft. With a non-fluffy cloth moistened with petrol, clean the piston, suction chamber interior, and venturi section.
6    Remove the float chamber lid screws and withdraw the lid and gasket. Clean any sediment from the float chamber bowl, and use a tyre pump to clear the internal passages and connecting tube to the metering jet.
7    Check the needle valve and seat for wear, clean them, and then refit the lid to the float chamber and tighten the securing screws.
8    Before refitting the piston assembly, carry out a 'drop test' by assembling the piston to the chamber without the spring, fitting the damper screw, and plugging the piston transfer holes with plasticine. Invert the suction chamber, hold the shank of the piston, and check the time taken for the suction chamber to drop freely from its fully inserted

position on the piston to the point where the piston outer diameter reaches the end of the suction chamber bore. If the time taken falls outside 5 to 7 seconds, suspect excessive carburettor wear and renew it. If the test is satisfactory, check that the needle shank is flush with the underside of the piston, and adjust the metering jet (Fig. 3.29) until it is flush with the bridge in the carburettor venturi. Then turn the adjusting screw a further two turns clockwise.
9    Refit the piston, spring and suction chamber noting the mating marks made previously, and top up the piston with engine oil to $\frac{1}{2}$ in (13 mm) above the top of the hollow piston rod. Check the piston for free movement by lifting it with the lifting pin and listening for a sharp 'click' as it falls onto the bridge.
10   Refit the damper and adjust the mixture and idling speed as described in Section 25.

## 27 Carburettor (Weber 40 DCOE – types 70 and 71) – general description

This carburettor has two throttle barrels of equal diameter, fed with fuel from a common float chamber. A single accelerator pump, and a single cold starting device, operate on both barrels. By fitting two carburettors to a four branch induction manifold, the advantages of having one carburettor for each cylinder are obtained.

## 28 Carburettor (Weber 40 DCOE – types 70 and 71) – removal and refitting

1    Removal of both carburettors at once is necessary because of the synchronising linkage between them. The method recommended is that of removing the assembly complete with the airbox and manifold.
2    Disconnect the hose from the airbox, the fuel pipe clip from the front carburettor and the fuel pipe at the unions on both float chambers.
3    Disconnect the accelerator cable, the choke cable and the brake servo hose at the rear carburettor T-connection.
4    Remove the manifold-to-cylinder head nuts and bolts, disconnect the exhaust pipe from the manifold, and lift the complete assembly away.
5    To remove the carburettors whilst leaving the manifold in place, disconnect the air cleaner hose, remove the airbox and studs, and disconnect the fuel pipe, the upper end of the throttle operating rod, and the choke lever operating cable. Remove both carburettor flange fixing nuts, double coil spring washers, and flat washers, removing the lower nuts first.
6    Refitting is the direct reversal of the removal procedure. However, if the carburettors have been removed from the manifold, the flange nuts must be tightened evenly until there is a gap of 0.020 to 0.025 in (0.5 to 0.6 mm) between the coils of the spring washers. In practice, if the nuts are fully tightened and then released by between a quarter and a half turn, the correct condition will be obtained.

## 29 Carburettor (Weber 40 DCOE – types 70 and 71) – adjustments

1    With the Weber arrangement which incorporates a separate venturi to each cylinder, it is sometimes possible to locate a carburettor fault by shorting out each spark plug in turn, and noting which cylinder gives the smallest decrease in engine speed. This assumes that the mechanical condition of the engine is good.
2    Run the engine until it reaches the normal operating temperature, stop the engine, and then remove the air intake box from the carburettors. Check the tightness of inlet and exhaust manifold securing nuts and bolts, and that there is a gap of 0.020 to 0.025 in (0.5 to 0.6 mm) between the spring washer coils at the carburettor flange (see Section 28).
3    Refer to Fig. 3.32 and screw the slow running mixture control screws onto their seats, then release them half a turn, for an initial setting.
4    Start the engine and adjust its speed to between 1000 and 1200 rpm by turning the throttle stop screw on the front carburettor.
5    Using a short length of plastic tubing compare the air flow 'hiss' at the front carburettor to that at the rear carburettor, and adjust the synchronising screw to equalise them.

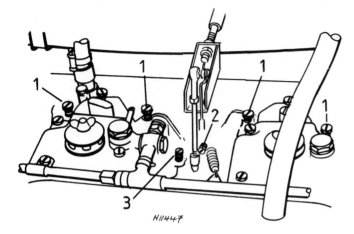

**Fig. 3.32 Weber DCOE carburettor – adjusting screws (Sec 29)**

1   Slow running mixture
    control screws

2   Synchronising adjusting
    screw
3   Throttle stop screw

6   Adjust each slow running mixture screw by equal amounts to give the highest engine speed; if necessary connect a tachometer to the engine, turning each screw 1/12th of a turn at a time. Turn clockwise to weaken the mixture, anti-clockwise to enrich.

7   If the idling speed is now incorrect, adjust the throttle stop screw. Shorting out each spark plug in turn should produce noticeable fall off of engine rpm for each cylinder, assuming good mechanical condition.

8   The choke control cable should be adjusted by ensuring that the starting device levers are fully against their stops. Then, with the choke control $\frac{1}{8}$ in (3 mm) from its fully returned position, tighten the cable securing screw. Check the operation.

## 30 Carburettor (Weber 40 DCOE – types 70 and 71) – servicing

1   The carburettor can be dismantled for cleaning whilst in-situ provided there is not an excessive amount of water or other impurities in the float chamber. Remove the carburettor to completely dismantle it, or if there is excessive sediment in the float chamber.

2   To clean in-situ, refer to Fig. 3.33 and slacken the fuel inlet filter cover plug. Unscrew and remove the fuel supply pipe. Remove the float chamber cover screws, with their brass washers and lift off the cover, being careful not to damage the float mechanism. Remove the fuel inlet plug and extract the filter. Unscrew the wing nut and remove the circular jet cover. Unscrew and remove the slow running jet assembly, main jet/emulsion tube/air correction jet assembly starter jets, and accelerator pumps jets.

3   Syphon as much fuel as possible from the float chamber and main jet well through the small well access holes. Blow through all the jets and internal passages using a tyre pump.

4   Refit the jets, float cover assembly, filter (after cleaning), filter cover, and fuel pipe in reverse order, and make sure that the special ring is correctly positioned beneath the cover before tightening the wing nut. Carry out the same procedure on each carburettor. Adjust and synchronise them as described in Section 29. With this type of carburettor it is particularly important to ensure that there are no air leaks between the intake and air cleaner, or the mixture strength will be upset. Check the cork gasket on the airbox, and inspect the flexible hose for damage, renewing as necessary.

5   To check the float level, remove the wing nut and cover, followed by the float chamber screws. Lift off the float chamber cover assembly.

6   Check the tightness of the needle valve assembly, and that the needle is free to move. Ensure that the float moves freely on its pin, and that the float lever is not pitted at the contact point with the needle valve.

7   Check the float weight against the Specifications.

8   Hold the cover vertically (see Fig. 3.34) with the float lever just touching the needle valve but without moving the spring-loaded end. Dimension 'A' disregarding the soldered seam, should be 0.335 in (8.50 mm) and if incorrect, should be rectified by carefully bending the

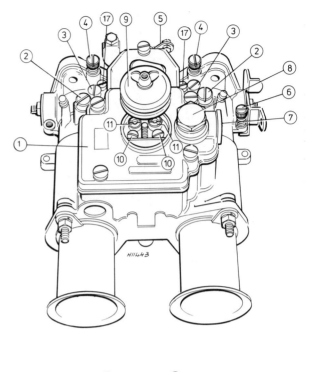

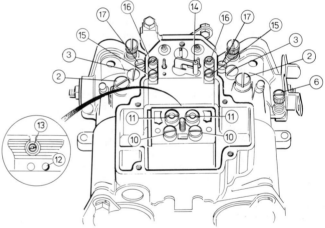

**Fig. 3.33 Weber DCOE carburettor – detail parts (Sec 30)**

1   Float chamber cover
2   Accelerator pump jets
3   Progression inspection
    cover screws
4   Idle mixture volume
    control screws
5   Cold start device lever
6   Idle speed adjusting screw
7   Fuel inlet
8   Filter cover plug
9   Cover

10  Slow running jet assemblies
11  Main jet/emulsion tube/
    air correction jet
    assemblies
12  Well access hole
13  Accelerator pump inlet
    valve
14  Accelerator pump
15  Pump outlet valves
16  Starter jets
17  Blanking plugs

tab. Make sure, however, that the contact area of the tab remains at 90° to the needle centre line.

9   When the float level is correct, check that the float movement is 0.256 in (6.50 mm) or alternatively that the float is 0.591 in (15.00 mm) from the cover gasket in its lowest position (dimension 'B'). Adjust if necessary by bending the lug.

10  Carefully enter the floats into the body as the cover is refitted. Refit all parts.

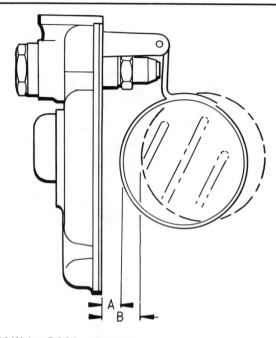

Fig. 3.34 Weber DCOE carburettor – checking the float level – see text (Sec 30)

## 31 Exhaust emission control system (single carburettor) – general description

This system is fitted to enable vehicles employed in certain territories to conform to local regulations which require a very low emission of hydrocarbon and carbon monoxide in the exhaust gas. A Stromberg CDSE or CDSET carburettor is employed, together with a control valve and suitable distributor. The components are shown in Fig. 3.35. The control valve operates by inlet manifold and when open it allows inlet vacuum to operate the throttle bypass valve and the ignition retard capsule. The distributor used with the Stromberg CDSE and CDSET carburettor has a tandem capsule, this additional chamber retards the ignition timing twelve crankshaft degrees during overrun conditions. The combined operations of these additional components overcomes the pollution normally present during overrun, where the slow running mixture is excessively diluted by exhaust gases causing incomplete combustion.

## 32 Exhaust emission control system (single carburettor) – servicing and fault diagnosis

1   To maintain the efficiency of the system, servicing must be carried out regularly. The items listed should be serviced at the recommended intervals, in the order in which they are listed, this being very important:

(a)   Check valve clearances
(b)   Check spark plug gaps
(c)   Check distributor contact point gap
(d)   Check idle speed and quality
(e)   Check ignition timing using a stroboscope
(f)   Check deceleration of engine, from 2500 rpm to idle, with gearbox in neutral

Details of certain of these operations will be found in the following paragraphs.
2   If a fault is found the following procedure should be carried out in sequence, preferably with the aid of proper diagnostic equipment where relevant.
3   Check the valve clearances, the spark plug gaps, and the contact breaker gap. Check the ignition timing by hand (see Chapter 4).
4   Remove the large control valve pipe, and plug the manifold connection. If practicable, check the ignition system performance on diagnostic equipment, with reference to the following points:

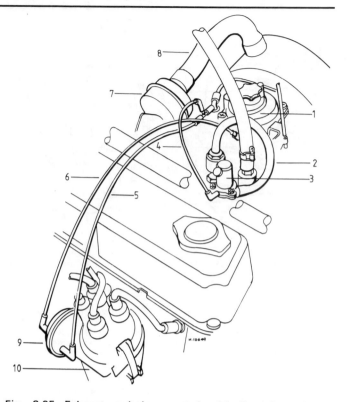

Fig. 3.35 Exhaust emission control with Stromberg CDSE carburettor – system components (Sec 31)

1   Carburettor
2   Large bore connection pipe from inlet manifold to control valve
3   Control valve
4   Small bore connection pipe from control valve to control valve
5   Small bore connection pipe to vacuum retard capsule
6   Connection pipe from carburettor to vacuum advance capsule
7   Crankcase emission flame trap
8   Crankcase emission pipe from flame trap to air filter
9   Vacuum advance and retard
10   Distributor

(a)   Distributor centrifugal advance curve
(b)   Vacuum advance curve
(c)   Vacuum retard movement
(d)   Distributor points dwell angle
(e)   Plug voltages
(f)   Coil and capacitor efficiency

Rectify all faults.
5   Check the idle speed and quality, adopting the procedures which follow as relevant. Rich mixture is indicated by lumpiness during idling or by the emission of black smoke from the exhaust. Check that the starter box rich mixture control is fully off, or on CDSET instruments that the automatic choke is operating properly (see Section 18). Check for air bubbles in the fuel pump glass cover where fitted and rectify air leaks in fuel line or pump gaskets or unions if necessary.
6   Slight enrichment may be corrected by adjustment of the idle air adjustment screw (Fig. 3.26). Where this does not effect a correction remove the carburettor depression cover (noting lug position for refitting). Lift out the air valve and needle assembly. Check that the spring bias is toward the inlet manifold, and that the needle shoulder is exactly level with the piston face as shown in Fig. 3.36. Correct assembly of the needle allows it to lean 3° by spring-loading towards the inlet manifold. Do not overtighten the needle fixing screw.
7   Reassemble the carburettor and check that the air valve piston falls freely. Should the mixture still be too rich, remove the plastic cover shown in Fig. 3.37 and gently feel that the temperature controlled valve is free to move. With the engine at operating temperature the valve should not be seated. Any stickiness must be

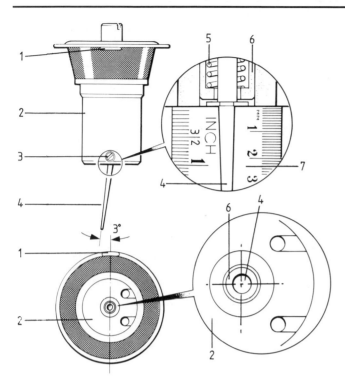

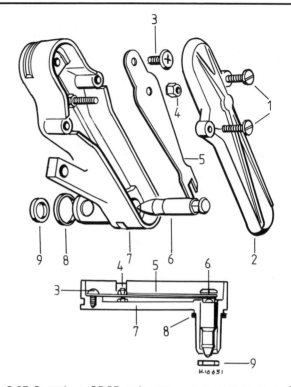

Fig. 3.36 Stromberg CDSE carburettor – needle fitting details (Sec 32)

Fig. 3.37 Stromberg CDSE carburettor – temperature controlled valve (Sec 32)

1  Diaphragm locating lug
2  Air valve piston
3  Needle holder retaining screw
4  Metering needle
5  Bias spring – metering needle
6  Needle holder
7  Six inch steel rule – used to set needle position with needle held square to piston face

1  Cover fixing screws
2  Plastic cover
3  Bimetal spring fixing screw plate
4  Bimetal spring adjusting nut plate
5  Bimetal spring plate
6  Valve – operated by (5)
7  Valve body
8  Rubber seating washer
9  Rubber seating washer

cleaned away after dismantling the valve assembly. When reassembling the valve, ensure that the letters stamped on the bi-metal spring are uppermost. Ensure the spring is not bent or twisted. Set the adjusting nut so that at room temperature 70°F (21°C) the valve is just on its seat. To test, immerse the valve in hot water, when it should open. Refit the valve and recheck idling. Should the mixture still be too rich remove the carburettor from the engine. Remove the float chamber cover, the float and needle valve and check the float level, all as described for type CDS carburettors. With a tyre pump blow any dirt from the components.

8  Reassemble and refit the carburettor but check that the heat insulator and flange joint are correctly positioned as shown in Fig. 3.38.

9  Should the mixture be weak, causing misfiring, check individual cylinders for blown gaskets, and for air leaks at flange and manifold joints. If the mixture is only slightly weak, a correction may be possible by turning the idle air adjusting screw (Fig. 3.19) in a clockwise direction until even running is obtained. Dismantle the carburettor, clean the components and examine the diaphragm for splits. Check the air valve piston for free movement. Check the temperature controlled valve. If by pressing it home on its seat an improvement in mixture strength is obtained, then service the assembly as previously described.

10  Check the fuel pump, the fuel lines, and the float chamber for water. Check that, with the fuel feed pipe removed from the carburettor, a full flow of fuel issues from the pipe when the starter is operated.

11  If weakness persists, remove the carburettor, and remove the float chamber cover, float and needle valve seat. Check for cleanliness and proper operation of the valve. Invert the carburettor and check that the float level dimensions (as given in Fig. 3.14 for the 150CDS instrument) are correct. To reset if necessary, bend the float arm extension where it contacts the needle valve. Reassemble all parts.

12  Check the ignition timing using a stroboscopic light, with the engine at idling speed (automatic cars should be in 'D').

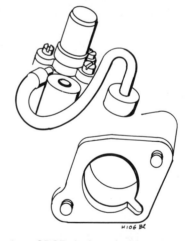

Fig. 3.38 Stromberg CDSE single carburettor – correct location of heat insulator and flange gasket (Sec 32)

13  Refit the pipe to the control valve, when the idle speed and quality should be unchanged. If the idle quality does alter, renew the control valve.

14  Check the time taken by the engine, when running at a constant 2500 rpm, to drop to idling speed. Use a stop-watch; if the time is between 4 and 6 seconds, the emission control system is working correctly. If the engine stays at about 2000 rpm, the suction retard capsule is not working. If the engine stays at 1500 to 1700 rpm, the engine may have become too hot, or the control valve may be faulty. Should the engine slow down in 2½ seconds or less, the throttle bypass valve is not opening. Check the security of all hoses and the condition of rubber sealing washers (Fig. 3.37) and renew if necessary.

15 If the preceding test has been properly carried out, the fault may lie with the throttle bypass valve (Fig. 3.19). Remove the three screws which retain it to the carburettor and remove it; remove the three countersunk screws which hold the valve base and cover together, and separate the parts taking care not to lose the spring, screw and O-ring seal.

16 Drive out the brass sealing disc from the valve outer body and reassemble the valve. Adjust the adjuster screw as far as it will go in a clockwise direction and then back off one complete turn (normal setting).

17 Recheck the time taken for the engine to drop from 2500 rpm to idling, and if within the specified time limits, reseal the valve with brass sealing disc. If the drop is still outside the limits renew the valve.

18 Certain parts of the Stromberg CDSE and CDSET carburettors are not renewable, and if the jet, air valve piston, depression chamber cover or carburettor body become unserviceable an exchange carburettor must be obtained.

### 33 Exhaust emission control system (twin carburettors) – general description

The general comments in Sections 31 and 32 are applicable to this version, but the layout differs in that two Stromberg CDSEV carburettors are employed, whilst no control valve, distributor retard capsule, or connecting pipes are employed. Normal distributor centrifugal and vacuum advance is fitted.

### 34 Exhaust emission control system (twin carburettors) – servicing and fault diagnosis

1 At 5000 mile intervals, service the system as described in Section 32, paragraph 1, but omit the last item, relating to deceleration time. At 25 000 mile intervals, service the carburettors as described in Section 20, paragraph 1. Also at this interval remove the temperature compensator assembly (see Fig. 3.37). Remove the inner seal from the body and the outer seal from the valve. Press the valve end to test the free movement. Do not interfere with the bi-metal blade. Refit, with new inner and outer seals. Top up the air valve piston damper and renew the sealing ring.

2 At 50 000 mile intervals, check and renew any worn moving parts, cams, links etc throughout the emission control system. In severe cases of general wear, renew the affected unit.

3 If a fault is found, the procedure outlined in Section 32, paragraphs 2 to 6 should be carried out in the given sequence, omitting the reference to removal of the control valve pipe. In addition, as the last item of the checking sequence, the throttle bypass valve should be

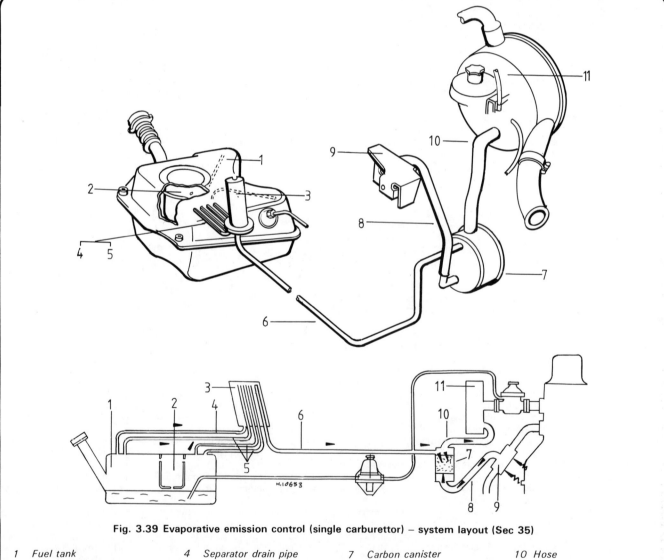

**Fig. 3.39 Evaporative emission control (single carburettor) – system layout (Sec 35)**

| | | | |
|---|---|---|---|
| 1 Fuel tank | 4 Separator drain pipe | 7 Carbon canister | 10 Hose |
| 2 Fuel tank inner chamber | 5 Vent pipes | 8 Hose | 11 Air cleaner |
| 3 Separator | 6 Vapour and tank vent pipe | 9 Air heating stove | |

serviced if necessary.

4    The setting of idle speed and quality is as outlined in Section 32 for single carburettors, and the method of dealing with the throttle bypass valve is described in Section 20.

## 35 Evaporative emission control system – general

1    This system is fitted to vehicles which operate in certain territories where regulations forbid the venting of fuel systems to atmosphere. The layout of the single carburettor version is illustrated in Fig. 3.39 and consists of a fuel tank without vent, a fuel tank inner chamber to prevent over-filling, a carbon canister to adsorb – not absorb – the fuel vapour on the surface of the granules, a heating stove to heat air for purging the carbon of fuel vapour, and necessary hoses and connections.

2    Servicing consists of renewing the carbon canister every five years or 50 000 miles operation, whichever occurs first. Check regularly for security of connections and renew any defective hoses. Ensure that the vapour and tank vent pipe does not become flattened as this will cause a fuel stoppage to the engine due to the tank being fitted with a non-vented type filler cap. Should the carbon canister become contaminated by flood water, renew the unit immediately (one bolt).

3    The system used in conjunction with twin carburettors differs from the single carburettor version in that no heating stove is used. Additionally, the vent outlets from the twin carburettor float chambers are connected by pipes to the carbon canister (Fig. 3.40), and the outlet positions of the carbon canisters differ between the two systems.

4    Servicing of the twin carburettor system is similar to the procedure described for single carburettor systems.

5    Fuel tank removal is described in Section 41.

## 36 Exhaust gas recirculating system – general description

This system is fitted to vehicles, operating in certain territories where stringent emission control regulations apply. Its purpose is to reduce oxides of nitrogen in the exhaust by recirculating a quantity of exhaust gas into the inlet manifold, thereby lowering the combustion temperature. The system consists of an exhaust gas recirculating control valve, throttle connecting linkage and the necessary pipework.

The principle of operation is that, as the throttle is opened, the control valve disc rotates uncovering a port and permitting recirculation of the exhaust gases. The port remains open until a wide throttle position is reached when it closes to ensure optimum engine

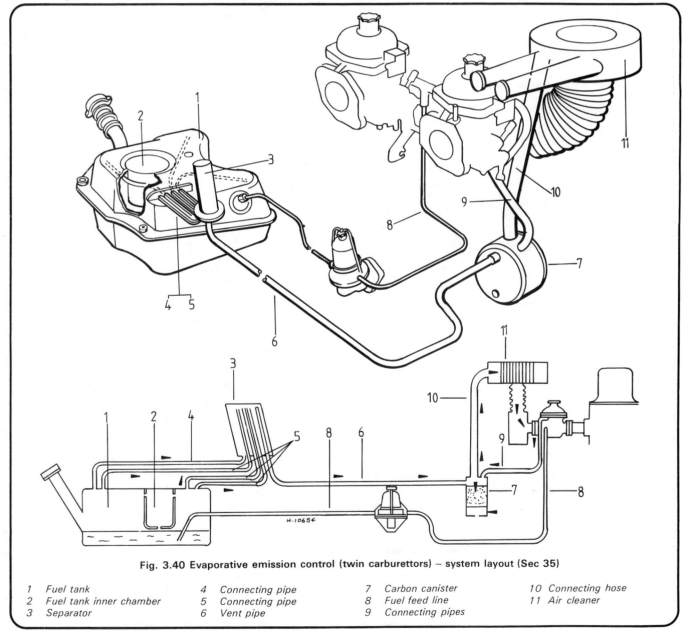

**Fig. 3.40 Evaporative emission control (twin carburettors) – system layout (Sec 35)**

| | | |
|---|---|---|
| 1  Fuel tank | 4  Connecting pipe | 7  Carbon canister | 10  Connecting hose |
| 2  Fuel tank inner chamber | 5  Connecting pipe | 8  Fuel feed line | 11  Air cleaner |
| 3  Separator | 6  Vent pipe | 9  Connecting pipes | |

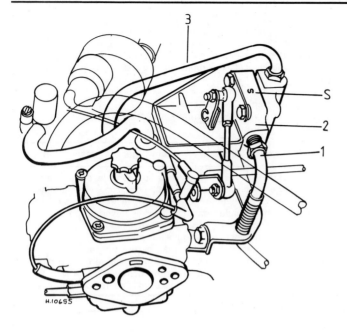

**Fig. 3.41 Exhaust gas recirculating system – Stromberg CDSET single carburettor (Sec 36)**

1   *Exhaust gas pipe to recirculating valve*
2   *Recirculating valve*
3   *Exhaust gas pipe from valve to inlet manifold*
S   *Single carburettor identification*

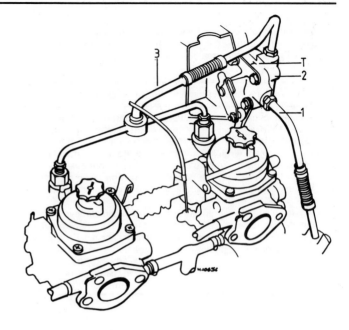

**Fig. 3.42 Exhaust gas recirculating system – Stromberg CDSET twin carburettors (Sec 36)**

1   *Exhaust gas pipe to recirculating valve*
2   *Recirculating valve*
3   *Exhaust gas pipe from valve to inlet manifold*
T   *Twin carburettor identification*

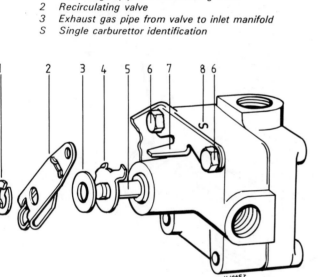

**Fig. 3.43 Exhaust gas recirculating valve (Sec 36)**

1   *Circlip*
2   *Operating lever and override spring*
3   *Spacer*
4   *Travel limiter (restrictor)*
5   *Operating shaft*
6   *Securing setscrew*
7   *Travel limiter stop*
8   *Identification symbol*

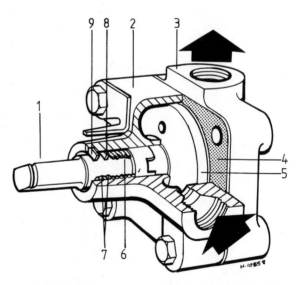

**Fig. 3.44 Exhaust gas recirculating valve (Sec 37)**

1   *Operating shaft*
2   *Front body*
3   *Rear body*
4   *Gasket*
5   *Ceramic disc valve*
6   *Spring*
7   *Brass rings*
8   *Seal*
9   *Circlip*

performance. A safety feature is provided by the inclusion of an override spring in the lever (Fig. 3.43) to ensure that the throttle linkage will function normally even if the valve sticks or jams through any cause.

## 37 Exhaust gas recirculating system – maintenance and fault diagnosis

1   Every 10 000 miles (16 000 km) the system and valve should be inspected for exhaust deposit build-up. Should there be symptoms of difficult starting, bad idling or stalling or lack of performance at full throttle opening, the maintenance procedure should be carried out

immediately as the recirculating valve is probably sticking.
2   Check all pipe connections for deterioration. Remove the pipe between the valve and the inlet manifold. If the adaptor into the inlet manifold is blocked or restricted with exhaust deposits, clear it using a $\frac{5}{16}$ in (7.94 mm) drill.
3   Operate the throttle linkage and observe the end of the valve

spindle which should rotate. If it does not, the interior of the valve is choked with exhaust deposits and must be dismantled to clear.

4   Remove the valve from its location by disconnecting the throttle link and the pipes to the inlet manifold and exhaust pipe.

5   Refer to Fig. 3.43 and withdraw the two bolts (6). Separate the two halves of the valve but take care not to drop the ceramic disc valve (Fig. 3.44).

6   Lift the disc valve from its location in the front body. Remove the circlip (Fig. 3.43), lever arm, spacer and restrictor.

7   Press the operating shaft through the front body and withdraw the brass rings, seal and spring.

8   Clean all components in paraffin and scrape away any deposits without damaging the surfaces. Dry the components with compressed air and spray them with an approved high temperature silicone lubricant before reassembling, which is a reversal of dismantling.

9   The valves used in single or twin carburettor installations vary in detail, but are identified by the letter S (single) or T (twin) stamped on the upper surface of the body. The single carburettor valve employs a ceramic disc having two 0.141 in (3.58 mm) diameter holes while the twin carburettor disc has two of 0.250 in (6.35 mm) diameter. The single carburettor valve driveshaft slot is at 45° to the shaft flats which engage with the override spring in the operating lever while the twin carburettor valve has the slot in the same plane as the flats.

## 38  Fuel tank (saloon car up to and including 7 Series) – removal and refitting

1   To remove the tank, disconnect and remove the battery earth (negative) lead.

2   Referring to Fig. 3.45, remove the drain plug and washer from the fuel tank and drain the contents.

3   Pull off the vent hose connector, disconnect the electrical leads from the tank level unit, and disconnect the fuel line from the tank level unit.

4   Pull the filler neck tube outwards from the rubber bush which is located in the tank face.

5   Unscrew the tank securing bolts and nuts and lower the tank.

6   Refit in reverse order. Take care not to trap electrical leads. *Never attempt to repair a leaking tank by soldering. This is very dangerous.* Consult specialist repairers or fit a new tank.

## 39  Fuel tank (saloon car, 7 Series on) – removal and refitting

1   To remove the tank, disconnect the battery negative terminal.

2   Open the filler cap cover on the right-hand side rear panel, and remove the two filler neck screws.

3   Jack-up the rear of the car, place it on stands, and syphon out any fuel in the tank.

4   Pull off the vent hose connector and disconnect the level sensor electrical leads.

5   Disconnect the fuel line from the level sensor unit. Unscrew and remove the retaining nuts and bolts and carefully lower the fuel tank while easing the filler neck through the rubber seal.

6   Refit in the reverse order. Smear a little rubber grease or silicone onto the filler neck to ease entry into the rubber seal.

## 40  Fuel tank (estate car) – removal and refitting

1   The tank fitted to the estate version incorporates a restrictor valve in the breather pipe (Fig. 3.47). To remove the tank, disconnect the battery negative terminal.

2   Remove the carpet retaining strips, fold the carpet forward, and remove the access plate.

3   Prise the right-hand trim panel away, and remove the floor finisher and filler pipe grommet.

4   Disconnect the breather pipe. Remove the filler cap, grommet, and filler tube.

5   There is no provision for draining the fuel tank, and any remaining fuel should be syphoned out at this stage.

6   Disconnect the fuel supply pipe and tank level sensor lead, remove the retaining bolts, and lower the tank from the car.

7   Refit in the reverse order.

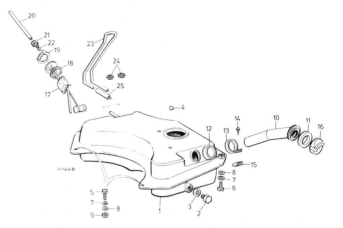

**Fig. 3.45 Fuel tank – saloon car up to and including series 7 (no evaporative emission system fitted) (Sec 38)**

| | | | |
|---|---|---|---|
| 1 | Tank | 14 | Screw |
| 2 | Plug | 15 | Clip |
| 3 | Washer | 16 | Cap |
| 4 | Buffer | 17 | Gauge unit |
| 5 | Setscrew | 18 | Seal |
| 6 | Setscrew | 19 | Locking ring |
| 7 | Washer | 20 | Fuel pipe |
| 8 | Washer | 21 | Nut |
| 9 | Nut | 22 | Olive |
| 10 | Filler | 23 | Pipe |
| 11 | Grommet | 24 | Grommet |
| 12 | Seal | 25 | Vent hose connector |
| 13 | Clip | | |

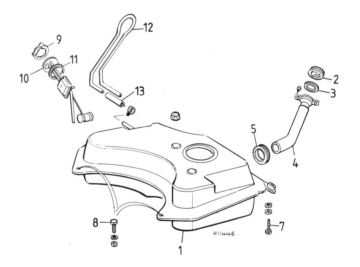

**Fig. 3.46 Fuel tank – saloon car 7 series on (no evaporative emission system fitted) (Sec 39)**

| | | | |
|---|---|---|---|
| 1 | Tank | 8 | Securing bolt |
| 2 | Filler cap | 9 | Locking ring |
| 3 | Seal | 10 | Level sensor unit |
| 4 | Filler neck | 11 | Seal |
| 5 | Seal | 12 | Breather pipe |
| 6 | Mounting | 13 | Connector |
| 7 | Securing bolt | | |

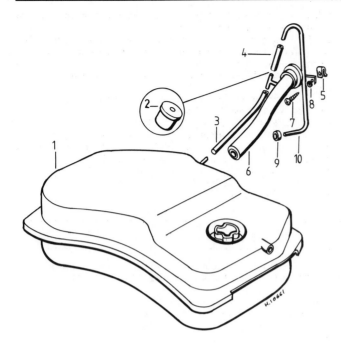

**Fig. 3.47 Fuel tank – estate car (no evaporative emission system fitted) (Sec 40)**

| | |
|---|---|
| 1  Tank | 6  Filler pipe |
| 2  Restrictor | 7  Clip retaining screw |
| 3  Breather pipe | 8  Washer |
| 4  Breather pipe | 9  Grommet |
| 5  Clip | 10  Breather pipe |

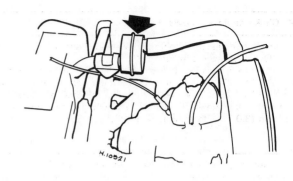

**Fig. 3.48 Flame trap – crankcase ventilation system (Sec 42)**

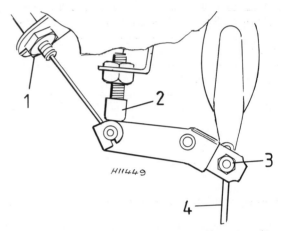

**Fig. 3.49 Accelerator connections – twin carburettors (Sec 43)**

| | |
|---|---|
| 1  Cable nut | 3  Trunnion nut |
| 2  Relay lever stop | 4  Link rod |

## 41 Fuel tank (saloon and estate cars fitted with evaporative emission control) – removal and refitting

1   Disconnect the battery earth lead, and remove the drain plug to drain the tank.
2   Disconnect the outlet pipe from the separator (Fig. 3.39), remove the three securing screws which retain the separator at the boot floor and draw it downward.
3   Disconnect the fuel pipe from the tank union and the electrical leads from the tank unit.
4   Pull the tank filler tube outwards from its rubber bush in the tank rear face, remove the two bolts and two nuts which retain the tank in position and lower it with its four flexible plastic pipes in position.
5   Refer to Fig. 3.39 and disconnect the pipes from the separator. The fuel tank may then be withdrawn.
6   Refit in the reverse order.

## 42 Crankcase emission control system

1   The engine crankcase is ventilated by a rubber tube connection between the rocker cover and the air filter. A flame trap is interposed between the two components, and requires regular servicing. Referring to Fig. 3.48, slacken the retaining clip screws and pull off the rubber tube from both sides of the flame trap. Soak and agitate the trap in paraffin (never fuel) and after draining, apply a tyre pump to dry the interior. Check the bores of the rubber tubing and clean out any moisture before fitting the flame trap in its original position. The correct alignment of the W or S marks according to season on the air filter intake will ensure the minimum of condensation occurring in the flame trap and connecting pipes.
2   The only difference between the systems employed on single and twin carburettor installations is that the hoses employed between the flame trap and air cleaner body are of different lengths.

## 43 Accelerator control rods and cables – removal, adjustment and refitting

1   On single carburettor models, a rod system is employed to control the butterfly valve. To adjust, detach the control rod running behind the cylinder block by pulling the plastic balljoints off the metal balls.
2   Loosen the locknuts, and screw the control rod until the end of the threaded portion can just be seen through the cut-out in the plastic balljoint.
3   Refit the control rod, but do not retighten the locknuts at this stage.
4   Loosen the trunnion nut in Fig. 3.17 and have an assistant fully depress the accelerator pedal. At the same time, fully open the throttle plate on the carburettor and tighten the trunnion nut.
5   Align the control rod balljoints in their correct planes, and tighten the locknuts. Check that, when the accelerator pedal is fully depressed, the throttle plate is fully open.
6   When the control rods have been set and the idling speed adjusted, check the throttle linkage adjustment screw (B), as described in Section 13.
7   On twin carburettor models, a cable system is employed to control the butterfly valves. To adjust, check that with both throttle plates fully closed the accelerator cable has a little slackness.
8   Adjust the relay lever stop (Fig. 3.49) to mid position and loosen the trunnion nut. Ensure that there is no obstruction beneath the accelerator pedal, and have an assistant depress it fully to the floor. At the same time turn the relay lever to the full throttle position, and tighten the trunnion nut.
9   Operate the accelerator pedal a few times and check that full throttle is obtainable with the pedal fully depressed.
10  To remove the cable, disconnect the inner and outer at the carburettor, and the inner from the other end. Remove the nut on the outer cable beneath the servo unit. (Use a box spanner, and feed the cable through it). Draw the cable from behind the servo.

## 44 Choke cable – renewal and adjustment

1   Remove the steering column cowls and unscrew the nut retaining the choke cable to the lower cowl.
2   Disconnect the inner and outer cables from the carburettor(s).
3   Withdraw the cable(s) through the bulkhead and lower cowl.
4   Refitting is the reversal of removal, but before tightening the carburettor adjustment screw(s) make sure that the control knob is 0.125 in (3.0 mm) from its fully returned position.

## 45 Exhaust systen – description, removal and refitting

1   The system is mounted flexibly at the ends of both the silencer and tailpipe, and consists of a front exhaust pipe complete with expansion chamber, a silencer, and a tailpipe.
2   To remove the tailpipe, undo the flexible supports at the tailpipe and at the silencer. Support the silencer, remove the tailpipe and withdraw it over the rear axle.
3   To remove the exhaust silencer, remove the tailpipe and then the silencer.
4   The front exhaust pipe and expansion box can be removed after withdrawing the silencer and tailpipe.
5   It should be mentioned that difficulty can be experienced in separating the component parts of the exhaust system if it has been in position for any length of time, and it may be necessary to employ penetrating oil, or even to cut the items apart in severe cases. If a certain part of the system is to be renewed, then there is no reason why this should not be cut down, with a probable saving in time.
6   Refitting is the reverse of removal.

## 46 Fault diagnosis – fuel and emission control systems

| Symptom | Reason(s) |
| --- | --- |
| Excessive fuel consumption | Air filter(s) choked |
| | Leaks in fuel tank or fuel lines |
| | Float level setting too high |
| | Mixture too rich |
| | Incorrect valve clearances |
| | Dragging brakes |
| | Tyres underinflated |
| | Choke adjustment incorrect |
| | Automatic choke faulty |
| Insufficient delivery or weak mixture | Sticking inlet needle valve |
| | Faulty fuel pump |
| | Leaking inlet manifold gasket |
| | Leaking carburettor flange gasket |
| | Mixture too weak |
| | Split air valve diaphragm |
| | Faulty carburettor temperature control valve |

# Chapter 4  Ignition system

## Contents

## Specifications

### Ignition system, conventional type (up to 7 Series)
#### Spark plugs
Type:
| | |
|---|---|
| Up to 6 Series ................................................ | Champion N7Y |
| 7 Series (1.50 carburettor) ................................. | Champion N9Y (N7Y for sustained high speeds) |
| 7 Series (1.75 carburettor) ................................. | Champion N7Y (N9Y for slow (city) driving) |
| Spark plug gap .............................................. | 0.030 in (0.75 mm) |

**Firing order** ................................................ 1-3-4-2

**Ignition advance control** .................................. Automatic, centrifugal and vacuum

**Ignition timing marks** ..................................... 5° speed notches on crankshaft pulley. Cast-in pointer on timing cover

#### Distributor (up to and including 7 Series models)
Type:

| | Direction of rotation | Contact breaker gap | Dwell angle |
|---|---|---|---|
| Lucas 25D4 ........................................ | Anti-clockwise | 0.015 in (0.38 mm) | 60° ± 5° |
| Lucas 45D4 and 43D4* ...................... | Anti-clockwise | 0.015 in (0.38 mm) | 51° ± 5° |
| AC Delco D204 ................................ | Anti-clockwise | 0.016 in (0.41 mm) | 39° ± 1° |
| Ducellier ........................................ | Anti-clockwise | 0.016 in (0.41 mm) initial then set dwell angle | 56° ± 1° |

**Coil** ........................................................ Lucas 11 C 12 or AC Delco 7992170

### Ignition timing – Pre 5 Series models
| Engine type | Distributor | Static timing | Dynamic timing at 3000 rpm† |
|---|---|---|---|
| 1250 single carburettor (HC) ..................... | Lucas 41302 Lucas 41467 AC Delco 7992447 | 6° to 8° | 29.° to 31° |
| 1250 twin carburettor (HC) ....................... | Lucas 41396 Lucas 41468 | 6° to 8° | 29° to 31° |
| 1500 single carburettor (N America) ............. | Lucas 41301 | 7° | 29° to 31° |
| 1500 single carburettor, early engines (HC) ..... | Lucas 41304 | 6° to 8° | 29° to 31° |

| Engine type | Distributor | Static | Dynamic timing at 3000 rpm† |
|---|---|---|---|
| 1500 twin and single carburettor, (later engines (HC) .......................... | Lucas 41364§ Lucas 41463 AC Delco 7992448 | 7° to 9° | 30° to 32° |
| 1500 single carburettor (LC) N America only ............................... | Lucas 41492 Lucas 41455 | 7° | 27° to 29° |
| 1500 single carburettor (LC) ............................................ | Lucas 41303 Lucas 41464 | 6° to 8° | 30° to 32° |
| 1500 twin carburettor (LC) N America only ............................... | Lucas 41365 Lucas 41466 | 9° to 11° | 30° to 32° |
| 1300 single carburettor (HC and LC) ...................................... | Lucas 41559 AC Delco 7992730 | 9° to 11° | 32° to 34° |
| 1300 twin carburettor (HC) ............................................ | Lucas 41561 AC Delco 7992731 | 9° to 11° | 29° t 31° |
| 1600 single carburettor (HC and LC) ...................................... | Lucas 41560 AC Delco 7992732 | 9° to 11° | 27° to 29° |
| 1600 twin carburettor (HC) ............................................ | Lucas 41562 AC Delco 7992733 | 9° to 11° | 29° to 31° |

## Ignition timing – 5 Series models

| Engine type | Distributor | Static timing | Dynamic timing at 3000 rpm† |
|---|---|---|---|
| 1300 single carburettor (HC) ............................................ | Lucas 41597 Ducellier 6617 | 9° to 11° | 29° to 31° |
| 1300 twin carburettor (HC) ............................................ | Lucas 41561 AC Delco 7992731 | 9° to 11° | 29° to 31° |
| 1300 single carburettor (LC) ............................................ | Lucás 41598 | 9° to 11° | 32° to 34° |
| 1600 single carburettor (HC) except Sweden ............................... | Lucas 41596 Ducellier 6616 | 9° to 11° | 27° to 29° |
| 1600 twin carburettor ................................................ | Lucas 41562 AC Delco 7992733 | 9° to 11° | 29° to 31° |
| 1600 single carburettor (LC) ............................................ | Lucas 41560 Lucas 41596 Ducellier 6616 | 9° to 11° | 27° to 29° |

## Ignition timing – 6 Series models

| Engine type | Distributor | Static timing | Dynamic timing at 3000 rpm† |
|---|---|---|---|
| 1300 1.50 carburettor (HC) ............................................ | Lucas 41597 Ducellier 6617 Lucas 41652‡ Ducellier 525020‡ | 9° to 11° | 29° to 31° |
| 1300 1.75 carburettor (HC) ............................................ | Lucas 41627 Ducellier 525001 | 9° to 11° | 31° to 33° |
| 1300 1.50 carburettor (LC) ............................................ | Lucas 41651‡ Ducellier 525019‡ | 9° to 11° | 35° to 37° |
| 1600 1.50 carburettor (HC) except Sweden ............................... | Lucas 41596 Ducellier 6616 Lucas 41653‡ Ducellier 525021‡ | 9° to 11° | 27° to 29° |
| 1600 1.75 carburettor (HC) ............................................ | Lucas 41628 Ducellier 525002 | 9° to 11° | 29° to 31° |
| 1600 1.50 carburettor (LC) ............................................ | Lucas 41596 Ducellier 6616 | 9° to 11° | 27° to 29° |

## Ignition timing – 7 Series models

| Engine type | Distributor | Static timing | Dynamic timing at 3000 rpm† |
|---|---|---|---|
| 1300 1.50 carburettor (HC) ............................................ | Lucas 41652 Ducellier 525020 | 9° to 11° | 29° to 31° |
| 1300 1.75 carburettor (HC) ............................................ | Lucas 41627 Ducellier 525001 | 9° to 11° | 31° to 33° |
| 1300 1.50 carburettor (LC) ............................................ | Lucas 41651 Ducellier 525019 | 9° to 11° | 35° to 37° |

| Engine type | Distributor | Static timing | Dynamic timing at 3000 rpm† |
|---|---|---|---|
| 1600 1.50 carburettor (HC) except Sweden ............................... | Lucas 41690 Ducellier 525094 | 9° to 11° | 32° to 34° |
| 1600 1.75 carburettor (HC) except Sweden ............................... | Lucas 41628 Ducellier 525002 | 9° to 11° | 29° to 31° |
| 1600 1.50 carburettor (LC) ................................................... | Lucas 41688 | 9° to 11° | 27° to 29° |

### Ignition timing – Swedish models

| Engine type | Distributor | Static timing | Dynamic timing at 3000 rpm† |
|---|---|---|---|
| 1600 single carburettor (HC) 5 Series ................................ | Lucas 41560 | 9° to 11° | 27° to 29° |
| 1600 1.50 carburettor (HC) 6 and 7 Series ......................... | Lucas 41647 | 7° to 10° | 23° to 26° |

## Ignition system, electronic type (8 Series onwards)
### Spark plugs
Type:
    1.50 carburettor ........................................................ Champion RN9Y (RN7Y for mainly sustained high speed driving)
    1.75 carburettor ........................................................ Champion RN7Y (RN9Y for mainly low speed (city) driving)
Spark plug gap ................................................................ 0.030 in (0.75 mm)

### Firing order ................................................................ 1-3-4-2

### Ignition advance control ........................................... Automatic, centrifugal and vacuum

### Distributor

| | Lucas | Bosch |
|---|---|---|
| Type ......................................................................... | 45DM4 | JGFU-4 |
| Rotation ................................................................... | Anti-clockwise | Anti-clockwise |
| Gap-reluctor to pick-up (for service purposes) ................ | 0.006 to 0.008 in (0.15 to 0.20 mm) | 0.006 to 0.008 in (0.15 to 0.20 mm) |

### Coil
Primary resistance .......................................................... 1.4 to 1.6 ohms
Secondary resistance ...................................................... 8000 to 10 000 ohms
Ballast resistor .............................................................. 0.50 to 0.60 ohms
Control unit auxiliary resistor ........................................... 4.75 to 5.75 ohms

### Ignition timing

| Engine type | Distributor | Static timing | Dynamic timing at 3000 rpm† |
|---|---|---|---|
| 1300 1.50 carburettor (HC) ............................................... | Lucas 41716 Bosch 0237002 032 | 9° to 11° | 29° to 31° |
| 1300 1.75 carburettor (HC) ............................................... | Lucas 41720 Bosch 0237002 043 | 9° to 11° | 31° to 33° |
| 1300 1.50 carburettor (LC) ............................................... | Lucas 41718 Bosch 0237002 036 | 9° to 11° | 35° to 37° |
| 1600 1.50 carburettor (HC) except Sweden ......................... | Lucas 41717 Bosch 0237002 031 | 9° to 11° | 32° to 34° |
| 1600 1.75 carburettor (HC) except Sweden ......................... | Lucas 41721 Bosch 0237002 037 | 9° to 11° | 29° to 31° |
| 1600 1.50 carburettor (LC) ............................................... | Lucas 41719 Bosch 0237002 044 | 9° to 11° | 27° to 29° |
| 1300 1.50 carburettors (HC) Sweden only ........................... | Lucas 41749 | 9° to 11° | 27° to 29° |
| 1600 1.50 carburettor (HC) Sweden only ............................ | Lucas 41750 | 9° to 11° | 26° to 28° |
| 1600 1.75 carburettor (HC) ............................................... | Lucas 41751 | 9° to 11° | 28° to 30° |

\*   *No vacuum unit fitted to the type 43D4 distributor*
†   *This figure is arrived at by adding the mean values of static and centrifugal advance, and apply with the vacuum advance pipe removed*
‡   *Fitted to ECE 15-01 engines*
§   *Use this unit when making a replacement*

### Torque wrench settings

| | lbf ft | Nm |
|---|---|---|
| Spark plugs ..................................................................... | 12 | 16 |
| Distributor bracket to cylinder block ................................... | 7 | 9.5 |
| Distributor clamp ............................................................ | 4 | 5.5 |

## 1  General description

A conventional ignition system is fitted to all models up to and including 7 series, and an electronic ignition system is fitted to 8 series models onwards.

### Conventional ignition system

This system comprises a battery, coil, distributor and spark plugs, and an ignition switch provides the means to switch the system on and off. Low and high tension circuits are incorporated into the system in order to provide a spark at the spark plugs to ignite the fuel/air mixture in the combustion chambers. The correct timing of the spark at each spark plug is important for the engine to run correctly.

The low tension or primary circuit consists of the battery, lead to the ignition switch, lead from the ignition switch to the low tension or primary coil windings, and the lead from the low tension coil windings to the contact breaker points and condenser in the distributor.

The high tension circuit consists of the high tension or secondary coil windings, high tension lead from the coil to the distributor cap, the rotor arm, spark plug leads and spark plugs.

The low tension voltage in the coil low tension windings is changed to high tension voltage in the coil high tension windings by the opening and closing of the contact breaker points. High tension voltage is then fed via the carbon brush in the distributor cap to the rotor arm, then via the metal segments in the distributor cap and spark plug leads to the spark plugs where it discharges to earth in the form of a spark across the plug electrodes. The rotor arm ensures that the spark occurs at the correct spark plug relative to the engine cycle. The condenser (or capacitor) prevents excessive arcing at the contact breaker points and also helps collapse the magnetic field in the coil.

The ignition timing is controlled by centrifugal weights and (except 43D4 distributors) by a vacuum capsule in order to provide the most efficient timing at different engine operating conditions.

### Electronic ignition system

This system comprises a battery, coil, control unit, distributor and spark plug. Operation is similar to the conventional system except that the contact breaker points are replaced by a rotating reluctor, a pick-up pole and coil, and a control unit. As there are no contact breaker points, a condenser is not fitted.

When the reluctor rotates, the signal from the pick-up is amplified in the control unit, and the current flowing through the coil primary windings is interrupted. This causes a spark at the spark plug as described for the conventional system. The reluctor has four teeth, one for each cylinder. As each tooth passes the magnetic pole piece, voltage is induced in the pick-up coil and fed to the control unit.

Centrifugal and vacuum advance are similar to the conventional system.

## 2  Routine maintenance

1    Every 5000 miles (8000 km) remove and clean the spark plugs, and check their gaps as described in Section 17. At the same time check the ignition timing and contact points (where fitted) as described in the relevant Sections.
2    Check the security of LT and HT leads and terminals periodically, and also wipe the distributor cap and plug leads clean.
3    Every 5000 miles (8000 km) remove the distributor cap and rotor and apply two or three drops of engine oil to the recess in the top of the distributor shaft. On early 25D4 distributors a screw head is visible in the recess, but on later types a felt pad is provided.
4    At the same time apply a smear of high melting point grease to the high points of the cam on conventional ignition systems. Also on conventional systems apply one or two drops of engine oil to the moving contact pivot; wipe away any excess oil.
5    Periodic lubrication of the distributor shaft varies between distributors and, in the case of electronic type distributors, is non-existent.

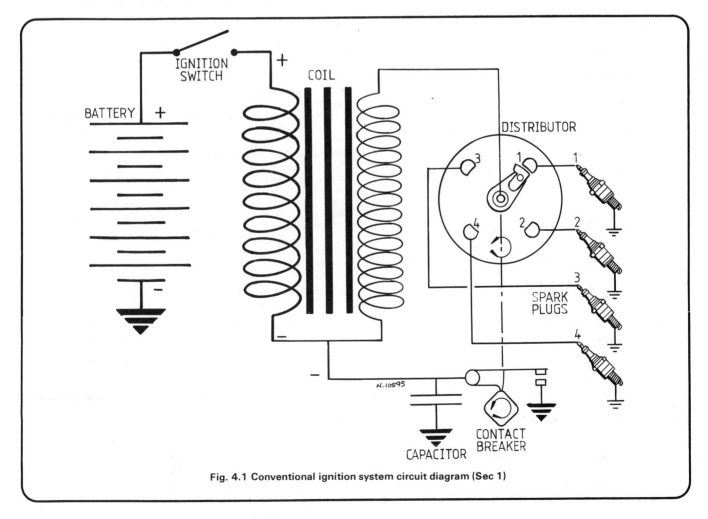

**Fig. 4.1 Conventional ignition system circuit diagram (Sec 1)**

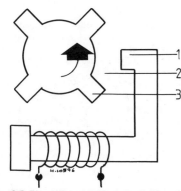

Fig. 4.2 Electronic ignition system – reluctor tooth approaching pole piece (Sec 1)

1  Pick-up pole piece        3  Reluctor
2  Air gap

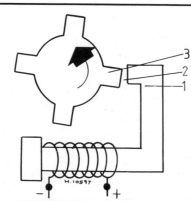

Fig. 4.3 Electronic ignition system – reluctor tooth and pole piece close, resulting in strong magnetic field (Sec 1)

1  Pick-up pole piece        3  Reluctor
2  Air gap

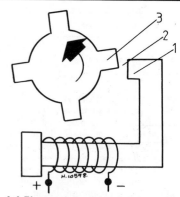

Fig. 4.4 Electronic ignition system – reluctor tooth moving away from pole piece resulting in change of polarity in pick-up coil (Sec 1)

1  Pick-up pole piece        3  Reluctor
2  Air gap

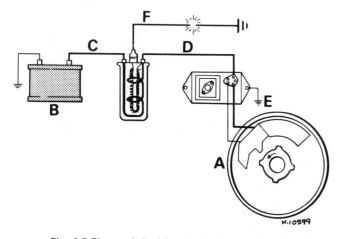

Fig. 4.5 Electronic ignition circuit diagram (Sec 1)

A  Pick-up coil inducing          D  Coil LT to control unit
   negative voltage               E  LT open circuit in control
B  Battery                           unit
C  Supply to ignition coil        F  HT induced in coil secondary

On Lucas and Ducellier types apply one drop of engine oil through the baseplate holes. On AC Delco types inject 5 cc of engine oil through the 0.25 in (6 mm) diameter hole in the baseplate. Lubricate the shaft every 5000 miles (8000 km).
6  Every 5000 miles (8000 km) on electronic ignition systems check the low tension leads for cracked insulation, and also wipe clean the rotor arm, arc shield and distributor cap, especially between the metal segments.
7  On all distributors except AC Delco, check that the carbon brush is free to move in the distributor cap every 5000 miles (8000 km).

## 3  Contact breaker points (conventional ignition system) – examination and adjustment

1  Spring back the retaining clips and withdraw the distributor cap. Lift off the rotor arm.
2  Prise the contact breaker points apart and examine their faces for pitting and deterioration. If necessary remove the points and dress them with an oilstone. On Lucas and AC Delco types make sure that the faces are kept level so that they will make good contact on reassembly. On Ducellier types it is possibe to dress the points provided the original contours are retained, although it is generally recommended that they are renewed.
3  Where excessive burning or pitting is found, renew the points as described in Section 4.

4  To adjust the points first turn the engine (with a spanner on the crankshaft pulley or by pushing the car in top gear) until the heel of the movable contact is located on the highest point of a cam lobe.
5  Insert a feeler blade of the specified thickness between the two contact points and check that it is a firm sliding fit without causing the moving contact to move from its rest position. If adjustment is necessary, loosen the fixed contact securing screw and reposition the fixed contact using a screwdriver in the adjusting slots on Lucas types, or the special tool if available on Ducellier types.
6  Tighten the securing screw and recheck the adjustment, then refit the rotor arm and distributor cap.
7  Using a dwell meter check the dwell angle (see Specifications) while turning the engine on the starter with the coil HT lead disconnected. Any final adjustment must be made by repositioning the fixed contact. If the angle recorded is too great, the points gap should be increased, and vice versa.

## 4  Contact breaker points (conventional ignition system) – removal

1  Remove the distributor cap and rotor arm.

### Lucas 25D4 distributor
2  With Lucas Quickafit contacts remove the terminal nut and two leads, the retaining screw and washer, and withdraw the assembly.
3  With earlier contacts, remove the terminal nut, insulator and two leads, and lift off the moving contact and fibre washer. Remove the retaining screw and washer and withdraw the fixed contact. Remove the insulating washer from the terminal post.

### Lucas 43D4 and 45D4 distributors
4  Push the moving contact spring out of the nylon insulator, then slide out the lead connecting plate.
5  Remove the retaining screw and washer and withdraw the assembly.

### AC Delco D204 distributor
6  Press the moving contact spring from the terminal and withdraw the moving contact.
7  Prise the capacitor and LT leads from the terminal insulator, remove the retaining screw, and withdraw the fixed contact.
8  Remove the insulator by pressing the two ears together.

### Ducellier distributor
9  Disconnect the coil LT lead at the distributor connector, and the capacitor lead from the insulator.
10  Withdraw the insulator from the body.
11  Remove the clip and washer from the moving contact pivot point, disengage the spring from the insulator and withdraw the moving contact together with the lead.
12  Remove the retaining screw and withdraw the fixed contact.

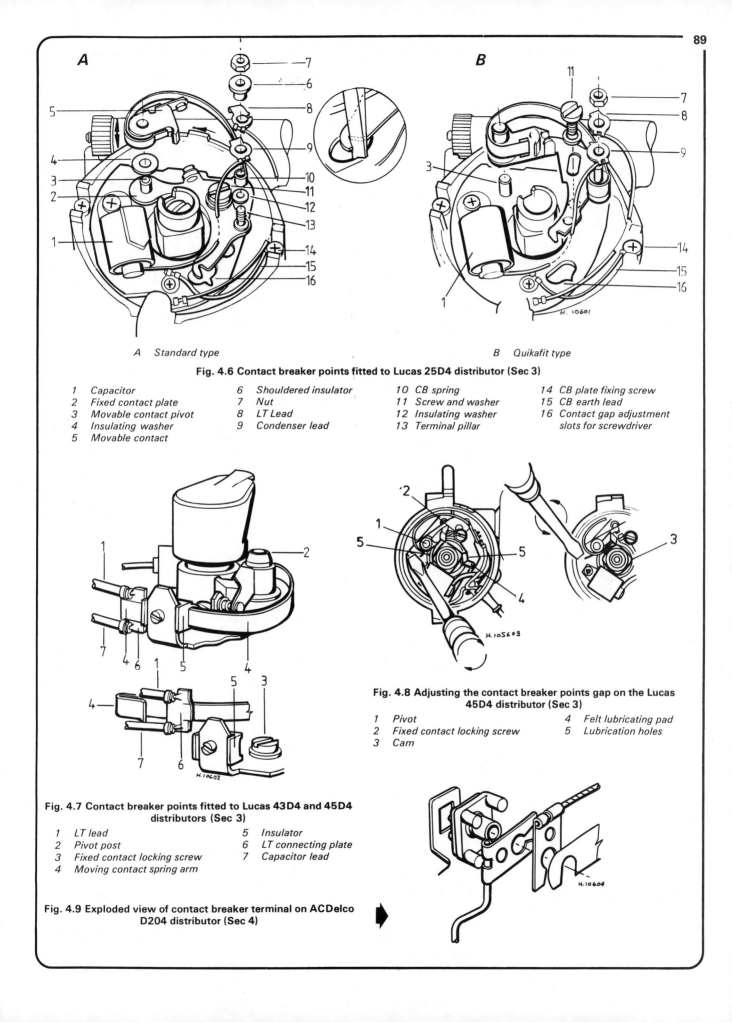

*A    Standard type*

*B    Quikafit type*

**Fig. 4.6 Contact breaker points fitted to Lucas 25D4 distributor (Sec 3)**

1   Capacitor
2   Fixed contact plate
3   Movable contact pivot
4   Insulating washer
5   Movable contact

6   Shouldered insulator
7   Nut
8   LT Lead
9   Condenser lead

10  CB spring
11  Screw and washer
12  Insulating washer
13  Terminal pillar

14  CB plate fixing screw
15  CB earth lead
16  Contact gap adjustment
    slots for screwdriver

**Fig. 4.7 Contact breaker points fitted to Lucas 43D4 and 45D4 distributors (Sec 3)**

1   LT lead
2   Pivot post
3   Fixed contact locking screw
4   Moving contact spring arm

5   Insulator
6   LT connecting plate
7   Capacitor lead

**Fig. 4.8 Adjusting the contact breaker points gap on the Lucas 45D4 distributor (Sec 3)**

1   Pivot
2   Fixed contact locking screw
3   Cam

4   Felt lubricating pad
5   Lubrication holes

**Fig. 4.9 Exploded view of contact breaker terminal on ACDelco D204 distributor (Sec 4)**

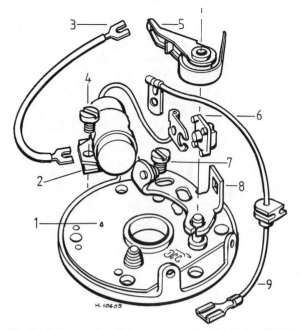

**Fig. 4.10 Contact breaker components on AC Delco D204 distributor (Sec 4)**

1   Contact breaker plate
2   Condenser and lead
3   Earth lead
4   Condenser securing screw
5   Moving contact point
6   Insulator
7   Fixed contact securing screw
8   Fixed contact
9   LT lead with grommet

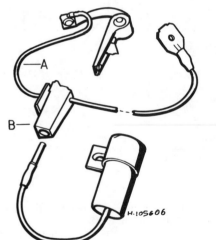

**Fig. 4.11 Moving contact supply lead (A) and insulator (B) on Ducellier distributor (Sec 4)**

*All distributors*
13  Refitting is a reversal of removal. If difficulty is experienced inserting the square insulator in the terminal post on AC Delco distributors, warm the insulator between the fingers to make it more flexible. Adjust the points gap as described in Section 3 before refitting the rotor arm and cap. Note that the terminal nut on Lucas 25D4 distributors should only be tightened finger tight plus a further half turn.

**5   Condenser (conventional ignition system) – testing, removal and refitting**

1   Failure of the condenser (or capacitor) will automatically cause failure of the ignition system as the points will be prevented from interrupting the low tension circuit.

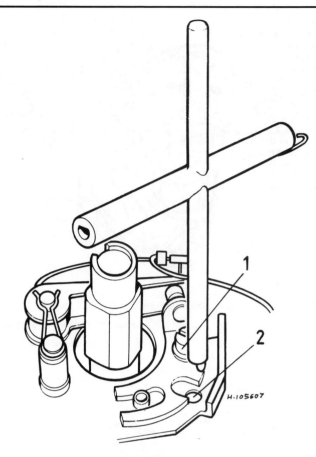

**Fig. 4.12 Dwell angle adjusting tool for Ducellier distributor (Sec 4)**

1   Screw                        2   Tool location hole

2   A quick test of the condenser can be made by switching on the ignition with the contact points closed, then separating the points by hand. If this is accompanied by a strong blue flash, condenser failure is indicated. A faulty condenser will also cause difficult starting and misfiring.
3   If the test is inconclusive, substitute the condenser for a new unit.
4   To remove the condenser first remove the distributor cap and rotor except on Ducellier distributors.

*Lucas 25D4 distributor*
5   Disconnect the lead from the terminal as described in Section 4.
6   Unscrew the crosshead screw and remove the condenser.

*Lucas 43D4 and 45D4 distributors*
7   Disconnect the lead connecting plate as described in Section 4.
8   Unscrew the crosshead screw, remove the earth lead, and withdraw the condenser.

*AC Delco D204 distributor*
9   Remove the moving contact as described in Section 4.
10  Prise the leads from the terminal insulator.
11  Remove the retaining screw and withdraw the condenser. Note that the retaining screw also secures the fork shaped earth lead.

*Ducellier distributor*
12  Disconnect the condenser lead from the insulator and clip.
13  Remove the retaining screw and withdraw the condenser.

*All distributors*
14  Refitting is a reversal of removal.

## 6  Air gap (electronic ignition system) – adjustment

1   The reluctor to pick-up air gap is only adjustable on the Lucas type 45DM4 distributor, no adjustment is provided on the Bosch type JGFU-4 distributor.

2   The air gap between the reluctor and the pick-up does not change in use, and only requires adjustment if one or the other has been moved. The gap quoted in the Specifications Section of 0.006 in to 0.008 in is a guide only, and if a different clearance exists it may be the result of the setting-up procedure employed during production to provide a pre-determined signal strength. However, if a case of difficulty of non-starting occurs, and after first checking that the fuel system and the rest of the ignition system are in order, the air gap may be reset. Remove the distributor cap, rotor arm and arc shield, and rotate the engine until a tooth on the reluctor lines up with the pick-up link (Fig. 4.13). Use a non-magnetic feeler gauge to check the gap and, if necessary, reset to the specified figure by slackening the two barrel nuts (2) and moving the pick-up assembly in or out. Tighten the nuts and recheck the gap.

## 7  Distributor – removal and refitting

1   Spring back the retaining clips and withdraw the distributor cap.

2   Pull the vacuum pipe from the distributor (except Lucas 43D4).

3   Disconnect the low tension lead (conventional system) or pick-up leads (electronic system).

4   Scribe mating marks on the distributor body, clamp plate and cylinder block.

5   Note the direction in which the rotor arm is pointing and mark the distributor body with pencil if necessary.

6   Remove the screw which secures the distributor clamp to the cylinder block, and withdraw the distributor from the engine.

7   Refitting is a reversal of removal, but note the following additional points:

   (a)  Clean the clamp and cylinder block mating surfaces
   (b)  On electronic system distributors inspect and if necessary renew the rubber O-ring on the distributor body
   (c)  With wear it is possible to insert the distributor with the rotor arm 180° out. However if the precaution given in paragraph 5 was heeded this will not occur
   (d)  Check the ignition timing as described in Section 14

## 8  Distributor (Lucas type 25D4) – dismantling, inspection and reassembly

1   Detach the spark plug leads, remove the distributor cap and withdraw the rotor. Withdraw the distributor as described in Section 7. Refer to Fig. 4.14 remove the two screws from the contact breaker baseplate and pull off the Lucar connector attached to the LT wire. Withdraw the contact breaker assembly, complete with external LT terminal.

2   Remove the circlip adjacent to the vernier adjustment nut. Rotate the nut until the screw and vacuum unit assembly are freed. Retain the ratchet and coil springs located under the micrometer nut. Remove the driving dog screw pin. Withdraw the distributor shaft assembly, complete with centrifugal timing control and cam foot, from the distributor body, after marking the dog and shaft in relation to each other.

3   Dismantle the centrifugal timing mechanism by lifting off the springs from the counterweights, removing the screw from inside the cam and withdrawing the cam and cam foot (mark the cam and shaft for position first). Lift off the counterweight, noting the collar fitted to the shaft beneath the baseplate.

4   Check the number stamped on the distributor body below the vernier control and ensure that it corresponds with the type specified in the Specifications Section. If the wrong unit is fitted, obtain a replacement.

5   Examine the condition of the dismantled parts. The most likely component requiring renewal will be the bearing bush. This is of sintered copper and a replacement item should be soaked in clean engine oil for a least 24 hours before fitting. Use a suitable shouldered mandrel to press out the worn bush from the distributor body tapered end, and insert the new bush from the drive end with the smaller

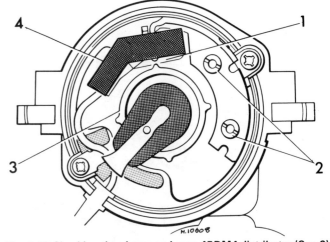

**Fig. 4.13 Checking the air gap on Lucas 45DM4 distributor (Sec 6)**

| | |
|---|---|
| 1  Air gap | 3  Reluctor |
| 2  Nuts | 4  Pole piece |

diameter leading. It should be a push fit until the larger diameter starts to enter the distributor body, when a vice will be required. Use jaw protectors. The bush is correctly fitted when it is flush with the shank at the drive end and slightly protruding at the top end. It must be a tight fit in the body. Drill the shaft oil drain hole and remove all metal cuttings.

6   Insert the driveshaft, continually and generously lubricating the new bearing bush in the process. Ensure the shaft does not bind. Should it do so, withdraw the shaft and tap the bearing lightly at the drive end. Repeat until the tightness disappears. Never bore or ream the bush.

7   Place the distance collar over the driveshaft. Smear the shaft with oil and insert it into the bearing bush. Refit the thrust washer and driving dog and pin. Refit the vacuum unit onto its housing. Fit the spring, milled nut and circlip.

8   Reassemble the centrifugal weights, the cam and the cam foot to the driveshaft and secure with the retaining screw. Engage the springs with the pillars. Refit the contact breaker baseplate into the distributor body, complete with contacts. Engage the link from the vacuum unit and secure the baseplate with its two retaining screws, noting that the screw securing the contact breaker earthing cable should be really tight. Refit the capacitor and slide the terminal block into position.

9   Check the contact breaker gap as described in Section 3. Insert the distributor assembly into its location in the crankcase as described in Section 7.

## 9  Distributor (Lucas types 43D4 and 45D4) – dismantling, inspection and reassembly

1   Remove the rotor arm and felt lubrication pad. On 45D4 units remove the vacuum unit screws (note the two baseplate prongs which locate beneath one screw). Disengage the vacuum unit link from the moving plate pin and remove the unit.

2   Push back the LT lead and rubber sleeve into the centre of the distributor. Remove the wedge screw. Note that later distributors have two such screws (see Fig. 4.16), whilst a later design still has locating lugs at each side of the baseplate, for securing the plate to the distributor (see Fig. 4.19). Use a small screwdriver to prise the expanded segment of the baseplate inwards, to release it from its trapped position and lift the complete baseplate assembly from the body.

3   Refer to Fig. 4.17 and drive out the drive dog securing pin. Pull off the dog and thrust washer, noting the position of the tongue in relation to the rotor. The shaft complete with centrifugal advance mechanism, can now be withdrawn through the body. Retain the O-ring.

4   If the centrifugal advance mechanism is worn, renewal as a complete shaft/advance mechanism assembly. Servicing should be limited to renewal of the springs. Check the shaft for side movement in the bearings. If evident the distributor should be renewed on an exchange basis.

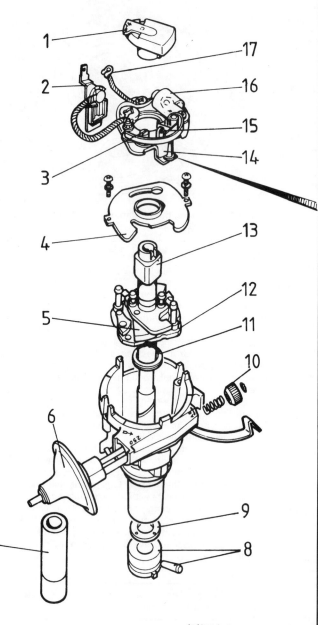

H11440

**Fig. 4.14 Exploded view of the Lucas 25D4 distributor (Sec 8)**

| | | | | |
|---|---|---|---|---|
| 1 | Rotor arm | 7 | Bearing bush | 14 |
| 2 | LT terminal | 8 | Driving dog and pin | |
| 3 | Fixed contact plate securing | 9 | Thrust washer | 15 |
| | screw | 10 | Vernier adjustment nut | 16 |
| 4 | Contact breaker baseplate | 11 | Distance collar | 17 |
| 5 | Centrifugal advance control | 12 | Baseplate | 18 |
| | weights and mechanism | 13 | Cam | 19 |
| 6 | Vacuum advance control unit | | | 20 |

1   Rotor arm
2   LT terminal
3   Fixed contact plate securing
    screw
4   Contact breaker baseplate
5   Centrifugal advance control
    weights and mechanism
6   Vacuum advance control unit

7   Bearing bush
8   Driving dog and pin
9   Thrust washer
10  Vernier adjustment nut
11  Distance collar
12  Baseplate
13  Cam

14  Contact breaker moving
    plate
15  Contacts
16  Condenser
17  CB earth connector
18  Contact breaker lever
19  Insulating washer
20  Fixed contact plate

21  Contact breaker pivot post
22  Nut
23  Shouldered insulator
24  Movable contact point spring
25  Insulating washer
26  Terminal pillar
27  Quikafit contact breaker
    point assembly

93

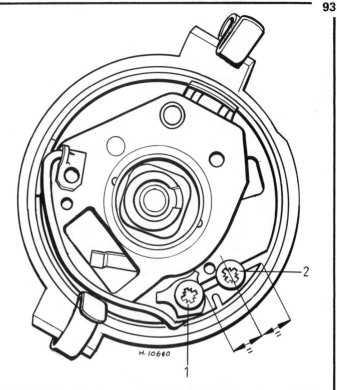

**Fig. 4.16 Bearing plate securing screw locations on Lucas 43D4 and 45D4 distributors (Sec 9)**

1   Original screw, early type
2   Additional screw on modified type

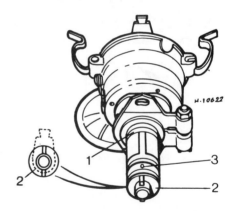

**Fig. 4.17 Driving dog and rotor arm positions on Lucas 43D4 and 45D4 distributors (Sec 9)**

1   O-ring seal
2   Driving dog
3   Pin

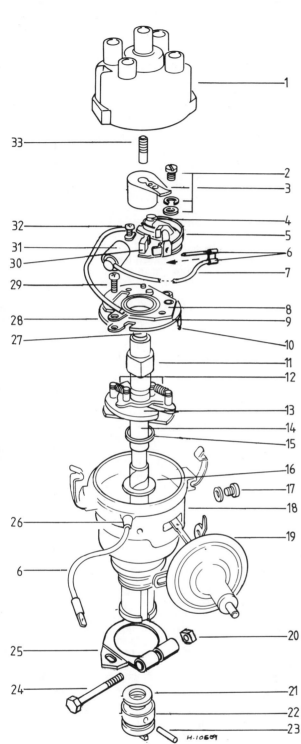

**Fig. 4.15 Exploded view of the Lucas 45D4 distributor (Sec 9)**

*Note: Applicable also to Lucas type 43D4, except that item 19 is replaced by a blanking plate*

| | | | |
|---|---|---|---|
| 1 Cap | 10 Baseplate locating prongs | 17 Vacuum capsule or blanking plate screws | 25 Clamp plate |
| 2 Contact securing screw | 11 Cam | 18 Body | 26 Insulating sleeve |
| 3 Rotor | 12 Centrifugal advance springs | 19 Vacuum capsule | 27 Felt lubricating pad |
| 4 Pivot post | 13 Centrifugal advance mechanism | 20 Pinch bolt nut | 28 Baseplate expanding section |
| 5 Movable contact arm | 14 Shaft | 21 Thrust washer | 29 Wedge screw |
| 6 LT lead and terminal plate | 15 Nylon washer | 22 Driving dog | 30 Cam lubricating wick |
| 7 Condenser (capacitor) lead | 16 Steel washer | 23 Pin | 31 Capacitor (condenser) |
| 8 Movable baseplate | | 24 Pinch bolt | 32 Retaining screw |
| 9 Fixed baseplate | | | 33 Carbon brush |

5    Reassemble in the reverse order but observe the following points: Smear all friction surfaces of internal components with a molybdenum type grease before assembly. Insert the baseplate assembly in its approximate position in the distributor body so that the two prongs are located either side of the hole through with the vacuum unit screw passes. On type 45D4 distributors, connect and screw the vacuum unit into position. Snap the baseplate into position in the body ensuring that it is pressed down against the ledge so that the chamfered edges will engage the undercut in the body side. Should there be any tendency for the baseplate not to be a tight fit in its groove, renew the plate. Fit and tighten the securing screw. If movement of the baseplate exists, it is feasible to fit a second wedge screw (Fig. 4.16) in the centre of the slot, as on later distributors. Baseplate movement has been eliminated on the latest distributors by the two locating lugs and fixing screws (Fig. 4.19).

6    Fit the thrust washer (raised side of pips towards dog) and the drive dog, noting the alignment of the segments in relation to the rotor arm (Fig. 4.17). Fit the dog securing pin and stake the holes at both ends. A new shaft will be supplied undrilled and should be drilled to accept the pin using a $\frac{3}{16}$ in (4.76 mm) twist drill. Use the dog as a guide to position the hole and press down on the cam end of the shaft whilst drilling to compress the dog and washer against the shank. Where a new thrust washer is installed, assemble the drive dog, washer and pin, and tap the end face of the drive dog to slightly flatten

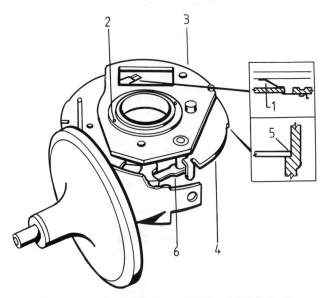

**Fig. 4.18 Baseplate (early) on Lucas 43D4 and 45D4 distributors (Sec 9)**

1  Bearing spring
2  Lubrication holes
3  Movable plate
4  Fixed plate
5  Locating groove in distributor body
6  Vacuum unit connecting link

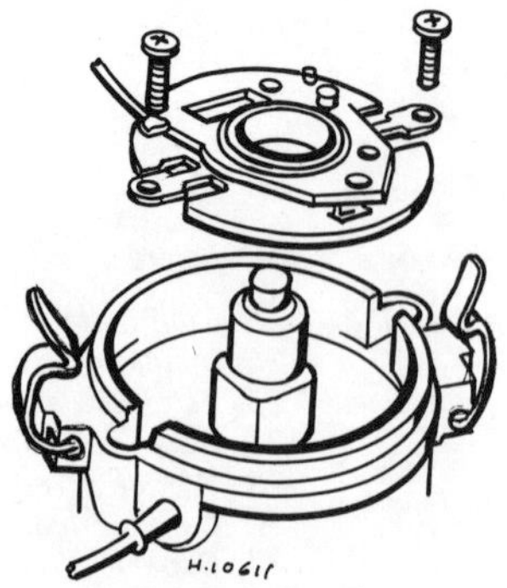

**Fig. 4.19 Baseplate (late) on Lucas 43D4 and 45D4 distributors (Sec 9)**

the 'pips' on the thrust washer to provide the specified shaft endfloat of between 0.010 and 0.020 in (0.25 to 0.51 mm).

## 10 Distributor (AC Delco type D204) – dismantling, inspection and reassembly

1    Remove the rotor arm, and contact breaker as described in Section 4 and pull the LT lead and support grommet away from the distributor body. Unscrew and remove the capacitor retaining screw. Lift the capacitor and lead out of the body. Remove the vacuum unit retaining screw from the side of the body, thus releasing the baseplate earth lead. Remove the lead with the distributor cap securing clip. Turn the vacuum unit slightly to disengage its arm from the slot in the body, and pull the unit out until the baseplate is turned to the fully advanced position. Unhook the vacuum unit from the body. Remove the two remaining baseplate screws together with the second distributor cap clip, and lift the plate out of the body. Further dismantling is not recommended, except for the renewal of the centrifugal advance mechanism springs. The distributor mainshaft, centrifugal weights, and cam are one assembly and, if the items are worn, the body will also be worn. However, should the mainshaft be seized or the shaft bearing surfaces need inspecting, proceed as described in the following paragraph.

2    Note the relationship of the driving dog to the rotor arm. With a suitable drift, drive the securing pin out of the driving dog and shaft end, and withdraw the dog from the shaft. Before pulling the mainshaft out of the body inspect the end for burrs which may have been made when driving the pin out and carefully remove them with a file and oilstone. Retrieve the two thrust washers located at top and bottom of the shaft. Remove the felt pad and spring clip from the cam recess and lift the cam away from the shaft plate. Withdraw the O-ring from the distributor body shank.

3    Clean all parts and examine them for wear. Check particularly the rotor arm for signs of insulation breakdown indicated by a thin grey-white line across the moulded base, and also that the spring blade is set at the correct height. The distance from the upper face of the moulding to the top of the contact button should be 0.3 to 0.35 in (7.6 to 8.9 mm), dimension 'A' in Fig. 4.21. Slight burning of the cap electrodes and rotor arm segment is normal and no attempt should be made to remove it, as this would increase the HT air gap and overload the igniton coil.

## 11 Distributor (Ducellier) – dismantling, inspection and reassembly

1    Remove the rotor arm and contact breaker as described in Section 4. Remove the capacitor securing screw and lift the capacitor away. Note the position of the serrated cam in relation to the vacuum unit spring plate, and then turn it fully clockwise to release the spring tension. Extract the hairspring clip from the D-shaped post. Remove the vacuum unit securing screw and cap clip, and holding the unit, release the operating rod and serrated cam from the D-post. Withdraw the unit from the distributor body, and do not on any account rotate the D-post from its existing position. Remove the remaining baseplate screw together with the cap clip. Prise the baseplate out of the distributor body, at the same time pressing the spring-loaded slipper away from the shaft, so that it clears the cam. Release the lever arm from the baseplate. Prise the felt pad from the cam recess and remove the cam retaining screw and washers. Extract the circlips from the centrifugal weight pivot posts, and unhook the centrifugal advance springs from the camplate. Remove the circlips from the centrifugal weight pins and, noting the relationship of the rotor arm slot to the dog drive, withdraw the cap from the shaft. Extract the springs from the fixed post, and lift the balance weights out of the body.

2    Further dismantling is not recommended unless the mainshaft bearing surfaces need inspecting or the shaft is partially seized. To further dismantle the distributor, wind the spring off the driving dog by lifting the bottom coil first. Mark the dog in relation to the shaft, and then drive the securing pin out with a suitable drift. Remove the dog from the shaft and retrieve the shims and fibre washer. Before pulling the mainshaft out of the distributor body, inspect the shaft end for burrs which may have been made when driving the securng pin out, and carefully remove them with a file and oilstone. Withdraw the O-ring from the body shank.

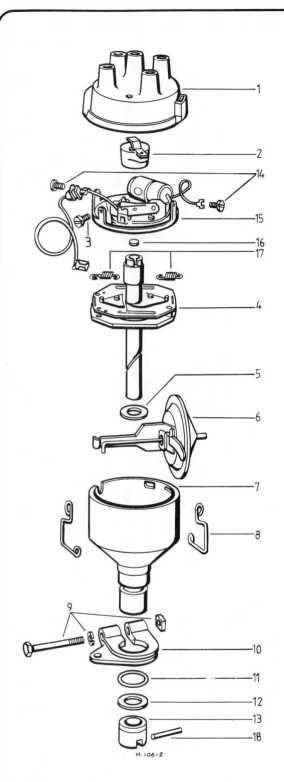

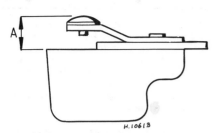

Fig. 4.21 Rotor arm setting dimension (A) on AC Delco D204 distributor – see text (Sec 10)

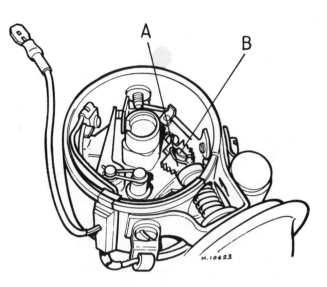

Fig. 4.22 Vacuum advance setting serrated cam (A) and D-post (B) on Ducellier distributor (Sec 11)

Fig. 4.20 Exploded view of the AC Delco D204 distributor (Sec 10)

1  Distributor cap
2  Rotor arm
3  Baseplate retaining screw
4  Mainshaft and centrifugal weight assembly
5  Upper thrust washer
6  Vacuum advance capsule
7  Distributor body
8  Distributor cap securing clip
9  Clamp plate assembly bolt
10  Clamp plate
11  O-ring
12  Lower thrust washer
13  Drive dog
14  Baseplate and cap clip retaining screws
15  Contact breaker and baseplate assembly
16  Felt lubricating pad
17  Centrifugal advance springs
18  Drive dog securing pin

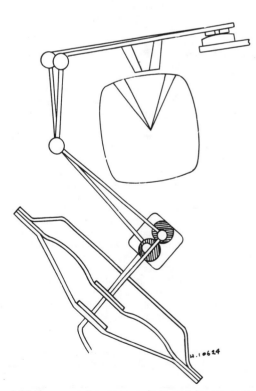

Fig. 4.23 Vacuum advance capsule-to-moving contact point linkage diagram on the Ducellier distributor (Sec 11)

3   Clean the components and examine them for wear. Clean the distributor cap with a soft cloth, and check the condition of the carbon brush which should protrude 5/32 in (4 mm) from its locating hole when correctly fitted. Slight burning of the cap electrodes and rotor arm segment is normal, and no attempt should be made to remove it. To do so will increase the HT air gap and overload the ignition coil. Check the rotor arm for signs of insulation breakdown indicated by a thin grey-white line across the moulded base. Renew the rotor if a fault is suspected.

4   Reassemble in the reverse order, observing the following points. Smear the friction surfaces of internal components with a molybdenum type oil before assembly. Lubricate the distributor mainshaft and cam bushes with engine oil before assembly and apply a few drops of engine oil to the felt pad within the cam recess. When refitting the drive dog check that the shaft endfloat of 0.008 in (0.2 mm) is not exceeded, but if it is, adjust the endfloat with shims fitted between the distributor body and the dog. Ensure that the serrated cam is refitted in the same position as when removed, as it is not possible to adjust the vacuum advance commencement without specialised equipment. Adjust the initial contact breaker gap as described in Section 3.

## 12  Distributor (Lucas type 45DM4) – dismantling, inspection and reassembly

1   Refer to Fig. 4.24 and remove the rotor arm and arc shield. Remove the circlip, lift out the washer and O-ring and remove the reluctor. Remove the two vacuum capsule fixing screws and washers, tilt the vacuum capsule slightly and disengage the pullrod from the underside of the pick-up baseplate.

2   Detach the pick-up lead grommet, remove the two baseplate fixing screws and washers, and the guide brackets. Lift off the pick-up and baseplate assembly, which need not be separated. Remove the coupling ring. Further dismantling is not recommended other than renewal of the centrifugal advance springs if worn, and if considerable wear is present a reconditioned unit is advised.

3   Inspect the distributor cap for damage caused by incorrect location of the rotor on the shaft, such as defects in the brush and spring. Inspect the cap for breakdown, indicated by greyish-white lines or burning. Renew the affected parts. Note that slight burning of the cap segments is normal and that this should not be removed or the entire system will be adversely affected. Check the brush for freedom of movement and wear, and renew both items if the brush protrusion is less than 5/32 in (4 mm). Brush wear is normally slight, the most likely causes being deliberate stretching of the spring, or a poor finish on the rotor top. The rotor top must be smooth, but not necessarily bright. No attempt may be made to smooth it with emery cloth or glasspaper as this will cause scoring which will engender rapid brush wear. Check that the upper pick-up plate revolves smoothly on the lower plate without tilting.

4   Reassemble in reverse order, noting the following points. Use a heavy duty molybdenum oil to lubricate the bearing surfaces of the body and shaft, the moving parts of the centrifugal advance mechanism, and the pin on the pick-up baseplate locating in the vacuum pullrod. Lubricate the pick-up mounting plate and baseplate with molybdenum grease. Fit the baseplate assembly into the distributor body with the guide bracket on the far side from the pick-up. Tighten the baseplate screws evenly. Rotate the pick-up plate clockwise to the fully advanced position and engage the end of the vacuum pullrod on the pin in the pick-up plate. Fit the vacuum capsule screws and washers.

5   Fit the coupling ring, correctly locating the dogs, and fit the reluctor which has similar dogs. Fit the O-ring, washer and circlip. Check the air gap (Section 6) using a non-magnetic feeler gauge. Apply two drops of clean engine oil to the felt pad in the top of the shaft. Refit the arc shield rotor arm and distributor cap.

## 13  Distributor (Bosch type JGFU-4) – dismantling, inspection and reassembly

1   Refer to Figs. 4.25, 4.26 and 4.27. Unscrew the vacuum advance capsule retaining screws, tilt the capsule to disengage the pullrod and withdraw the capsule.

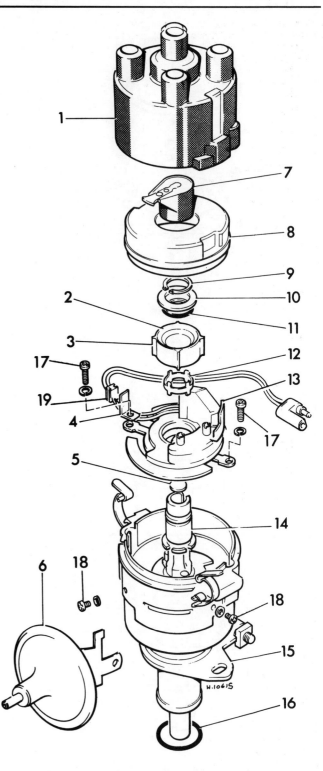

**Fig. 4.24 Exploded view of the Lucas 45DM4 distributor (Sec 12)**

|   |   |   |   |
|---|---|---|---|
| 1  | Cap            | 11 | O-ring                |
| 2  | Reluctor       | 12 | Coupling              |
| 3  | Reluctor tooth | 13 | Pick-up and baseplate |
| 4  | Bracket        | 14 | Reluctor carrier      |
| 5  | Lubrication pad| 15 | Clamp plate           |
| 6  | Vacuum capsule | 16 | O-ring                |
| 7  | Rotor arm      | 17 | Baseplate fixing screws |
| 8  | Arc shield     | 18 | Vacuum capsule screw  |
| 9  | Circlip        | 19 | Cable grommet         |
| 10 | Washer         |    |                       |

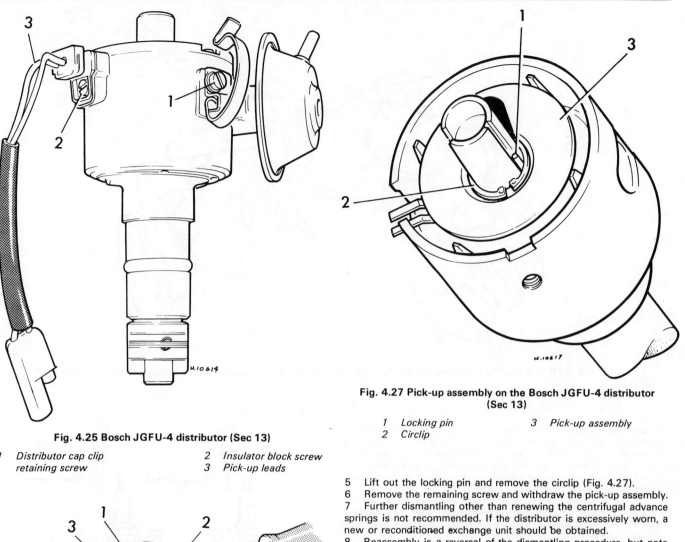

Fig. 4.25 Bosch JGFU-4 distributor (Sec 13)

1   *Distributor cap clip*        2   *Insulator block screw*
    *retaining screw*             3   *Pick-up leads*

Fig. 4.27 Pick-up assembly on the Bosch JGFU-4 distributor
(Sec 13)

1   *Locking pin*           3   *Pick-up assembly*
2   *Circlip*

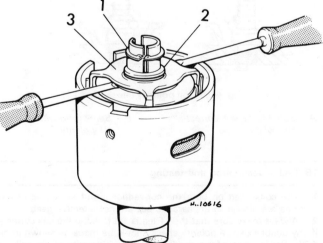

Fig. 4.26 Removing the reluctor on the Bosch JGFU-4 distributor
(Sec 13)

1   *Circlip*                  3   *Reluctor*
2   *Belleville washer*

2   Remove the two distributor cap retaining clip screws and withdraw the spring clips.
3   Remove the terminal block securing screw and withdraw the pick-up terminal block together with the pick-up leads.
4   Extract the circlip and the Belleville washer and withdraw the reluctor from the shaft using two suitable levers.

5   Lift out the locking pin and remove the circlip (Fig. 4.27).
6   Remove the remaining screw and withdraw the pick-up assembly.
7   Further dismantling other than renewing the centrifugal advance springs is not recommended. If the distributor is excessively worn, a new or reconditioned exchange unit should be obtained.
8   Reassembly is a reversal of the dismantling procedure, but note the following additional points:

(a)   *Make sure that the circlips are fully entered into their locating grooves*
(b)   *Do not fully tighten the capsule and pick-up securing screws until a check has been made that the air gaps between each reluctor tooth and the pick-up pole are equal. If necessary, move the pick-up assembly then tighten the screws*
(c)   *Check the baseplate for free movement by applying vacuum to the capsule*

## 14  Ignition timing – adjustment

*One of two methods may be used to time the ignition, ie static or dynamic. On electronic ignition systems the static method will provide an initial setting to be made, but this should always be followed by a further check using the dynamic method.*

### Static method
1   On the Lucas 25D4 distributor set the vernier adjustment nut to the mid-range position.
2   Remove No 1 spark plug and rotate the engine with a spanner on the crankshaft pulley nut until pressure is felt (using the thumb placed over the plug hole) indicating that No 1 piston is on its compression stroke.
3   Continue to turn the engine until the correct notch on the pulley (refer to Specifications) is opposite the timing mark on the timing case. The notches are spaced at 5° intervals covering a total of 60°, and TDC (top dead centre) is obtained when the last peak (during clockwise rotation) is aligned with the mark on the timing case.

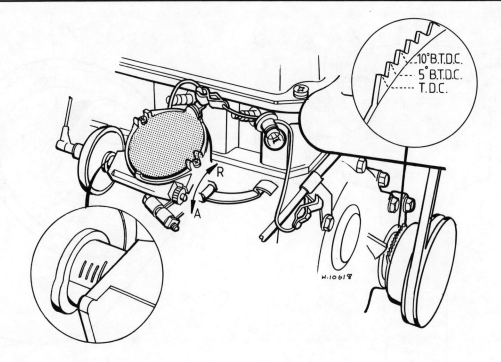

**Fig. 4.28 Checking the static ignition timing with a 12 volt test lamp – Lucas 25D4 distributor shown (Sec 14)**

4   On conventional ignition systems connect a 12 volt bulb and leads between the distributor LT terminal and earth. Loosen the clamp plate to cylinder block securing screw and switch on the ignition. If the timing light is already lit, turn the distributor body anti-clockwise until it goes out. Turn the distributor slowly clockwise until the timing light *just* lights then tighten the securing screw.

5   On electronic ignition systems remove the distributor cap and check that the reluctor tooth is in exact alignment with the pick-up link when the rotor arm is pointing in the direction of the No 1 spark plug lead segment in the distributor cap.

6   On both types of system if there is insufficient adjustment within the elongated hole, the clamp plate bolt should be loosened and the plate repositioned.

7   Tighten the securing and clamp screws as necessary and on electronic ignition systems refit the distributor cap. Switch off the ignition on conventional systems and remove the 12 volt bulb and leads.

*Dynamic method*

8   Connect a timing light and tachometer to the engine in accordance with the manufacturer's instructions. Note that certain tachometers triggered by the coil LT circuit are not suitable for use with electronic ignition.

9   Disconnect and plug the vacuum advance pipe at the distributor end (except Lucas 43D4 type).

10  Refer to the Specifications and use chalk to mark the appropriate point on the crankshaft pulley.

11  Start the engine and maintain a speed of 3000 rpm. Point the timing light at the timing marks and check that they are in alignment. If necessary, loosen the clamp plate to cylinder block securing screw and reposition the distributor. On Lucas 25D4 distributors, adjustment can be made using the vernier nut.

12  Tighten the clamp screw and recheck the timing.

13  Check the centrifugal advance mechanism by observing the timing marks while increasing the engine speed from idling. As the speed is increased the timing should advance simultaneously.

14  To check the vacuum advance operation, hold the engine speed as 1500 rpm, then refit the vacuum advance pipe. The timing must advance as the pipe is connected.

15  Switch off the ignition and remove the timing light and tachometer.

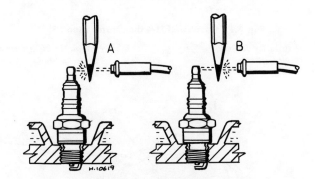

**Fig. 4.29 Coil polarity check (Sec 15)**

A   *Spark form with correct HT polarity*  B   *Spark form with incorrect HT polarity*

## 15  Coil – description and testing

1   The coils used on both the conventional and electronic ignition systems are similar in appearance but are not interchangeable.

2   Always make sure that the LT leads are fitted to the coil correctly. If any doubt exists, a polarity check should be made as shown in Fig. 4.29. The location of the spark indicates the polarity of the coil, and the HT current should always be negative at the spark plug terminals. Incorrect location of the LT leads can cause up to 60 per cent loss of spark efficiency with rough idling and misfiring at speed.

3   If a coil is renewed because of burning at the HT tower do not re-use the old rubber boot. This will have become carbonised and will probably cause the new coil to fail.

## 16  Resistor block (electronic ignition system) – description and renewal

1   The block contains the ballast resistor for the coil and an auxiliary resistor in series with the supply to the control unit. The ballast resistor

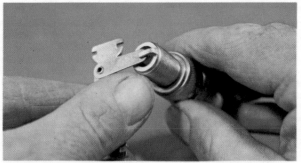

**Measuring plug gap.** A feeler gauge of the correct size (see ignition system specifications) should have a slight 'drag' when slid between the electrodes. Adjust gap if necessary

**Adjusting plug gap.** The plug gap is adjusted by bending the earth electrode inwards, or outwards, as necessary until the correct clearance is obtained. Note the use of the correct tool

**Normal.** Grey-brown deposits, lightly coated core nose. Gap increasing by around 0.001 in (0.025 mm) per 1000 miles (1600 km). Plugs ideally suited to engine, and engine in good condition

**Carbon fouling.** Dry, black, sooty deposits. Will cause weak spark and eventually misfire. Fault: over-rich fuel mixture. Check: carburettor mixture settings, float level and jet sizes; choke operation and cleanliness of air filter. Plugs can be re-used after cleaning

**Oil fouling.** Wet, oily deposits. Will cause weak spark and eventually misfire. Fault: worn bores/piston rings or valve guides; sometimes occurs (temporarily) during running-in period. Plugs can be re-used after thorough cleaning

**Overheating.** Electrodes have glazed appearance, core nose very white – few deposits. Fault: plug overheating. Check: plug value, ignition timing, fuel octane rating (too low) and fuel mixture (too weak). Discard plugs and cure fault immediately

**Electrode damage.** Electrodes burned away; core nose has burned, glazed appearance. Fault: pre-ignition. Check: as for 'Overheating' but may be more severe. Discard plugs and remedy fault before piston or valve damage occurs

**Split core nose (may appear initially as a crack).** Damage is self-evident, but cracks will only show after cleaning. Fault: pre-ignition or wrong gap-setting technique. Check: ignition timing, cooling system, fuel octane rating (too low) and fuel mixture (too weak). Discard plugs, rectify fault immediately

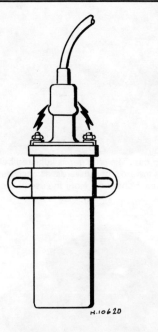

**Fig. 4.30 Electronic ignition coil possible arcing paths (Sec 15)**

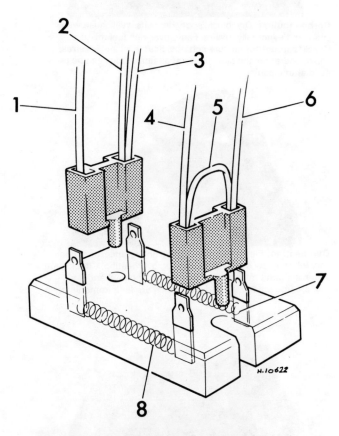

**Fig. 4.31 Electronic ignition resistor block (Sec 16)**

*1   Blue with orange wire, to control unit No 3 cavity*
*2   White with blue wire, from starter solenoid*
*3   White with blue wire, to coil positive*
*4   White wire, to control unit No 1 cavity*
*5   White wire, supply to auxiliary resistor*
*6   White wire, from ignition switch*
*7   Ballast resistor, 0.5 ohm*
*8   Auxiliary resistor, 5 ohm*

maintains constant primary current in the ignition coil despite variations in engine speed, and thus protects the coil against high current flow at low engine speed. The ballast resistor is, however, bypassed when the starter motor is operated, thus ensuring that full battery voltage is applied to the coil for ease of starting. The auxiliary resistor protects the control unit, by limiting the current flow in the related part of the circuit.

2   To remove the block, note the location of the two terminal plugs then pull them off the terminals.

3   Remove the single retaining screw and withdraw the block.

4   Refitting is a reversal of removal but make sure that the block is the correct way round and that the wires are connected to the correct terminals. Do not overtighten the retaining screw, otherwise the porcelain may crack.

### 17   Spark plugs and HT leads – general

1   Correct operation of the plugs and leads is vital. The correct type are listed in the Specifications Section. At intervals of 5000 miles the plugs should be removed, examined, cleaned and, if worn excessively, renewed. The condition of the spark plug will also tell much about the overall condition of the engine.

2   If the insulator nose of the spark plug is clean and white, with no deposits, this indicates a weak mixture, or too hot a plug. (A hot plug transfers heat away from the electrode slowly – a cold plug transfers it away quickly). If the top and insulator nose are covered with hard black looking deposits, then the mixture is too rich. Should the plug be black and oily, then it is likely that the engine is worn, as well as the mixture being too rich. If the insulator nose is covered with light tan to greyish brown deposits, then the mixture is correct and the engine is probably in good condition. If there are traces of long brown tapering stains on the outside white portion of the plug this shows that there is a faulty joint between the body and the insulator, and compression is being allowed to leak away. Renew the plug.

3   Plugs should ideally be cleaned by a sandblasting machine which will free them from carbon more thoroughly than cleaning by hand, and which will also test the condition of the plugs under compression. Any plug that fails to spark at the recommended pressure should be renewed. The plug gap has considerable effect on engine efficiency and should be set to the specified dimension for the best results. Measure the gap with a feeler gauge, and bend the outer plug electrode until the correct gap is achieved. The centre electrode should never be bent as this may crack the insulation.

4   When refitting the plugs, remember to use new washers and refit the leads from the distributor in the correct order. No 1 cylinder is nearest the radiator. The plug leads require no routine attention other than being kept clean.

### 18   Fault diagnosis – conventional ignition system

*Engine fails to start*

1   If the engine fails to start and the car was running normally when it was last used, first check there is fuel in the fuel tank. If the engine turns over normally on the starter motor and the battery is evidently well charged, then the fault may be in either the high or low tension circuits. **Note:** *If the battery is known to be fully charged, the ignition light comes on, and the starter motor fails to turn the engine, check the tightness of the leads on the battery terminal and also the secureness of the earth lead to its connection to the body. It is quite common for the leads to have worked loose, even if they look and feel secure. If one of the battery terminal posts get very hot when trying to work the starter motor this is a sure indication of a faulty connection to that terminal.*

2   One of the commonest reasons for bad starting is wet or damp spark plug leads and distributor. Remove the distributor cap; if condensation is visible internally, dry the cap with a rag and also wipe the leads. Refit the cap.

3   If the engine still fails to start, check that current is reaching the plugs by disconnecting each plug lead in turn at the spark plug end, and hold the end of the cable about $\frac{1}{8}$ in (3 mm) away from the cylinder block. Spin the engine on the starter motor.

4   Sparking between the end of the cable and the block should be fairly strong with a regular blue spark. (Hold the lead with a dry cloth or rubber glove to avoid electric shocks). If current is reaching the

plugs, remove them, clean and regap them. The engine should now start .

5    If there is no spark at the plug leads, take off the HT lead from the centre of the distributor cap and hold it to the block as before. Spin the engine on the starter once more. A rapid succession of blue sparks between the end of the lead and block indicates that the coil is in order and that the distributor cap is cracked, the rotor arm faulty, or the carbon brush in the top of the distributor cap is not making good contact with the spring on the rotor arm.

6    If there are no sparks from the end of the lead from the coil, check the connections at the coil end of the lead. If it is in order start checking the low tension circuit.

*Engine misfires*

7    If the engine misfires regularly, run it at a fast idling speed. Pull off each of the plug caps in turn and listen to the note of the engine. Hold the plug cap in a dry cloth or with a rubber glove as additional protection against a shock from the HT supply.

8    No difference in engine running will be noticed when the lead from the defective circuit is removed. Removing the lead from one of the good cylinders will accentuate the misfire.

9    Remove the plug lead from the end of the defective plug and hold it about $\frac{1}{8}$ in (3 mm) away from the block. Restart the engine. If the sparking is fairly strong and regular, the fault must lie in the spark plug.

10   The plug may be loose, the insulation may be cracked, or the electrodes may have burnt away giving too wide a gap for the spark to jump. Worse still, one of the electrodes may have broken off. Either renew the plug, or clean it, reset the gap, and then test it.

11   If there is no spark at the end of the plug lead, or if it is weak and intermittent, check the ignition lead from the distributor to the plug. If the insulation is cracked or perished, renew the lead. Check the connections at the distributor cap.

12   If there is still no spark, examine the distributor cap carefully for tracking. This can be recognised by a very thin black line running between two or more electrodes or between an electrode and some other part of the distributor. These lines are paths which conduct electricity across the cap thus letting it run to earth. The only remedy is a new distributor cap.

13   Apart from the ignition timing being incorrect, other causes of misfiring have already been dealt with under the section dealing with the failure of the engine to start. To recap – these are that:

(a)   The coil may be faulty giving an intermittent misfire
(b)   There may be a damaged wire or loose connection in the low tension circuit
(c)   There may be a mechanical fault in the distributor

14   If the ignition timing is too far retarded, it should be noted that the engine will tend to overheat, and there will be a quite noticeable drop in power. If the engine is overheating and the power is down and the ignition timng is correct, then the carburettor should be checked, as it is likely that this is where the fault lies.

## 19  Fault diagnosis – electronic ignition system

The complex nature of the system puts most diagnostic work outside the scope of the average home mechanic, and the work will probably need to be entrusted to a main dealer, who will possess the special equipment required. However, the following points may be checked, and corrected if necessary:

(a)   Battery voltage sufficient
(b)   Battery, earth and starter solenoid connections clean and tight
(c)   Control unit properly earthed, and the securing bolts tight
(d)   Low tension connections clean and tight
(e)   No arcing evident at the coil HT tower
(f)   HT leads clean, in good condition, and all terminals tight
(g)   Spark plugs clean and properly gapped
(h)   Distributor cap and rotor free from cracks and arcing
(j)   The pick-up leads are not touching any metal part of the engine

# Chapter 5 Clutch

## Contents

## Specifications

| **Type** ........................................................................... | Single plate diaphragm spring, cable operated |
| --- | --- |

**Clutch driven plate**
Diameter:

| | |
| --- | --- |
| 1250 models ........................................................ | 7.25 in (184 mm) |
| 1500 models ........................................................ | 7.50 in (190 mm) |
| 1300 model (twin carb 1.50) .............................. | 7.50 in (190 mm) |
| 1300 model (single carb 1.75) ........................... | 7.50 in (190 mm) |
| 1600 model (twin carb 1.50) .............................. | 7.50 in (190 mm) |
| 1600 model (single carb 1.75) ........................... | 7.50 in (190 mm) |
| 1300 engine (single carb 1.50) .......................... | 7.25 in (184 mm) or 7.50 in (190 mm) |
| 1600 engine (single carb 1.50) .......................... | 7.50 in (190 mm) |

| **Release bearing type** ....................................................... | Ball race |
| --- | --- |

**Free movement**

| | |
| --- | --- |
| At the bellhousing release lever ...................................... | $\frac{3}{16}$ in (4.8 mm) |
| At the clutch foot pedal (except 8 Series) ..................... | 0.80 in (20.3 mm) |

**Torque wrench settings**

| | lbf ft | Nm |
| --- | --- | --- |
| Clutch cover assembly bolts ........................................ | 16 | 22 |
| Locknut on free movement adjuster | 3 | 4 |

## 1 General description

A $7\frac{1}{4}$ in (184 mm) or a $7\frac{1}{2}$ in (190 mm) single dry plate diaphragm spring clutch is fitted. The unit consists of the following:

(a) *A steel cover, dowelled and bolted to the rear face of the flywheel, and containing the pressure plate, diaphragm spring and fulcrum rings*

(b) *A clutch disc, mounted on the splined gearbox first motion shaft, and held between the flywheel and the pressure plate by the pressure plate spring. Friction material is riveted to the disc, and it has a spring cushioned hub to absorb transmission shocks and to help ensure a smooth take-up*

(c) *The release mechanism, consisting of a release fork and bearing in contact with the release fingers on the pressure plate. Wear of the friction material in the clutch is adjusted out by a cable adjuster nut on the outer end of the release fork*

In operation, the clutch pedal actuates the clutch release arm by means of the cable. The arm pushes the release bearing against the release fingers, moving the centre of the diaphragm spring inwards. As the centre of the spring is pushed in the outside of the spring is pushed out, moving the pressure plate backwards and disengaging it from the clutch disc. When the clutch pedal is released the diaphragm spring forces the pressure plate into contact with the linings on the disc, and also pushes the disc fractionally forwards on its splines, so engaging the disc with the flywheel. The clutch disc is now sandwiched between the pressure plate and the flywheel, and can transmit the drive.

## 2 Clutch adjustment

1 When correctly adjusted there should be $\frac{3}{16}$ in (4.8 mm) of free movement at the outer end of the clutch release arm and also 0.8 in (20.3 mm) free play at the clutch pedal (up to and including Series 7 models). On Series 8 models the clutch pedal should be level with the brake pedal and approximately 7.0 in (177.0 mm) from the floor.
2 To adjust loosen the locknut and turn the adjusting nut until the clutch release arm will move $\frac{3}{16}$ in (4.8 mm) away from the nut or until the pedal is correctly positioned. Ensuring that the adjuster nut or cable does not turn, tighten the locknut.
3 When fitting a new friction plate the cable may need fairly extensive adjustment, particularly if the old plate was well worn.

## 3 Clutch pedal – removal and refitting

### Up to and including Series 7 models

1 To remove the clutch pedal, free it from the cable by removing the circlip and clevis pin from the clevis assembly inside the car. Gain access to the clutch pedal cross-shaft by undoing the two nuts, bolts and washers which hold the pedal stop plate in position. Remove the plate together with the stop light switch. With a thin punch drift out at the outer end of the cross-shaft adjacent to the pedal, remove the washers, and push the cross-shaft towards the brake pedal. Lift off the clutch pedal.

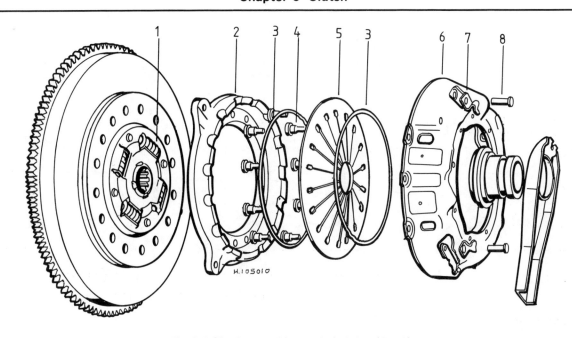

**Fig. 5.1 Clutch assembly – exploded view (Sec 1)**

| | | | |
|---|---|---|---|
| 1 | Driven plate (friction plate) | 3 | Fulcrum ring |
| 2 | Pressure plate | 4 | Shouldered rivet |

| | | | |
|---|---|---|---|
| 5 | Diaphragm spring | 7 | Retractor clip |
| 6 | Cover plate | 8 | Rivet |

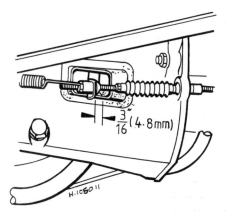

**Fig. 5.2 Free play at the release arm (Sec 2)**

### Series 8 models onwards
2 Disconnect the battery and disengage the return spring from the pedal.
3 Release the cable from the top of the pedal.
4 Extract the split pin and withdraw the pedal from the shaft noting the location of the plain and Belleville washers (where fitted).
5 Remove the return spring from the pedal and note which way round it is fitted.

### All models
6 Refitting of the clutch pedal is a reversal of removal but lubricate the shaft with a little grease.

### 4 Clutch – removal and refitting

1 Remove the gearbox, as described in Chapter 6.
2 Scribe a mark on the clutch cover and the flywheel to aid correct refitting, and remove the cover by unscrewing the bolts in diagonal sequence half a turn at a time to prevent distortion to the flange. Lift the clutch assembly off the locating dowels at the same time watching for the clutch disc, which may fall out. Do not allow oil or grease to

contaminate the clutch disc friction linings, the pressure plate or the flywheel face.
3 When refitting, ensure that the hands and all the clutch components are clean. Place the clutch disc against the flywheel, ensuring that it is the correct way round. The flywheel side is clearly marked near the centre. If the disc is fitted the wrong way round, the clutch will not operate. Refit the clutch cover assembly (photo) loosely on the dowels, and fit the six bolts and washers only finger tight, so that the clutch disc is gripped but can still be moved.
4 The clutch disc must now be centralised, so that when the engine and gearbox are mated the gearbox shaft is properly in line with the splined hole in the centre of the friction plate. Ideally, either a proper centralising tool, or an old gearbox input shaft, placed through the friction plate centre and into the crankshaft spigot bearing, are the easiest way to achieve this. However, it is possible to centralise the plate by inserting a round bar or long screwdriver through the centre of the clutch, resting it in the crankshaft spigot bearing, and moving it in whichever direction is necessary, thereby pushing the friction plate where it is required. Remove the bar and view the driven plate hub in relation to the hole in the centre of the clutch cover plate diaphragm spring and crankshaft spigot bearing. When all are in line, centralisation is achieved.
5 Tighten the clutch cover bolts in diagonal sequence and in progressive stages, to avoid distortion of the flange (photo).
6 Refit the gearbox as described in Chapter 6.

### 5 Clutch – dismantling and inspection

**Note:** *Clutch component design details vary slightly from model to model. Interchangeability of parts of different design is not possible.*

1 It is not practicable to dismantle the pressure plate assembly, and if this requires renewal an exchange unit must be purchased. This will have been accurately set up. If a new clutch disc is being fitted it is a false economy not to renew the release bearing, which may then have to be renewed soon after when wear on the clutch linings is still slight.
2 Examine the clutch disc friction linings for wear and loose rivets, and the disc for rim distortion, cracks, broken hub springs and worn splines. Compare the lining wear with a new clutch disc at your supplier, and decide whether or not to renew it while the unit is dismantled. It is far more satisfactory to renew the disc complete than to try and economise by only fitting new friction linings, but if this is attempted do not knock the rivets out with a punch, drill them out carefully (photos).

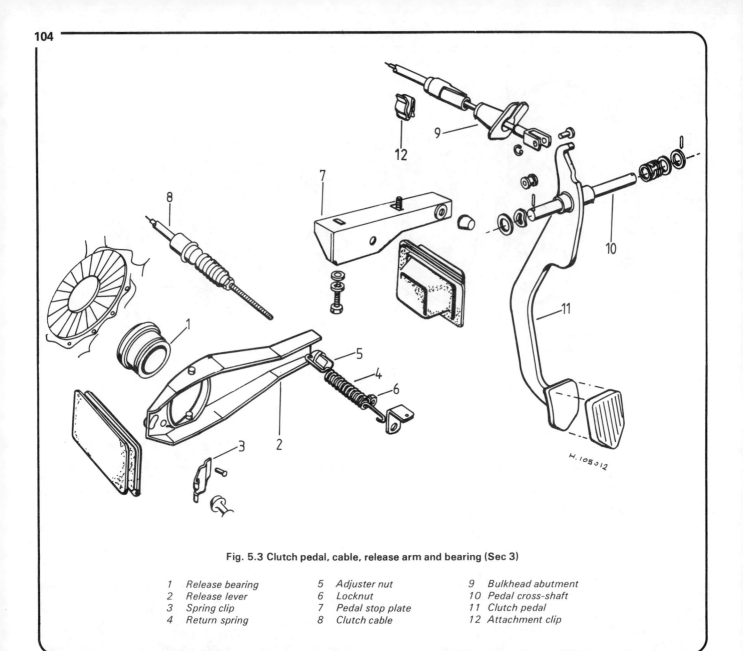

**Fig. 5.3 Clutch pedal, cable, release arm and bearing (Sec 3)**

| | | | | | |
|---|---|---|---|---|---|
| 1 | Release bearing | 5 | Adjuster nut | 9 | Bulkhead abutment |
| 2 | Release lever | 6 | Locknut | 10 | Pedal cross-shaft |
| 3 | Spring clip | 7 | Pedal stop plate | 11 | Clutch pedal |
| 4 | Return spring | 8 | Clutch cable | 12 | Attachment clip |

4.3 Fitting the friction plate and cover assembly to the flywheel

4.5 Fitting the cover securing bolts

5.2a A friction plate, with the linings worn down to the rivets (arrowed)

5.2b A new friction plate

3   Check the machined faces of the flywheel and pressure plate. If either are grooved, cracked or split, or if the diaphragm spring is suspect, fit a replacement unit. Check the release bearing for smoothness of operation. There should be no harshness and no slackness. It should spin reasonably freely bearing in mind it has been pre-packed with grease.

## 6   Clutch cable – removal and refitting

1   Chock behind the rear wheels, jack up the front of the car and place stands under the front crossmember.
2   Remove the locknut and cable adjuster nut from the clutch cable. Pull out the threaded end of the inner cable from the release arm, unclip the cable, and withdraw it from the bellhousing aperture and through the engine mounting.
3   Inside the car, free the cable from the pedal by removing the circlip and clevis pin at the pedal hook.
4   Pull back the outer cable from the nylon bulkhead abutment, and remove the abutment by squeezing it together and pulling it into the engine compartment. Withdraw the cable.
5   Refit by inserting the inner cable through the aperture in the bulkhead. Push the nylon abutment off the end of the outer cable, squeeze the ends of the abutment together, and push it into place in the bulkhead, sandwiching it with the abutment slot. Refit the outer cable to the nylon bulkhead abutment, gently pushing the cable fully home whilst ensuring that the key is in line with the abutment slot.
6   Refit the remaining items in the reverse order, and adjust the cable as described in Section 2.

## 7   Clutch release bearing - removal and refitting

1   Separate the engine and gearbox, as described in Chapter 6. The release bearing is a relatively inexpensive but important component and unless nearly new, should always be renewed during clutch overhaul.

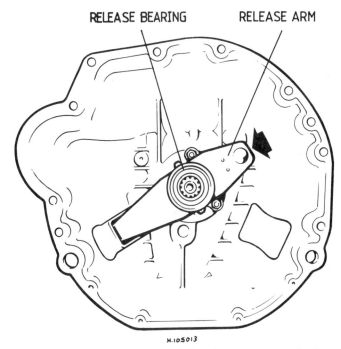

RELEASE BEARING            RELEASE ARM

H.105013

Fig. 5.4 Direction of movement of the release arm, when freeing the clip from the pivot (Sec 7)

2   Pull off the release arm rubber gaiter and the return spring. Free the release arm from the round-headed stud on which it pivots by pulling the arm in the direction of the arrow in Fig. 5.4. Unhook the bearing from the arm. Press the bearing from the hub, using blocks of wood and a vice.
3   Refit all parts in the reverse order.

See overleaf for 'Fault diagnosis – clutch'

## 8 Fault diagnosis – clutch

| Symptom | Reason(s) |
| --- | --- |
| Judder when taking up the drive | Defective engine or gearbox mountings<br>Worn or contaminated friction linings<br>Worn splines on friction plate hub or gearbox shaft<br>Worn crankshaft spigot bush<br>Defective pressure plate assembly |
| Clutch slip | Defective pressure plate assembly<br>Friction plate linings contaminated |
| Noise when depressing the clutch pedal | Defective clutch release bearing<br>Excessive play in input shaft splines |
| Noise on releasing the clutch pedal | Defective friction plate assembly<br>Defective pressure plate assembly<br>Defective gearbox input shaft<br>Defective clutch release bearing |
| Clutch disengagement difficult | Adjustment incorrect<br>Friction linings contaminated<br>Driven plate or gearbox shaft splines worn or sticky |

# Chapter 6 Manual
# gearbox and automatic transmission

*For modifications, and information applicable to later models, see Supplement at end of manual*

## Contents

## Specifications

*Manual gearbox*
**Number of gears** ................................................. 4 forward, 1 reverse

**Synchromesh** .................................................... On all forward gears

**Oil capacity (refill)** .......................................... 3 Imp pints (3.6 US pints, 1.7 litres)

**Primary shaft**
Bearing type ....................................................... Four spot ball bearing
Selective washers available ........................................ 0.051 to 0.053 in (1.30 to 1.35 mm)
            0.056 to 0.058 in (1.42 to 1.47 mm)
            0.060 to 0.062 in (1.52 to 1.57 mm)
End clearance between circlip and washer ........................... 0.001 to 0.007 in (0.03 to 0.18 mm)
Shaft spigot bearing ............................................... Oilite bush in rear of crankshaft (early cars)
            Needle rollers in rear of crankshaft (later cars)

**Layshaft**
Bearing type ....................................................... Needle roller at each end
Laygear endfloat ................................................... 0.006 to 0.010 in (0.15 to 0.25 mm)
Front thrust washer (selective fit) ................................ 0.058 to 0.060 in (1.47 to 1.52 mm)
            0.061 to 0.063 in (1.55 to 1.60 mm)
            0.064 to 0.066 in (1.63 to 1.68 mm)
Rear thrust washer (non-selective) ................................. 0.070 to 0.072 in (1.78 to 1.83 mm)

**Mainshaft**
Bearing type – front ............................................... Spigot – needle roller
Bearing type – rear ................................................ Two spot ball bearing
1st speed gearwheel endfloat ....................................... 0.005 to 0.0085 in (0.12 to 0.21 mm)
2nd speed gearwheel endfloat ....................................... 0.004 to 0.0075 in (0.10 to 0.19 mm)
3rd speed gearwheel endfloat ....................................... 0.004 to 0.0075 in (0.10 to 0.19 mm)

**Speedometer drive pinion**

| Axle ratio | Manual | | Automatic BW35 | | Automatic BW45 |
|---|---|---|---|---|---|
| | Number of teeth | Colour | Number of teeth | Colour | Number of teeth |
| 3.89 : 1 ........................ | 17 | White | 17 | Pink | 37 |
| 4.37 : 1 ........................ | 19 | Light green | 19 | Blue | N/A |
| 4.11 : 1 ........................ | 18 | Red | N/A | N/A | 39 |
| 3.70 : 1 ........................ | 17 | White | N/A | N/A | 37 |
| 3.54 : 1 ........................ | 17 | White | N/A | N/A | 35 |

*N/A – not applicable*

## Gearbox ratios (to chassis number R4 184358)

| | |
|---|---|
| 4th | 1.000 to 1 |
| 3rd | 1.366 to 1 |
| 2nd | 2.029 to 1 |
| 1st | 3.317 to 1 |
| Reverse | 3.450 to 1 |

## Gearbox ratios (from chassis number RH 184359)

| | |
|---|---|
| 4th | 1.000 : 1 |
| 3rd | 1.387 : 1 |
| 2nd | 2.165 : 1 |
| 1st | 3.538 : 1 |
| Reverse | 3.680 : 1 |

## Torque wrench settings

| | lbf ft | Nm |
|---|---|---|
| Clutch housing to engine | 30 | 41 |
| Crossmember to bodyshell | 12 | 16 |
| Detent plunger cover plate | 4 | 5 |
| Drain and filler plugs | 34 | 46 |
| Front cover nuts | 6 | 8 |
| Gearbox mounting to crossmember | 26 | 35 |
| Mainshaft front nut | 70 | 95 |
| Mainshaft rear nut (using special tool) | 69 | 94 |
| Mainshaft rear nut (without special tool) | 80 | 108 |
| Rear cover to casing | 14 | 19 |
| Reverse fulcrum pivot screw | 25 | 34 |
| Top cover | 4 | 5 |

## *Automatic transmission type 35*

**Type** ............ 3 speed, epicyclic with 3 element hydrokinetic torque converter

**Fluid capacity (including converter)** ............ $11\frac{1}{4}$ Imp pints (6.39 litres/13.5 US pints)

### Speed ratios

| | |
|---|---|
| 1st | 2.393 : 1 |
| 2nd | 1.450 : 1 |
| 3rd | 1.000 : 1 |
| Reverse | 2.094 : 1 |

**Torque converter diameter** ............ 9.5 in (241.3 mm)

**Operating temperature** ............ 100 to 115°C (212 to 236°F)

### Approximate shift speeds

| Speed shift | Light throttle: mph (kph) | Full throttle: mph (kph) | Kickdown: mph (kph) |
|---|---|---|---|
| 1 to 2 | 7 to 11 (11 to 17) | 30 to 40 (48 to 64) | – |
| 2 to 3 | 10 to 15 (16 to 24) | 56 to 65 (88 to 104) | – |
| 3 to 2 | – | – | 50 to 62 (80 to 93) |
| 2 to 1 | – | – | 20 to 30 (32 to 48) |

## *Automatic transmission type 45*

**Type** ............ 4 speed, epicyclic with 3 element hydrokinetic torque converter

**Fluid capacity (including converter)** ............ 10.5 Imp pints (6 litres/12.68 US pints)

### Speed ratios

| | |
|---|---|
| 1st | 3.00 : 1 |
| 2nd | 1.94 : 1 |
| 3rd | 1.35 : 1 |
| 4th | 1.00 : 1 |
| Reverse | 4.69 : 1 |

**Torque converter diameter** ............ 9.5 in (241.3 mm)

### Approximate shift speeds (final drive ratio 3.89 : 1/single carburettor)

| Speed shift | Light throttle: mph (kph) | Full throttle: mph(kph) | Kickdown: mph (kph) |
|---|---|---|---|
| 1 to 2 | 6 to 9 (9 to 14) | 23 to 27 (37 to 43) | – |
| 2 to 3 | 8 to 13 (13 to 21) | 40 to 47 (65 to 76) | – |
| 3 to 4 | 13 to 20 (21 to 32) | 58 to 68 (94 to 110) | – |
| 4 to 3 | – | – | 66 to 51 (107 to 82) |
| 3 to 2, 4 to 2 | – | – | 37 to 30 (60 to 49) |
| 2 to 1, 4 to 1 | – | – | 22 to 16 (35 to 26) |

## Approximate shift speeds (final drive ratio 4.11 : 1/single carburettor)

| Speed shift | Light throttle: mph (kph) | Full throttle: mph (kph) | Kick-down: mph (kph) |
|---|---|---|---|
| 1 to 2 | 6 to 9 (9 to 14) | 22 to 27 (35 to 43) | — |
| 2 to 3 | 8 to 13 (13 to 21) | 38 to 45 (61 to 73) | — |
| 3 to 4 | 13 to 20 (21 to 32) | 54 to 65 (87 to 105) | — |
| 4 to 3 | — | — | 62 to 48 (100 to 77) |
| 3 to 2, 4 to 2 | — | — | 36 to 28 (58 to 45) |
| 2 to 1, 4 to 1 | — | — | 20 to 16 (32 to 25) |

## Approximate shift speeds (final drive ratio 3.89 : 1/twin carburettor)

| Speed shift | Light throttle: mph (kph) | Full throttle: mph (kph) | Kick-down: mph (kph) |
|---|---|---|---|
| 1 to 2 | 6 to 9 (9 to 14) | 23 to 27 (37 to 43) | — |
| 2 to 3 | 8 to 13 (13 to 21) | 43 to 49 (69 to 79) | — |
| 3 to 4 | 13 to 20 (21 to 32) | 62 to 71 (100 to 115) | — |
| 4 to 3 | — | — | 68 to 55 (110 to 89) |
| 3 to 2, 4 to 2 | — | — | 40 to 32 (65 to 51) |
| 2 to 1, 4 to 1 | — | — | 22 to 17 (35 to 27) |

## Torque wrench settings

| | Type 35 | | Type 45 | |
|---|---|---|---|---|
| | lbf ft | Nm | lbf ft | Nm |
| Centre support to transmission core | 12 | 16 | 19 | 26 |
| Valve body to transmission case (small) | 5 | 7 | 7 | 9 |
| Valve body to transmission case (large) | 5 | 7 | — | — |
| Sump to transmission case | 5 | 7 | 5 | 7 |
| Inhibitor switch to transmission case | 4 | 5 | 4 | 5 |
| Converter to driveplate | 32 | 43 | 32 | 43 |
| Driveplate to crankshaft | 40 | 54 | 40 | 54 |

### 1  Manual gearbox – general description

The gearbox fitted to all models contains four constant mesh, helically cut forward gears and one spur reverse gear. Synchromesh is fitted to all forward gears. The bellhousing cannot be separated from the gearbox. Attached to the rear of the gearbox casing is an aluminium alloy extension which supports the rear of the mainshaft and the gearchange rod. The gearbox casing is also cast in aluminium and is fitted with a removable top cover. The drain plug is at the bottom right-hand side of the casing and the filler plug is half way up the same side.

Although they look identical, mainshafts with different diameter spigots have been used in production. Up to gearbox CH****91987 a mainshaft with a spigot diameter of 0.625 in (15.875 mm) was used. From gearbox CH****91988 the spigot diameter was increased to 0.875 in (22.225 mm). Ensure that the correct exchange shaft is used. Different primary shafts have been used, the later type with a deeper bore and identified by a longitudinal groove. Whilst early mainshafts can be used with later primary shafts, later mainshafts cannot be used with early primary shafts. All the mainshaft gears are bushed internally and wear normally takes place in the bushes and not on the shaft itself.

### 2  Gearbox (up to Series 7 inclusive) – removal and refitting

1  The gearbox can be removed in unit with the engine through the engine compartment as described in Chapter 1. Alternatively the gearbox can be separated from the rear of the engine and lowered from the car. The latter method is easier and quicker than the former.
2  Run the car over a pit or onto ramps. Alternatively jack up the car and fit stands.
3  Undo the drain plug and drain the oil from the gearbox.
4  Unscrew the gear lever knob after loosening the nut which secures it. Undo the four screws which hold the metal surround at the base of the lever. Note that on some models a console is fitted. Undo the screw which holds the front end and lift it off. Lift the metal surround and rubber gaiter from the transmission tunnel and gear lever.
5  Undo the three screws which secure the gear lever ball plate to the gearbox extension (photo). The gear lever can then be lifted from the extension (photo). Refit the three screws so that they are not lost.

2.5a Removing gear lever ball plate

2.5b Lifting out the gear lever

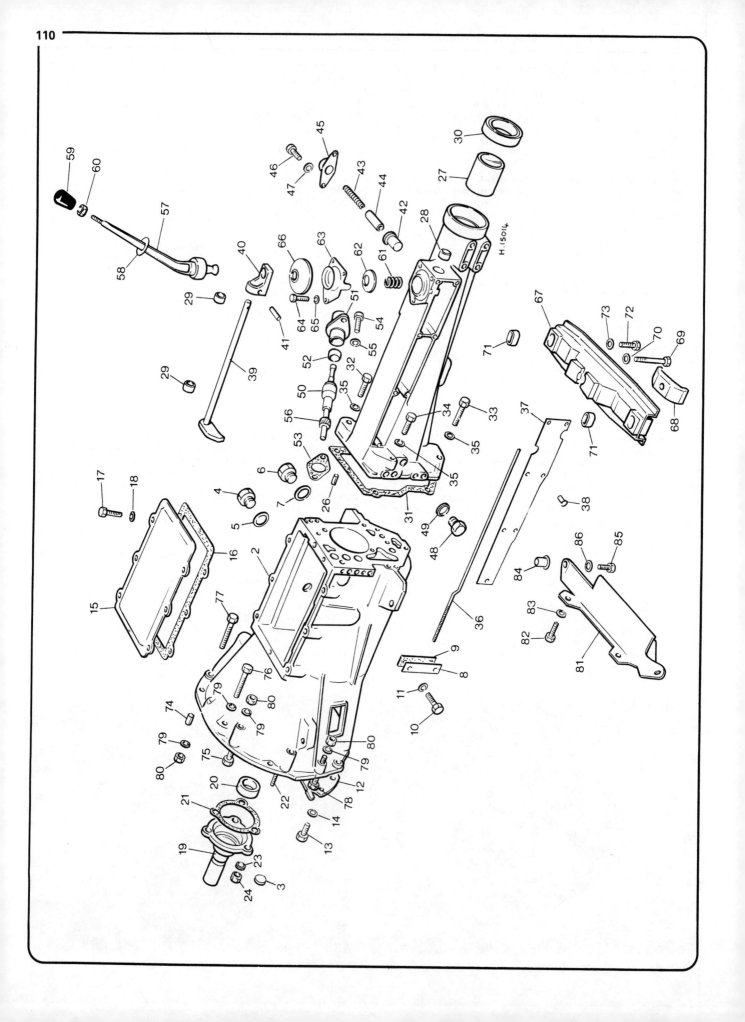

H.15014

**Fig. 6.1 Manual gearbox – exploded view (Sec 1)**

| | | | | |
|---|---|---|---|---|
| 2 Gearbox casing | 19 Front cover | 37 Plate | 54 Setscrew – adaptor to rear cover | 70 Washer |
| 3 Sealing disc | 20 Front cover oil seal | 38 Screw | 55 Washer | 71 Spacer |
| 4 Filler plug | 21 Gasket | 39 Gearchange shaft | 56 Speedometer drive pinion | 72 Bolt |
| 5 Washer | 22 Stud | 40 Swing lever | 57 Gear lever | 73 Washer |
| 6 Drain plug | 23 Washer | 41 Pin | 58 Washer | 74 Dowel |
| 7 Washer | 24 Nut | 42 Reverse stop plunger | 59 Knob | 75 Bolt |
| 8 Detent cover | 25 Rear cover | 43 Spring | 60 Locknut | 76 Bolt |
| 9 Cover gasket | 26 Dowel | 44 Rubber sleeve | 61 Spring | 77 Bolt |
| 10 Setscrew | 27 Rear bush | 45 Retainer | 62 Closing disc | 78 Bolt |
| 11 Washer | 28 Sealing cup | 46 Setscrew | 63 Retaining cap | 79 Washer |
| 12 Cover plate | 29 Gearchange shaft bush | 47 Washer | 64 Cap to cover screw | 80 Nut |
| 13 Setscrew | 30 Rear oil seal | 48 Reverse light switch blanking hole plug | 65 Washer | 81 Shield |
| 14 Washer | 31 Gasket | 49 Washer | 66 Grommet | 82 Screw |
| 15 Top cover | 32 Bolt | 50 Speedometer pinion bearing | 67 Rear mounting | 83 Washer |
| 16 Gasket | 33 Bolt | 51 Speedometer cable adaptor | 68 Rebound plate | 84 Rawl nut |
| 17 Setscrew | 34 Long bolt | 52 Oil seal | 69 Bolt | 85 Screw |
| 18 Washer | 35 Washer | 53 Adaptor gasket | | 86 Washer |
| | 36 Oil transfer tube | | | |

6 Isolate the battery by disconnecting the earth lead.

7 Undo the two nuts and bolts which hold the starter motor and its shield in place, noting the earth strap secured to the top bolt. Pull the motor clear.

8 Undo the nuts and bolts from the top of the clutch housing.

9 Free the throttle control rod from the carburettor by snapping the clip from the rod. Remove the rod from the coupling.

10 From under the car undo and remove the four bolts securing the propeller shaft to the rear axle flange, having marked both flanges to ensure correct reassembly. Separate the flanges and lower the propeller shaft, at the same time pulling the shaft out of the gearbox extension.

11 Free the front of the exhaust pipe from the manifold by undoing the nuts from the flanges. Pull the pipe away.

12 Undo the speedometer drive cable. Disconnect the clutch cable from the release arm by undoing the locknut and adjuster nut and pull the threaded rod portion of the cable forwards.

13 If a reverse light switch is fitted pull the wires from the terminals.

14 Undo the bolts which hold the semicircular plate to the bottom front of the bellhousing.

15 Place a jack under the gearbox (preferably trolley type) and undo the bolt at each end of the crossmember. If the crossmember is to be removed, also undo the centre bolt.

16 Place a jack under the front of the engine to prevent it tilting and undo the remaining bellhousing nuts and bolts. Carefully pull the gearbox from the engine, taking the weight (unless it is on a trolley jack) during the whole of this operation until the primary shaft is clear of the clutch hub. This happens when the gearbox has moved back 3 to 4 inches. The gearbox is now clear and can be lowered to the ground.

17 Refitting is a direct reversal of the removal procedure. Note that on no account should the gearbox be allowed to hang on the primary shaft when it is in the half-on position. The best way to refit it is to slide it forwards supported on a trolley jack. If the clutch has been renewed ensure that it has been properly centralised as described in Chapter 5. Refit the earth strap on the top starter motor bolt. Ensure that the marks on the propeller shaft and rear axle flanges are in line, or vibration may occur. Refill the gearbox with the correct amount and grade of oil, and reset the clutch pedal clearance as described in Chapter 5.

## 3 Gearbox (to Series 7 inclusive) – dismantling and reassembly

1 Wash the exterior of the gearbox casing with paraffin or a suitable grease solvent.

2 Disengage the clutch release arm from its pivot post by pushing it towards the aperture in the bellhousing. Remove the release bearing (photo).

3 Remove the setscrews and washers from the top cover and lift the cover, with its gasket, off the gearbox (photo).

4 Stand the gearbox on the bellhousing flange. Remove the two bolts retaining the speedometer gear housing, and withdraw the housing and gear.

5 Remove the reverse gear stop plate spring and plunger by undoing the two bolts and washers. Undo the five bolts which hold the rear extension to the back of the gearbox (photo).

6 Turn the gearshift lever shaft anti-clockwise to the stop and move it as far to the rear as possible so it disengages the cut-outs in the ends of the three selector rods. The rear extension can now be removed (photo).

7 Undo the bolt from the centre of the keep plate between the layshaft and the reverse idler gear shaft. Slide the plate out from the slots in the layshaft and reverse idler shaft. If it is stiff drift it out (photo).

8 Undo the two bolts which hold the selector spring cover plate in position on the rear top corner of the gearbox casing, left-hand side. Lift off the plate and take out the three springs. Remove the plungers if they will slip out easily, otherwise leave them in place. Keep these parts together (photo).

9 To drive out the roll pins which hold the selector forks in place use a $\frac{1}{8}$ in (3.2 mm) pin punch. If one is not available cut the sharp end off a round-headed $1\frac{1}{2}$ in nail. The nail makes an excellent punch. Drive out the roll pin which secures the 3rd/4th gear selector fork to its selector rod and also the pin which secures the 1st/2nd gear selector fork to its rod. Remove the forks and pins (photo).

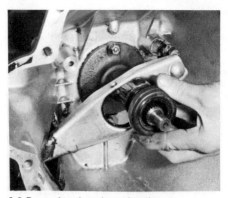

3.2 Removing the release bearing

3.3 Removing the top cover

3.5 Removing the gearbox extension bolts

3.6 Removing the gearbox extension

3.7 Removing the keep plate

3.8 Removing the selector spring cover plate

3.9 Driving out the selector fork pins

3.11 Removing the interlock plungers

3.16a Drifting out the primary shaft bearing assembly

10  The selector rods can now be removed from the rear of the gearbox. Label them to ensure correct reassembly.

11  With a piece of wire push out the interlock plungers from their drillings in the rear face of the gearbox. Plungers are fitted between the 3rd/4th and 1st/2nd selector rod holes and also between 1st/2nd and reverse (photo).

12  Before the reverse gear selector rod can be removed undo and remove the lever pivot bolt and lever.

13  Before proceeding further, check the endfloat of 1st, 2nd and 3rd gears with a feeler gauge (see Fig. 6.4) placed between the gear and its flange.

14  Undo the nuts and washers holding the front cover and remove it.

15  Drive the layshaft rearwards, and gently lower the laygear assembly to the bottom of the gearbox.

16  Drift out the primary shaft bearing very carefully from inside the gearbox, removing it complete with the primary shaft. Ensure that the gear does not interfere with the laygear on removal (photos).

17  At the rear of the gearbox undo the two bolts and washers which

secure the rear bearing clamp plate in position.

18  Clamp the long exposed portion of the mainshaft between soft jaws in a vice. In the absence of a large enough spanner ($1\frac{5}{8}$ AF) start the self-locking nut by holding a drift to the lower or left-hand side of one of the nut's six faces, hitting the drift smartly until the nut starts to turn (photo).

19  Release the shaft from the vice and drive it forward with a heavy mallet, or hammer with a block of wood interfaced, until the shoulder on the shaft is free from the rear bearing (photo).

20  The bearing must now be removed from the casing and, although free from the shaft, it can usually be started by drifting the front of the shaft rearwards. The shaft will tend to push the bearing out rather than enter the bore in the bearing it has just left (photo).

21  Once the bearing has started to move it can be levered out of the rear of the casing with the aid of two open-ended spanners (photo). When the bearing is free, lift it from the tail end of the mainshaft.

22  The mainshaft assembly can now be lifted out, front end first, through the hole in the top of the gearbox casing (photo).

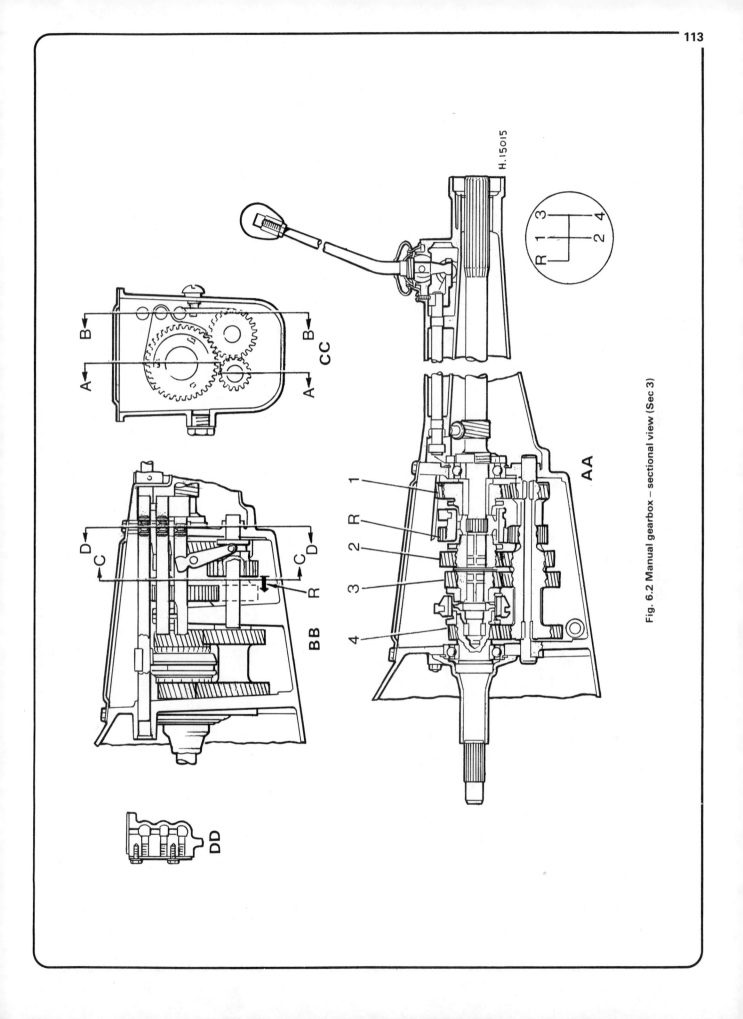

H.15015

Fig. 6.2 Manual gearbox – sectional view (Sec 3)

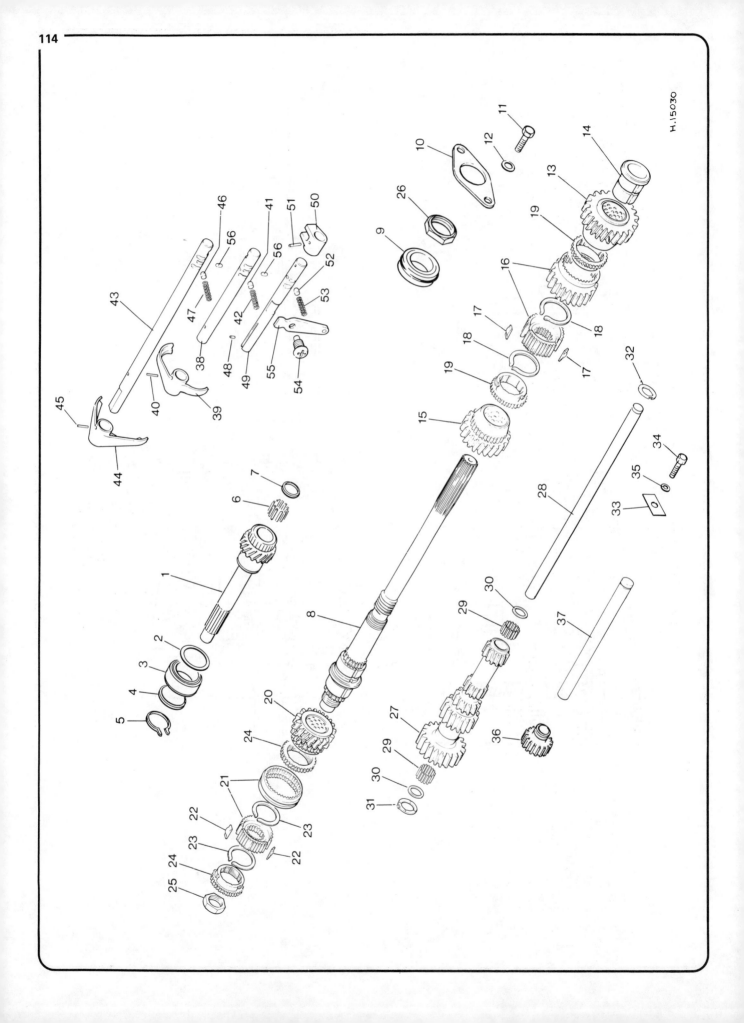

H.15030

**Fig. 6.3 Manual gearbox internal components – exploded view (Sec 3)**

1  Primary shaft
2  Chip shield
3  Bearing and snap ring
4  Selective washer
5  Circlip
6  Spigot needle roller bearing
7  Bearing collar
8  Mainshaft
9  Mainshaft rear bearing and snap ring
10  Bearing retainer
11  Setscrew
12  Washer

13  1st gear
14  Spacer
15  2nd gear
16  Reverse gear and 1st and 2nd gear synchroniser hub
17  Blocker bar (shifting plate)
18  Circlip
19  Baulk ring (synchro ring)
20  3rd gear
21  3rd and 4th gear synchroniser hub
22  Blocker bar
23  Circlip

24  Baulk ring (synchro ring)
25  Mainshaft front nut
26  Mainshaft rear nut
27  Laygear
28  Layshaft
29  Rollers
30  Abutment ring
31  Thrust washer (selective)
32  Rear thrust washer
33  Lockplate
34  Setscrew
35  Washer

36  Reverse idler gear
37  Reverse idler shaft
38  1st and 2nd gear selector rod
39  1st and 2nd gear selector fork
40  Pin
41  Plunger
42  Spring
43  3rd and 4th gear selector rod
44  3rd and 4th gear selector fork
45  Pin

46  Plunger
47  Spring
48  Reverse shaft locating peg
49  Reverse selector rod
50  Reverse shaft operating boss
51  Pin
52  Plunger
53  Spring
54  Reverse gear selector pivot bolt
55  Fulcrum lever
56  Shaft interlocking plunger

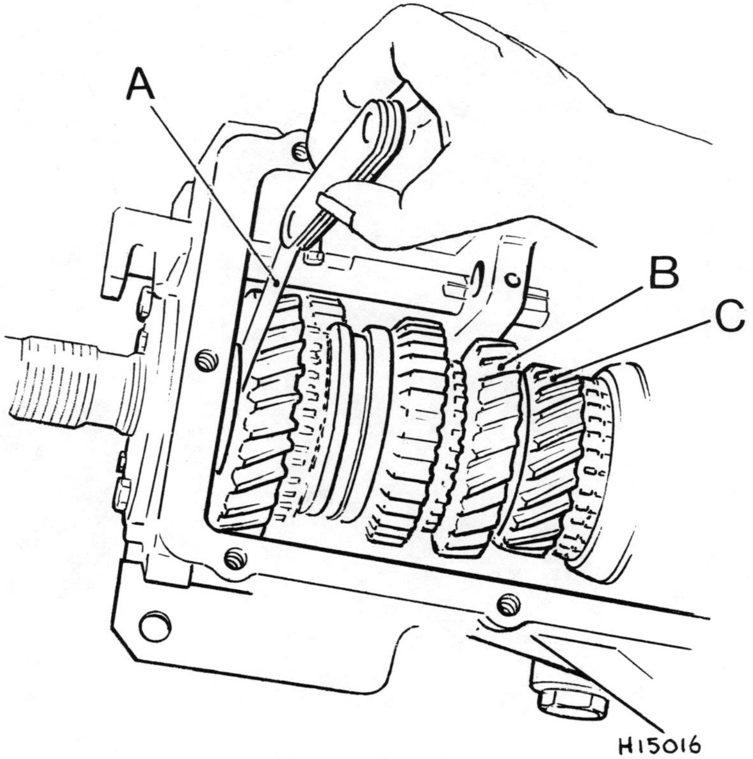

**Fig. 6.4 Method of measuring endfloat — see Specifications (Sec 3)**

A  1st gear
B  2nd gear
C  3rd gear

H15016

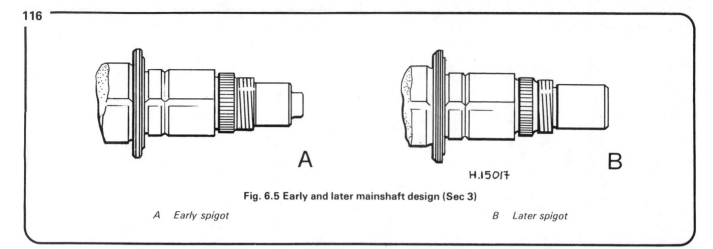

Fig. 6.5 Early and later mainshaft design (Sec 3)

A    Early spigot                                          B    Later spigot

3.16b Removing the primary shaft bearing assembly

3.18 Removing the mainshaft nut

3.19 Driving the mainshaft forward

3.20 Drifting back the mainshaft bearing

3.21 Levering out the mainshaft bearing

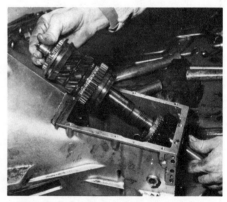

3.22 Lifting out the mainshaft assembly

3.23 Lifting out the laygear

3.25 Removing the extension oil seal

3.26 Fitting a new extension oil seal

23 Lift out the laygear and thrust washers from the bottom of the gearbox (photo).

24 Remove the reverse idler gear and shaft by removing the reverse selector shaft guide peg, and pulling out the shaft from the rear of the gearbox.

25 The rear oil seal should be renewed as a matter of course. Prise out the old seal with a drift or broad screwdriver. It comes out quite easily (photo).

26 With a piece of wood, to spread the load evenly, carefully tap a new seal into place ensuring that it enters the bore in the extension squarely (photo).

27 The only reason for dismantling the primary shaft is to fit a new bearing. If the gear on the shaft is worn the bearing will be worn too. With circlip pliers remove the circlip from the primary shaft, and place it vertically in a vice so the gear faces down and is free of the vice jaws. The sides of the bearing will now lie across the top of the vice. Carefully drift the shaft out of the bearing with a mallet (photo).

28 To fit the new bearing, fit the oil thrower and then the bearing with the groove for the circlip away from the gear. Using the jaws of a vice as a support behind the bearing drift the shaft into place (photo).

29 Fit the selective washer, and, with the edge of the circlip in the groove, measure the clearance with a feeler gauge, check against the specifications, and fit a washer of appropriate thickness. Fit a new circlip.

30 The mainshaft has to be dismantled before some of the synchroniser rings can be inspected. With a soft-faced hammer tap the splined end of the shaft while gripping on to 2nd gear (photo).

31 Slide off from the splined end of the shaft 1st gear and then, as shown, the 1st/2nd gear synchroniser hub (reverse is on its periphery) and 2nd gear. Ensure all the parts are kept in their relative positions (photo).

32 Mount the plain portion of the shaft between two pieces of wood in a vice and undo the nut which retains the 3rd/4th gear synchroniser assembly. Slide off the synchroniser hub followed by 3rd gear. Note that on the 3rd/4th gear synchro sliding sleeve the selector fork groove is fitted opposite the hub wide face boss. If during removal of one of the synchroniser hubs the outer sleeve slips off the inner hub, reassembly is straightforward. Fit the sleeve to the hub and then the three blocker bars (photo).

33 Retain the blocker bars to the outer sleeve by fitting the two internal springs with their ends evenly spaced between two blocker bars. Note that the 1st/2nd gear synchro hub can be fitted either way round (photo).

34 Throughout reassembly lightly lubricate all the components as they are fitted together. To reassemble the mainshaft, slide 3rd gear onto the short end until it abuts the flange. Fit a new synchro ring (photo).

35 Fit the 3rd/4th gear synchro hub so the wide face hub boss is adjacent to 3rd gear, and the selector fork groove, which is offset, is towards the nose of the shaft (photo). Note that when the synchro hub is fitted it is essential that the cut-outs in the periphery of the synchroniser ring mate with the blocker bars on the inside of the synchroniser sleeve (photo).

36 Place the mainshaft between two blocks of wood in a vice and refit the self-locking nut with its plain side against the synchro hub. Tighten the nut to the specified torque setting (photo).

37 Moving to the longer end of the mainshaft fit second gear with its flat side towards the flange on the shaft. Follow with a new synchro ring and the 1st/2nd gear synchroniser hub (photo). Note when fitting the 1st/2nd gear synchro hub that the end of the hub with the groove on its periphery is fitted facing the tail end of the shaft (photo).

38 Ensure that the blocker bar on the inside of the synchroniser sleeve (arrowed) fits onto the cut-out on the synchro ring (photo), and with a drift gently tap alternate sides of the synchro hub until the hub is on as far as possible.

39 Fit a further synchro ring, 1st gear with the cone side facing the 1st/2nd gear synchroniser hub, and finally the distance piece. The mainshaft is now reassembled (photo).

40 When reassembling the gearbox, ensure that the interior of the gearbox is spotlessly clean. Hold the reverse gear idler in place with the groove for the selector fork towards the rear of the gearbox. Drift in the reverse gear idler shaft until the slot is adjacent to the gearbox outer end face.

41 Assemble the needle roller bearings at either end of the laygear.

3.27 Drifting out the primary shaft from the bearing

3.28 Refitting the primary shaft bearing

3.30 Tapping the mainshaft end

3.31 Sliding off the mainshaft parts

3.32 Fitting the blocker bars

3.33 Fitting the synchro springs

3.34 Fitting 3rd gear end synchro ring

3.35a Fitting the 3rd/4th gear synchro hub

3.35b Aligning the synchro ring cut-outs

3.36 Tighten the mainshaft nut

3.37a Fitting 2nd gear, synchro ring and hub

3.37b Correct assembly of the 1st/2nd gear synchro hub

3.38 Fitting the blocker bar

3.39 Mainshaft final assembly

3.41 Fitting the layshaft needle rollers

3.42 Fitting a laygear abutment ring

3.43 Fitting the laygear in the gear case

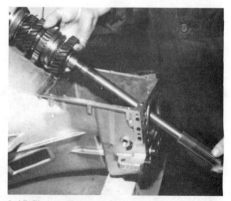

3.45 Fitting the mainshaft assembly

Spread grease round the orifice at each end, then fit 26 needle rollers to each end of the shaft. Press them well into the grease so they will not drop out (photo).

42 With the rollers assembled, fit a steel abutment ring at each end of the laygear (photo). Slide in a dummy layshaft so the needle rollers will not drop out of place. Use a length of mild steel a fraction under the length of the laygear, and the same diameter or very slightly less than that of the layshaft.

43 Grease the backs of the laygear thrust washers and fit the thickest washer to the rear with its tag in the cut-outs in the casing and the thinner washer similarly to the front of the casing. Fit the laygear, larger end to the front (photo).

44 Temporarily refit the layshaft from the rear of the gearbox, pushing out the dummy shaft as this is done. Measure the endfloat between the front of the laygear and the thrust washer (0.006 to 0.010 in). Fit a different washer if necessary and refit the dummy layshaft.

45 Fit the mainshaft assembly to the gearbox through the top cover, holding on to 1st gear and the distance piece to prevent them from slipping down the mainshaft (photo).

46 Fit the rear bearing to the gearbox casing from the tail end of the mainshaft, with the retainer ring to the rear of the bearing (photo).

47 With a broad drift tap the bearing into place in the gearbox until the retainer ring is fully home and in contact with the casing. Support the underside of the bearing and with a soft-faced hammer tap the mainshaft fully into the bearing. Make sure that the gears do not foul the laygear and that the blocker bars and synchro cut-outs are all in line.

48 Fit a new self-locking nut to the rear of the mainshaft bearing. Tighten to the recommended torque setting. If a torque wrench is not available use a ring or open-ended spanner, or a pipe wrench, and tighten very firmly. To prevent the shaft from turning grip it between soft jaws in a vice (photo).

49 Refit the rear bearing retainer plate and tighten the two bolts. With a feeler gauge recheck the endfloat of 1st, 2nd and 3rd gears between the gears and their abutment flanges (see Fig. 6.4).

50 Slide the abutment ring over the nose of the mainshaft. If this is fitted to the bore in the rear of the primary shaft after the needle roller bearings have been fitted, it tends to drop when fitting the primary shaft in place. Grease the annulus in the end of the primary shaft and fit the 23 needle rollers, pressing them firmly into the grease so they will not fall out when the primary gear is refitted (photo).

51 Carefully offer up the primary shaft to the mainshaft, so that the nose of the latter seats squarely in the needle rollers. Do not forget the remaining synchro ring which lies between 3rd and 4th gears (photo). With a broad-faced drift, tap the bearing evenly and lightly on its outer track into position in the gearbox casing. Ensure it enters the casing squarely.

52 Turn the gearbox upside down so the laygear falls into mesh with the mainshaft and primary gears.

53 Insert the layshaft from the rear of the gearbox. Keep the forward end of the layshaft up against the dummy shaft as the latter is driven out. Coat the front end of the layshaft where it enters the bellhousing with a sealing compound.

54 Turn the layshaft and reverse idler shafts until the slots are vertical and facing each other. Slip the retainer plate into the slots in the layshaft and reverse gear idler shaft (photo).

55 Refit and tighten the bolt and washer which secures the plate to the gearbox end face.

56 To avoid oil leaks from the front of the gearbox always fit a new oil seal to the front cover. With a broad-bladed screwdriver, lever the old seal out. Select a socket of the same diameter as the new seal and, with the jaws of the vice extended and the front cover and socket placed between them, press the seal into place (photo). Grease the new seal with a multi-purpose grease, and spread the non-setting jointing compound on the front cover and gearbox casing face.

57 Fit a new gasket and position the front cover in place over the studs. Tighten down the three securing nuts and washers.

58 Slide the reverse gear selector rod into place in the bottom holes in the rear of the casing, ensuring that the cut-out in the front of the rod faces upwards (photo), and insert the guide peg for the reverse gear selector rod through the hole in the top of the lug.

59 With a piece of thin wire manipulate the guide peg so that it enters the narrower bore in the bottom of the larger hole and seats in the reverse gear selector rod cut-out (photo).

3.46 Fitting the rear bearing

3.48 Fitting the mainshaft nut

3.50 Fitting the needle rollers

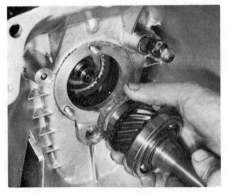

3.51 Fitting the primary shaft

3.54 Fitting the layshaft/reverse idler shaft plate

3.56 Fitting the front cover oil seal

3.58 Fitting the reverse gear selector rod

3.59 Positioning the guide peg

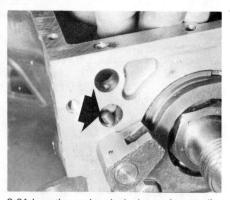

3.61 Inserting an interlock plunger (arrowed)

3.62 Positioning the 1st/2nd gear selector rod

3.63 Fitting the 1st/2nd gear selector fork

3.64 Fitting the interlock plunger

3.65 Fitting the 3rd/4th gear selector fork

3.70 Fitting the middle detent plunger

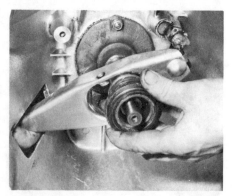

3.75 Fitting the clutch release arm and bearing

60  Coat the underside of the head of the reverse gear selector pivot bolt and the adjacent area on the gearbox casing with jointing compound. Screw the bolt into the gearbox case, whilst holding the fulcrum lever, so that the pivot enters the hole in the lever. As the bolt is tightened make sure that the lower end of the lever enters the groove on the periphery of the reverse idler gear, and that the broader upper end locates in the cut-out in the reverse gear selector rod.

61  Insert an interlock plunger into the hole in the end of the casing between the reverse gear selector rod and the 1st/2nd gear selector rod (photo).

62  Slide the 1st/2nd gear selector rod into the middle hole and at the same time fit the 1st/2nd gear selector fork with its boss to the rear, so its forks enter the groove in the 1st/2nd gear synchro hub (photo).

63  Line up the small hole in the 1st/2nd gear selector rod with the hole in the boss of the fork and drift the roll pin into place (photo).

64  Place an interlock plunger in the small hole between the 1st/2nd gear selector rod and the 3rd/4th gear selector hole (photo).

65  Slide the 3rd/4th gear selector rod into the top hole, and at the

same time fit the remaining selector fork with its boss towards the rear of the gearbox. Secure the fork to the rod with a roll pin (photo).

66  Check that the primary shaft, mainshaft and layshaft all turn freely, and if not check that two gears have not been engaged simultaneously.

67  Ensure that the slots in the end of the three selector rods face inwards, are in line, and are in neutral.

68  Make sure the gearbox and extension mating faces are clean, smooth and smear them with jointing compound. Grease the rear oil seal in the end of the gearbox extension and offer up the extension to the gearbox. Carefully feed the mainshaft through the seal and the oil pipe through the hole in the casing. While the extension is being fitted, hold the gearshift shaft as far anti-clockwise and to the rear of the extension as possible.

69  Fit the extension bolts finger tight. Move the gearshift shaft forwards and turn it clockwise so that the shaft locates in the slots in the selector rods. Tighten the bolts to the specified torque.

70  Insert detent plungers into the three holes in the side of the

gearbox casing. The middle plunger is shown being fitted (photo). Fit the springs, one on top of each detent plunger.

71 Make sure that the joint face is clean and free from burrs. Refit the detent springs cover plate, insert and tighten the two bolts and washers which hold the plate in place.

72 Refit the reverse gear plunger, spring and cover and tighten the two bolts and washers which hold the cover in place.

73 Fit a new gasket to the gearbox top face and lubricate the gears well. Check that the oil feed pipe is 1 in (25.4 mm) below the level of the gearbox top cover face and bend it carefully up or down as necessary.

74 Refit the top cover. Refit the bolts and washers holding the cover in position and tighten to the specified torque. Do not overtighten.

75 The source of an annoying squeal when the clutch pedal is pressed can be a dry release arm pivot post. Smear the head of the pivot post with multipurpose grease. Slide the clutch release arm into the bellhousing so the narrower portion of the arm enters the bellhousing cut-out. Fit the groove in the release bearing to the two pivot points in the release arm (photo). Finally push the arm into place on the release arm pivot post so that the spring clip rests behind the head of the post. Gearbox reassembly is now complete.

## 4 Gearbox (up to Series 7 inclusive) – inspection

1 It is assumed that the gearbox has been dismantled for reasons of excessive noise, lack of synchromesh, or for failure to stay in gear. If any more drastic trouble exists, it may be better to obtain a replacement unit.

2 Examine all gears for excessively worn, chipped or damaged teeth. Any such gears should be renewed. Check all synchromesh cones for wear on the bearing surfaces, which normally have clearly machined oil reservoir lines in them. If these are smooth or obviously uneven, renewal is essential. Also, when the cones are put together – as they would be when in operation – there should be no rock. This would signify ovality, or lack of concentricity. A satisfactory way of checking is by comparing the fit of a new cone on the hub with the old one. If the teeth of the ring are obviously worn or damaged (causing engagement difficulties) they should be renewed. All ball race bearings should be checked. It is advisable to renew these as a matter of course. Circlips should be checked to ensure that they are undistorted and undamaged. A selection of new selective washers of varying thicknesses should be obtained to compensate for variations in new components fitted, or wear in old ones (see Specifications). The thrust washers at the ends of the laygear should also be renewed as they will almost certainly have worn if the gearbox is of any age. Needle roller bearings between the input shaft and mainshaft and in the laygear are usually found in good order, but if in doubt renew them.

3 The sliding hubs are subject to wear. Where the fault has been failure of a gear to remain engaged, or difficulty in engagement, the hub is one of the likely suspects. Check that the blocker bars (sliding keys) are not sloppy and move freely. If there is rock or backlash between the inner and outer sections of the hub the whole assembly should be renewed, particularly if jumping out of gear has been occurring.

4 The selector fork ends should be examined for signs of excessive or uneven wear. Compare with new forks and renew if the wear exceeds 0.005 in. Worn selector forks are one of the more common reasons for a gear lever repeatedly jumping out of gear.

5 If the bush in the rear of the gearbox extension is worn, take the extension to a main agent to have a new bush fitted and bore in position. Alternatively obtain a new extension complete. The mainshaft is prone to wear on high mileage cars at the spigot, on the splines, or on the areas against which 2nd and 3rd gears rotate. Renew the shaft if necessary.

## 5 Gearbox (up to Series 7 inclusive) – gear ratio changes

1 The different gearbox ratios and the applicable chassis number change points are given in the Specifications, but if in doubt, the gearbox can be identified by engaging first gear and counting the number of turns required at the primary shaft to rotate the output shaft one turn. Early versions require 3.3 turns and later versions 3.5 turns, a difference of almost a quarter of a turn.

2 The lower ratio laygear is identified with a small groove cut in its outer diameter, between the primary shaft gear and third gear meshing gears. The lower ratio primary shaft and mainshaft third gears are identified with a small groove cut in the middle of the gear teeth outer circumference.

3 When ordering spare parts, full details of the vehicle should be given.

## 6 Gearbox (commencing Series 8 vehicles) – removal and refitting

1 Disconnect the battery earth lead, and remove the starter motor upper bolt and earth strap.

2 Drain the gearbox oil. Partially drain the radiator, to just above the level of the water pump.

3 Remove the upper hose, and unclip the heater hoses from the cylinder head.

4 If a clock is fitted, push it out towards the rear of the vehicle and disconnect the lead and lampholders.

5 Remove the console by taking out the five screws, remove the gear lever knob, the gaiter and dust pad. slide off the rubber boot, remove the three screws securing the retaining cap, and take out the lever complete with the cap, and spring.

6 Remove the bolts from the exhaust pipe joint next to the propeller shaft guard. Remove the propeller shaft (Chapter 7) and the guard.

7 Detach the clutch cable from the clip, note the protruding thread length for refitting, and withdraw the cable.

8 Remove the speedo cable from the gearbox, and remove the sump to clutch housing stiffeners (if fitted) together with any shims, noting their positions.

9 Remove the flywheel dust cover, and release the stabiliser bar to give approximately $\frac{3}{8}$ in (10 mm) clearance between brackets and chassis members.

10 Pull off the reversing light connections, support the gearbox end, and remove the rear support bracket bolts.

11 Lower the gearbox gently until the upper part of the engine almost touches the bulkhead, and place a protective pad in position at this point.

12 Remove the two top bolts securing the engine to the gearbox, and retrieve the clip. Remove the retaining starter motor bolt and withdraw the motor.

13 Place a small jack under the engine front, with a piece of wood interposed, to prevent tilting.

14 Support the gearbox, remove the remaining bolts, and withdraw the gearbox straight back.

15 To refit the gearbox, lightly grease the input shaft splines and spigot with high melting point grease. Engage a gear, lift the unit to the engine, keeping it in a straight line and engage the input shaft in the clutch plate. Turn the output shaft to assist engagement and do not allow the gearbox to hang on the input shaft before it is bolted up.

16 Locate the dowels, then fit and lightly tighten the two upper bolts, remembering to fit the clip under the right-hand bolt.

17 Refit the remaining bolts and tighten them all to the specified torque. Select gearbox neutral.

18 Offer up the starter motor and refit the lower fixings. Refit the upper bolt but not the nut.

19 Refit the reverse light wires through the clip. Offer the gearbox mounting up to the body, check the spacer positions, refit the bolts, remove the jack, and tighten the bolts to the specified torque. Reconnect the reverse light leads.

20 Refit the dust cover, fit the stiffener bolts through the adjustment shims and cover, and secure finger tight to the clutch housing. Tighten the screws at the sump, followed by the bolts of the dust cover.

21 Note that if the gearbox or engine has been changed the stiffeners will require adjustment, and, with the sump screws tight and the bolts removed from the stiffener to dust cover, the clearance between the stiffener and gearbox should be measured. Shims to take up the clearance should be selected and fitted. Fit the securing bolts and tighten to the specified torque.

22 Refit the clutch cable to approximately the correct position, and clip to the front engine bearer. Tighten the stabiliser bracket bolts to the correct torque loading.

23 Refit the propeller shaft (see Chapter 7), the guard, and the speedometer cable.

24 Refit the drain plug and refill the gearbox.

25 Refit the earth strap to the starter motor upper bolt, and secure both bolts to the specified torque.
26 Adjust the clutch cable (see chapter 5), and refit the exhaust pipe.
27 Reconnect the heater pipes, refit the top hose, and top up the radiator.
28 Apply grease to the gear lever bearing surfaces and refit, together with the retaining plate, gaiter, console, clock and gear lever knob.
29 Connect the battery, then start and reset the clock.

## 7 Gearbox (commencing Series 8 vehicles) – overhauling procedure

1 Overhauling procedures are similar to those described in Sections 3 and 4 for the earlier gearbox. However, certain variations apply and are covered in the paragraphs which follow.
2 The reverse bias assembly may be removed with the gearbox in position as described in Section 3, paragraph 5. Lubricate the plunger with grease when refitting.
3 The reversing light switch should be removed or adjusted as described in Chapter 10, Section 46.
4 The speedometer pinion assembly is removed as described in Section 3, paragraph 4. If the teeth are broken, the gearbox should be drained and the rear cover removed and cleaned out. To renew the oil seal, separate the pinion and housing and remove the old seal. Oil the new seal and seating, and press the seal home, lip inward towards the pinion. Fit a new dry joint, and reassemble all parts.
5 The rear cover oil seal can be renewed as described in Section 3 paragraphs 25 and 26 if the cover is off the car. The seal may be renewed with the cover in position using special tools RG 553A and 7657, by screwing the tool into the seal and tightening the extractor bolt. Refit with tools RG 554A and 550, and pack the oil seal with grease between the sealing lips. Check the gearbox oil level.
6 To remove the rear cover with the gearbox in situ, carry out the operations described in Section 2, paragraphs 2 to 5 inclusive. Isolate the battery, and remove the propeller shaft as described in Section 2, paragraph 10. Remove the propeller shaft guard. Remove the speedometer drive assembly by disconnecting the cable, removing the bolts and pulling out the assembly. Remove the reverse bias assembly as described in paragraph 2, and pull the wires from the reverse light switch. Place a jack under the gearbox case, remove the bolts retaining the gearbox rear mounting to the floor, and remove the five bolts holding the cover to the main case. Place the gearbox in neutral, turn the gear change shaft anti-clockwise to the stop, and move it backwards to disengage it from the selectors. Withdraw the cover rearwards in a straight line, to prevent damage to the oil tube. To refit the cover, grease the inner lips of the oil seal, and ensure that the oil transfer tube is positioned with the double bend facing forward and angled upwards. Use jointing compound and a new joint between the cover and the gear case faces. Move the gearchange shaft fully backwards, rotate it anti-clockwise as far as possible, and hold it there as the cover is fitted. Whilst fitting, locate the oil transfer pipe in the hole in the gearbox. Lightly secure the cover with the bolts, and move the gearchange shaft forward and clockwise to engage it in the selector shaft slots. Tighten the cover bolts to the specified torque and refit the remaining parts in the reverse order. Refit the drain plug and fill with oil.
7 To remove the gearchange shaft, remove the rear cover, and the gearbox side cover plate. Drive out the roll pin securing the swing lever to the shaft for a short distance only, line up the pin with the reverse bias bolt hole, and drive the pin out via this hole, ensuring that the threads are not damaged. Pull the shaft forward to disengage it from the lever. To refit, oil the shaft, and grease the forward seal in the cover. Insert the shaft and secure the lever temporarily on it with a pin through the front bolt hole of the reverse plunger assembly. Drive a new roll pin in flush from the main cover side, pushing out the temporary pin as this is done. Grease the shaft socket, and refit all parts in the reverse order to dismantling.
8 The detent plungers and springs can be removed with the gearbox in the vehicle, the procedure being as described in Section 3, paragraphs 8, 70 and 71.

## 8 Gearbox (commencing Series 8 vehicles) – dismantling and reassembly

The procedure is as for the earlier gearboxes, and the information supplied in Section 13 should be followed.

## 9 Automatic transmission – general description

There are two types of automatic transmission available as an option on Avenger and Cricket models; the Borg-Warner 3-speed (type 35), and the Borg-Warner 4-speed (type 45). The automatic transmission is installed with either a 1500 cc capacity engine (early models) or a 1600 cc capacity engine (later models).
The system comprises two main components:

(a) A three element hydrokinetic torque converter coupling capable of torque multiplication at an infinitely variable ratio between approximately 2 : 1 and 1 : 1
(b) A torque/speed responsive and hydraulically operated epicyclic gearbox comprising a planetary gearset, providing three (type 35) or four (type 45) forward ratios and one reverse ratio

Due to the complexity of the automatic transmission unit, if performance is not up to standard, or overhaul is necessary, it is imperative that this be left to the local main agents who will have the special equipment for fault diagnosis and rectification. The content of the following Sections is therefore confined to supplying general information and any service information and instruction that can be used by the owner.

## 10 Automatic transmission fluid

1 It is important that transmission fluid manufactured only to the correct specification is used. Refer to the Specifications Section for details of the capacity of the complete unit. Drain and refill capacity will be less, as the torque converter cannot be completely drained, but this operation should not be necessary except for repairs. Periodic routine fluid changes are not required.
2 Every 5000 miles (8000 km) or more frequently, check the fluid level in the automatic transmission. To do this, ensure that the transmission fluid is at normal operating temperature, which will only be attained after a minimum of 6 miles (10 km) operation on the road.
3 In the case of the type 35 transmission, place the car on level ground, move the speed selector lever slowly through all positions and then select 'P'. Switch off the engine and wait two minutes for the fluid to drain from the filler tube. Withdraw the dipstick, wipe it, re-insert it, withdraw it again and read off the level. The fluid level should be between the 'low' and 'full' marks, but check on certain versions that the correct side of the dipstick is being read according to the transmission fluid temperature. The distance between the 'low' and 'full' marks represents a quantity of fluid of approximately 1 Imp pint (0.56 litres). Top up as necessary using the correct type fluid poured through the filler tube. If the unit has been drained, it is recommended that only new fluid is used. Fill up to the correct level by gradually refilling the unit. The exact amount will depend on how much was left in the converter after draining.
4 In the case of the type 45 transmission, place the car on level ground, move the selector lever slowly through all positions, finally selecting 'P'. Switch off the engine, remove the dipstick and wipe it with clean paper or lint-free cloth, and re-insert it fully. Wait 30 seconds, and then remove the dipstick, checking the level on the side marked 'hot'. If necessary, top up to the 'full' mark, repeating the foregoing procedure to check the level. If the level must be checked without taking the vehicle on the road, run the engine at fast idle for 5 minutes, and then follow the procedure given except that readings should be taken on the 'warm' side of the dipstick.

## 11 Automatic transmission – general maintenance

1 Ensure that the exterior of the converter housing and gearbox is kept clear of dust or mud or overheating will occur. Occasionally brush the air intake grilles and check that the air duct slot is clear.
2 Where automatic transmission is installed the starter motor drive is more prone to stick, due to the formation of rust on its sliding surfaces. The rust is caused by the ingress of water through the cooling air grilles. It should be a regular three monthly operation to remove the starter motor, to wash the drive in paraffin and very lightly oil it before refitting. If the starter jams on an automatic vehicle there is no easy alternative method of starting the engine.

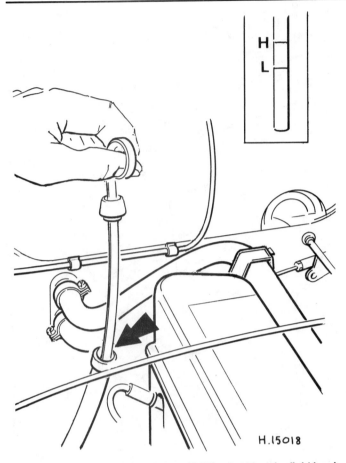

Fig. 6.6 Automatic transmission type 35 – checking the fluid level (note the direction of the dipstick hook) (Sec 10)

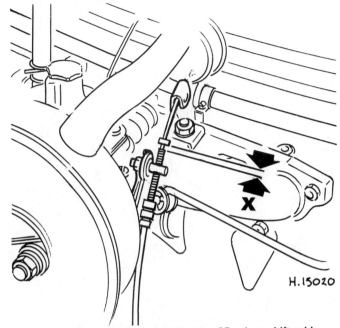

Fig. 6.8 Automatic transmission type 35 – downshift cable adjustment gap (X) (Sec 13)

the throttle pedal linkage and cable are operating correctly, particularly that with the throttle pedal fully depressed, the carburettor butterfly is fully open. If adjustment is required, refer to Chapter 3.

## 13 Automatic transmission – downshift cable renewal

1    The new cable will be supplied with its sleeve loose on the inner cable for subsequent crimping in position when installed.
2    Disconnect the cable at the carburettor end together with the securing clip.
3    Drain the fluid and retain for replenishment (speed selector in position 'P').
4    On models fitted with an oil cooler, identify and disconnect the hoses at the transmission, and plug the ends.
5    Remove the oil pan, after disconnecting the oil filler tube and its support bracket, and disconnect the downshift cable on type 35 transmissions.
6    Identify the inhibitor switch supply leads, disconnect them and remove the inhibitor switch (type 45 only).
7    From within the transmission unit remove the detent bracket and leaf spring, and the filter screen (type 45 only).
8    Remove a valve body securing bolt from the front and rear of the valve body and insert dummy threaded bolts with wing nuts. This is necessary because the valve body must be lowered sufficiently to allow access to the downshift cable operating cam (type 45 only).
9    Remove the remaining valve body securing bolts, and lower the valve body until the downshift cable can be disconnected from the cam (type 45 only).
10   Detach the downshift outer cable from the transmission housing.
11   Fitting the new cable is a reversal of the removal procedure, but adjustment must be carried out to position the inner cable crimp correctly.
12   Refill the transmission unit and operate on the road until it reaches normal temperature.
13   Switch off the engine and remove the socket screw (pressure take-off plug) located at the rear of the transmission housing just above the oil pan joint. In place of the plug, screw in a pressure gauge using an adaptor if necessary.
14   Connect a tachometer to the engine and chock the rear wheels against forward movement. Apply the handbrake.
15   Start the engine and with 'P' selected, run the engine until any transmission heat loss has been replaced.
16   Select 'D' and note the reading on the pressure gauge when the engine is at idling speed (refer to the Specifications and use a tachometer).

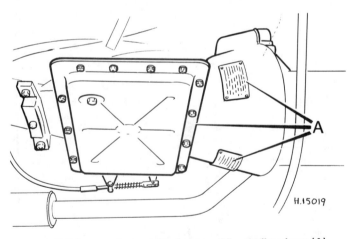

Fig. 6.7 Automatic transmission type 35 – cooling ducts (A) (Sec 11)

## 12 Automatic transmission – downshift cable adjustment

1    Ensure that the idling speed is correctly set. The correct position of the production-set crimped sleeve on the downshift cable is when a 0.030 to 0.060 in (0.76 to 1.52 mm) feeler for type 35 transmissions or a 0.010 to 0.020 in (0.25 to 0.50 mm) feeler for type 45 transmissions, will pass between its lower face and the end face of the threaded outer cable conduit.
2    Where adjustment of the downshift cable is required, slacken the locknut on the outer cable conduit and rotate as necessary. Retighten the locknut. When the adjustment has been correctly set, check that

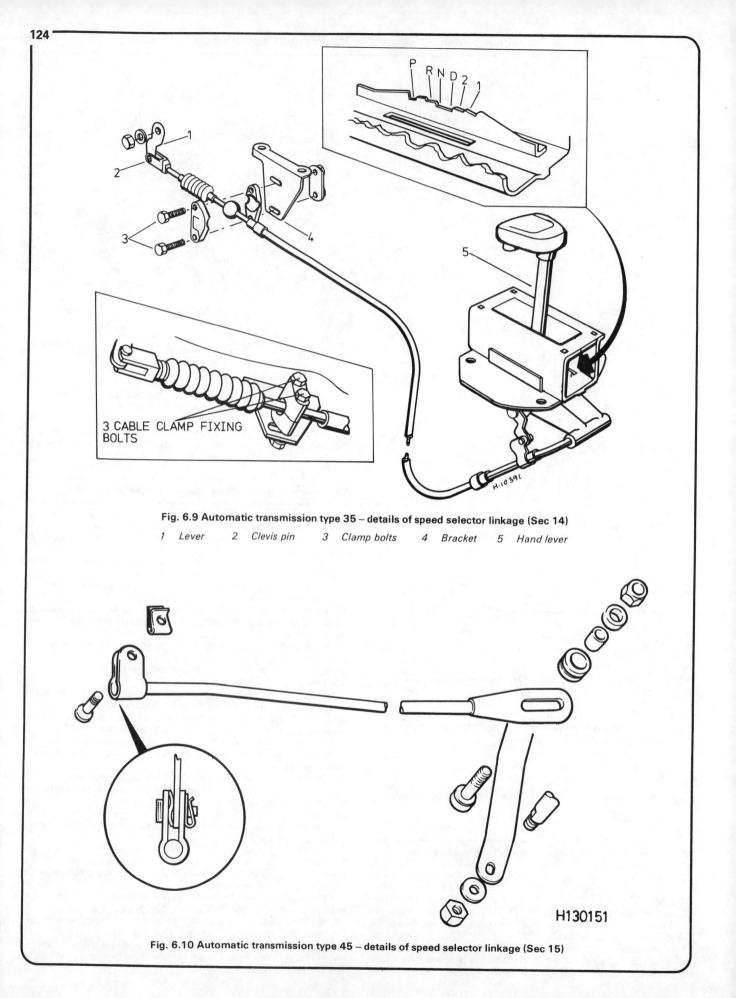

**Fig. 6.9 Automatic transmission type 35 – details of speed selector linkage (Sec 14)**

1 *Lever*    2 *Clevis pin*    3 *Clamp bolts*    4 *Bracket*    5 *Hand lever*

3 CABLE CLAMP FIXING BOLTS

H.10391

H130151

**Fig. 6.10 Automatic transmission type 45 – details of speed selector linkage (Sec 15)**

17 Increase the engine speed to 1100 rpm (type 35) or 1200 rpm (type 45) and note the pressure increase, which should be between 10 and 20 lbf/in² higher than with the engine at idling speed.

18 Adjust the downshift cable to obtain the correct pressure readings, and then recheck them following the exact sequences described in the previous paragraphs 16 and 17.

19 Securely crimp the sleeve onto the inner cable so that there will be the required gap between it and the end of the cable conduit as described in Section 12, making sure that the throttle pedal is fully released and the carburettor butterfly fully onto its stop.

20 Switch off the engine, tighten the downshift cable conduit locknut, and recheck the gap.

21 Remove the pressure gauge and refit the plug. Remove the tachometer and wheel chock, and road test for satisfactory downshift and kickdown operation.

### 14 Automatic transmission (type 35) – selector lever linkage adjustment

1 Disconnect the lower cable end from the gearbox lever, and place the lever in the 'D' position by moving it fully forward, and bringing it back three 'clicks'. Place the selector lever in the 'D' position (Fig. 6.9).

2 Slacken the clamp fixing bolts. Reconnect the cable to the gearbox lever, push the outer cable lightly forward to take up slack in the cable, and tighten the two clamp bolts. Check that a distinct click can be felt at each selector lever position.

### 15 Automatic transmission (type 45) – selector lever linkage adjustment

1 Push the hand lever into the 'P' position.

2 Underneath the vehicle, loosen the self-locking nut securing the transmission lever to the selector rod. Check that the transmission lever is in its rearmost detent by moving the lever as far backwards as possible, then rocking it to confirm that the roller is firmly in the detent.

3 With the hand lever still in the 'P' position, tighten the self-locking nut without moving the operating rod or transmission lever.

4 Move the hand lever to all positions, and check that a distinct click can be heard at each position as the detents engage. Check that the key start only operates with the hand lever in 'N' or 'P'.

### 16 Automatic transmission (type 35) – adjustment of front and rear brake bands

1 It is unlikely that adjustment of these components will be required, but if as a result of reference to Section 18 the symptoms indicate a possible need of attention, it is worth carrying out the following operations before pursuing any other course.

2 To adjust the rear band, loosen the locknut, and using an open-ended spanner of 4 in (100 mm) length (essential to ensure correct torque is not exceeded) tighten the centre adjuster bolt fully and back off one complete turn. Tighten the locknut without moving the centre bolt.

3 This method of adjustment is used as it is impossible to obtain clearance for a torque wrench. Where the transmission is removed from the vehicle, however, the adjuster bolt should be tightened to a torque of 10 lbf ft (1.4 kgf m) and then backed off one turn.

4 To adjust the front band, drain the fluid and remove the oil pan. Loosen the adjuster bolt locknut and move the servo lever outwards so that a $\frac{1}{4}$ in (6.35 mm) thick flat bar can be placed between the piston pin and the adjuster bolt contact faces. Tighten the adjuster bolt to a torque of 10 lbf ft (1.4 kgf m) only. Tighten the locknut to a torque of between 15 and 20 lbf ft (2.1 to 2.8 kgf m). Remove the bar, refit the oil pan and refill the transmission unit.

### 17 Starter inhibitor/reversing light switch (automatic transmission) – description and adjustment

1 The switch fitted to the type 45 transmission is non-adjustable. Removal is effected by disconnecting the leads, undoing the single screw, and withdrawing the switch.

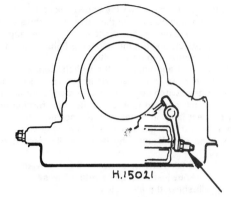

**Fig. 6.11 Automatic transmission type 35 – front band adjustment (Sec 16)**

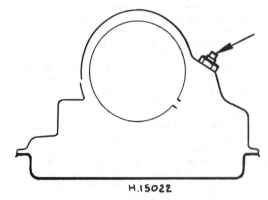

**Fig. 6.12 Automatic transmission type 35 – rear band adjustment (Sec 16)**

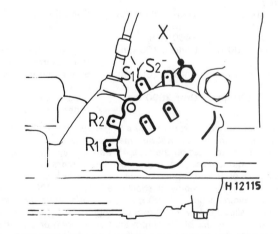

**Fig. 6.13 Automatic transmission type 45 – location of starter inhibitor/reversing light switch terminals (Sec 17)**

| | | | |
|---|---|---|---|
| R1 | Green | S2 | White/Red |
| R2 | Green/Brown | X | Switch retaining screw |
| S1 | White/Red | | |

2 The switch fitted to the type 35 transmission can be either adjustable, or in the case of later switches, non-adjustable. The adjustable switches are identifiable in that they have a locknut – also they may be found fitted either horizontally or vertically, and are directly replaceable by the later non-adjustable switch in either position.

3 To adjust the early type, place the speed selector lever in the 'D' position, and identify and disconnect the cables from the switch, which is screwed into the side of the transmission. The angled Lucar terminals on the switch are for the reversing lights, and the vertical terminals for the solenoid inhibitor switch.

4 Loosen the locknut and unscrew the switch. Connect a test lamp in series with the reverse switch angled terminals and switch on the ignition. Screw in the switch until the lamp just goes out and mark the position of the switch body in relation to the transmission housing.

5 Connect the test lamp in series with the solenoid inhibitor switch vertical terminals; with the ignition switched on, the lamp should not light. Screw in the switch until the lamp just lights and mark this second position.

6 Unscrew the switch midway between the two marked positions and tighten the locknut just enough to retain the switch in position. Overtightening will shear the alloy stem.

7 Reconnect the paired cables to their correct terminals on the switch, and check that the starter motor operates only with the selector lever in 'P' or 'N'; also that the reversing lights only operate with the lever in the 'R' position.

## 18 Automatic transmission – performance testing

1 The following procedures are given to enable the owner to satisfy himself that the transmission is operating correctly. It is not intended that he should diagnose or rectify faults, but a detailed report of the nature of the malfunction may enable a main dealer to quickly ascertain the trouble at reduced cost to the owner. Before carrying out the tests, ensure that the fluid level, and other adjustments described earlier, are correct.

2 A stall test, to determine that the torque converter and gearbox are operating satisfactorily, should be carried out on the type 35 transmission by first checking the engine condition. An engine not developing full power will affect the stall test readings.

3 Allow the engine and transmission to reach correct working temperature, connect a tachometer to the vehicle, chock the wheels and apply the handbrake and footbrake.

4 Select '1' or 'R' and depress the throttle to the 'kickdown' position. Note the reading on the tachometer, and compare the results with the following table:

| Single carburettor models | Twin carburettor models | Condition of transmission |
|---|---|---|
| 2000 rpm | 2400 rpm | Normal |
| Under 1800 rpm | Under 2100 rpm | Engine underpowered and requires tuning |
| Under 1500 rpm | Under 1700 rpm | Stator one-way clutch slipping |
| Over 2200 rpm | Over 2600 rpm | Transmission or converter slipping |

**Note**: *Do not carry out a stall test for a longer period than 10 seconds, otherwise the transmission will become overheated.*

5 Carry out a stall test on the type 45 transmission by making the initial preparations discussed in the preceding paragraphs.

6 Select 'D' or 'R' and depress the throttle to the kick-down position. The reading on the tachometer should be between 2300 and 2650 rpm. If the reading is below 1800 rpm suspect the converter of stator sprag clutch slip; if below 2100 rpm the engine is not developing full power, and if in excess of 2800 rpm the transmission or converter is slipping. **Note**: *Do not carry out a stall test for a longer period than 10 seconds, or the transmission will become overheated. Consecutive tests must be separated by at least 30 minutes.*

7 An inability to start on steep gradients, combined with poor acceleration from rest and low stall speed (1000 rpm), indicates that the converter stator uni-directional clutch is slipping. This condition permits the stator to rotate in an opposite direction to the impeller and turbine, and torque multiplication cannot occur. Poor acceleration in high gear above 30 mph (48 kph) and reduced maximum speed indicate that the stator uni-directional clutch has seized. The stator will not rotate with the turbine and impeller and the 'fluid flywheel' phase cannot occur. This condition will also be indicated by excessive overheating of the transmission although the stall speed will be correct.

## 19 Automatic transmission (type 35) – road test procedure

1 Check that the engine will only start with the selector lever in 'P' or 'N' and that the reverse light operates only in 'R'.

2 Apply the handbrake, and with the engine idling select 'N' – 'D', 'N' – 'R' and 'N' – '2', 'N' – '1'. Engagement should be positive.

3 With the transmission at normal running temperature select 'D', release the brakes and accelerate with minimum throttle. Check 1 – 2 and 2 – 3 shift speeds and quality of change.

4 Stop the vehicle, select 'D' and restart, using full throttle. Check 1 – 2 and 2 – 3 shift speeds and quality of change.

5 At 25 mph (40 kph) apply 'full throttle'. The vehicle should accelerate in third gear and should not downshift to second.

6 At a maximum of 45 mph (72 kph) kickdown fully, when the transmission should downshift to second.

7 At a maximum of 31 mph (50 kph) in third gear kickdown fully. The transmission should downshift to first gear.

8 Stop the vehicle, select 'D' and restart using kickdown. Check the 1 – 2 and 2 – 3 shift speeds.

9 At 40 mph (64 mph) in third gear, select '2' and release the throttle. Check 3 – 2 downshift and engine braking.

10 With the '2' still engaged stop the vehicle and accelerate to over 25 mph (40 kph) kickdown. Check for slip, 'squawk' and absence of upshifts.

11 Stop the vehicle and select 'R'. Reverse using full throttle if possible. Check for slip and clutch 'squawk'.

12 Stop the vehicle on a gradient. Apply the handbrake and select 'P'. Check the parking pawl hold when the handbrake is released. Turn the vehicle around and repeat the procedure. Check that the selector lever is held firmly in the gate in 'P'.

## 20 Automatic transmission (type 45) – road test procedure

1 Check that the engine will only start with the selector lever in 'P' or 'N', and that the reverse light operates only in 'R'.

2 Apply the handbrake and, with the engine idling, select 'N' – 'R' and 'N' – 'D'. Engagement should be positive and felt.

3 With the transmission at normal running temperature select 'D', release the brakes and accelerate with minimum throttle. Check 1 – 2, 2 – 3 and 3 – 4 shift speeds and compare the results with the information given in the Specifications. The 3 – 4 shift may be difficult to detect, in which case manually select '3' at the 3 – 4 shift speed range. If a slight increase in engine speed occurs, the transmission was engaged in 4th speed.

4 With 'D' selected and 4th speed engaged, decelerate and check the 4 – 3 and 3 – 1 shift speeds.

5 Stop the vehicle, select 'R', release the brakes and reverse with light and then full throttle to check the reverse driven operation with particular reference to slip.

6 Stop the vehicle, select 'D' and restart, using full throttle. Check 1 – 2, 2 – 3, and 3 – 4 shift speeds and quality of change. Compare with the Specifications.

7 At 45 mph (73 kph) release the throttle and select '3'. There should be an immediate 4 – 3 shift change.

8 At 30 mph (48 kph) in 3rd speed release the throttle and select '2'. The 3 – 2 shift change should occur as the speed falls.

9 Stop the vehicle and accelerate from standstill with the throttle pedal fully depressed to the kickdown position. Check the 1 – 2, 2 – 3 and 3 – 4 shift speeds and quality of change. Compare with the Specifications.

10 As speed reduces, check that the kickdown changes are obtainable within the speed ranges given in Specifications. To do this, ascertain the gear engaged by manually engaging 3rd or 2nd as previously described, and then, within the speed range given, fully depress the throttle pedal to the kickdown position.

11 Stop the vehicle on a gradient. Apply the handbrake and select 'P'. Check the parking pawl hold when the handbrake is released. Turn the vehicle around and repeat the procedure. Check that the selector lever is held firmly in the gate in 'P'.

12 Select 1/2 from standstill and drive away, checking that the transmission does not change up to 3rd. Similarly select '3' from standstill and drive away, checking that the transmission does not change up to 4th.

### 21 Automatic transmission (type 35) – removal and refitting

1 Suspected faults should be referred to the main agent for confirmation on specialist equipment, before the unit is removed from the vehicle.
2 Removal is similar to the procedure described for removal of the manually operated gearbox in this Chapter but with the following differences.
3 Drain the fluid into a container of adequate size.
4 Disconnect the downshift cable from its connection at the carburettor and from its converter housing support bracket.
5 Disconnect the leads from the starter inhibitor/reversing light switch (wider terminals for reversing lights).
6 Disconnect the speed selector cable at the operating lever by removing the split pin and clevis pin.
7 Unscrew and remove the upper bolts which secure the torque converter housing to the engine, noting that two of these bolts secure the starter motor and engine earthing strap.
8 Unscrew the bolt from the filler tube upper support bracket and then, with earlier models, unscrew the filler tube coupling nut and remove from the transmission. Plug the open hole with a piece of rag. With later models the filler tube is a snap-in fit in the transmission housing and simply requires a sharp pull to remove it. Retain the sealing O-ring.
9 Remove the semi-circular plate which covers the lower half of the torque converter housing and unscrew and remove the bolts which secure the torque converter to the crankshaft drive plate. These bolts are accessible one at a time by rotating the engine with a spanner applied to the crankshaft pulley bolt.
10 Support the rear of the engine sump on a jack and place a trolley jack under the base of the transmission oil pan. Use a piece of wood between the jack and oil pan to prevent damage.
11 Remove the remaining torque converter housing to engine securing bolts, and lower and withdraw the transmission unit as for a manually operated gearbox.
12 Refitting is the reverse of removal. If the torque converter has been removed, it will be necessary before installation to align the front drive tangs with the slots in the inner gear and then slide the torque converter into position. Take great care not to damage the oil seal.
13 When installation is complete check and adjust the speed selector cable, the downshift cable setting and the operation of the starter inhibitor/reverse light switch.
14 Refill the unit with the correct quantity of fluid.

### 22 Automatic transmission (type 45) – removal and refitting

1 Note paragraph 1 of the preceding Section. Place the car over a pit or on ramps, as considerable clearance is required beneath the car to allow the torque converter to clear the body.

2 Disconnect the battery negative terminal.
3 Drain the radiator and disconnect the top hose.
4 Disconnect the downshift cable from its connection at the carburettor.
5 Mark the propeller shaft rear flange in relation to the rear axle input flange, unscrew and remove the securing bolts and withdraw the propeller shaft from the transmission.
6 Drain the transmission fluid into a container of adequate size by loosening the oil filler tube union nut; when completed detach the oil filler tube from the transmission and support bracket and withdraw it.
7 Disconnect the oil cooler pipe unions at the transmission, and plug the pipe ends to prevent entry of dirt.
8 Unscrew and remove the exhaust manifold flange nuts and, on twin carburettor models, disconnect the exhaust downpipe-to-exhaust pipe joint. Lower the front section of the exhaust pipe.
9 Disconnect the throttle linkage at the carburettor and bulkhead.
10 Unbolt and remove the transmission guard plate, and remove the sump stiffener brackets and dirt shield.
11 Note the location of the selector rod on the transmission lever, mark its position in the elongated adjustment slot, and disconnect the rod from the lever.
12 Identify and disconnect the leads from the starter inhibitor/reversing light switch. Release them from the retaining clip.
13 Disconnect the speedometer cable and tie it up out of the way.
14 Remove the bolts which secure the torque converter to the crankshaft driveplate. These bolts are accessible one at a time by rotating the engine with a socket spanner on the crankshaft pulley bolt. If necessary jam the starter ring gear with a screwdriver.
15 Support the rear of the engine sump on a jack. Place a trolley jack under the base of the transmission oil pan. Use a piece of wood of cradle construction between the jack and the pan to prevent damage.
16 Remove the rear crossmember mounting bolts, insulating rubber and sleeves.
17 Unscrew and remove the remaining torque converter housing-to-engine securing bolts, but leave the starter motor bolts in position. Note the location of the engine earthing strap.
18 Lower the jacks together, until the weight of the transmission is just supported. A further jack placed under the front of engine sump will prevent the engine lifting when the transmission is removed.
19 Withdraw the transmission unit, making sure that the torque converter disengages from the driveplate and stays fully engaged with the transmission oil pump, otherwise there will be considerable loss of fluid and possible damage to the torque converter oil seal. The use of a cranked lever or length of wood will help during this operation.
20 Refitting is the reverse of removal. If the torque converter has been removed, it will be necessary before installation to align the front drive tangs with the slots in the inner gear and then slide the torque converter into position. Make sure that the oil seal is not damaged.
21 Refill the unit with the correct quantity of fluid, and carry out the necessary adjustments to the downshift cable and the selector lever linkage.

### 23 Fault diagnosis – manual gearbox

| Symptom | Reason(s) |
| --- | --- |
| Weak or ineffective synchromesh | Wear in baulk ring or synchro hubs |
| Jumping out of gear | Weak detent spring<br>Selector fork wear<br>Worn gears |
| Noisy and rough operation | Worn bearings<br>Oil level too low<br>Wrong grade of oil used<br>Worn or damaged gear teeth |
| Noisy and difficult gear engagement | Clutch faults |

**Note:** *It can be difficult to decide whether to remove and dismantle a gearbox for a fault which is only a minor irritant. Gearboxes which howl, or where the synchromesh can be 'beaten' by a quick gear change, may continue to perform for a long time in this state. A worn gearbox usually needs a complete rebuild to eliminate noise because the various gears, if re-aligned on new bearings, will continue to howl when different wearing surfaces are presented to each other. It may, therefore, be decided that the noise or malfunction will be ignored until a replacement gearbox can be afforded.*

## 24  Fault diagnosis – automatic transmission

| Symptom | Reason(s) |
| --- | --- |
| Speed shifts too high or too low | Driveshaft cable incorrectly adjusted |
| No kick-down | Downshift cable incorrectly adjusted |
| No forward or reverse drive | Low fluid level |
| Transmission slip | Low fluid level<br>Downshift cable disconnected |

**Note**: *Refer also to Section 18*

# Chapter 7 Propeller shaft

## Contents

## Specifications

### Propeller shaft type
Manual transmission ........................................................  Single steel tube, damped
Automatic transmission ...................................................  Single steel tube, undamped

### Universal joints type ............................................  Needle roller bearing, sealed

### Torque wrench settings

|  | lbf ft | Nm |
|---|---|---|
| Propeller shaft flange nuts ........................................... | 17 | 23 |

## 1  General description

The drive from the gearbox to the rear axle is via a tubular propeller shaft. With the need to accommodate angular variations of the rear axle relative to the gearbox, universal joints are fitted to each end of the shaft. This movement also varies the distance between the rear axle and gearbox, and this is absorbed by the splined sleeve at the front of the propeller shaft sliding on the gearbox mainshaft. The sleeve runs in an oil seal in the gearbox rear cover, and is supported by the gearbox rear bearing. The splines are lubricated by oil from the gearbox.

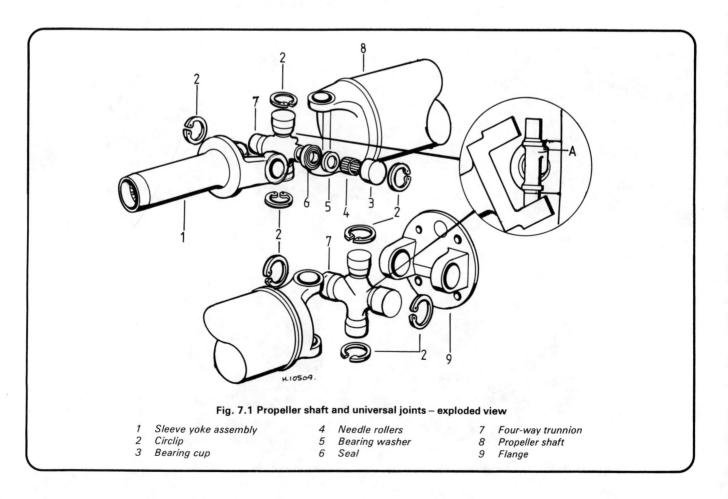

**Fig. 7.1 Propeller shaft and universal joints – exploded view**

| | | | | | |
|---|---|---|---|---|---|
| 1 | Sleeve yoke assembly | 4 | Needle rollers | 7 | Four-way trunnion |
| 2 | Circlip | 5 | Bearing washer | 8 | Propeller shaft |
| 3 | Bearing cup | 6 | Seal | 9 | Flange |

The universal joints each comprise a four-way trunnion, or 'spider', each leg of which runs in a needle roller bearing race, prepacked with grease and fitted into the bearing journal yokes of the sliding sleeve and propeller shaft and flange. The joints are renewable as a kit. All universal joints are of the sealed type and require no maintenance.

## 2    Routine maintenance

1    No lubrication of the universal joints is required as they are prepacked with grease. The sliding sleeve on the forward end of the propeller shaft is lubricated from the gearbox.
2    A periodic check of the universal joints and the rear flange bolts is recommended.

## 3    Propeller shaft – removal, inspection and refitting

1    Raise the rear of the car and support it on stands.
2    The propeller shaft is connected to the rear axle by a flange held by four nuts and bolts. Mark the flanges relative to each other and undo the bolts.
3    Move the propeller shaft forward to disengage it from the pinion flanges and lower it to the ground.
4    Draw the splined sleeve out of the rear of the gearbox cover. Do not permit it to fall.
5    Place a receptacle under the gearbox rear cover to catch the oil which will come out if the gearbox is tilted.
6    Examine the bore of the two flanges which mate at the rear. If they are damaged or a slack fit eccentric running of the shaft at the flange can occur, causing vibration in the drive. If vibration exists, but with no obvious defect, reconnect the flanges with one turned through 180° relative to the other. This may stop the vibration.
7    Refit in the reverse order. Clean the sliding sleeve and invert it carefully into the gearbox end cover, taking care that the oil cover seal is not damaged.

8    Connect the flanges in accordance with the marks made, and fit the bolts with their heads towards the universal joint.
9    Check and, if necessary, top up the gearbox oil level.

## 4    Universal joints – inspection, removal and refitting

1    With the propeller shaft still on the car, grasp each side of the universal joint and, with a twisting action, attempt to reveal any backlash in the joint. Rock up and down, and recheck. If any play is observed the joint must be renewed.
2    To renew a joint, remove the propeller shaft as described in Section 3.
3    Clean all dirt from the bearings on the yokes. Remove the circlips using a pair of contracting circlip pliers. If they are very tight, tap the bearing race inside the circlip with a drift and hammer to relieve the pressure (photo).
4    With the circlips removed, tap the joints at the yoke with a soft hammer. The bearings and races will then come out of their housings. If they are tight, they can be gripped in a self-locking wrench for final removal (assuming that they are to be renewed). Disengage the four-way trunnion (photos).
5    Fitting the new trunnions, needle rollers and races is the reversal of the removal procedure. Keep the grease seals on the inner ends of each trunnion as dry as possible. Locate the journal in the yoke as shown at 'A' in the inset to Fig. 7.1. Place the needles in each race, fill the race one-third full with grease, place it over the trunnion and tap home with a brass drift. Any grease exuding from the further bearing journal after three have been fitted should be renewed before fitting the fourth race. Refit the circlips, ensuring that they are properly located in their grooves (photos).
6    In cases of extreme wear, the bearing housings in the propeller shaft, sliding sleeve or rear flange may be so worn that the bearing cups are too loose to fit. In such cases, the affected item must be renewed. Ensure also that there is not excessive backlash of the sliding sleeve on the gearbox shaft.
7    Refit the propeller shaft.

4.3 Tap the race to release the circlip

4.4a Using a self-locking wrench to remove the bearing

4.4b Disengaging the trunnion

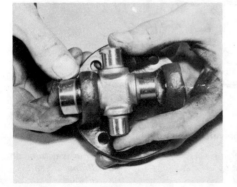

4.5a Refitting the needle races

4.5b Refitting a circlip

## 5   Fault diagnosis – propeller shaft

| Symptom | Reason(s) |
| --- | --- |
| Vibration | Propeller shaft distorted or out of balance<br>Backlash in splined shaft<br>Loose flange securing bolts<br>Worn universal joint bearings |
| Noise when taking up drive | Loose rear flange bolts<br>Worn universal joint bearings<br>Worn differential gears in rear axle<br>Loose roadwheel nuts |

# Chapter 8  Rear axle

**Contents**

**Specifications**

**Type** .................................................................................... Semi-floating, hypoid bevel gears

**Ratio identification**
Early models:
    1250 engine ...................................................................... 4.37 : 1
    1500 engine ...................................................................... 3.89 : 1
Later models:
    Up to and including 6 Series models .................................. The second letter or number in the 'Service Code' box on the chassis identification plate indicates the rear axle ratio
    7 Series models and onwards ............................................ The third from last number of the 'Vehicle Service Number' on the chassis identification plate indicates the rear axle ratio

| Code number or letter | Ratio |
|---|---|
| A ............................................................ | 3.89 : 1 (1500 engine) |
| N ............................................................ | 4.37 : 1 (1250 engine) |
|  | 3.89 : 1 (1500 engine) |
| 1 and 2 .................................................. | 4.37 : 1 |
| 3 and 4 .................................................. | 4.11 : 1 |
| 5 and 6 .................................................. | 3.89 : 1 |
| 7 and 8 .................................................. | 3.70 : 1 |
| 9 and 0 .................................................. | 3.54 : 1 |

**Number of teeth**

| | Ratio | | | | |
|---|---|---|---|---|---|
| | 3.89 : 1 | 4.37 : 1 | 4.11 : 1 | 3.70 : 1 | 3.54 : 1 |
| Crownwheel | 35 | 35 | 37 | 37 | 39 |
| Pinion | 9 | 8 | 9 | 10 | 11 |

**Road speed (in top gear, per 1000 rpm of the engine)**

| | mph | km/h |
|---|---|---|
| With 4.37 : 1 axle ratio | 15.5 | 25 |
| With 4.11 : 1 axle ratio | 16 | 26 |
| With 3.89 : 1 axle ratio | 17 | 27 |
| With 3.70 : 1 axle ratio | 17.5 | 28 |
| With 3.54 : 1 axle ratio | 18.5 | 30 |

**Bearings**
Pinion and differential ............................................................... Taper roller
Rear wheel hub .......................................................................... Ball with combined oil seal

**Adjustment**
Crownwheel to pinion backlash .................................................. 0.005 to 0.009 in (0.13 to 0.23 mm)

**Oil capacity** ........................................................................ 1.5 Imp pints (0.85 litres)

**Torque wrench settings**

| | lbf ft | Nm |
|---|---|---|
| Halfshaft retaining plate | 18 | 24 |
| Rear cover securing bolt | 14 | 19 |
| Panhard rod to frame | 44 | 59 |
| Panhard rod to axle | 32 | 43 |

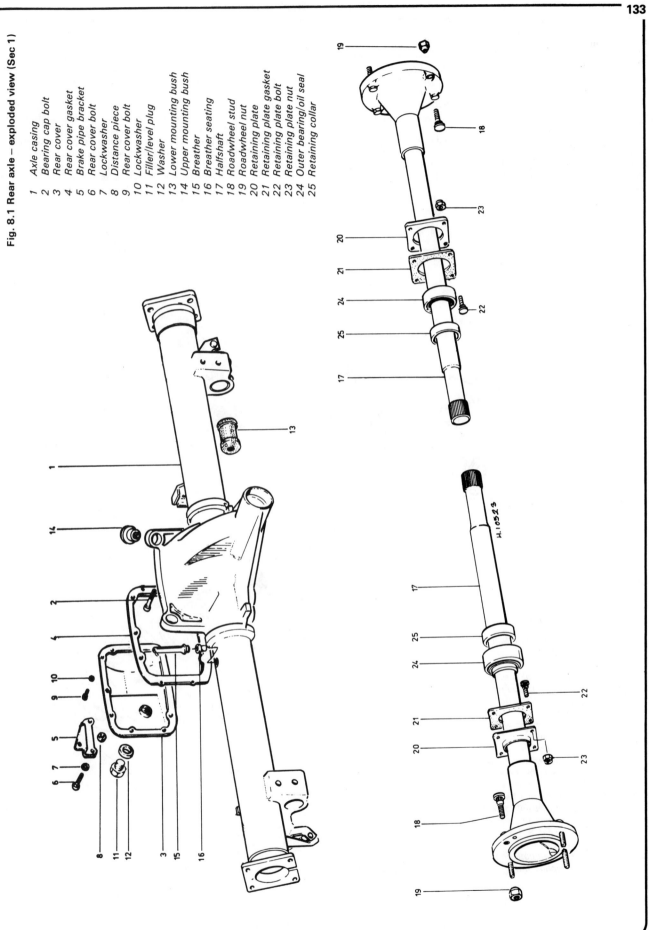

Fig. 8.1 Rear axle – exploded view (Sec 1)

1  Axle casing
2  Bearing cap bolt
3  Rear cover
4  Rear cover gasket
5  Brake pipe bracket
6  Rear cover bolt
7  Lockwasher
8  Distance piece
9  Rear cover bolt
10 Lockwasher
11 Filler/level plug
12 Washer
13 Lower mounting bush
14 Upper mounting bush
15 Breather
16 Breather seating
17 Halfshaft
18 Roadwheel stud
19 Roadwheel nut
20 Retaining plate
21 Retaining plate gasket
22 Retaining plate bolt
23 Retaining plate nut
24 Outer bearing/oil seal
25 Retaining collar

## 1  General description

The semi-floating axle incorporates a hypoid gear final drive. The unit construction axle casing embodies a differential carrier and welded-in axle tubes. The casing has four rubber bushed mounting points to which the suspension links are attached. The pinion is carried on two taper roller bearings adjusted to a specified preload by a compressible spacer.

A single, cast, differential unit with hypoid gear assembly is carried in the axle casing by adjustable taper roller bearings. Crownwheel-to-pinion meshing is accurately attained by the use of lockable screwed adjusters. Thrust washers are fitted between the differential gears and casing. The halfshafts are one piece flanged forgings, each carried on sealed, combined ball-bearings and oil seals. No provision is made for regular draining. A plastic breather unit is located on the top of the right-hand axle tube.

## 2  Routine maintenance

1    Every 5000 miles (8000 km) clean the area around the rear axle filler plug (Fig. 8.3) ensure that the car is standing level and remove the plug. If necessary, add gear oil to bring the level up to the filler plug threads. Although regular oil changes are not specified, it is considered good policy to do this at 25 000 mile intervals to remove metal particles resulting from normal wear. Drain when the oil is warm after a run by removing the cover bolts and pulling away the rear cover (Fig. 8.1). Some oil will remain in the base and this should be mopped from the casing. Refit the rear cover, using a new gasket and noting carefully the location of the longer bolts. Tighten the bolts to the specified torque and refill the unit. Refit the filler plug.
2    Check that the breather is clear, to avoid pressure build-up and the consequent loss of oil, past the hub seals.

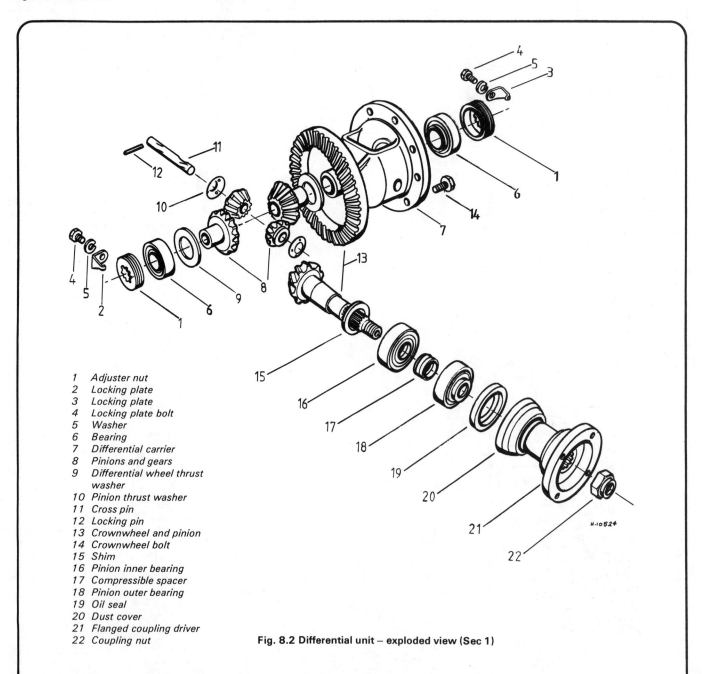

1    Adjuster nut
2    Locking plate
3    Locking plate
4    Locking plate bolt
5    Washer
6    Bearing
7    Differential carrier
8    Pinions and gears
9    Differential wheel thrust
      washer
10   Pinion thrust washer
11   Cross pin
12   Locking pin
13   Crownwheel and pinion
14   Crownwheel bolt
15   Shim
16   Pinion inner bearing
17   Compressible spacer
18   Pinion outer bearing
19   Oil seal
20   Dust cover
21   Flanged coupling driver
22   Coupling nut

Fig. 8.2 Differential unit – exploded view (Sec 1)

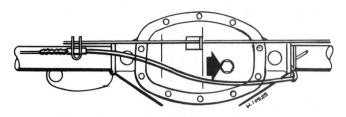

Fig. 8.3 Rear axle filler/level plug (Sec 2)

### 3  Rear axle and road springs – removal and refitting

1    Chock the front wheels, jack up the rear of the vehicle and place the stands under the jacking points. Place a jack under the differential housing.
2    Remove the roadwheels, and disconnect the Panhard rod (estate cars only).
3    Mark the pinion and propeller shaft flanges to ensure exact refitting.
4    Remove the four flange coupling bolts and tie the propeller shaft to one side. Avoid the propeller shaft moving rearwards or the front sliding joint will become disengaged from the rear of the gearbox.
5    On saloon cars, release the handbrake and detach the clevis pin from the handbrake lever below the floor. Detach the rubber boot from the handbrake outer cable and the outer cable from its abutment and retainer. On estate cars, loosen the nut on the yoke of the main cable to the compensator, withdraw the clevis pin and unscrew the yoke and nut. Undo the clip on the vehicle body and pull the cable forward from the abutment on the axle tube.
6    Place a piece of polythene underneath the cap of the brake master cylinder, disconnect the brake flexible hose (see Chapter 9) and plug the line to prevent the ingress of dirt.
7    Disconnect the hydraulic damper lower mountings and carefully lower the axle jack sufficiently to permit removal of the coil springs (Fig. 8.4).
8    Slacken the upper front pivot nuts and bolts.
9    Remove the four nuts and bolts which connect the suspension links to the axle pivot points.
10   Push the upper links off the axle. Lower the axle carefully and draw it rearwards off the lower links.
11   Refitting is largely a reversal of the removal procedure. When refitting the coil springs, ensure that the sealing rubber is correctly located. Employ a spring compression clamp on one side of the spring,

Fig. 8.4 Rear coil spring removal (Sec 3)

tightened just enough to give it a slight curve, and place the spring into position with the compressor facing towards the front of the vehicle and the adjuster end through the centre hole in the lower link. Raise the axle until the shock absorber can be connected. Progressively release the spring compressor, allowing the spring to engage its seat properly.
12   Refit the propeller shaft, ensuring that the flange marks are aligned. Tighten the pivot nuts and bolts to the specified torque with the vehicle standing level on its wheels.
13   Remove the polythene from the brake master cylinder, bleed the brakes and refill the axle with the correct oil.

### 4  Halfshafts – removal and refitting

1    Chock the front wheels of the car and jack up the rear under the differential casing, taking care that the jack does not bear upon the lower lip of the axle cover or it may be distorted, causing oil leakage.
2    Remove the rear roadwheel and brake drum and brush the dirt from the brake backing plate and axle flange.
3    Remove the four self-locking nuts which secure the halfshaft plate (Fig. 8.1).
4    A slide hammer attached to the roadwheel studs will now normally be required. However; refitting a roadwheel and tapping the inner side with a wooden or rubber faced hammer will remove the halfshaft from its housing without damaging the wheel. Place a short plank of wood across the rim and tap firmly but equally along its length.
5    Never lever the shaft out against the brake backing plate or the plate will be distorted.
6    Refit ensuring that the shaft is quite clean and lightly lubricated.
7    Check the condition of the brake backplate gasket and renew if necessary.
8    Smear sealant on the outer surface of the bearing. Pass the halfshaft into the casing, keeping it level and rotating slightly until the splines on the shaft engage with the differential gear.
9    Push the shaft in, and engage the outer bearing in its recess in the casing.
10   Position the halfshaft retaining plate over the four securing studs and gently drive the halfshaft fully home.
11   Fit the four self-locking nuts and tighten in the specified torque. Do not use the retaining plate as a means of drawing in the halfshaft, or excessive endfloat will be apparent on final assembly.
12   Fit the brake drum and roadwheel. Lower the car. The loss of oil during halfshaft removal and refitting is normally small, but a check should be made.

### 5  Halfshaft outer bearings and oil seals

These are of combined type and must be renewed as an assembly when failure occurs. The combined bearings/oil seals are a press fit on the halfshaft and removal and fitting should be left to a garage having the appropriate press and gauge. The security of the halfshaft is solely dependent upon the interference fit of the bearing on the halfshaft and the importance of correct fitting within the specified tolerances cannot be over-emphasised.

### 6  Pinion oil seal, removal and refitting with axle in position

1    Jack up the rear of the car and support the axle on stands.
2    Mark the propeller shaft and pinion coupling flanges to ensure exact refitting.
3    Remove the four coupling bolts, detach the propeller shaft at the axle pinion flange and tie the propeller shaft to one side.
4    Remove both rear wheels and brake drums to eliminate drag.
5    Wind a cord round the pinion flange coupling and, exerting a steady pull, note the reading on a spring balance as shown in Fig. 8.5. The reading indicates the pinion bearing preload.
6    Mark the coupling in relation to the pinion splines for exact refitting.
7    Hold the pinion coupling flange still with a length of flat steel bolted to it, and unscrew and remove the self-locking nut. Using a suitable two- or three-legged puller, withdraw the coupling flange from the pinion shaft splines.

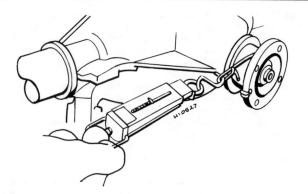

**Fig. 8.5 Bevel pinion bearing – preload check (Sec 6)**

8   Remove the defective oil seal by drifting in one side of the seal as far as it will go to force the opposite side of the seal from the housing (see Fig. 8.6). Hook out the seal.
9   Fit the new oil seal, having greased the mating surfaces of the seal and the axle housing. The flanges of the seal must face inwards. Using a piece of brass or copper tubing of suitable diameter, carefully drive the seal into the axle housing (Fig. 8.7). Make sure that the end of the pinion is not knocked during this operation.
10  Refit the coupling to its original position on the pinion splines after first having located the dust cover.
11  Fit a new pinion nut and, holding the coupling still with the screwdriver or tyre lever, tighten the nut until the pinion endfloat only just disappears. Do not overtighten, or overcompression of the spacer will result in it being necessary to dismantle the axle to fit a new one.
12  Rotate the pinion to settle the bearings. Check the preload using the cord and spring balance method previously described and by slight adjustment of the nut and rotation of the pinion obtain a pre-load figure to match that which applied before dismantling.
13  Remove the two holding bolts and refit the propeller shaft making sure to align the mating marks. Refit the brake drums and roadwheels. Lower the car to the ground.

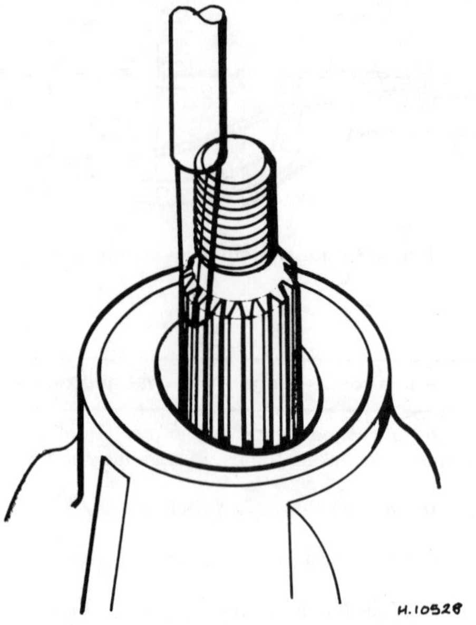

## 7   Differential unit

It is not within the scope of the home mechanic to service the differential unit due to the need for special tools and gauges. It is therefore recommended that the complete assembly is removed and taken to a specialist repairer or exchanged for a factory replacement.

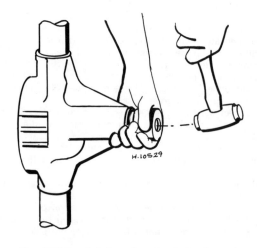

**Fig. 8.6 Bevel pinion oil seal removal (Sec 6)**

**Fig. 8.7 Bevel pinion oil seal refitting (Sec 6)**

## 8   Fault diagnosis – rear axle

| Symptom | Reason(s) |
|---|---|
| Vibration | Worn axleshaft bearing<br>Loose pinion flange bolts<br>Roadwheels out of balance<br>Propeller shaft out of balance |
| Noise on turns | Worn differential gear<br>Worn or incorrectly adjusted crownwheel and pinion |
| Noise on acceleration or deceleration | Excessive backlash in differential gears<br>Worn axleshaft splines<br>Worn propeller shaft joints<br>Loose pinion flange bolts |

# Chapter 9 Braking system

## Contents

## Specifications

**Type** .......................................................... Hydraulic; single or dual circuit; all-drum or disc front, drum rear; cable operated handbrake to rear wheels

**Master cylinder**
Type .......................................................... Single or tandem, depending on model
Diameter .......................................................... 0.625 in (15.9 mm), 0.75 in (19.0 mm) or 0.812 in (20.6 mm) depending on model

**Servo type** .......................................................... 28 or 38 depending on model
*For identification purposes, note that the outside diameter of the type 28 servo unit is 7 in (178 mm) and that of the type 38 is 8 in (203 mm)*

**Rear wheel cylinder diameter** .......................................................... 0.625 in (15.9 mm), 0.6875 in (17.4 mm), 0.7 in (17.8 mm) or 0.75 in (19.0 mm) depending on model

**Front wheel cylinder diameter (all-drum system)** .......... 0.75 in (19.0 mm)

**Brake disc run-out (max)** .......................................................... 0.004 in (0.1 mm)

**Brake pad minimum thickness** .......................................................... $\frac{1}{8}$ in (3 mm) of friction material

**Shoe lining minimum thickness** .......................................................... 0.04 in (1 mm) above rivet heads

## Torque wrench settings

| | lbf ft | Nm |
|---|---|---|
| Disc to hub ....................................................................................... | 33 | 45 |
| Caliper to stub axle carrier ............................................................... | 60 | 81 |
| Backplate to axle casing ................................................................... | 18 | 24 |
| Pressure differential warning actuator: | | |
|    Plug to body ................................................................................. | 16 to 20 | 22 to 27 |
|    Adaptor to body ............................................................................ | 16 to 20 | 22 to 27 |
| Tandem master cylinder, tipping valve nut ........................................ | 35 to 40 | 47 to 54 |
| Handbrake fixing to body .................................................................. | 15 | 20 |
| Backplate to stub axle (all-drum system) ......................................... | 46 | 62 |

## 1 General description

The braking system may consist of either disc brakes at the front wheels and drum brakes at the rear or, in certain cases, drum brakes on all wheels. The brakes are operated by application of a front pedal attached to a hydraulic cylinder. The hydraulic pressure is then distributed through rigid and flexible brake pipes to the operating cylinders at the wheels. In some countries safety regulations require a dual system, and this is fitted to Avenger models by installing an in-line tandem master cylinder. This operates through separate front and rear pipe circuits to give 50 per cent braking efficiency even in the event of a failure in either a front or rear brake. A vacuum servo unit is available as a factory option. A mechanically operated handbrake operates on the rear wheels only.

The all-drum brake layout has front brakes of the two leading shoe type. Each shoe is actuated by an individual wheel cylinder and adjustment is provided by an eccentric pin terminating in a squared adjuster on the brake backplate. The rear brakes comprise leading and trailing shoes actuated by a double acting wheel cylinder. A single wedge type adjuster is used and adjustment of the rear shoes automatically adjusts the handbrake.

## 2 Routine maintenace

1  On disc/drum layouts, no adjustment of the brakes is required. Wear in the front pads is taken up by fluid in the hydraulic system. The rear shoes are automatically adjusted by the action of the handbrake.

2  Every 5000 miles (8000 km) remove a front wheel and check the thickness of the disc pads. They should be renewed when the friction material has been reduced to $\frac{1}{8}$ in (3 mm) thick. At a similar mileage remove a rear wheel and brake drum and examine the brake linings. The shoes should be renewed before the rivets are flush with the friction material surface, or scoring of the drum is inevitable. In practice if the linings are less than $\frac{1}{16}$ in (1 mm) above the rivets, the shoe should be renewed.

3  To adjust the brakes on all-drum layouts, chock the rear wheels and apply the handbrake. Raise one front wheel at a time and rotate each of the two adjusters on the brake backplate in the normal direction of wheel rotation until each brake shoe is locked against the drum. Back off each adjuster until the wheel will revolve without drag. Depress the brake pedal hard several times to centralise the shoes and recheck the adjustment. To adjust the rear brakes, chock the front wheels, release the handbrake, and raise one rear wheel at a time. There is only one adjuster on each backplate and they must be rotated clockwise to lock the shoes to the drum.

4  Maintain the fluid in the brake master cylinder at $\frac{1}{4}$ in (6 mm) below the rim. Do not overfill, and ensure that the cap and surround is clean before the cap is removed. Use the correct fluid, ensuring that it is clean, that is has been stored in an airtight container, and that it has not been shaken for at least 24 hours. Brake fluid which has been exposed to the atmosphere, or agitated, quickly absorbs moisture and will corrode the internal surface of the hydraulic system. Take care when adding brake fluid that none is spilled on the paintwork or damage will be caused. Periodically, check that the brake master cylinder fluid reservoir filler cap vent is not clogged. Probe the hole with wire. Restriction can cause a pressure build-up, and the brakes to bind.

5  Periodically check the condition of the two front and one rear flexible hoses for deterioration. Renew if necessary.

6  Occasionally check the security of unions and bleed valves but do not overtighten. More than a slight lowering of the level of the fluid in the reservoir (due to lining or pad wear) must be immediately investigated and indicates a leak in the hydraulic system.

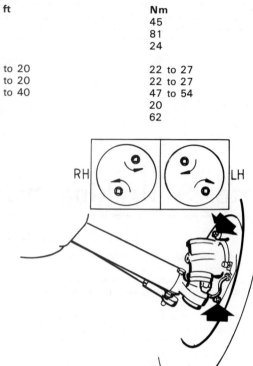

Fig. 9.1 Front brake adjustment – all-drum system (Sec 2)

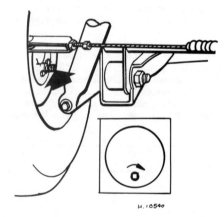

Fig. 9.2 Rear brake adjustment – all-drum system (Sec 2)

7  Fluid renewal is required at 18 month or 24 000 mile (48 000 km) intervals. Continually top up the master cylinder whilst bleeding from each bleed screw in turn, until clean fluid is seen to flow from the screws. Details of the procedure for bleeding the system are given in this Chapter.

8  If the hydraulic system becomes contaminated with any unsuitable fluid, it should not be used until rectification work is complete. The system should be flushed through with new fluid, and all units then removed for dismantling (see the relevant sections). All rubber items (including flexible hoses) must be renewed, and all metal parts cleaned and examined. Any unsatisfactory items should be renewed. Reassemble, refill with new fluid, and bleed the system.

9  Regularly apply a small quantity of oil to the handbrake clevis forks, one at each rear brake drum operating lever and one at the handbrake lever connection below the car floor.

## 3   Disc brake pads – removal, inspection and refitting

1    Apply the handbrake, jack up the front of the car and remove the wheels.

1    Renew the pads when reduced to $\frac{1}{8}$ in (3 mm) thick. Refer to Fig. 9.3 and remove the pad retaining pins and spring clips.

3    Withdraw the friction pads with any anti-squeak shims which may be fitted. Note the position and the directional arrow stamped on the shims for exact refitting.

4    Clean the surfaces of the caliper pistons and ensure that the dust covers are in good condition.

5    Before fitting the new pads, release the caliper bleed screw half a turn and press in the caliper pistons squarely to the bottom of their bores in order to accommodate the new thicker pads.

6    Retighten the brake bleed screws and fit the new pads with the anti-squeal shims positioned as originally located.

7    Fit the pins and spring clips.

8    Bleeding is not required after this operation but pump the foot brake pedal until solid resistance indicates that the pistons are repositioned against the pads.

9    Top up the fluid reservoir, refit the wheel and remove the jack.

## 4   Rear brake shoes (disc/drum system) – removal, inspection andd refitting

1    Chock the front wheels, release the handbrake, jack up the rear of the car and remove the roadwheel and brake drum (countersunk screw). Do not operate the brake pedal. (If the drum proves difficult to remove, see Section 10).

2    The linings must be renewed if they have worn level with their securing rivets. Factory reconditioned exchange shoes are recommended. These will be ground to the brake drum contour to facilitate immediate operating efficiency with quicker bedding-in.

3    Refer to Fig. 9.4 and remove the shoe steady springs and pins.

4    Note the proper positions of both the shoes and the return springs, making sketches where necessary to assist reassembly.

5    Prise the leading shoe away from the fixed abutment on the backplate. Extract the trailing shoe from the handbrake lever mechanism. By pulling outwards against the return springs remove both brake shoes and return springs together with the threaded pushrod. Clean the handbrake lever mechanism and backplate. Check the wheel cylinders, and service if necessary as described in Section 13.

6    Examine the tip of the lever which rotates the adjuster nut and the spindle roller which bears against the backplate. If the roller shows signs of wear on its outer surface it may be rotated 90° to present a new wearing surface. Should the tip of the lever be worn, then a complete new lever assembly should be fitted.

7    Lightly smear the moving parts of the lever mechanism, (not the tip of the lever nor the adjuster nut serrations), the shoe bearing surfaces of the backplate, the engagement slots in the backplate fixed abutment and the wheel cylinder piston slots with high melting point grease. Use the grease sparingly and keep it away from the shoe linings.

8    Position the new shoes on a flat surface and engage the return springs, as noted in paragraph 4. Return the adjustment nut to the end of the thread.

9    Exert outward pressure against the return springs, offer up the brake shoes to the backplate and engage the ends of both shoes in the fixed abutment slots. With the screwed adjuster rod engaged in its tube, prise the brake shoes outwards to engage the upper ends with the wheel cylinder unit piston slots. Refit the shoe steady pins and springs.

10   Clean the interior of the brake drum, refit it, and secure with the countersunk screw.

11   Operate the handbrake lever repeatedly, to bring the brake shoes to their correct adjustment. Test for a firm foot pedal. Rotate the wheel to check for binding. Slight drag should be ignored. Lower the car.

## 5   Handbrake (saloon) – adjustment, removal and refitting

1    The handbrake is set during manufacture and normally no adjustment is required other than to compensate for cable stretch or when the assembly had been dismantled. Operation of the handbrake

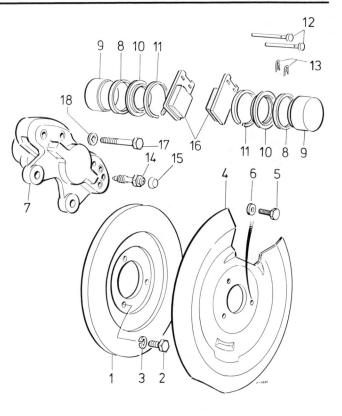

**Fig. 9.3 Front disc brake assembly (Sec 3)**

| | |
|---|---|
| 1   Disc | 11  Dust cover retaining |
| 2   Disc-to-hub bolt |       ring |
| 3   Lockwasher | 12  Pad retaining pin |
| 4   Guard plate | 13  Spring clip |
| 5   Guard plate screw | 14  Bleed screw |
| 6   Lockwasher | 15  Dust cap |
| 7   Caliper unit | 16  Friction pad |
| 8   Piston seal | 17· Caliper mounting bolt |
| 9   Piston | 18  Lockwasher |
| 10  Dust cover | |

automatically adjusts the position of the rear brake shoes through a lever and ratchet assembly housed within the drums on disc/drum brakes.

2    To remove the handbrake assembly, chock the front wheels and release the handbrake. Refer to Fig. 9.5 and remove either the console or rear floor mat, whichever is fitted.

3    Withdraw the clevis pin, remove the two setscrews and lift away the handbrake lever assembly.

4    Remove the rear cable jaw by withdrawing the pin.

5    Unscrew the cable jaw from the adjuster and withdraw the cable from the slot in the mounting bracket.

6    Release the strap which locates the cable to the rear axle and pull the cable from the securing clip attached to the floor.

7    Withdraw the handbrake cable from inside the car.

8    The rod section of the handbrake operating mechanism is removed by withdrawing the bolts at one end, and spring pin and clip at the other.

9    Refitting is a reversal of the removal and dismantling procedure. On completion the cable must be adjusted.

10   Set the handbrake lever in the off position, then lift it one notch only.

11   Slacken the cable adjuster right off and disconnect the cable jaw.

12   Pull the two handbrake levers at the backplates inwards to check that the wheel cylinders are not seized and that the springs are returning the brake shoes to their fully-off position.

13   Rotate the cable adjuster just enough to remove the slack from the

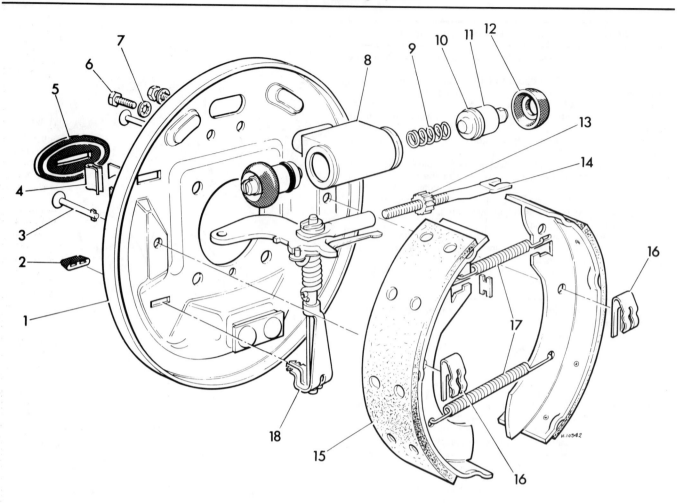

**Fig. 9.4 Rear brake assembly (disc drum system) (Sec 4)**

| | | | |
|---|---|---|---|
| 1 Backplate | 6 Backplate-to-hub bolt | 11 Piston | 16 Shoe steady spring |
| 2 Dirt excluder | 7 Lockwasher | 12 Dust cover (boot) | 17 Shoe return spring |
| 3 Shoe steady pin | 8 Wheel cylinder body | 13 Adjuster nut | 18 Automatic adjuster |
| 4 Handbrake lever support | 9 Centering spring | 14 Pushrod | assembly |
| 5 Dirt excluder | 10 Seal | 15 Brake shoe | |

cable, so that with the backplate levers in the fully released position the clevis pin freely enters the cable jaw without any need to pull on the levers or cable.

14  Use new split pins in the clevis pins. Adjustment is correct when the wheels are locked by pulling the handbrake lever up five notches.

## 6  Handbrake (estate) – adjustment, removal and refitting

1  The handbrake linkage on estate models is different to that of the saloon models.

2  Removal of the handbrake assembly is as described in Section 5, but removal of the cable differs in that it can be disconnected from the compensator swivel, and the outer cable is not located in a slotted hole.

3  To adjust the cable, chock the front wheels and jack up the rear of the car.

4  Disconnect the left-hand rear cable at the wheel end and the main cable at the compensator end by removing their respective split pins and clevis pins.

5  Pull the handbrake levers on each rear wheel backplate in turn, and check that each wheel rotates freely when they are released. This will ensure that the wheel cylinders and internal handbrake linkage is operating correctly. The rear brakes are self-adjusting and, if there is

any sign of stiff action or seizure, the fault will have to be rectified before proceeding.

6  Refer to Fig. 9.6 and position the compensator vertically, with the handbrake clevis pin hole centre $\frac{3}{4}$ in (19 mm) to the rear of a line drawn parallel to the rear axle and passing through the compensator pivot centre.

7  Hold the compensator in this position, and offer the left-hand rear cable to the operating lever on the backplate. The clevis pin jaw should be adjusted on the cable until the clevis pin locates exactly with the lever. Enter the clevis pin, assemble the washer and spring clip, and tighten the cable locknut.

8  Fully release the handbrake lever and then lift it one notch.

9  Adjust the main handbrake cable jaw so that the clevis pin locates exactly with the compensator arm, push the pin fully down and assemble the washer and spring clip.

10  Operate the handbrake a few times and check that the brakes do not bind with the lever fully released. Check that the handbrake is fully applied by five notches of the handbrake ratchet, and that, when fully applied, the compensator operating arm clevis pin centre does not move further forward than an imaginary line drawn parallel to the rear axle and passing through the compensator pivot centre. Make minor adjustments at the rear of the cable.

11  Tighten the handbrake cable locknut at the compensator end and lower the car to the floor.

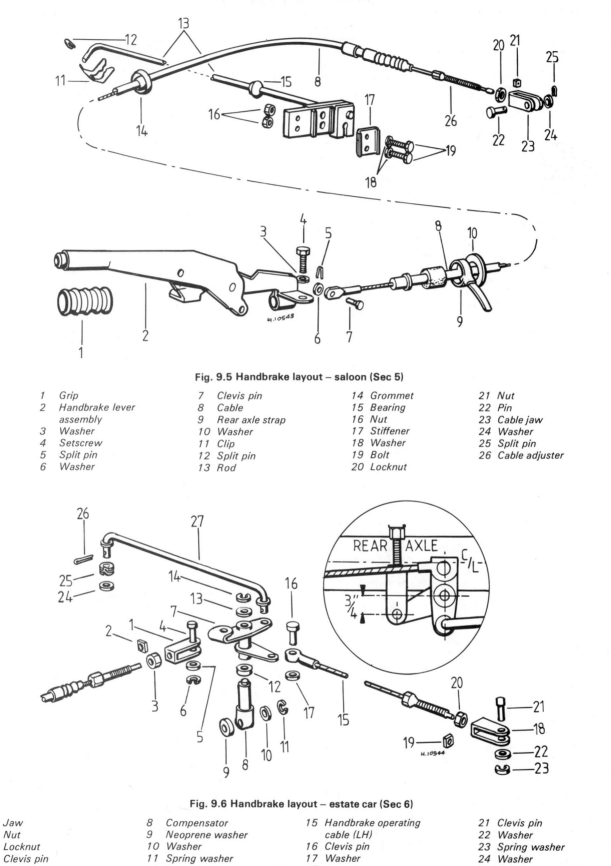

**Fig. 9.5 Handbrake layout – saloon (Sec 5)**

| | | | | | | | |
|---|---|---|---|---|---|---|---|
| 1 | Grip | 7 | Clevis pin | 14 | Grommet | 21 | Nut |
| 2 | Handbrake lever assembly | 8 | Cable | 15 | Bearing | 22 | Pin |
| 3 | Washer | 9 | Rear axle strap | 16 | Nut | 23 | Cable jaw |
| 4 | Setscrew | 10 | Washer | 17 | Stiffener | 24 | Washer |
| 5 | Split pin | 11 | Clip | 18 | Washer | 25 | Split pin |
| 6 | Washer | 12 | Split pin | 19 | Bolt | 26 | Cable adjuster |
| | | 13 | Rod | 20 | Locknut | | |

**Fig. 9.6 Handbrake layout – estate car (Sec 6)**

| | | | | | | | |
|---|---|---|---|---|---|---|---|
| 1 | Jaw | 8 | Compensator | 15 | Handbrake operating cable (LH) | 21 | Clevis pin |
| 2 | Nut | 9 | Neoprene washer | 16 | Clevis pin | 22 | Washer |
| 3 | Locknut | 10 | Washer | 17 | Washer | 23 | Spring washer |
| 4 | Clevis pin | 11 | Spring washer | 18 | Jaw | 24 | Washer |
| 5 | Washer | 12 | Neoprene washer | 19 | Nut | 25 | Double coil washer |
| 6 | Spring washer | 13 | Washer | 20 | Locknut | 26 | Split pin |
| 7 | Compensator arm assembly | 14 | Spring washer | | | 27 | Handbrake operating rod (RH) |

## 7 Backplates (rear) (disc/drum system) – removal and refitting

1   Refer to Chapter 8, and remove the relevant halfshaft. Withdraw the backplate after disconnecting the hydraulic pipe connection on the wheel cylinder, and the handbrake cable or rod.

2   Refit in reverse order, renewing both sealing joints. Bleed the hydraulic system and adjust the brakes.

## 8 Brake pedal – adjustment

The correct free play at the brake foot pedal is essential for two reasons. Firstly, to ensure correct operation of the plunger type brake warning light switch, and secondly, to prevent any pressure being continuously applied to the brake master cylinder when in the fully recuperated state. Fig. 9.7 shows the correct and two incorrect positions of adjustment:

(a)   *Pedal against the rubber stop and having a minimum of $\frac{1}{8}$ in (3 mm) free play at the pad*

(b)   *Pedal against the rubber stop but no free play at the pad. To correct, loosen the switch locknut and move the switch/bracket assembly in the direction X to the dotted line position. Maintain light finger pressure behind the brake pedal during the adjustment. Tighten the locknut*

(c)   *Free play at the pad, but the pedal not against its rubber stop and the switch plunger not compressed. To correct, loosen the switch locknut and move switch/bracket assembly in direction Y to the dotted line position. Maintain light finger pressure behind the brake pedal during the adjustment. Tighten the locknut*

## 9 Brake disc – checking, removal and refitting

1   The condition of the brake discs is a vital factor in braking efficiency. The disc should run true to within 0.004 in (0.1 mm) between the brake pads. The disc must run equidistant between the caliper cylinders and checking should be done with feeler gauges placed between the pad abutments and the disc face while the disc is rotated. The gap on opposite sides of the disc may differ by 0.010 in (0.25 mm) but on the same side of the disc there should be no difference between the gaps at the two abutments. This ensures that the caliper is in line and that the pads and the pistons are square with the discs. Any discrepancy should be corrected by shims behind the caliper mounting bolts.

2   Where the discs are found not to be running true and in line, they should be renewed. Regrinding is not recommended. Light scratching or scoring is normal.

3   To remove a disc, first remove the caliper unit as described in Section 12. Remove the hub and disc assembly as described in Chapter 11. Separate the disc from the hub by removing the four securing bolts and washers.

4   Refit in the reverse order. Ensure that the new disc is clean, and that burrs and any protective coating have been removed. Secure all fixings to the specified torque.

## 10 Brake drums (damaged) – method of removal

1   In cases of neglect where brake lining rivets have been permitted to score the drum, the drum can be difficult to remove where self-adjusting brakes are fitted unless the adjustment can be backed off.

2   To deal with this situation, disconnect the handbrake cable from the lever at the backplate, remove the clip acting as a lever stop, pull the lever towards the backplate as far as possible, and remove the drum.

3   If the method in paragraph 2 proves unsuccessful, refer to Fig. 9.8 and drill the drum as indicated. Turn the drum until the adjuster nut and small lever are visible through the drilled hole, and with a small screwdriver rotate the nut to increase the lining to drum clearance.

4   Replacement drums are recommended if this condition is encountered. Skimming is not advised.

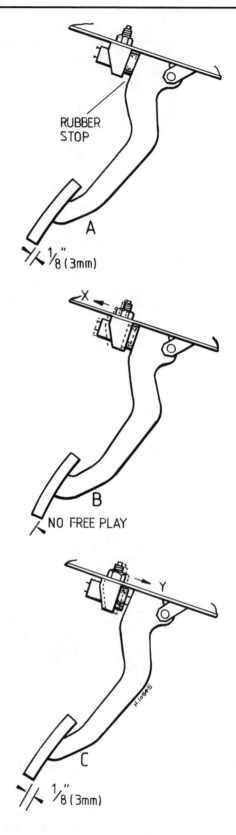

**Fig. 9.7 Brake pedal adjustment (see text) (Sec 8)**

A   *Correct adjustment*
B   *Incorrect adjustment*
C   *Incorrect adjustment*

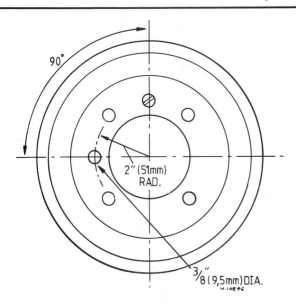

Fig. 9.8 Brake drum drilling details (Sec 10)

## 11  Hydraulic master cylinder (Single circuit braking system) – removal, servicing and refitting

1    The master cylinder is mounted on the bulkhead within the engine compartment. A screwed-top reservoir is mounted on the cylinder body. When pressure is applied to the brake pedal the pushrod contacts the plunger and propels it along the cylinder. The movement of the plunger cuts off the supply of hydraulic fluid from the reservoir and pressurises fluid through the outlet port and pipelines to the wheel caliper or cylinder units. Figs. 9.9 and 9.10 illustrate the master cylinders.

2    To remove the non-servo type, disconnect the rigid hydraulic pipe from the master cylinder by unscrewing the union. Catch the escaping fluid but do not reuse. Detach the pushrod (Fig. 9.9) from the brake pedal beneath the facia, inside the car, by removing the split pin and washer. Remove the two cylinder retaining nuts and withdraw it forwards.

3    To remove the servo type master cylinder, disconnect the fluid pipe and unscrew the two cylinder retaining nuts from the front of the servo unit.

4    Prior to dismantling, clean the exterior of the unit. With the non-servo type peel back the rubber dust cover (2) (Fig. 9.9) and remove the circlip (3).

5    With both types of cylinder, extract the internal components and note the sequence in which they emerge. Knock the end of the cylinder

Fig. 9.9 Master cylinder, single hydraulic line type
(non servo-assisted) – exploded view (Sec 11)

| | | | |
|---|---|---|---|
| 1 | Pushrod | 9 | Valve stem |
| 2 | Dust cover | 10 | Circlip |
| 3 | Circlip | 11 | Seal |
| 4 | Piston | 12 | Body |
| 5 | Seal | 13 | Baffle |
| 6 | Spring retainer | 14 | Seal |
| 7 | Spring | 15 | Cap |
| 8 | Spacer | | |

Fig. 9.10 Master cylinder, single hydraulic line type
(servo assisted) – exploded view (Sec 11)

| | | | |
|---|---|---|---|
| 1 | Piston | 10 | Reservoir |
| 2 | Seal | 11 | Washer |
| 3 | Spring retainer | 12 | Bolt |
| 4 | Spring | 13 | Baffle |
| 5 | Spacer | 14 | Cap |
| 6 | Seal | 15 | Seal |
| 7 | Valve stem | 16 | Baffle |
| 8 | Circlip | 17 | Adaptor |
| 9 | Body | 18 | Seal |

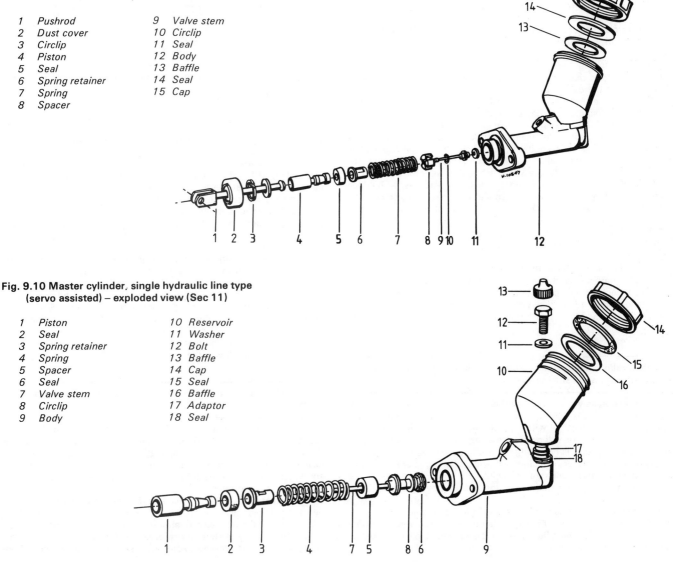

on a piece of wood to eject the internal assemblies. Examine the piston, the bore and all the components for defects. Renew where necessary.

6   Obtain the correct servo or non-servo service kit. Discard the old seals and fit the new using only the fingers. Note carefully the correct orientation of the seals.

7   Flush and lubricate the interior of the master cylinder with clean hydraulic fluid. Insert the components in their correct order, taking care not to nip or distort the seals. Refitting is a reversal of the removal procedure. Fit a new split pin to the pushrod clevis at its connection with the foot brake pedal (as applicable). Bleed the system.

## 12 Disc brake calipers – removal, inspection, servicing and refitting

1   Apply the handbrake, jack up the front of the car and remove the wheel.

2   Fit a piece of polythene sheeting beneath the lid of the fluid reservoir.

3   Disconnect the caliper rigid pipe at the suspension strut brackets. Remove the two mounting bolts and lockwashers which retain the caliper unit to the stub axle. Withdraw the caliper unit complete with short rigid fluid pipe. The caliper can be withdrawn complete with disc pads, or they may be removed earlier.

4   Carefully clean all dirt from the exterior of the unit. **Do not split the caliper in two.**

5   Refer to Fig. 9.3 and remove the piston dust covers and retaining rings.

6   Dismantling operations must be undertaken in completely clean conditions. The internal components and rubber items must be cleaned in clean hydraulic fluid or methylated spirit. The use of any other medium will cause corrosion, swelling and deterioration of the seals.

7   Pack clean rag between the opposing surfaces of the caliper pistons and eject them carefully by applying a tyre pump to the inlet connection of the caliper body.

8   Extract the piston seal from the cylinder bore, using a non-metallic probe to avoid scratching the operating surfaces.

9   Discard the original seals and dust covers and thoroughly examine the surfaces of pistons and cylinders for scoring or wear. The pistons may be renewed as separate items, but where scoring has occurred in the cylinder bores the caliper unit must be renewed as an assembly.

10  Obtain the correct service kit, which will include the appropriate seals and components. Lubricate the cylinder interiors with clean hydraulic fluid and fit the new piston seals in their grooves. Use the fingers only to manipulate the seals, as the use of tools will damage them.

11  Insert each piston fully into its cylinder and fit the dust covers and retaining rings. Assembly of these components is easier if they are fitted dry.

12  Refit the caliper unit to the stub axle carrier, refit the friction pads, any antii-squeal shims, the retaining pins and springs.

13  Reconnect the rigid pipe at the suspension leg bracket, remove the polythene from the fluid reservoir and bleed the caliper.

14  Check the fluid level and top up as required. Refit the roadwheel. Lower the jack.

## 13 Hydraulic wheel cylinders (drum brakes) – removing, inspection, servicing and refitting

1   The rear brake wheel cylinders should be inspected periodically for leaks and seizure. The latter will be detectable if the brake pedal is applied and then released with the rear wheel jacked up. If the brake drum is stiff to turn or will not rotate at all, then almost certainly the wheel cylinder piston is not being returned by the shoe return springs. A similar but less severe condition can exist when air is present in the wheel cylinder, and bleeding is required.

2   To remove, jack up the rear of the car. Remove the wheel and brake drum.

3   Remove the brake shoes as described in Section 4.

4   Disconnect the hydraulic pipe at its union with the wheel cylinder and plug the pipe to avoid fluid loss. A rubber bleed nipple cap is useful for this.

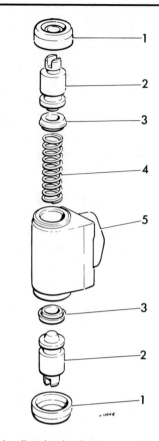

**Fig. 9.11 Hydraulic wheel cylinder – exploded view (Sec 13)**

| | |
|---|---|
| 1   Dust cover | 4   Spring |
| 2   Piston | 5   Wheel cylinder body |
| 3   Seal | |

5   Unscrew the wheel cylinder to backplate securing bolts or remove the spring clips.

6   Clean the exterior of the wheel cylinder and withdraw the dust covers (Fig. 9.11) the pistons, the seals and the spring. If necessary, use a tyre pump at the fluid connection to eject the piston.

7   Examine the pistons and cylinder bores, and renew the complete cylinder if scoring is in evidence.

8   Obtain a service kit of the appropriate seals and dust covers. Note that wheel cylinders are left and right-handed and that, if they are renewed complete, the correct item must be used.

9   Lubricate the cylinder bore with clean brake fluid. Fit the new seals to the pistons with the wider end of the seal furthest from the slotted end. Dip the assembled piston in clean brake fluid and insert it into the cylinder (seal end first) ensuring that the seal is not ripped or damaged.

10  Fit the new rubber boots in position. Refit the wheel cylinder to the backplate, bleed screw uppermost. Check the correct location of the seal between the wheel cylinder and the backplate.

11  Refit the brake drum, bleed the cylinder, top up the reservoir, refit the roadwheel and lower the jack.

## 14 Hydraulic pipes and flexible hoses – inspection, removal and refitting

1   Periodically, examine all brake pipes, both rigid and flexible for rusting, chafing and deterioration. Check the security of connections.

2   Examine for signs of leakage at the pipe unions. Examine the flexible hoses for signs of chafing, fraying and leakage. Exterior condition does not necessarily indicate their interior condition which will be considered later.

3   The steel pipes must be cleaned off and examined for any signs of dents, other percussive damage and corrosion. Corrosion should be scraped off, and if the depth of pitting is significant, the pipes renewed. This is particularly likely in those areas underneath the car body and along the rear axle where the pipes are exposed to severe conditions.

4   If a section of pipe is to be taken off, first remove the fluid reservoir cap, line it with a piece of polythene film to make it airtight and refit it. This will minimise the fluid loss, when a section of pipe is removed.
5   Rigid pipes are removed by undoing the unions at each end, undoing body clips as necessary, and removing the pipe. However, exposed unions can be very tight, and in these cases a self-locking wrench rather than an ordinary spanner may be needed. In severe cases, pipe breakage is not uncommon. Rigid pipes are now available for many vehicles ready made, but in some cases it may be be necessary to ask a motor engineer to make them up. Most local garages have the necessary tools, and it is helpful to supply them with the old pipe assembly as a pattern. Acute bends should be put in the pipes by the supplier. Gentle bends may be put in carefully by the owner, but if when doing this a pipe becomes kinked, it must be discarded.
6   Flexible hoses are mounted in a bracket attached to the body or to a sub-assembly. To remove them, grip the hexagon on the flexible hose and undo the pressure pipe nut. Still gripping the flexible hose, undo and remove the locknut and washer, and hence withdraw the hose from the mounting. Exposure can cause seizing of the fastenings, and an application of penetrating oil may assist. Care must be taken to ensure that twisting does not occur, or the mounting brackets may be wrenched off. A self-grip wrench can assist with both holding, and with preventing the assembly from twisting. With the flexible hose removed, blow through it and look through the bore. Any sign of restriction, or specks of rubber coming out, mean that the lining is breaking up and the pipe must be renewed. Refit flexible pipes in the reverse order of removal, noting that very great care must be taken to position the run of the hose away from other parts of the vehicle to prevent chafing. Check this at all stages of suspension travel. When tightening fixings the specified torque figures should be observed, or stripping of threads may result.
7   With the pipes refitted, remove the polythene film from the reservoir cap and bleed the system. It is not necessary always to bleed at all four wheels. It depends which pipe has been removed. If the main one from the master cylinder is removed, air can reach any line from the later distribution of pipes. If, however, a flexible hose at a front wheel is renewed, only that wheel needs to be bled.

## 15 Servo unit – general description

The servo unit is designed to assist the effort applied by the driver's foot to the brake pedal. The unit is independent, so that in the event of its failure, the normal braking effort of the master cylinder is retained. Vacuum is created in the servo unit by its connection to the engine inlet manifold, and with this condition applying on one side of a diaphragm, atmospheric pressure applied on the other side is harnessed to assist the foot pressure on the master cylinder.

Refer to Fig. 9.13. With the brake pedal released the diaphragm is fully recuperated and held against the rear shell by the return spring. The valve rod assembly is also fully recuperated by the brake pedal return spring. With the valve rod in this position, the vacuum port is fully open and there is a vacuum each side of the diaphragm.

With the brake applied, the valve rod assembly moves forward until the control valve closes the vacuum port. Atmospheric pressure enters behind the diaphragm and is assisted by the valve rod to push the diaphragm plate forward enabling the pushrod to actuate the master cylinder plunger.

With the pressure on the brake pedal released the vacuum port is opened and the atmospheric pressure in the rear chamber is extracted to the front chamber and thence to the inlet manifold via the non-return valve. The atmospheric pressure port remains closed whilst the valve rod assembly returns to its original position, assisted by the diaphragm return spring. The diaphragm then remains suspended in vacuum until the brake pedal is next depressed, when the operating cycle is repeated.

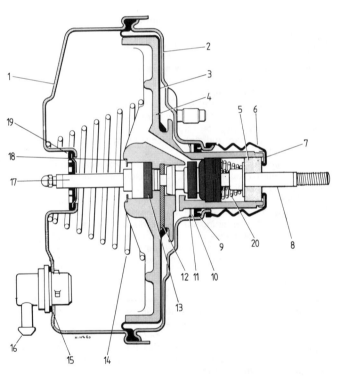

**Fig. 9.13 Vacuum servo unit – sectional view (Sec 15)**

| | | | |
|---|---|---|---|
| 1 | Front shell | 11 | Retainer |
| 2 | Rear shell | 12 | Valve retaining plate |
| 3 | Diaphragm | 13 | Reaction disc |
| 4 | Diaphragm plate | 14 | Diaphragm return spring |
| 5 | Air filter | 15 | O-ring seal |
| 6 | Dust cover | 16 | Non-return valve |
| 7 | End cap | 17 | Hydraulic push-rod |
| 8 | Valve operating rod assembly | 18 | Sprag washer |
| 9 | Seal | 19 | Seal and plate assembly |
| 10 | Bearing | 20 | Brake pedal return spring |

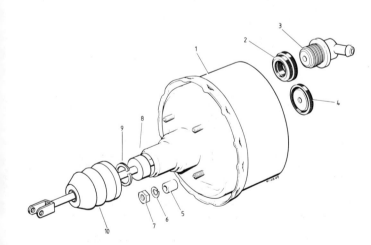

**Fig. 9.12 Vacuum servo unit – external details (Sec 15)**

| | | | |
|---|---|---|---|
| 1 | Servo unit body | 6 | Washer |
| 2 | Rubber grommet | 7 | Nut |
| 3 | Non-return valve | 8 | Air filter |
| 4 | Seal and plate assembly | 9 | Circlip |
| 5 | Spacer | 10 | Dust cover |

## 16  Servo unit – maintenance and servicing

1    The only regular maintenance required is to change the filter element every 30 000 miles (48 000 km) or every 30 months, whichever occurs first.
2    Disconnect the operating rod from the brake foot pedal by removing the split pin and clevis.
3    Unscrew the four nuts and washers from the servo unit mounting studs.
4    Detach the four-way connector from the wing valance by removing the screw and washer.
5    Pull the servo unit just sufficiently forward to provide access to the filter. Do not lose any spacers fitted behind the unit.
6    Peel back the dust cover and withdraw the old filter from the diaphragm plate neck.
7    Fit the new filter. This will be easier if it is first cut diagonally from its outer edge to the centre hole. Reposition the dust cover.
8    Refit the four-way connector securing screw and refit the servo unit mounting nuts. Connect the operating rod to the brake pedal using a new split pin.
9    Major servicing of the servo unit is not recommended and a new unit should be obtained if deterioration has occurred. Service kits are available, however, to permit the non-return valve and the seal and plate assembly to be renewed.
10   Note the exact position of the non-return valve in relation to the front shell of the servo unit. Remove the hose from the valve nozzle. The new valve must be fitted in exactly the same attitude. Then, while pressing down on the valve, turn the valve with a suitable spanner, one-third of a turn anti-clockwise to release the fixing rings.
11   Fit a new O-ring (from the service kit) to the new non-return valve. Do not lubricate.
12   Place the new valve complete with O-ring in position on the front shell, press down to compress the O-ring and turn one-third of a turn clockwise to engage the securing lugs (Fig. 9.14). A straight type of non-return valve (Fig. 9.15) may be encountered. It should be removed by pulling and at the same time exerting a side pressure. It may be found easier to remove if the hose is left clipped in position to give more purchase and leverage.
13   Lubricate the grommet used with the straight type valve using a little brake fluid and locate it in the front shell of the servo unit. Insert the new (straight type) non-return valve.
14   To renew the seal and plate assembly remove the complete servo unit assembly from the car.
15   Disconnect the operating rod from the brake pedal, unscrew the four servo unit mounting stud nuts, disconnect the fluid pipe and vacuum pipe connections.
16   Withdraw the unit noting the location of the four spacers.
17   Remove the seal and plate assembly from the front recess of the servo unit shell by gripping the centre rib with pliers.
18   Using only the grease supplied in the service kit, lubricate the new seal and plate assembly and press into the servo unit recess.
19   Refitting the unit to the car is a reversal of the removal procedure. Bleed the hydraulic system.

## 17  Bleeding – single circuit hydraulic system

1    Use only clean fluid from a sealed container during bleeding operations. Discard fluid expelled from the bleed nipples. Keep the reservoir well topped up during the whole of the bleeding operation or air may be drawn into the system, in which case the operation will have to be repeated.
2    Where a servo unit is fitted, destroy all vacuum by repeated operation of the brake pedal with the ignition switched off.
3    Fit a bleed tube to the front caliper bleed nipple opposite to the master cylinder, and immerse the free end in a jar containing sufficient fluid to keep the end of the tube covered.
4    Unscrew the bleed nipple $\frac{1}{2}$ to $\frac{3}{4}$ of a turn and, with the assistance of another person, watch fluid being expelled from the end of the tube while the brake pedal is depressed firmly to the full extent of its travel. Both slow long strokes and sharp ones should be given until air bubbles cease to emerge. It is essential that the tube in the jar is kept covered with fluid and that the master cylinder reservoir is kept filled. After each stroke of the pedal it should be allowed to fly back to its stop with the foot removed.

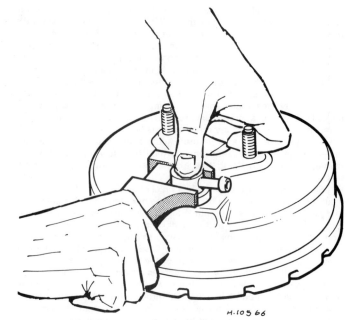

Fig. 9.14 Refitting an angled-type non-return valve on the servo unit (Sec 16)

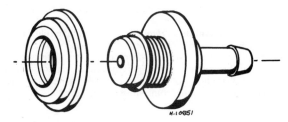

Fig. 9.15 Servo non-return valve – alternative straight type (Sec 16)

5    Tighten the bleed screw on a downward stroke of the pedal using a spanner of short length. Do not overtighten. Remove the bleed tube.
6    Repeat the operations at the other front caliper bleed nipple and then the rear left-hand wheel cylinder bleed nipple, in that order. (Note: *The estate car has two bleed nipples, and should be bled first on the side opposite to the master cylinder*). Top up the master cylinder.

## 18  Hydraulic master cylinder (dual circuit braking system up to Series 6 vehicles – certain territories only) – removal, servicing and refitting

1    The dual line braking system fitted to cars for use in certain territories comprises a direct acting, servo assisted, tandem master cylinder with separate outlets and braking circuits to front and rear brakes. The master cylinder (Fig. 9.17) accommodates two pistons which are supplied with fluid from a divided reservoir. Both the primary and secondary systems operate through a pressure differential warning actuator.
2    To remove and dismantle the master cylinder refer to Fig. 9.16 and disconnect the fluid pipes by unscrewing the unions. Catch the fluid, but do not re-use. Remove the two cylinder retaining nuts, and remove the unit.
3    Clean the exterior of the master cylinder and remove the four reservoir securing setscrews and reservoir.
4    Unscrew the tipping valve nut and remove the seal.
5    Depress the primary plunger and withdraw the tipping valve.
6    Expel the internal components by shaking the unit. Separate the plungers and primary spring.
7    Lift the tag on the spring retainer and withdraw the secondary spring and valve sub-assembly from the secondary plunger.

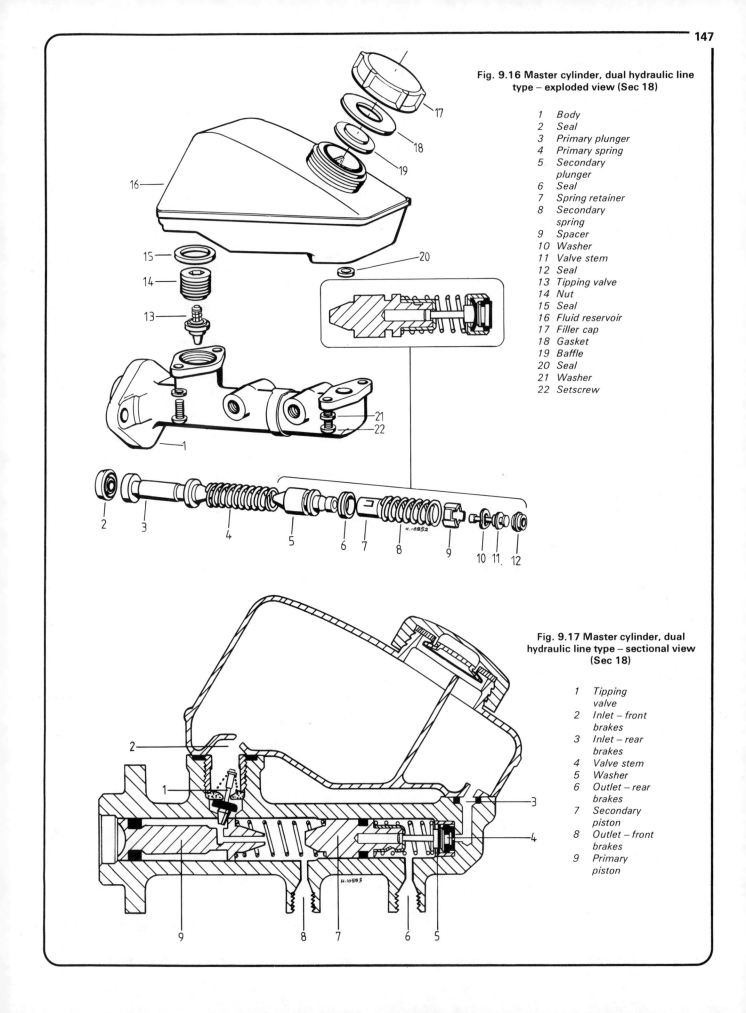

Fig. 9.16 Master cylinder, dual hydraulic line
type – exploded view (Sec 18)

1   Body
2   Seal
3   Primary plunger
4   Primary spring
5   Secondary
    plunger
6   Seal
7   Spring retainer
8   Secondary
    spring
9   Spacer
10  Washer
11  Valve stem
12  Seal
13  Tipping valve
14  Nut
15  Seal
16  Fluid reservoir
17  Filler cap
18  Gasket
19  Baffle
20  Seal
21  Washer
22  Setscrew

Fig. 9.17 Master cylinder, dual
hydraulic line type – sectional view
(Sec 18)

1   Tipping
    valve
2   Inlet – front
    brakes
3   Inlet – rear
    brakes
4   Valve stem
5   Washer
6   Outlet – rear
    brakes
7   Secondary
    piston
8   Outlet – front
    brakes
9   Primary
    piston

8   Dismantle the components of the valve sub-assembly. Remove all rubber seals and discard them. Remove the baffle and washer from the filler cap.

9   Examine the surfaces of plungers and cylinder bores. If scored or worn, renew the unit. If in order, obtain the correct service kit and renew all pistons and valve seals. Use only the fingers to manipulate them into position and ensure that they are the right way round.

10   Refer to the inset in Fig. 9.16 and check that the new valve seal has its smallest internal diameter nearest the secondary spring. Position the spring washer with its concave side nearest the coil spring.

11   Fit the spacer and the spring retainer and slide the secondary spring over the retainer.

12   Position the valve sub-assembly on the secondary plunger pressing the tag on the spring retainer down behind the plunger head. The

simplest way to carry out this operation is to compress the spring in a vice until it is nearly coil bound, and with the use of a small screwdriver, press the spring retainer right back against the secondary plunger (Fig. 9.18). Using pliers (Fig. 9.19), depress the tag on the spring retainer behind the plunger head.

13   Fit the primary spring between primary and secondary plungers and lubricate the cylinder bore with clean hydraulic fluid.

14   Insert the plunger assembly into the cylinder bore, valve end first. Depress the primary plunger in order to fit the tipping valve.

15   Fit the seal, and screw in the tipping valve securing nut and tighten to the specified torque.

16   Refit the reservoir. Refit the baffle and washer to the filler cap.

17   Refit the unit and couple the fluid lines to it. Bleed the system as described in Section 20.

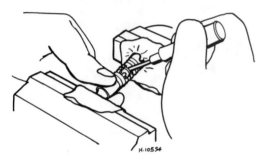

**Fig. 9.18 Positioning the spring retainer against the secondary plunger (Sec 18)**

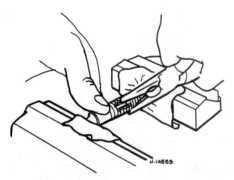

**Fig. 9.19 Depressing the spring retainer tag behind the secondary plunger head (Sec 18)**

### 19 Pressure differential warning actuator (PDWA) dual circuit system up to Series 6 vehicles – (certain territories only) – removal, servicing and refitting

1   Each circuit of the tandem braking system operates through the actuator. The unit is operated by the movement of a double-ended plunger in the fluid lines (Fig. 9.21). If both hydraulic circuits are functioning correctly the piston will remain in balance. Should failure occur in either, the piston will be displaced and depress a warning light switch plunger. Resetting will be automatic after the fault has been corrected and the system bled as described in Section 16.

2   To remove the actuator disconnect and plug the fluid lines, unscrew the retaining nut, and withdraw the actuator. To service the actuator refer to Fig. 9.20 and unscrew the end plug and switch assembly, retaining the ball carefully. Unscrew and remove the adaptor. Push out the pistons and remove the seals. Discard the seals and copper gaskets.

3   Clean all parts in clean brake fluid and obtain a service kit.

4   Fit the new seals to the pistons with the chamfers correctly located. Lubricate the interior of the actuator with clean brake fluid.

5   Insert the longer piston into the bore with its slotted end outwards, until the radiused groove is opposite the switch assembly aperture. Screw in the switch assembly and ball and tighten to the specified torque.

6   Insert the shorter piston into its bore with the slotted end outwards and fit the plug and adaptor using new copper gaskets. Tighten to the specified torque. Bleed the system as described in Section 20 after refitting the actuator. Note that neither seal must pass the centre point of the actuator (switch and ball assembly removed) or they will be damaged and must be renewed.

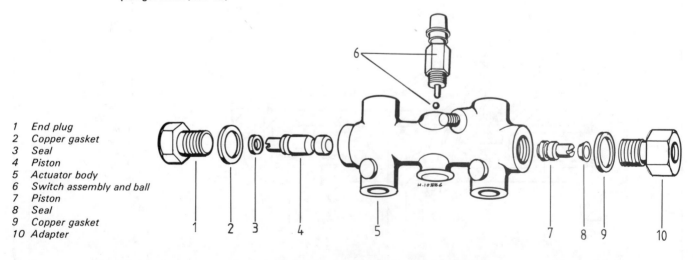

1   End plug
2   Copper gasket
3   Seal
4   Piston
5   Actuator body
6   Switch assembly and ball
7   Piston
8   Seal
9   Copper gasket
10   Adapter

**Fig. 9.20 Pressure differential warning actuator, dual circuit braking system up to Series 6 – exploded view (Sec 19)**

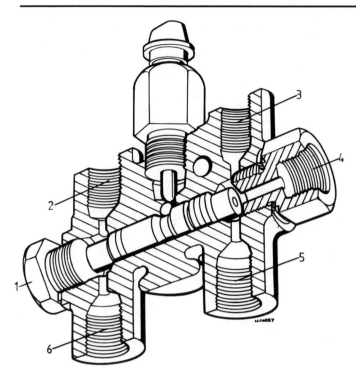

Fig. 9.21 Pressure differential warning actuator, dual circuit braking system up to Series 6 – sectional view (Sec 19)

| | | | |
|---|---|---|---|
| 1 | Cap | 4 | Outlet – LH front |
| 2 | Outlet – rear | 5 | Inlet – front |
| 3 | Outlet – RH front | 6 | Inlet – rear |

## 20 Bleeding – dual circuit hydraulic system up to Series 6

1   Keep both components of the master cylinder topped up during bleeding operations.

2   Bleed in the manner described in Section 17, but first from the bleed screw at the nearside rear wheel. Follow with the front brakes, nearside first.

3   Unscrew each bleed screw only enough ($\frac{1}{2}$ turn) to permit the fluid to be pumped out. Depress the brake pedal lightly until resistance is felt and allow it to return slowly by foot control.

4   Do not test the brakes by depressing the foot pedal until the complete bleeding process is finished.

5   Should the brake failure warning light come on during bleeding, then close the bleed nipple which is open at the time and open the one at the opposite end of the car. Apply a steady pressure at the foot pedal until the light goes out when the pedal should be released and the bleed nipple closed. When the brake failure light goes out a click will be felt through the brake pedal indicating that the piston in the actuator has moved to its point of balance.

6   Continue bleeding, then top up the master cylinder compartments.

## 21 Front brake shoes (all-drum system) – removal and refitting

1   Chock the rear wheels, jack up the front of the vehicle and remove the front wheels. Back off the shoe adjusters fully by turning them in the opposite direction to wheel forward rotation. Remove the brake drum retaining screw and withdraw the drum. Should the drum be stuck tight to the hub, tap it off from the rear using a hardwood block positioned at two or three equidistant points on the rim.

2   Examine the lining condition, and obtain replacement shoes if the rivet heads are close to the surfaces. Check for hydraulic leaks. Clean the area thoroughly, but avoid contaminating the friction linings. Renew the return springs if they are weak.

3   To dismantle further, sketch the location of the shoe return springs (or scribe the shoe webs), and note the correct layout of the shoes.

4   Pull the end of each shoe, against the spring tension, out of engagement with the wheel cylinder piston or abutment slots. Remove

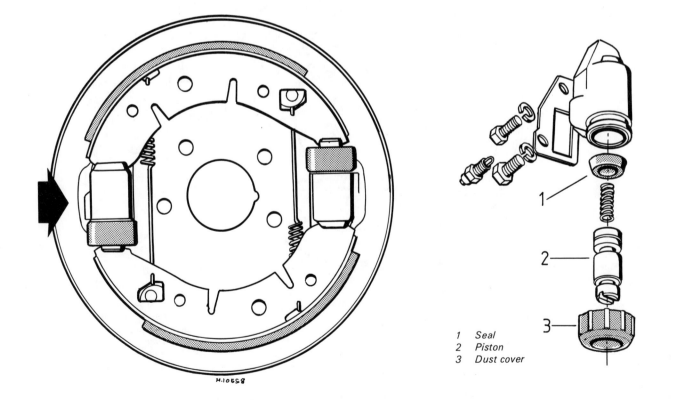

| | |
|---|---|
| 1 | Seal |
| 2 | Piston |
| 3 | Dust cover |

Fig. 9.22 Front brake and wheel cylinder details – all-drum system (Sec 21)

the shoes. To prevent the pistons dropping out, place elastic bands round the cylinder or retain the pistons in some other way. *Do not depress the brake pedal.*

5    Apply a smear of high melting point grease to the slots in the wheel cylinder pistons and abutments, and to the adjuster eccentric pins.

6    Lay the new shoes on the bench, correctly orientated, and engage the shoe return springs in their original positions. Remove the retainers from the wheel cylinders and engage the lower shoe in the cylinder slots, exerting slight upward pressure on the upper shoe to ensure that the return springs do not jump out of engagement. Pull the upper shoe against the tension of the return springs and prise it into engagement with the piston and abutment slots. Check that the eccentric adjusters are correctly engaged in the cut-outs in the shoe webs.

7    Wipe or brush out any dust from the brake drums and refit them.

8    Adjust the shoes as described in Section 2, refit the wheels and lower the vehicle to the ground.

## 22  Rear brake shoes (all-drum system) – removal and refitting

This is similar to the procedure for the front brakes but the following differences apply:

(a)  Only one adjuster is used

(b)  A single (but double acting) wheel cylinder is used

(c)  Shoe steady springs and posts are incorporated and these must be removed before the shoes can be withdrawn from the backplate. Depress the retaining cup and turn it through 90° to release the cup from the steady post

(d)  The handbrake cross lever is engaged with the webs of the shoes and it will be found easier to disengage it during dismantling if the clevis pin is first removed from the handbrake cable connecting fork.

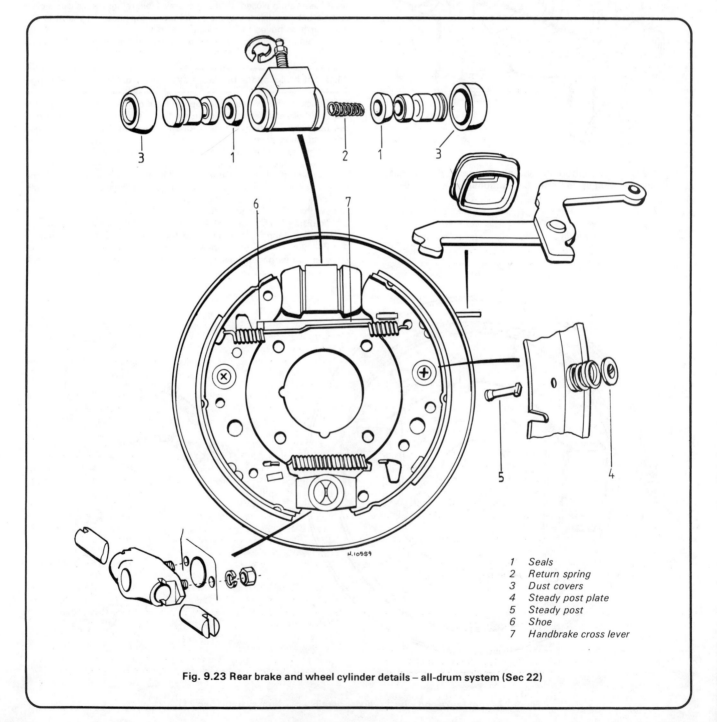

H.10559

1   Seals
2   Return spring
3   Dust covers
4   Steady post plate
5   Steady post
6   Shoe
7   Handbrake cross lever

**Fig. 9.23 Rear brake and wheel cylinder details – all-drum system (Sec 22)**

## 23 Backplate and rear brake adjuster (all-drum system) – removal and refitting

1   To remove the front backplates, remove the drum retaining screw and remove the drum. Remove the grease cap, the split pin, locking cap, nut and washer. Withdraw the hub assembly.
2   Place a piece of polythene under the master cylinder filler cap. Loosen the pipe at the wheel cylinder, disconnect it from the flexible hose, and cap the hose to prevent fluid loss.
3   Remove the four screws and washers, and take off the backplate. Remove the shoes and wheel cylinders.
4   Refit in the reverse order. Adjust the hub endfloat (see Chapter 11) and adjust the brakes (do not operate the pedal until bleeding has been carried out). Bleed the brakes, operate the pedal several times, and readjust the brakes.
5   To remove a rear backplate, first remove the halfshaft as described in Chapter 8.
6   Tape over the vent hole in the brake fluid reservoir cap, place a tray beneath the backplate, and undo the hydraulic pipes from the wheel cylinder. Disconnect the handbrake linkage, withdraw the backplate and remove the shoes, wheel cylinder and adjuster (two nuts).
7   Refit in the reverse order. Remember to remove the tape from the reservoir cap. Adjust the brakes, bleed the hydraulic system, operate the brake pedal several times, and readjust the brakes.

## 24 Hydraulic master cylinder and bleeding procedure (all-drum system)

1   The procedures relating to the master cylinder are as given in Section 11.
2   The procedures relating to bleeding the system are as given in Section 17.

## 25 Hydraulic wheel cylinders (all-drum system) – servicing

1   The front wheel cylinders are bolted to the backplate, whereas the rear wheel cylinders are retained by circlips.
2   Stick tape over the master cylinder fluid reservoir to reduce the loss of fluid when the hydraulic pipes are disconnected.
3   In the case of the front wheel cylinders, note the location of the bridge pipe between the cylinders and the position of the ports to which the rigid pipes connect.
4   Remove the brake shoes. Unscrew the hydraulic pipe unions at the wheel cylinders and plug the lines.
5   Unbolt the wheel cylinders (or remove the circlip) from the backplate.
6   Clean the exterior of the cylinder head and pull off the rubber dust excluders.
7   Apply air pressure from a tyre pump the the cylinder fluid port and eject the piston, seals and return springs.
8   Wash all internal components in clean hydraulic fluid or methylated spirit. Discard all seals and obtain a repair kit. However, first examine the piston and cylinder bore for defects and renew the complete assembly if evident.
9   Manipulate the new seals into place with the fingers only, ensuring that they are the correct way round as indicated in Figs. 9.22 and 9.23.
10   Dip the piston assembly in clean hydraulic fluid, and insert in the cylinder bore.
11   Reassemble in the reverse order. Use a new circlip for the rear wheel cylinder. Remove the tape from the reservoir vent. Adjust and bleed the brakes.

## 26 Split circuit hydraulic system (commencing Series 7) – description

1   This system is fitted to all Series 7 models onwards. It operates in an identical manner to the dual circuit system described in Section 1, although individual components have been modified.
2   The system incorporates a pressure differential warning actuator which operates if there is a loss of fluid pressure in either the front or

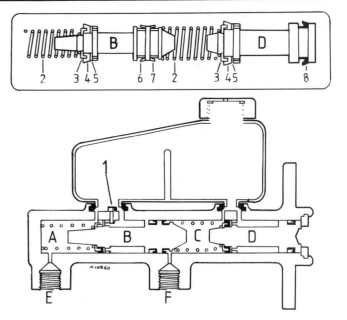

**Fig. 9.24 Master cylinder, split circuit system commencing Series 7 (Sec 27)**

| | |
|---|---|
| 1   Secondary plunger stop pin | A   Secondary pressure chamber |
| 2   Plunger return springs | B   Secondary plunger |
| 3   Seal retainers | C   Primary pressure chamber |
| 4   Seals | |
| 5   Seal support washer | D   Primary plunger |
| 6   Interchamber seal | E   Front brake outlet |
| 7   Interchamber seal | F   Rear brake outlet |
| 8   Primary seal | |

rear hydraulic lines. In certain countries this unit is fitted with a pressure reducing valve which controls the hydraulic pressure to the rear brakes in proportion to that on the front brakes.

## 27 Hydraulic master cylinder (split circuit braking system commencing Series 7) – removal, servicing and refitting

1   Referring to Fig. 9.24, disconnect the fluid pipes, Catch the fluid, but do not re-use.
2   Remove the two nuts which retain the cylinder to the front of the servo unit, retrieve the spring washers and withdraw the unit.
3   Clean the exterior of the cylinder and remove the reservoir by extracting the two clips and pins at the sides.
4   Depress the primary plunger fully and withdraw the secondary plunger stop pin from the fluid inlet aperture using a pair of pliers.
5   Extract the plunger retaining circlip from the cylinder bore. Remove the primary and secondary plungers and springs by tapping the end of the cylinders with a piece of wood.
6   Lay the components on a clean bench as they are removed. Identify the primary and secondary return springs with adhesive tape as they have different characteristics.
7   Dismantle the springs, retainers, seals, and washers. If necesssary use a wooden or plastic lever.
8   Examine the surfaces of plungers and cylinder bores. If scored or worn, renew the unit.
9   Obtain a service kit and renew the seals. All items should be cleaned with fresh hydraulic fluid or methylated spirit, and should be lubricated with unused brake fluid prior to assembly. Renew the reservoir filler cap washer.
10   Refer to Fig. 9.24 and assemble the seals to the plungers using the fingers only ensuring that the seals are the correct way round.
11   Check that the springs are fitted with the small coil abutting the plunger, and that each spring locates with the correct plunger.
12   Insert the assembly into the cylinder bore, being careful not to damage the leading edges of the seals, and fit the circlip to the end of the bore.

13 Depress the primary plunger fully and fit the secondary plunger stop pin into the fluid inlet aperture.

14 Refit the fluid reservoir and secure with the two pins and clips, and assemble the master cylinder to the servo unit, tightening the two securing nuts onto the spring washers.

15 Refit the hydraulic fluid pipes and tighten the union nuts.

16 Bleed the brakes, as described in Section 31.

## 28 Pressure differential warning actuator (PDWA) (split circuit system commencing Series 7) – description, removal and refitting

1 The unit is fitted in the brake hydraulic line between the master cylinder and the wheel cylinder, and consists of a floating double

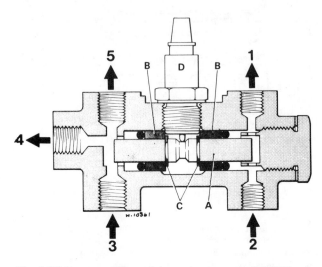

Fig. 9.25 Pressure differential warning actuator (PDWA) split circuit system commencing Series 7 (Sec 28)

| | |
|---|---|
| 1 Rear brake outlet | A Floating plunger |
| 2 Rear brake inlet (primary circuit) | B Sleeves |
| 3 Front brake inlet (secondary circuit) | C Circlip stops |
| 4 Front brake outlet (LH) | D Pressure differential actuator switch |
| 5 Front brake outlet (RH) | |

acting plunger which is only displaced if there are unequal pressures in the front and rear brake lines. Should a brake fault develop, resulting in loss of fluid from one circuit, the plunger will move and cause the switch contacts to close. This will illuminate a warning light on the car instrument panel. When the fault has been rectified and the brakes bled the plunger will return to its central position. The unit cannot be dismantled, and servicing is confined to renewing the unit as an assembly and renewing the actuator switch.

2 To remove the PDWA, disconnect the battery negative terminal and pull the lead from the actuator switch.

3 Place some plastic sheeting beneath the brake fluid reservoir filler cap and tighten the cap to minimise loss of fluid.

4 Unscrew the hydraulic pipe unions from the PDWA and catch any escaping fluid.

5 Detach the actuator from the wheel valance by removing the securing bolt. Do not spill any fluid on the bodywork.

6 Refitting is a reversal of the removal procedure. Remove the plastic sheeting, and bleed as described in Section 31.

## 29 Pressure differential warning actuator switch (split circuit system commencing Series 7) – description, removal and refitting

1 A loss of pressure in either hydraulic circuit will cause the plunger in the PDWA to become displaced. The switch plunger will therefore lift, and cause the dashboard warning light to illuminate.

2 To remove the switch, disconnect the battery, remove the switch lead and unscrew the switch from the actuator. Take care not to damage the ceramic part of the switch, or the Lucar connector.

3 To refit the switch, check that the floating plunger in the actuator is in its central position. If not, the movable sleeves will prevent the switch from being fully entered.

4 Tighten the switch, and reconnect the supply lead and battery negative terminal earth lead.

## 30 Pressure conscious reducing valve (PCRV) (split circuit system commencing Series 7) – description, removal and refitting

To comply with legislation in certain countries a pressure differential warning actuator which embodies a pressure conscious reducing valve is fitted to the brake hydraulic system. The pressure differential warning actuator section of the unit operates as described in Section 28. The pressure conscious reducing valve section of the unit effectively governs the maximum pressure which can be applied to the rear brakes by means of a spring tensioned shuttle valve.

Referring to Fig. 9.26, inset 1, the shuttle valve, under spring tension, allows hydraulic fluid to pass the rubber valve face. Hydraulic fluid pressure to the rear brakes is normal.

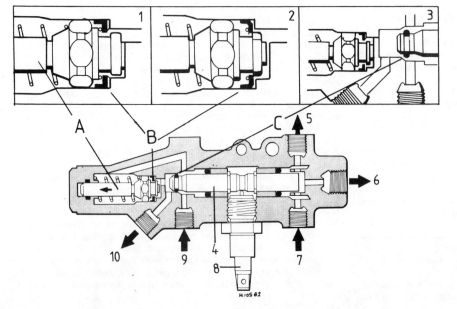

Fig. 9.26 Pressure conscious reducing valve (PCRV), split circuit system commencing Series 7 (Sec 30)

| | |
|---|---|
| 1 | Valve open |
| 2 | Valve shut |
| 3 | Pressure differential actuator plunger displaced |
| 4 | Pressure differential actuator plunger |
| 5 | Front brake outlet |
| 6 | Front brake outlet |
| 7 | Front brake inlet |
| 8 | Pressure differential actuator switch |
| 9 | Rear brake inlet |
| 10 | Rear brake outlet |

| | |
|---|---|
| A | Pressure conscious reducing valve plunger |
| B | Pressure conscious reducing valve sealing rubber |
| C | Warning actuator by-pass seal |

Once the predetermined hydraulic pressure has been reached, a condition which could occur in an emergency stop, the shuttle valve overcomes the spring tension and moves the valve head against the rubber seal (inset 2). The pressure in the rear hydraulic line then remains constant although the brake pedal may be depressed further, any further effort being directed to the front brakes. The action of the PCRV thus prevents the rear wheels from locking under hard braking and, by directing hydraulic pressure to the front wheels, improves all-round braking efficiency under these conditions.

Should a failure occur in the front brake hydraulic system, the pressure differential warning actuator plunger will be displaced and the end seal (inset 3) will allow full hydraulic pressure to be applied to the rear brakes, the pressure conscious reducing valve being bypassed.

Removal and refitting is as for the PDWA. The instructions in Section 28 apply, except that one extra securing bolt is used.

## 31  Bleeding – split circuit hydraulic system commencing Series 7

The instructions in Section 17 and 20 apply. However, use only slow movement when depressing the brake pedal and pause for 3 or 4 seconds between strokes. Employ the correct wheel sequence when bleeding, depending upon whether the vehicle is RHD or LHD. Should the pressure differential warning actuator be displaced during bleeding, it will be automatically centralised when the brake pedal is firmly applied.

## 32  Load conscious pressure reducing valve (certain Series 7 onwards vehicles only) – description and servicing

1   This valve is incorporated into the rear brake hydraulic line on certain models only, and its purpose is to regulate the hydraulic pressure to the rear brakes in relation to the load being carried by the rear axle. The amount of braking which can be applied to the rear wheels without locking will be proportional to the weight carried. The valve is mounted beneath the rear floor panel, and is connected to the rear axle by an extended coil spring and a rubber bushed linkage arm. The valve components consist of a spring-tensioned pushrod with a tapered ramp, and a steel ball valve actuated by the ramp. The pressure released to the rear brakes depends on the relative positions of the pushrod and the coil spring load sensor. Operation of the valve is by comparison of hydraulic pressures above and below the pushrod

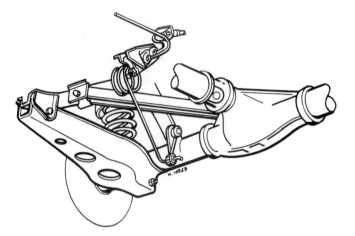

Fig. 9.27 Location of load conscious pressure reducing valve, and associated operating linkage (Sec 32)

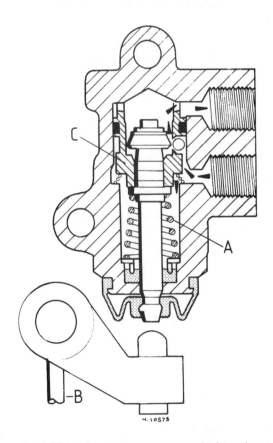

Fig. 9.28 Load conscious pressure reducing valve (ball valve open) – fluid flow (Sec 32)

A   Return spring
B   Sensing coil spring
C   Sleeve

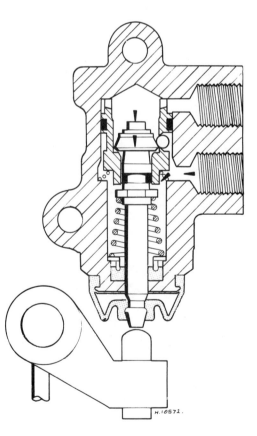

Fig. 9.29 Load conscious pressure reducing valve (ball valve closed) – fluid flow (Sec 32)

piston and, under heavy load conditions, greater pressure will be required to enable the pushrod to overcome the internal and load sensing spring pressures. The ball valve is therefore kept open and greater pressure is applied to the rear brakes. It is not possible to dismantle the load conscious pressure reducing valve, and adjustment entails the use of special gap gauges. Therefore this work should be entrusted to a suitably equipped garage. However, renewal of the valve unit and linkage is within the scope of the owner provided it is understood that adjustments will have to be carried out elsewhere.

2    To test the valve, the car should be unladen and standing on a level surface.

3    Disconnect the link from the rear axle and check the valve for fluid leaks by lifting the dust cover.

4    Have an assistant apply the brake pedal firmly and check that the valve piston rod rapidly moves out about $\frac{1}{16}$ in (1.5 mm) and then stops.

5    With the brake pedal held in the same position for 10 to 15 seconds, the rod should remain still. Slight movement after 15 seconds is permissible, but if it moves during the test period the ball valve is not seating correctly and the valve should be renewed.

6    Release the pedal. The piston rod should move slightly downwards and then return to its stop.

7    If the test is satisfactory, reconnect the link to the axle and tighten the securing nut. Make sure the link is inserted in the upper bracket hole, and have the adjustment checked.

8    Maintenance of the valve consists of checking the valve setting at the recommended intervals, and whenever the link is disconnected or

the road springs are renewed. Check for security of the fixings, and for any fluid leaks. Renew the unit every 3 years or 40 000 miles (64 000 km) whichever occurs first.

9    To remove the valve assembly, apply the handbrake, and place a piece of plastic sheet under the fluid reservoir cap to minimise loss of fluid. Identify the hydraulic hoses on the valve to assist correct refitting, disconnect them, and plug to prevent entry of dirt.

10   Unscrew and remove the mounting nuts and withdraw the valve from the bracket.

11   Refitting is a reversal of the removal procedure. Make sure that the hoses are fitted correctly (the line from the master cylinder connects to the lower port). Bleed the brakes.

12   To remove the sensing coil, link and lever arm, slacken the screw in the end of the pivot pin in the lever arm, and withdraw the sensing spring and dowel pin.

13   Drive the pivot pin out of the lever arm and bracket and withdraw the lever arm.

14   Disconnect the link from the rear axle bracket and lower the sensing spring and link from the car.

15   Dip the bush in water and ease the spring rod out.

16   Check each item for wear and renew as necessary.

17   Refitting is a reversal of the removal procedure. Use water to lubricate the link bush when inserting the sensing spring. The ends of the spring and dowel must not protrude from the pivot pin by more than 0.060 in (1.5 mm). The socket screw should be tightened to a torque of 10 lbf ft (1.35 kgf m).

## 33 Fault diagnosis – braking system

| Symptom | Reason(s) |
| --- | --- |
| Brake grab | Brake shoe linings or pads not bedded-in<br>Linings or pads contaminated with oil or grease<br>Scored drums or discs<br>Servo unit faulty |
| Brakes tend to bind, drag or lock-on | Master cylinder faulty<br>Brake foot pedal return impeded<br>Blocked filler cap vent<br>Master cylinder reservoir or components overfilled<br>Seized wheel caliper or cylinder<br>Incorrect adjustment of handbrake<br>Weak or broken shoe return springs<br>Crushed or blocked pipelines |
| Brake pedal feels hard | Friction surfaces contaminated with oil or grease<br>Glazed friction material surfaces<br>Rusty disc surfaces<br>Seized caliper or wheel cylinder<br>Faulty servo unit |
| Excessive pedal travel | Low fluid level in reservoir<br>Automatic rear shoe adjusters faulty<br>Excessive disc run-out<br>Worn front wheel bearings<br>System requires bleeding<br>Worn pads or linings<br>Leak in hydraulic system |
| Pedal creep during sustained application | Fluid leak<br>Faulty master cylinder<br>Faulty servo |
| Pedal spongy or springy | System requires bleeding<br>Perished flexible hose<br>Loose master cylinder nuts<br>Discs or drums in poor condition<br>Leaks in hydraulic system<br>Linings not bedded-in<br>Faulty master cylinder |

| Symptom | Reason(s) |
| --- | --- |
| Excessive effort required | Pads or shoes worn out |
| | New pads or shoes not bedded-in |
| | Harder than standard linings fitted |
| | Contamination of linings |
| | Servo unit inoperative |
| | One half of dual brake system inoperative |
| | Wheel cylinders faulty |
| Braking uneven | Contamination of linings |
| | Tyre pressures uneven |
| | Varying tyre types fitted |
| | Brake caliper loose |
| | Brake pads and shoes wrongly fitted |
| | Differing types of friction linings fitted |
| | Wear in suspension or steering |
| | Disc or drum condition poor |
| | Wheel cylinder faults |
| Fall in master cylinder fluid level | Normal disc pad wear |
| | Leak |
| | Internal fluid leak from master cylinder |

## 34 Fault diagnosis – servo unit

| Symptom | Reason(s) |
| --- | --- |
| Pedal hard, with lack of assistance with engine running | Lack of vacuum due to loose connections, restricted hose, blocked air filter or major fault in unit |
| Slow servo action | Faulty vacuum hose |
| | Blocked air filter |
| Lack of assistance during heavy braking | Air leaks in non-return valve O-ring, non-return valve, dust cover or hoses and connections |

# Chapter 10 Electrical system

*For modifications, and information applicable to later models, see Supplement at end of manual*

## Contents

## Specifications

**System** ...................................................................... 12V negative earth

**Battery** ........................................................ 30 to 55 amp hour capacity at 20 hour rate, depending on type

## Dynamo

| | |
|---|---|
| Type ............................................................ | Lucas C40-1 or C40-L |
| Maximum output ........................................... | 22 amps (C40-1) or 25 amps (C40-L) |
| Field resistance ........................................... | 6 ohms approx |
| Number of brushes ....................................... | 2 |
| Minimum brush length .................................. | 0.28 in (7 mm) |
| Brush spring pressure (new) ........................... | 30 ozf (850 gf) |

## Control box

| | |
|---|---|
| Type ............................................................ | Lucas RB340 |
| Open circuit settings at 0–25°C ..................... | 14.5 to 15.5 volts |
| Open circuit setting at 26–40°C .................... | 14.25 to 15.25 volts |

**Note**: *The voltage should be set to the upper or lower limit, depending which figure is closest to that obtained when checking*

## Alternator

| | Lucas 16ACR | Delco Remy DN460 | Mitsubishi AH-2040C-4 |
|---|---|---|---|
| Type | | | |
| Nominal rated output at 14V .......................... | 34 amps | 35 amps | 38 amps |
| Slip ring brush length (min) ........................... | 0.20 in (5 mm) | 0.20 in (5 mm) | 0.30 in (8 mm) |
| Regulated voltage ........................................ | 13.6 to 14.4V | 13.6 to 14.4V | 14.3 ± 0.3V |
| Brush spring tension ..................................... | 9 to 13 oz (255 to 368 gf) | | |

## Starter

| | Lucas M35J | M35J-PE | MEB02-0 or MEA16-0 |
|---|---|---|---|
| Make .......................................................... | | | |
| Type | | | |
| Minimum brush length .................................. | $\frac{3}{8}$in (9.5 mm) | $\frac{3}{8}$ in (9.5 mm) | 0.45 in (11.4 mm) |
| Brush spring pressure ................................... | 28 ozf (0.8 kgf) | 28 ozf (0.8 kgf) | 51 to 61 ozf (1.44 to 1.73 kgf) |
| Light running current ................................... | 65 amps at 8000 to 10 000 rpm | 65 amps at 8000 to 10 000 rpm | 55 amps at 7500 rpm |

## Fuse unit

| | |
|---|---|
| Up to and including Series 3 .......................... | 3 fuses |
| Series 4 to Series 7 ...................................... | 8 fuses |
| Series 8 onwards ......................................... | 12 fuses |

## Windscreen wiper

| | |
|---|---|
| Type ............................................................ | 15 w (single or two speed) |
| Light running current (transmission disconnected) warm: | |
|     Normal speed ........................................ | 1.5 amp |
|     High speed ........................................... | 2.0 amp |

## Bulbs and sealed beam units

**Lucas type**

| | Wattage |
|---|---|
| Twin headlamp RHD: | |
|     Outer sealed beam 54523632 .................. | $37\frac{1}{2}$/50 |
|     Inner sealed beam 54522973 ................... | $37\frac{1}{2}$ |
| Twin headlamp RHD: | |
|     Inner and outer bulbs 410 ...................... | 45/40 |
| Twin headlamp (France): | |
|     Outer and inner bulbs 411 ...................... | 45/40 |
| Single headlamp RHD 4FR ............................. | Sealed beam |
| Single headlamp LHD 410 .............................. | 45/40 |
| Single headlamp RHD (up to Series 7) 54526250 ... | Sealed beam |
| Single headlamp (Series 7 onwards) 410 or H4 ... | 45/40 or 60/55 |
| Single headlamp LHD 411 .............................. | 45/40 |
| Sidelamp 501 or 989 .................................... | 5 |
| Stoplamp 382 .............................................. | 21 |
| Stop and tail 380 ......................................... | 5/21 |
| Reverse lamp 382 ........................................ | 21 |
| Rear fog lamp 382 ....................................... | 21 |
| Front fog lamp (Series 7) H3 ......................... | 55 |
| Flashers 382 ............................................... | 21 |
| Side flasher lamp 254 (festoon) ..................... | 6 |
| Side flasher lamp 989 (repeater) ................... | 5 |
| Tail lamp (Series 7) 989 ............................... | 5 |
| Engine compartment lamp 989 ...................... | 5 |
| Number plate lamp 989 ................................ | 5 |
| Glovebox lamp 989 ...................................... | 5 |
| Luggage compartment lamp 501 .................... | 5 |
| Interior lamp 254 ........................................ | 6 |
| Instrument panel illumination 504 ................. | 3 |
| Instrument panel illumination 286 ................. | 1.5 |
| Instrument panel illumination 505 ................. | 3 |

## Torque wrench settings

| | lbf ft | Nm |
|---|---|---|
| Dynamo to engine and timing cover ................................................ | 16 | 22 |
| Lucas 16ACR alternator pulley nut ................................................ | 27 | 37 |
| Delco Remy DN460 alternator pulley nut ....................................... | 50 | 68 |
| Mitsubishi AH-2040C-4 alternator pulley nut ................................ | 40 | 55 |
| Lucas 16ACR alternator securing nuts and bolts .......................... | 16 | 22 |
| Mitsubishi AH-2040C-4 alternator securing nuts and bolts ................. | 16 | 22 |

## 1  General description

The electrical system is of the 12 volt earth return type. Earth polarity is negative. The main items employed are either a dc generator or an alternator for charging, an electro-mechanical starter motor, and a 12 volt battery.

Great care should be taken when fitting service replacements, to ensure that they are compatible with the electrical system polarity. If this is not done, irreversible damage could occur to certain units.

## 2  Battery – removal, refitting and maintenance

1    The battery is located at the front on the right-hand side of the engine compartment. Disconnect the negative terminal first by un-screwing the self-tapping screw.
2    Remove the positive terminal, remove the battery frame screws and lift the frame away. Lift the battery carefully to avoid spilling electrolyte on the paintwork.
3    Refitting is a reversal of the removal procedure but when reconnecting the terminals, clean off any deposits and smear with petroleum jelly. Do not overtighten the terminal post screws.
4    Ensure that the battery top is kept free from dirt and moisture, to prevent discharge by leakage.
5    On type D batteries, remove the manifold and check that the electrolyte level is just above the separator guard. On type A batteries the level can be seen through the transparent case, whereas the type F has a vent chamber cover similar to the type D. The correct electrolyte level for the type D is up to the perforated splash guard, for the type A to the level marks provided, and for the type F to the bottom of the filling tubes.
6    Top up the type D to the level of the perforated splash guard. To top up the type A, lift the vent cover vertically to its fullest extent and tilt to one side. Pour distilled water into the trough until all the rectangular tubes are full and the bottom of the trough is just covered. Press the vent cover firmly back, thereby causing the cells to be automatically topped up. On the type F battery, pour distilled water into the trough until the tubes are filled and water begins to lay in the trough. Refit the cover. Do not overfill when topping-up, or corrosion will be caused by electrolyte which subsequently overflows.
7    Once every three months, remove the battery and inspect the securing bolts, the clamp plate, tray and leads for corrosion. If this is found (white fluffy deposits on the metal) clean off the deposits with ammonia and paint the clean metal with an anti-rust/anti-acid paint.
8    Inspect the battery case for cracks. If a crack is found, clean and plug it with a proprietary compound marketed for this purpose. If leakage through the crack has been excessive it will be necessary to refill the appropriate cell with fresh electrolyte as detailed later. Cracks are frequently caused to the top of battery cases by adding distilled water in winter *after* instead of *before* a run. This gives the water no chance to mix with the electrolyte and so the former freezes and splits the case. If excessive topping-up is required, but no leaks are found, the battery is probably being overcharged. The voltage regulator should therefore be checked.
9    To check the state of charge, check each cell with a hydrometer. If one cell differs from the others by more than 0.040, either the electrolyte in that cell is of the wrong specific gravity, or an internal short circuit exists, in which case total battery failure is probably imminent. Hydrometer readings should be compared with the following tables:

### Types D and A batteries, at an electrolyte temperature of 60°F (15.6°C)

| | Climate below 80°F (26.7°C) | Climate above 80°F (26.7°C) |
|---|---|---|
| Fully charged ................ | 1.270 to 1.290 | 1.210 to 1.230 |
| Half charged ................. | 1.190 to 1.210 | 1.130 to 1.150 |
| Fully discharged ........... | 1.110 to 1.130 | 1.050 to 1.070 |

### Type F batteries, at an electrolyte temperature of 60°F (15.6°C)

| | Climate below 90°F (32°C) | Climate above 90°F (32°C) |
|---|---|---|
| Fully charged ................ | 1.277 to 1.297 | 1.227 to 1.247 |
| Half charged ................. | 1.190 to 1.220 | 1.160 to 1.180 |
| Fully discharged ........... | 1.100 to 1.130 | 1.080 to 1.100 |

The specific gravity of an electrolyte varies with temperature. For each 2.8°C (5°F) above 60°F, add 0.002 to the hydrometer readings, and for each 2.8°C (5°F) below 60°F, subtract 0.002 from the hydrometer reading. This will give the true specific gravity.

## 3  Battery – charging and electrolyte replenishment

1    In winter, when demand upon the battery can be heavy, it can be useful to occasionally have the battery fully charged from an external source at the rate of 3.5 or 4 amps. Charge at this rate until no further rise in specific gravity is noted over a four hour period. Alternatively, a trickle charger charging at the rate of 1.5 amps can be safely used overnight. Specially rapid 'boost' charges which are claimed to restore the power of the battery in 1 to 2 hours are not advised. These can cause serious damage to the battery plates.
2    The danger of explosion with a battery, particularly where it is well charged and gassing cannot be overemphasised. The battery should be kept well away from all naked lights and sources of sparks. A single spark can be enough to cause an explosion, with the battery being thrown in many pieces over a considerable distance. The danger to the person is therefore obvious.
3    Electrolyte replenishment should not normally be necessary unless spillage has occurred. Top up the cell with a solution of mixed electrolyte obtainable from a motor store or garage. If the cell is already fully topped up draw some electrolyte out with a pipette. When mixing sulphuric acid and water at home, NEVER ADD WATER TO SULPHURIC ACID – always pour the acid slowly onto the water in a glass container. IF WATER IS ADDED TO ACID IT WILL EXPLODE. The correct ratio is 1 part of acid to 2.5 parts of water by volume. Top up the cell with the freshly made electrolyte and then recharge the battery and check the hydrometer readings.

## 4  Dynamo – routine maintenance

1    Check the fanbelt tension and condition frequently, and lubricate the dynamo rear bearing every 5000 miles. The fanbelt should be tight enough to ensure no slip between the belt and pulley. A shrieking noise from the engine when the unit is accelerated rapidly may be due to the belt slipping. However, the belt must not be too tight or rapid wear of the bearings will result, and $\frac{1}{2}$ in total free movement should exist midway between the fan and the dynamo pulley.
2    To adjust the fanbelt tension, slightly slacken the three dynamo retaining bolts and swing the dynamo on the upper two bolts outwards to increase the tension, and inwards to lessen it. Leave the bolts fairly tight so that some effort has to be used to move the dynamo, otherwise it is difficult to get the correct setting. If the dynamo is being moved outwards to increase the tension and the bolts have only been slackened a little, a long spanner against the block, works very well in moving the dynamo outwards. Retighten the dynamo bolts and check that the dynamo pulley is correctly aligned with the fanbelt.
3    Lubricate the dynamo by inserting three drops of engine oil in the oil hole in the centre of the commutator end bracket. The front bearing is pre-packed with grease and requires no attention.

## 5  Dynamo – testing in the vehicle

1    Check that the fanbelt is in place and is not slipping, and that the leads from the control box to the dynamo are firmly attached. The lead

from the D terminal on the dynamo should be connected to the D terminal on the control box, and similarly the F terminals on the dynamo and control box should also be connected. Check that these are correct.

2   Pull the leads from the dynamo terminals, and join the terminals together with a short length of wire. Connect the positive terminal of a 0-20 volt voltmeter to the wire, and the negative terminal to earth on the dynamo yoke. Start the engine and allow it to idle at approximately 750 rpm. At this speed the dynamo should give a reading of about 15 volts on the voltmeter. There is no point in raising the engine speed above a fast idle as the reading will then be inaccurate. If a low reading (or no reading) is obtained, the dynamo will have to be removed for further examination. If, however, a radio suppressor is fitted between the D terminal and earth, a further check should be made with this removed, as the suppressor can be the cause of the fault.

## 6   Dynamo – removal and refitting

1   Slacken the two dynamo retaining bolts and the nut on the sliding link, and move the dynamo in towards the engine. Remove the fanbelt. Disconnect the two leads from the dynamo terminals.
2   Remove the nut from the sliding link bolt, remove the two upper bolts, and lift the dynamo away.
3   Refitting is a reversal of the above procedure. Do not finally tighten the fixings until the fanbelt has been tensioned.

## 7   Dynamo – dismantling, repair and reassembly

1   Mount the dynamo in a vice and remove the two through-bolts from the commutator end bracket.
2   Mark the end bracket and the dynamo casing so the bracket can be refitted in its original position. Pull the end bracket off the armature shaft. **Note**: *Some versions of the dynamo may have a raised pip on*

*the end bracket which locates in a recess on the edge of the casing. If so, marking the end bracket and casing is not necessary. A pip may also be found on the drive end bracket at the opposite end of the casing.*

3   Lift the two brush springs and draw the brushes out of the brush holders.
4   Measure the brushes, and, if worn down to 9/32 in or less, unscrew the screws holding the brush leads to the end bracket. Take off the brushes complete with leads.
5   If no locating pip can be found, mark the drive end bracket and the dynamo casing so that the drive end bracket can be refitted in its original position. Then pull the drive end bracket complete with armature out of the casing.
6   Check the ball bearing in the drive endplate by firmly holding the plate and noting if there is visible side movement of the armature shaft in relation to the plate. If play is present, the armature assembly must be separated from the endplate. If the bearing is sound there is no need to carry out the work described in the following paragraph.
7   Hold the armature in one hand (mount it carefully in a vice if preferred), undo the nut holding the pulley wheel and fan and pull them off. Remove the Woodruff key from its slot in the armature shaft. Remove the bearing locating ring. Place the drive end bracket across the open jaws of a vice, armature downwards, and gently tap the armature shaft from the bearing in the endplate with a suitable drift. Support the armature so that it does not fall.
8   Inspect the armature and check it for open or short-circuited windings. It is a good indication of an open-circuited armature when the commutator segments are burnt. If the armature has short-circuited the commutator segments will be very badly burnt and the overheated armature windings badly discoloured. If open or short circuits are suspected replace the suspect armature with a new one.
9   Check the resistance of the field coils. To do this connect an ohmmeter between the field terminal and the yoke and note the reading on the ohmmeter, which should be about 6 ohms. If the ohmmeter reading is infinity this indicates an open circuit in the field winding. If the ohmmeter reading is below 5 ohms this indicates that

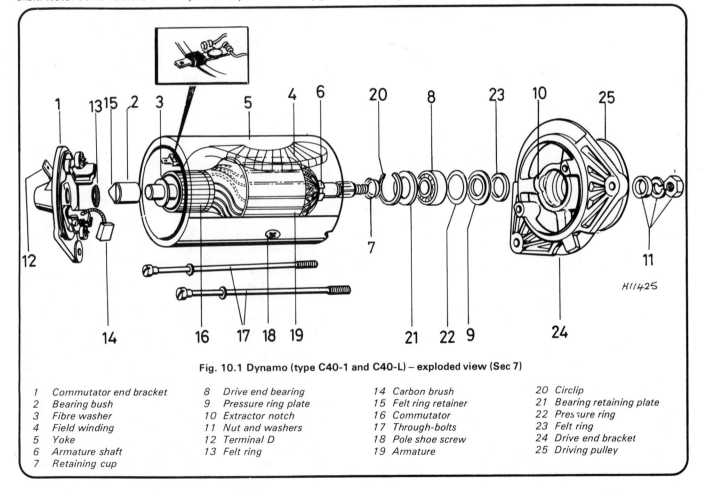

**Fig. 10.1 Dynamo (type C40-1 and C40-L) – exploded view (Sec 7)**

| | | |
|---|---|---|
| 1   Commutator end bracket | 8   Drive end bearing | 14   Carbon brush | 20   Circlip |
| 2   Bearing bush | 9   Pressure ring plate | 15   Felt ring retainer | 21   Bearing retaining plate |
| 3   Fibre washer | 10   Extractor notch | 16   Commutator | 22   Pressure ring |
| 4   Field winding | 11   Nut and washers | 17   Through-bolts | 23   Felt ring |
| 5   Yoke | 12   Terminal D | 18   Pole shoe screw | 24   Drive end bracket |
| 6   Armature shaft | 13   Felt ring | 19   Armature | 25   Driving pulley |
| 7   Retaining cup | | | |

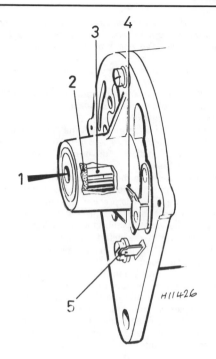

Fig. 10.2 Dynamo – end view (Sec 7)

1    Lubrication hole              3    Bearing bush
2    Felt ring                     4 and 5    Terminal connectors

one of the field coils is faulty and must be renewed.
10 Field coil renewal involves the use of a wheel operated screw-driver, a soldering iron, caulking and riveting and this operation is considered to be beyond the scope of most owners. Therefore, if the field coils are at fault either purchase a rebuilt dynamo, or take the casing to a dealer or electrical engineering works for new field coils to be fitted.
11 Check the condition of the commutator. If dirty and blackened, clean it with a petrol dampened rag. If the commutator is in good condition the surface will be smooth and quite free from pits or burnt areas, and the insulated segments clearly defined. If small traces of pitting remain after cleaning, these can be removed by wrapping a strip of glass paper (not emery paper) round the commutator and drawing it round evenly. Do not try to clean off too much in this way, and ensure that the commutator remains evenly circular.
12 In extreme cases of wear the commutator can be mounted in a lathe and, with the lathe turning at high speed, a very fine cut taken. Then polish with glass paper. Do not undercut the commutator.
13 Check the bush bearing in the commutator end bracket for wear by noting if the armature spindle rocks when refitted in it. If worn, it must be renewed. The bearing can be removed by a suitable extractor or by screwing a $\frac{5}{8}$ in tap four or five turns into the bush. The tap complete with bush is then pulled out. **Note**: *before fitting the new bush (which is of the porous type), it is essential that it is allowed to stand in SAE 30 engine oil for at least 24 hours before fitting. In an emergency the bush can be immersed in hot oil (100°C) for 2 hours.* Carefully fit the new bush into the endplate, pressing it in until the end of the bearing is flush with the inner side of the plate. It is recommended that a smooth-finished mandrel as shown in Fig. 10.4 should be employed.
14 To renew the ball bearing fitted to the drive end bracket, drill out the rivets which hold the bearing retainer plate to the bracket and lift off the plate.
15 Press out the bearing and remove the corrugated felt washers from the bearing housing.
16 Thoroughly clean the bearing housing and the new bearing. Pack the bearing with high melting point grease, place the felt washer and corrugated washer in that order in the end bracket bearing housing and fit the new bearing, gently tapping it into place with a suitable drift. Refit the bearing plate, fit three new rivets, open up their ends and peen them over with a small ball hammer.

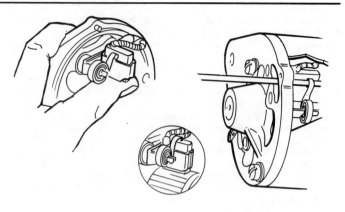

Fig. 10.3 Location of dynamo brushes (Sec 7)

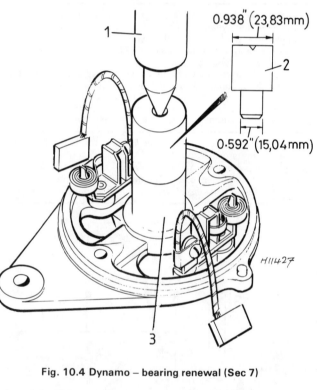

Fig. 10.4 Dynamo – bearing renewal (Sec 7)

1    Press                          3    Bush
2    Mandrel

17 Refit the drive end bracket to the armature shaft. Do not try and force the bracket on, but with the aid of a suitable socket abutting the bearing, tap gently, so pulling the bracket down with it.
18 Slide the spacer up the shaft and refit the Woodruff key. Refit the fan and pulley wheel and fit the spring washer and nut. Tighten the nut. Note that in some cases the bearing retaining plate is located not by rivets but by a circlip, and the procedure for bearing renewal is the same except that the riveting instructions should be ignored.
19 If the brushes are to be used again, ensure that they are placed in the same holders from which they were removed. When refitting brushes, either new or old, check that they move freely in their holders. If either brush sticks, clean with a petrol moistened rag and, if still stiff, lightly polish the sides with a very fine file until it moves freely. Refit the brushes by securing them with the retaining screws and washers. Refit the brushes in their holders, but keep them raised by allowing the springs to bear against their sides. This makes it a great deal easier to fit the endplate.
20 Refit the armature assembly through the casing, refit the commutator endplate, ensuring correct location, and secure with the two through-bolts. Hook the two springs up onto their heads, thereby pushing the brushes down onto the armature.

## 8 Control box (Lucas type RB340) – general

The control box is fitted to dynamo-equipped models, and is positioned on the right-hand wing valance. It comprises two separate vibrating armature-type single contact regulators and a cut-out relay. One of the regulators is sensitive to changes in current and the other to changes in voltage.

Adjustment can only be made with a special tool which resembles a screwdriver, with a multi-toothed blade. This can be obtained through Lucas agents.

The regulators control the output from the dynamo depending on the state of the battery and the demands of the electrical equipment, and ensure that the battery is not overcharged. The cut-out is really an automatic switch and connects the dynamo to the battery when the dynamo is turning fast enough to produce a charge. Similarly, it disconnects the battery from the dynamo when the engine is idling or stationary so that the battery does not discharge through the dynamo.

## 9 Control box (Lucas type RB340) – maintenance

1   Every 12 000 miles check the cut-out and regulator contacts. If they are dirty, rough or burnt, disconnect the battery and place a piece of fine glass paper (do not use emery paper or carborundum paper) between the cut-out contacts, close them manually and draw the glass paper through several times.
2   Clean the regulator contacts in exactly the same way, but use emery or carborundum paper and not glass paper. Carefully clean both sets of contacts with a rag moistened in methylated spirits. Reconnect the battery.

## 10 Control box (Lucas type RB340) – adjustment

1   Normally very little attention is required to this unit. Should there be any reason to suspect its correct functioning, tests of all circuits should be made to ensure that they are not the reason for the trouble.
2   These checks include the tension of the fanbelt, to make sure that it is not slipping and so providing only a very low charge rate. The battery should be carefully checked for possible low charge rate due to a faulty cell, or corroded battery connections.
3   The leads from the generator may have been crossed during refitting, and if this is the case then the regulator points will have stuck together as soon as the dynamo starts to charge. Check for loose or broken leads from the dynamo to the regulator.
4   If, after a thorough check, it is considered advisable to test the regulator, this should only be carried out by an electrician who is well acquainted with the correct method. Testing should be carried out quickly, or errors will arise due to heating of the unit.
5   To test the voltage regulator, connect a 0-20V moving coil voltmeter between control box terminal WL (remove the lead), and a good earth point (negative lead to earth).
6   Pull off the Lucar connections from the control box terminals B-B. Join together, and insulate the join in case they should short-circuit adjacent items and cause damage.
7   Start the engine and run it at about 2000 rpm, and compare the voltmeter reading with the Specifications. If the reading is unsteady this may be due to dirty contacts. If the reading is outside the specified limits stop the engine and adjust the voltage regulator.
8   To adjust, employ the proper setting tool to turn the cam until the setting is within the specified limits. Stop the engine. Start the engine again, and recheck the reading.
9   To test the current regulator, remove the cover and short circuit the voltage regulator contacts by closing them together with a clip. Pull the wires from terminals B-B. Join them together, connect a 0-40 amp moving coil ammeter to the join and insulate the connection against possible short-circuiting. Connect the remaining ammeter lead to B-B on the control box.
10  Start the engine and switch on all lights. Run the engine at 3000 rpm and check the ammeter reading against the Specification. If the needle flickers it is likely that the points are dirty. If the reading is too low turn the special Lucas tool clockwise to raise the setting and anti-clockwise to lower it. Stop the engine, re-start, and re-check the reading.
11  To test the cut-out setting, connect a voltmeter as described in

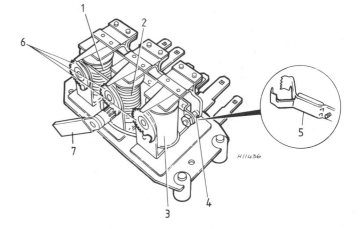

Fig. 10.5 Control box (Lucas RB340) – top cover removed (Sec 8)

| | | | |
|---|---|---|---|
| 1 | Cut-out relay | 5 | Clip |
| 2 | Current regulator | 6 | Adjustment cams |
| 3 | Voltage regulator | 7 | Setting tool |
| 4 | Contacts | | |

paragraph 5, switch on all lights, and start the engine. Slowly increase engine speed and observe the voltmeter reading, which should increase steadily, before dropping slightly at the point of contact closure. If the indicated voltage is outside the Specifications, adjust the cut-out relay clockwise to raise the reading or anti-clockwise to lower it, using the Lucas tool.
12  To check the cut-out relay drop-off voltage, leave the set-up as in paragraph 11, start the engine and run it at 3000 rpm. Observing the meter, reduce the engine speed and note the reading indicated immediately before it drops to zero. Check against the Specification. If adjustment is required bend the fixed contact bracket carefully, reducing the contact gap to raise the voltage, or increasing to lower the voltage. Re-check, and adjust again if necessary.
13  Air gap settings are accurately set in the factory and should not be disturbed. Renewal of the control box is advised if the unit does not respond to adjustment of the electrical settings.

## 11 Alternator (Lucas type 16ACR) – description and maintenance

1   The type 16ACR alternator incorporates its own built-in regulator and is shown in exploded form in Fig. 10.6.
2   Maintenance consists of occasionally wiping away any dirt or oil which may have collected around the apertures in the slip ring end bracket and moulded cover.
3   Check the fanbelt tension every 5000 miles (8000 km) and adjust as described in Chapter 2 by loosening the mounting bolts. Pull the alternator body away from the engine block. Do not use a lever as it will distort the alternator casing.
4   No lubrication is required as the bearings are grease-sealed for life.
5   Take extreme care when making connections to a vehicle fitted with an alternator. When making connections from a battery always match correct polarity. Before using electric-arc welding equipment to repair any part of the vehicle, disconnect the alternator leads and the positive battery terminal. Never start the car with a battery charger connected. Always disconnect both battery leads before using a mains charger. If boosting from another battery, always connect in parallel using heavy cable. It is not recommended that testing of an alternator should be undertaken at home due to the testing equipment required and the possibility of damage occurring during testing. It is best left to automotive electrical specialists.

## 12 Alternator (Lucas type 16ACR) – removal and refitting

1   Disconnect the battery. Disconnect the leads to the alternator.
2   Remove the radiator filler cap to depressurise the cooling system, to prevent a water leak at the strap bolt on the timing cover. Take great

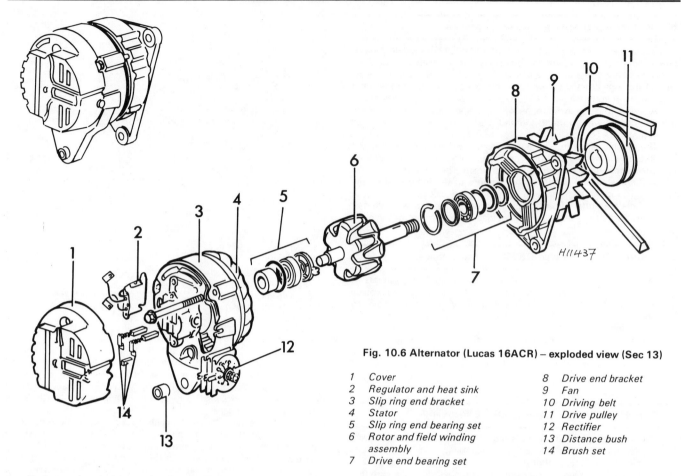

**Fig. 10.6 Alternator (Lucas 16ACR) – exploded view (Sec 13)**

1   Cover
2   Regulator and heat sink
3   Slip ring end bracket
4   Stator
5   Slip ring end bearing set
6   Rotor and field winding
    assembly
7   Drive end bearing set

8   Drive end bracket
9   Fan
10  Driving belt
11  Drive pulley
12  Rectifier
13  Distance bush
14  Brush set

care if the engine is hot, and refer to Chapter 2 for the correct procedure.

3   Loosen the alternator securing bolts, and push the unit towards the engine block sufficiently far to enable the fanbelt to be slipped off the alternator pulley. Remove the securing bolts, but avoid removal of the timing cover strap bolt or loss of coolant will occur. Lift away the alternator.

4   Refitting is a reversal of the removal procedure, but ensure that the connections are correctly made and that the fanbelt is adjusted as described in Chapter 2.

## 13 Alternator (Lucas type 16ACR) – servicing

1   Servicing other than renewal of the brushes is not recommended. The major components should normally last the life of the unit and in the event of failure a factory exchange replacement should be obtained.

2   To renew the brushes, refer to Fig. 10.6, remove the two cover screws and withdraw the moulded cover.

3   Unsolder the three stator connections to the rectifier assembly, noting carefully the order of connection.

4   Withdraw the two brush moulding securing screws, and slacken the nut on the rectifier assembly bolt. Remove the regulator securing screw and (if fitted) the suppressor cable at the rectifier. Withdraw the brush moulding and rectifier assembly complete with short linking cable.

5   Inspect the brushes which should protrude 0.2 in (5 mm) beyond the brush box moulding when in a free position. Renew if worn to, or below, this amount, and do not lose the leaf spring fitted at the side of the inner brush.

6   Should a brush stick, clean it with petrol or lightly rub with a smooth file.

7   The surfaces of the slip rings should be clean and smooth. If necessary, clean with a petrol moistened cloth. If there is evidence of burning, use very fine glass paper to clean (not emery).

8   Reassemble in reverse order to dismantling.

## 14 Alternator (Delco Remy type DN460) – description, maintenance, removal and refitting

The information given in Sections 11 and 12 applies equally to the Delco Remy alternator.

## 15 Alternator (Delco Remy type DN460) – servicing

1   Servicing, other than renewal of the brushes, is not recommended. The major components should normally last the life of the unit and, in the event of failure, a factory exchange replacement should be obtained.

2   To renew the brushes remove the alternator from the engine as described in Section 12.

3   Refer to Fig. 10.7 and remove the three clamp bolts which hold the two halves of the alternator together. Separate the pulley end cover from the rear cover assembly by inserting a screwdriver between the stator and the pulley end cover. The rotor will be withdrawn with the pulley and the brushes will be ejected from their holders in the rear cover. Place the rear cover on a bench and protect the rear bearing from dirt by placing a sheet of paper over it.

4   From within the rear cover unscrew and remove the screw securing the field diode lead to the brush holder and voltage regulator, and bend the connecting terminal up out of the way. Note the insulating washer under the screw head. Remove the remaining brush holder securing screw, noting the insulating washer and sleeve, and lift the brush holder out of the end cover assembly.

5   Examine the brushes, which should protrude 0.20 in (5 mm) beyond the brush holder moulding when in a free position. Renew them if necessary and check their movement in the holder. Clean them with petrol or lightly rub with a smooth file if there are any high spots.

6   The surfaces of the slip rings should be clean and smooth. If necessary, clean them with a petrol moistened cloth. If there is evidence of burning, use only very fine glass paper to clean (not emery paper or tape).

7   To reassemble the alternator, obtain a length of straight wire of 3/32 in (2.0 mm) diameter and file any sharp edges from each end. Fit the springs and brushes into the brush holder, depress them fully, and pass the wire through the hole in the holder to retain the brushes. Position the holder over the voltage regulator, at the same time passing the wire through the small hole in the end cover.

8   Bend the field diode connecting terminal over the brush holder and fit the two securing screws, tightening evenly to avoid uneven stress in the holder and regulator mouldings. Install the insulating washers and sleeves correctly.

9   Remove the paper from the end cover bearing and assemble the halves of the alternator together, making sure that the two mounting lugs are aligned.

10  Insert the three clamp bolts, and tighten them evenly. The rotor

should rotate without resistance. If not, slightly release the clamp bolts and tap the body lightly to reposition the rotor, then retighten the bolts. Release the brushes by removing the retaining wire and refit the alternator, as described in Section 12.

## 16 Alternator (Mitsubishi type AH-2040C-4) – description and servicing

1   This alternator is of a similar basic construction to the Delco Remy type described in Sections 14 and 15, and servicing, other than renewal of the brushes, is not recommended.

2   To remove the brush box, refer to Fig. 10.8 and remove the capacitor securing screw, the capacitor, the field terminal plug, the

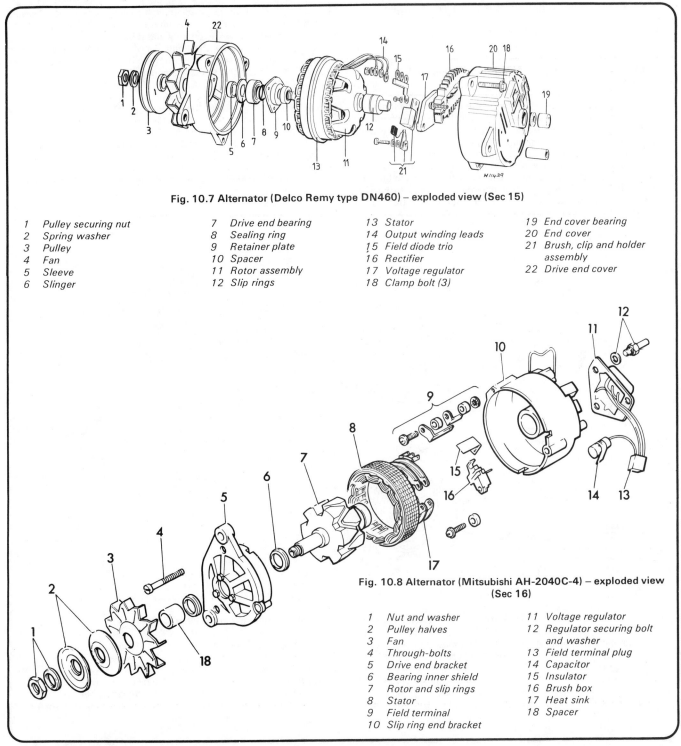

**Fig. 10.7 Alternator (Delco Remy type DN460) – exploded view (Sec 15)**

| | | | |
|---|---|---|---|
| 1  Pulley securing nut | 7  Drive end bearing | 13  Stator | 19  End cover bearing |
| 2  Spring washer | 8  Sealing ring | 14  Output winding leads | 20  End cover |
| 3  Pulley | 9  Retainer plate | 15  Field diode trio | 21  Brush, clip and holder |
| 4  Fan | 10  Spacer | 16  Rectifier |      assembly |
| 5  Sleeve | 11  Rotor assembly | 17  Voltage regulator | 22  Drive end cover |
| 6  Slinger | 12  Slip rings | 18  Clamp bolt (3) | |

**Fig. 10.8 Alternator (Mitsubishi AH-2040C-4) – exploded view (Sec 16)**

| | |
|---|---|
| 1  Nut and washer | 11  Voltage regulator |
| 2  Pulley halves | 12  Regulator securing bolt |
| 3  Fan |      and washer |
| 4  Through-bolts | 13  Field terminal plug |
| 5  Drive end bracket | 14  Capacitor |
| 6  Bearing inner shield | 15  Insulator |
| 7  Rotor and slip rings | 16  Brush box |
| 8  Stator | 17  Heat sink |
| 9  Field terminal | 18  Spacer |
| 10  Slip ring end bracket | |

three screws and the regulator. Mark the drive end bracket, the stator, and slip ring end bracket, to assist with reassembly. (These screws are normally very tight, and an impact tool may be required).

3   Prise at the slots provided to separate the main items.

4   Loosen the four heat sink and brush box assembly screws, but do not try to remove any where the head interferes with the stator winding. Release them evenly, separating the stator and end bracket, eventually removing the stator/heat sink assembly with the screws. Collect the washers between the positive heat sink and the end bracket.

5   Lift the insulator from the field terminal block, withdraw the brush box securing screws (avoiding damage to the winding), lift away the earth and capacitor blades, and withdraw the stepped insulators from the heat sink and brush box. Remove the brush box assembly.

6   Remove the brushes and compare with the length quoted in the Specifications.

7   Refitting is a reversal of dismantling.

## 17  Starter motor (Lucas type M35J, inertia engaged) – general description

The inertia engaged type of starter motor is mounted on the right-hand side of the engine, attached to a circular cut-out in the crankcase clutch bellhousing by two bolts. A separate electro-magnetically operated switch is actuated through the ignition system.

The principle of operation of the inertia type starter motor is as follows: when the ignition switch is turned, current flows from the battery to the starter motor solenoid switch which causes it to become energised. Its internal plunger moves inwards and closes an internal switch, so allowing full starting current to flow from the battery to the starter motor. This creates a powerful magnetic field in the field coils which causes the armature to rotate.

Mounted on helical splines is the drive pinion which, because of the sudden rotation of the armature, is thrown forwards along the armature shaft and so tinto engagement with the ring gear. The engine crankshaft will then be rotated until the engine starts to operate on its own and, at this point, the drive pinion is thrown out of mesh with the ring gear.

## 18  Starter motor (Lucas type M35J, inertia engaged) – testing in position

1   If the starter motor fails to operate, check the condition of the battery by turning on the headlamps. If they glow brightly for several seconds and then go dim, the battery is in an uncharged condition.

2   If the headlamps glow brightly and it is obvious that the battery is in good condition, check the tightness of the battery wiring connections (particularly the earth lead from the battery terminal to the body frame). Check the tightness of the connections at the relay switch and at the starter motor. Check the wiring for breaks or shorts.

3   If the wiring is in order, check that the starter motor switch is operating. To do this press the rubber covered button in the centre of the relay switch under the bonnet. If it is working the starter motor will be heard to 'click' as it tries to rotate.

4   If the motor fails to operate with the battery fully charged, the wiring in order, and the switch working, it will have to be removed from the car for examination. However, first ensure that the starter pinion has not jammed in mesh with the flywheel. Check by turning the square end of the armature shaft with a spanner. This will free the pinion if it is jammed.

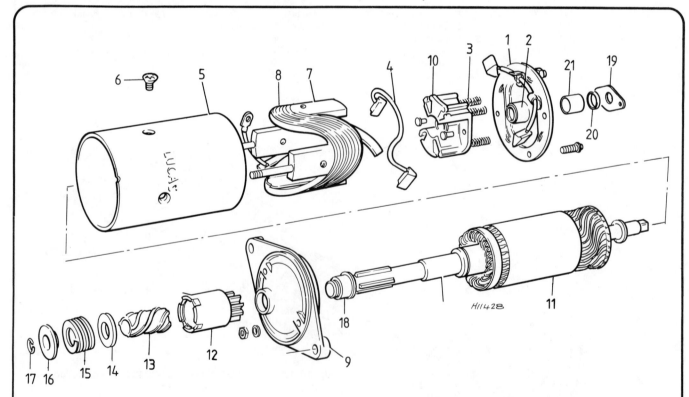

**Fig. 10.9 Starter motor (Lucas type M35J, inertia engaged) – exploded view (Sec 19)**

| | | |
|---|---|---|
| 1   Commutator end bracket | 7   Pole shoe | 12  Pinion and barrel | 17  Jump ring |
| 2   Bush housing | 8   Field coils | 13  Screwed sleeve | 18  Bearing bush |
| 3   Brush springs | 9   Drive end brackets | 14  Buffer washer | 19  Bush cover |
| 4   Brushes | 10  Brush box moulding | 15  Main spring | 20  Felt washer |
| 5   Yoke | 11  Armature | 16  Cup spring | 21  Bearing bush |
| 6   Pole screw | | | |

## 19 Starter motor (Lucas type M35J, inertia engaged) – removal, dismantling, reassembly and refitting

1   Disconnect the battery earth lead from the negative terminal. Disconnect the starter motor cable from the terminal on the motor endplate, and remove the upper motor securing bolt.
2   Working under the car loosen, and then remove, the lower securing bolt taking care to support the motor to prevent damage to the drive components. Lift the starter motor out of engagement with the flywheel ring gear. Remove the motor.
3   Referring to Fig. 10.9, and with the starter motor removed, remove the drive end bracket securing nuts followed by the bracket. Withdraw the armature complete with drive assembly and internal thrust washer. Remove the thrust washer.
4   Remove the commutator end bracket screws and withdraw the bracket. Disengage the field brushes from the brush box moulding.
5   Dismantle the drive assembly by using a spring compressor on the main starter spring until the jump ring is sufficiently exposed to be eased from its groove. Remove the remaining items.
6   Reassembly is a reversal of the dismantling procedure.
7   Refit the motor in the reverse sequence to removal.

## 20 Starter motor (Lucas type M35J, inertia engaged) – servicing

1   Clean any copper swarf from the dismantled parts.
2   Check that the brushes are free to move in the brush box. If not, clean with petrol. Check the brush length against the Specifications and renew if worn.
3   To renew the brushes note the arrangement of the long and short flexible connections relative to the end bracket and then cut them from their end bracket terminal.
4   Cut a groove in the terminal head suitable in depth to accommodate both flexible connections.
5   Solder the new flexibles to the terminal groove.
6   Cut the brushes from the field winding, leaving $\frac{1}{4}$ in (6 mm) stubs.
7   Solder a pair (long and short) of new brush connections to the stubs. Tape well to insulate.
8   Clean the surface of the commutator with a petrol moistened rag or if necessary with fine glass paper. *Do not undercut the mica insulators between the commutator segments.* If the commutator is in poor condition it may be skimmed in a lathe as long as the limits given in the Specifications are adhered to. The armature should be checked in a lathe for eccentricity, if there are signs of it touching the pole shoes. If no eccentricity is evident, the end bracket bearings will be at fault and in need of renewal.
9   With the starter motor dismantled, test the four field coils for an open circuit. Connect a 12 volt battery with a 12-volt bulb between the field terminal post and the tapping point on the field coils to which the brushes are connected. An open circuit is proved by the bulb not lighting.
10   If the bulb lights, it does not necessarily mean that the field coils are in order, as one of the coils may be earthing to the yoke or pole shoes. To check this, remove the lead from the brush connector and place it against a clean portion of the starter yoke. If the bulb lights the field coils are earthing.
11   Renewal of the field coils is beyond the scope of most owners, but if this is to be carried out, first drill out the rivet at the earth connection. Using a wheel operated screwdriver, slacken the four pole shoe screws. Remove two opposite screws and pole shoes. Slacken the remaining screws enough to permit withdrawal of the field winding. Wipe all parts clean, and insert the new field winding into the yoke, locating it under the pole shoe shoulders. Refit the remaining items in reverse order.
12   If wear is present in the end cover bushes, the use of shouldered and polished mandrels as shown in Fig. 10.10 is advised. On the commutator endplate, drill out the rivets and hence remove the bush cover and felt washer. Preferably employ extractors to withdraw the bushes. Alternatively a $\frac{1}{2}$ in (12.70 mm) tap may be screwed squarely into the commutator end bush to allow it to be pulled out.
13   The drive end may be carefully pressed out employing suitable sockets or other tubular items.
14   Prepare the porous bronze bush by soaking it for 24 hours in the specified oil, before fitting it. Soak the felt washer.
15   Press the bushes into place, using mandrel A for the commutator

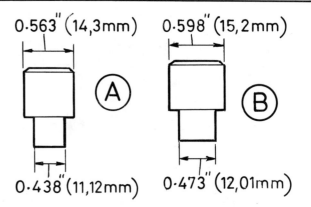

**Fig. 10.10 Mandrels for starter motor bush renewal (Sec 20)**

*A   Commutator end*                    *B   Drive end*

end, B for the drive end (Fig. 10.10).
16   Re-rivet the bush cover, complete with the felt washer, to the commutator end bracket. Note that reaming is not permissible.
17   To service the inertia drive assembly, refer to Fig. 10.9 and, using a spring compressor, remove the jump ring followed by the remaining items. Wash the components in paraffin, dry, and refit. Where the pinion and barrel and screwed sleeve are to be renewed, then renew as a matched pair.

## 21 Starter motor (Lucas type M35J-PE, pre-engaged) – general description

This motor has a solenoid mounted on the body, the solenoid serving to operate both switching contacts and a lever coupled to a roller clutch assembly. When the starter switch is operated, the solenoid plunger is actuated, engaging the starter pinion with the flywheel. The design is such that, once the pinion is engaged, the solenoid closes the contacts which connect the battery to the motor, thus turning the starter pinion. A hold-on winding in the solenoid keeps the pinion engaged whilst the ignition switch is in operation, but when the switch is released the winding no longer functions and the plunger returns to its normal position. This pre-engagement of the starting pinion results in much less wear on both the pinion and the starter ring than with the inertia-drive type.

## 22 Starter motor (Lucas type M35J-PE, pre-engaged) – removal, dismantling, reassembly and refitting

1   To remove the motor, disconnect the battery earth lead, and the supply cables. Remove the upper starter motor retaining bolt.
2   Working under the car, remove the lower bolt, taking care to support the motor to prevent damage to the drive. Withdraw the motor from the bellhousing.
3   To dismantle the motor, refer to Fig. 10.11 and remove the solenoid, then separate the solenoid plunger and drive return spring from the engagement lever.
4   Remove the grommet from between the drive end bracket and the motor yoke.
5   Remove the engagement lever pivot pin by removing the retaining ring.
6   Remove the drive end bracket bolts and withdraw the bracket.
7   Lift the engagement lever off the drive operating plate.
8   Remove the cotter pin, shim washers and thrust washer from the armature shaft.
9   Withdraw the armature complete with internal thrust washer and drive assembly from the drive end of the yoke. Remove the thrust washer from the commutator end of the armature shaft.
10   Remove the two commutator end bracket screws and lift it from the yoke, at the same time disengaging the brushes from the brush box.
11   Remove the drive assembly complete from the armature and dismantle into separate parts by using a tube to compress the coil spring, enabling the jump ring to be removed, from its groove.

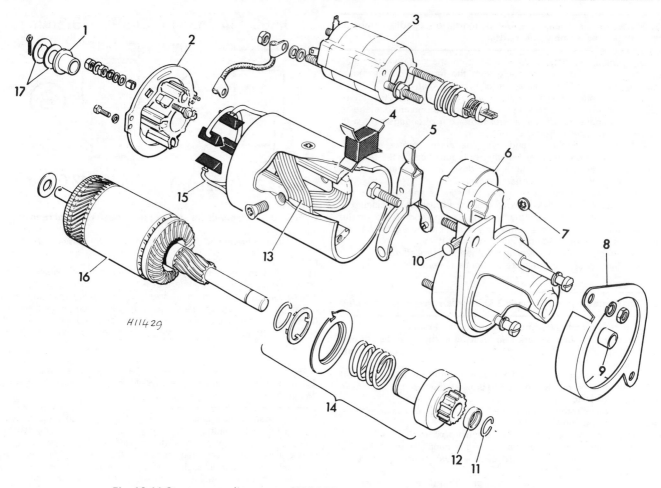

H11429

**Fig. 10.11 Starter motor (Lucas type M35J-PE, pre-engaged) – exploded view (Sec 22)**

| | | |
|---|---|---|
| 1 | Bush commutator end | 6 | Drive end bracket | 11 | Jump ring | 15 | Brush set |
| 2 | Commutator end bracket | 7 | Pivot pin retainer | 12 | Thrust collar | 16 | Armature |
| 3 | Solenoid | 8 | Dust cover | 13 | Field coil set | 17 | Thrust washer – shim |
| 4 | Grommet | 9 | Bush | 14 | Drive – roller clutch | | set |
| 5 | Engagement lever | 10 | Pivot pin | | assembly | | |

12  Reassembly is the reverse of dismantling, but note that the plunger attached to the top of the engagement lever is matched to the main part of the solenoid and is not interchangeable.

13  Refitting is a straightforward reversal of the removal procedure, but ensure that the engine earth strap is reconnected or serious damage will result.

---

**23  Starter motor (Lucas type M35J-PE, pre-engaged) – servicing**

1  Attention to the brushes and commutator is as described in Section 20 for inertia engaged motors. Do not undercut the mica insulation between the commutator segments.

2  Carry out a field winding check as described in Section 20. Should there be a fault, it is recommended that a factory reconditioned unit be obtained.

3  Starter motor bearings may be renewed as described in Section 20. The brush gear arrangement applicable to pre-engaged motors is shown in Fig. 10.12.

4  The roller clutch and drive mechanism of a pre-engaged starter motor provides instantaneous take-up of drive in one direction and freewheeling in the other. The assembly should move freely round and along the armature shaft splines without roughness. Where this condition is not apparent, a replacement unit should be fitted. Keep all moving parts (14) (Fig. 10.11) lubricated with light grease.

5  The setting of the pinion and correct function of the solenoid and

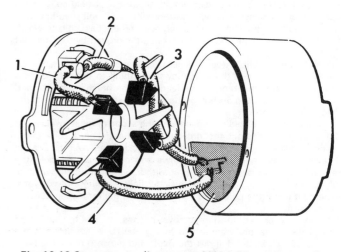

**Fig. 10.12 Starter motor (Lucas type M35J-PE, pre-engaged) – brush gear arrangement (Sec 23)**

1  *Short brush – flexible, commutator end bracket*
2  *Long brush – flexible, commutator end bracket*
3  *Long brush – flexible, field winding*
4  *Short brush – flexible, field winding*
5  *Yoke insulator – field connection joint*

drive depend upon clearances being maintained as originally manufactured. Where wear occurs, a new unit should be obtained.

### 24 Starter motor (Lucas type M35J-PE, pre-engaged) – solenoid servicing

1   Refer to Figs. 10. 13 and 10.14. The solenoid plunger is fitted with

a lost motion spring which provides a measure of lost motion in the drive operating mechanism. This lost motion takes place at the beginning of drive disengagement to ensure that the main solenoid contacts will always open prior to pinion retraction. Lost motion will also take effect if the pinion does not disengage from the flywheel ring gear when the solenoid switch is released.

2   Check the operation of the solenoid in position on the starter motor, but first disconnect the flexible link at the solenoid 'STA' terminal.

3   Check the continuity of the solenoid windings by connecting a 12 volt, 6 watt bulb between the terminal 'STA' and a good earth on the solenoid body. The lamp will light if both windings are in good order.

4   Check the resistance of the closing coil by connecting an ohmmeter between terminal (14) (Fig. 10.14) and earth on the solenoid body.

5   If the main solenoid contacts are suspect, the fixed contacts and the moving spindle and contact assembly must be renewed as a matched set. Check the operation of the contacts by connecting a 12 volt, 60 watt test lamp between the main terminals, when the lamp should not light. Energise the solenoid by connecting a separate 12 volt lead between the unmarked terminal and earth on the solenoid body. The solenoid should operate and the test lamp light to full brilliance.

6   Access to the contacts is obtained by withdrawing the two screws (12) (Fig. 10.14) which secure the moulded cover to the halves of the solenoid body. Unsolder the three winding connections from (i) the small unmarked terminal (ii) the terminal marked 'STA' (iii) the earth connection beneath one of the body screws. Withdraw the cover.

7   Where the solenoid body has been separated for coil renewal, a petrol resistant jointing compound must be used between the mating faces on reassembly. Ensure that the separated ends of the windings protrude through the insulated body slot. The thicker of the wires connects with the 'STA' terminal and the thinner to the earth strip.

8   Reassembly of the unit is a reversal of dismantling but take care to check the correct sequence of assembly when reassembling the drive engagement lever to the operating plate and the plunger assembly to the lever (Fig. 10.13). Always use a new pivot pin retainer (7) (Fig. 10.11).

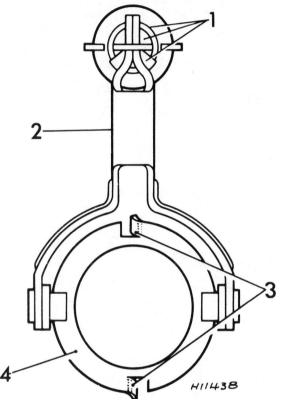

**Fig. 10.13 Engagement lever and solenoid plunger – assembly (Sec 24)**

1   Plunger, 'lost motion' spring and retaining plate
2   Drive engagement lever
3   Locking shoulders
4   Drive operating plate

### 25 Starter motor (Lucas type MEB02-0, pre-engaged) – general description

This motor is fitted to certain models, including the North American Cricket. It is of four pole, four brush construction with a series-parallel field. The drive gear operating solenoid has voltage and current coils, the latter being shorted out when the drive gear is fully engaged with the flywheel. The drive gear incorporates an over-running clutch and slides on a helical spline. The motor has an adjustable drive gear and whenever the unit has been dismantled or reassembled it must be adjusted as described in the relevant Section.

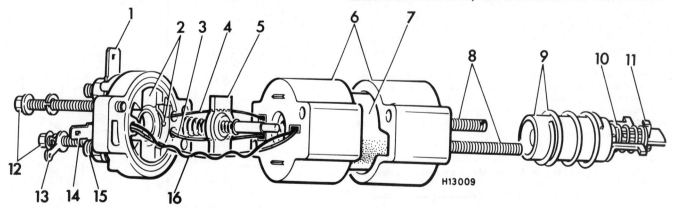

**Fig. 10.14 Solenoid (pre-engaged starter motor) – exploded view (Sec 24)**

1   Lucar terminal
2   Baseplate (fixed main contact)
3   'STA' terminal connection
4   Earth strip connection
5   Spindle and contact assembly
6   Body
7   Coil assembly
8   Fixing studs
9   Plunger and return spring
10  'Lost motion' spring
11  Spring retainer
12  Securing screws
13  Earth strip
14  Lucar terminal (unmarked)
15  'STA' terminal
16  Connection to unmarked Lucar

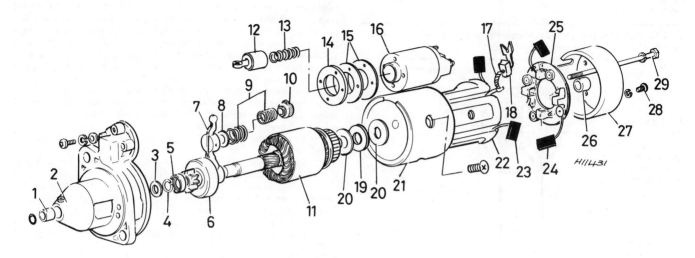

Fig. 10.15 Starter motor (type MEB020-0, pre-engaged) – exploded view (Sec 26)

| | | |
|---|---|---|
| 1 Bush | 9 Inner and outer springs | 17 Field lead | 24 Earth brush |
| 2 Drive end bracket | 10 Outer spring retainer | 18 Insulator | 25 Brush holder |
| 3 Thrust washer | 11 Armature | 19 Fibre thrust washer | 26 Bush |
| 4 Stop ring | 12 Solenoid plunger | 20 Steel thrust washer | 27 Commutator end bracket |
| 5 Stop collar | 13 Plunger return spring | 21 Yoke | 28 Brush holder retaining |
| 6 Drive gear/clutch assembly | 14 Packing plate (steel) | 22 Field coil assembly | screw |
| 7 Engagement lever | 15 Packing plate (fibre) | 23 Brush | 29 Tie bolt |
| 8 Inner spring retainer | 16 Solenoid | | |

## 26 Starter motor (Lucas type MEB02-0, pre-engaged) – removal, dismantling, servicing, reassembly and refitting

1   To remove and refit, refer to Section 22.
2   To dismantle, proceed basically as described in Section 22. There are detail differences in the component parts, but the basic dismantling procedure is similar. Note, however, when removing the clutch and drive gear assembly, that the armature shaft should be supported vertically (not, however, supported on the commutator). Drive the stop collar down with a piece of tube, remove the stop ring, and withdraw the stop collar and clutch/drive gear assembly.
3   To refit the earth brushes, clean the brackets, heat the solder joints and remove the leads. Tin the new brush leads and solder into place. A heavy duty soldering iron will be required for this operation. Do not permit solder to creep along the lead for more than $\frac{1}{4}$ in (6 mm).
4   To refit the field coil brushes, note how the leads are placed in the coil ends. Remove the leads as in paragraph 3, and open up the coil end.
5   Tin the new brush lead, and insert it in the field coil in the correct direction. Solder in position, clamp the joint with pliers, and re-solder. Other general instructions are as described in paragraph 3.
6   Reassembly of the starter motor is the reverse of dismantling. Lubricate both ends of the armature shaft, and the splines, with light engine oil before assembly.

## 27 Starter motor (Lucas type MEB02-0 pre-engaged) – drive gear adjustment

1   Connect a 12 volt battery between the 'S' (small) terminal of the solenoid and the motor body, to energise the solenoid and move the drive gear to the engaged position.
2   Check the clearance between the faces of the drive gear and stop collar with feeler gauges. This should be between 0.020 and 0.080 in (0.50 and 2.00 mm). To reset, disconnect the battery, remove the solenoid and add or withdraw fibre packing washers until, on refitting, the solenoid and energising it, the correct clearance is achieved.

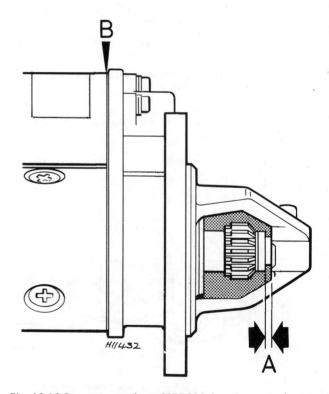

Fig. 10.16 Starter motor (type MEB020-0, pre-engaged) – drive gear adjustment diagram (Sec 27)

A   Drive gear to stop collar clearance 0.020 to 0.080 in (0.50 to 2.00 mm)
B   Location of adjustment packing shim

## 28 Starter motor (Mitsubishi type MEA16-0, pre-engaged – description and servicing)

1   This starter motor is similar in construction to the Lucas MEB02-0 with the following minor detail differences:

    *(a) Only one steel washer is fitted to the commutator end of the armature in addition to the thrust washer*
    *(b) Only one spring is fitted to the engagement lever*
    *(c) The solenoid is retained by two screws instead of three*

2   Servicing procedures are identical to those described in Section 26; however, the drive gear adjustment dimensions are different to those described in Section 27. With the starter motor de-energised, the distance from the surface of the mounting flange to the further edge of the pinion should be between 1.06 and 1.14 in (27.0 to 29.0 mm). With the motor energised as described in Section 27 the dimension should be between 1.58 and 1.66 in (40.0 and 42.0 mm).

## 29 Lighting system – general description

The lighting circuit is of single wire earth return type. The main wiring harness is located on the right-hand side of the car and connections are made by plug-in, snap or in-line connectors. The headlamp units are generally of sealed beam type, but renewable bulbs may be encountered in certain types.

## 30 Four headlamp system (Lucas round type) lamps and bulbs – removal and refitting

1   Disconnect the battery negative lead and remove the radiator grille by withdrawing the self-tapping screws located as shown in Chapter 12 according to headlamp style.
2   Slacken the three chrome retainer screws, rotate the retainer anti-clockwise and withdraw. Pull the light unit forward and disconnect the electrical connections.
3   The sealed beam unit will have to be renewed as a unit. Where a bulb type light unit is fitted the bulb holder is located separately at the rear of the reflector. The bulb may be replaced with a new one. The components of both sealed beam and bulb type light units are shown in Fig. 10.17.
4   Should the outer section of the headlight unit require removal, the four attachment rivets must be drilled out.
5   Refit all parts in the reverse order. Ensure that the sealing sleeves and gaskets are in good order and set the beams as detailed in Section 34.

## 31 Four headlamp system (Marchal round type) lamps and bulbs – removal and refitting

1   Remove the grille and the lamp finisher. Remove the light unit by snapping the three ball-ended screws out of the plastic shell by finger

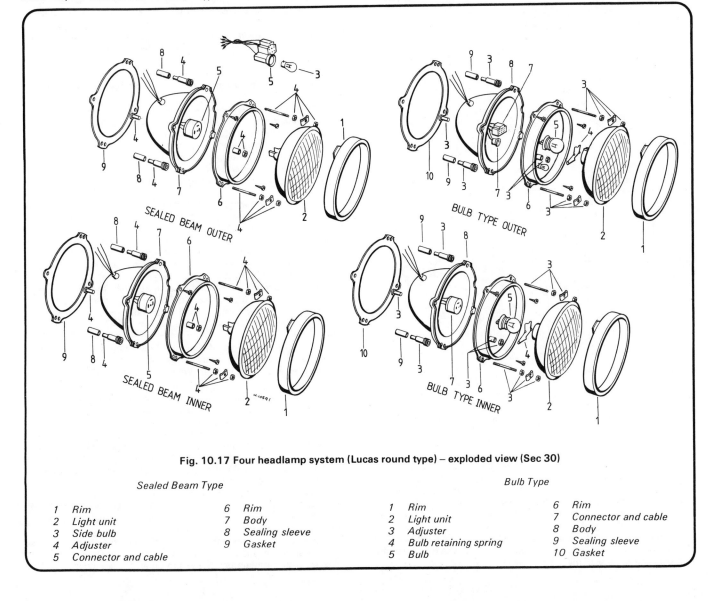

Fig. 10.17 Four headlamp system (Lucas round type) – exploded view (Sec 30)

| Sealed Beam Type | | | |
|---|---|---|---|
| 1 | Rim | 6 | Rim |
| 2 | Light unit | 7 | Body |
| 3 | Side bulb | 8 | Sealing sleeve |
| 4 | Adjuster | 9 | Gasket |
| 5 | Connector and cable | | |

| Bulb Type | | | |
|---|---|---|---|
| 1 | Rim | 6 | Rim |
| 2 | Light unit | 7 | Connector and cable |
| 3 | Adjuster | 8 | Body |
| 4 | Bulb retaining spring | 9 | Sealing sleeve |
| 5 | Bulb | 10 | Gasket |

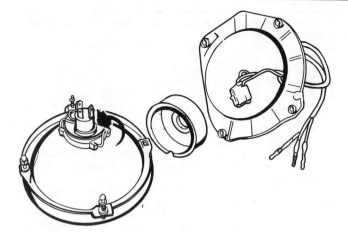

Fig. 10.18 Inner headlamp (Marchal type) – exploded view
(Sec 31)

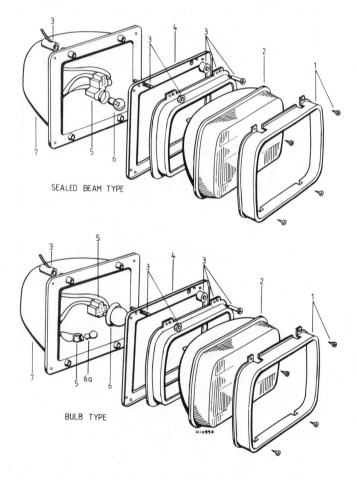

SEALED BEAM TYPE

BULB TYPE

Fig. 10.19 Headlamps (Lucas 4FR) – exploded view (Sec 32)

| 1 | Rim | 5 | Connection and cable |
|---|---|---|---|
| 2 | Light unit | 6 | Bulb |
| 3 | Rim | 6a | Side bulb |
| 4 | Mounting plate | 7 | Body |

and thumb pressure. Remove the connector plug and rubber cover. Ease the retaining spring clear of the bulb, and lift it out. Do not try to clean the reflector.

2    To refit, ensure that the glass envelope of the bulb is not handled. Clean with alcohol if it is touched. Refit all parts in the reverse order, and reset the lamp alignment if necessary.

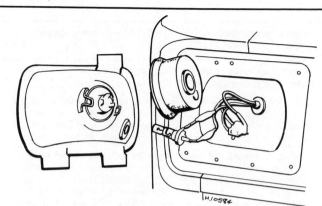

Fig. 10.20 Headlamp (Cibie type) – exploded view (Sec 32)

## 32  Headlamp (rectangular, Lucas type 4FR and Cibie) – bulb renewal

1    Disconnect the battery negative terminal and remove the radiator grille by withdrawing the self-tapping screws. Remove the four screws which secure the rim, at the same time supporting the light unit. In the case of the Cibie unit the headlamp frame must be 'snapped' off the ball-ended retaining screws. Withdraw the rubber seal and snap the bulb retaining clips away, and the bulb can then be extracted. To remove the outer section of a light unit the attachment rivets must be drilled out.

2    Refitting is a reversal of the removal procedure but ensure the headlamp beams are set as described in Section 35.

## 33  Headlamp (rectangular, commencing Series 7) – removal and refitting

1    The headlamps incorporate separate sidelamp bulbs clipped into the reflector assembly, which is itself mounted to a bracket by three ball and socket attachments.

2    To remove the reflector unit for bulb renewal, disconnect the battery negative terminal. Separate the plug and socket in the aperture behind the headlamp unit and remove the two star-headed screws from the flasher lens.

3    Using an angled length of flat steel or wheel cap remover, prise the headlamp reflector unit from its support bracket attachments while steadying the front lens. Make sure that the lever is inserted behind the bracket to avoid damaging the reflector. Partly withdraw the unit from its aperture and disconnect the green wire connector to the flasher assembly. The headlamp bulb socket connector and rubber seal can now be withdrawn from the headlamp.

4    Unhook the retaining clip and remove the bulb. The sidelamp bulb can also be removed after prising its holder out of the reflector. Note that the left-hand sidelamp bulb can be removed from within the engine compartment. Do not handle the envelope of bulbs with the fingers.

5    If further dismantling of the support bracket and flasher assembly is necessary, the grille assembly must be removed. Reassemble in reverse order, and check headlamp alignment before refitting the grille.

## 34  Four headlamp system – beam adjustment

1    Although it is preferable to have the headlamps set on optical equipment the following procedure will provide a good alternative. Set the car on level ground, 25 feet (7.62 metres) from, and at right-angles to, a flat surface. Load the vehicle with a full complement of fuel, oil and water, and check the tyre pressures.

2    Clean the glass of an inner lamp and mask the other three. Switch the headlamps to main beam. Refer to Figs. 10.25 and 10.26, and make the appropriate marks on the wall. Adjust each adjustment screw until the correct light pattern is obtained.

3    Repeat the operations for each lamp in turn, remembering to mask all lamps that are not being adjusted. During adjustment the inner lamps must be on main beam and the outer lamps dipped.

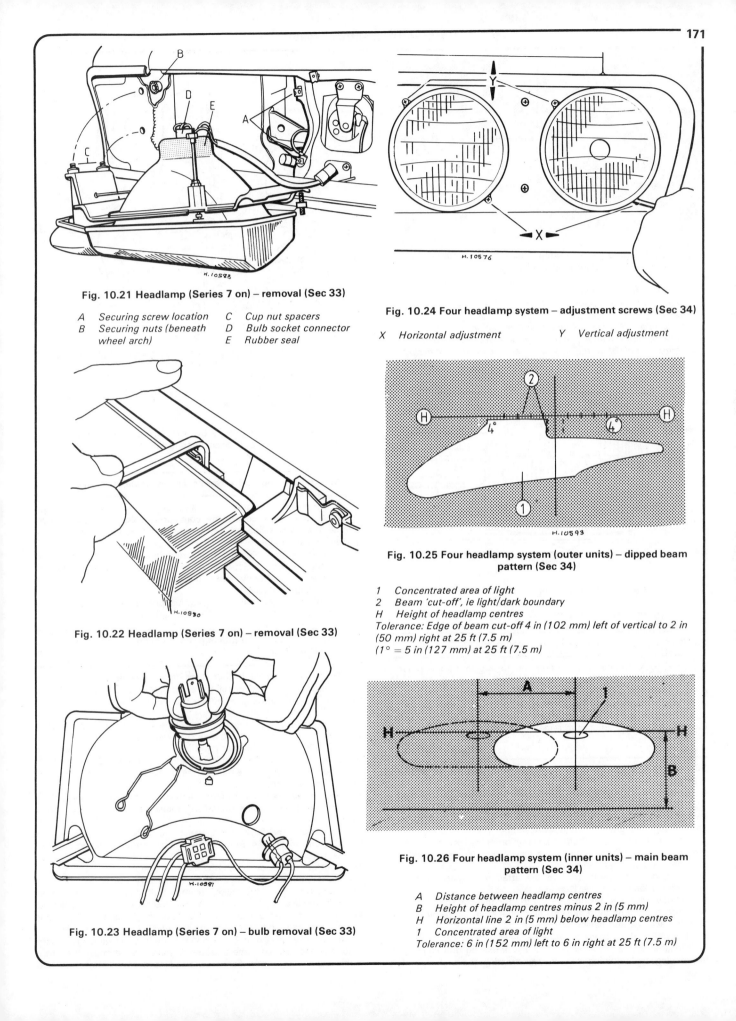

**Fig. 10.21 Headlamp (Series 7 on) – removal (Sec 33)**

A   Securing screw location
B   Securing nuts (beneath wheel arch)
C   Cup nut spacers
D   Bulb socket connector
E   Rubber seal

**Fig. 10.24 Four headlamp system – adjustment screws (Sec 34)**

X   Horizontal adjustment
Y   Vertical adjustment

**Fig. 10.22 Headlamp (Series 7 on) – removal (Sec 33)**

**Fig. 10.25 Four headlamp system (outer units) – dipped beam pattern (Sec 34)**

1   Concentrated area of light
2   Beam 'cut-off', ie light/dark boundary
H   Height of headlamp centres
Tolerance: Edge of beam cut-off 4 in (102 mm) left of vertical to 2 in (50 mm) right at 25 ft (7.5 m)
(1° = 5 in (127 mm) at 25 ft (7.5 m)

**Fig. 10.23 Headlamp (Series 7 on) – bulb removal (Sec 33)**

**Fig. 10.26 Four headlamp system (inner units) – main beam pattern (Sec 34)**

A   Distance between headlamp centres
B   Height of headlamp centres minus 2 in (5 mm)
H   Horizontal line 2 in (5 mm) below headlamp centres
1   Concentrated area of light
Tolerance: 6 in (152 mm) left to 6 in right at 25 ft (7.5 m)

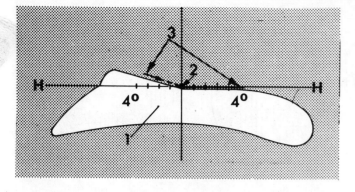

**Fig. 10.27 Rectangular headlamp (Lucas 4FR and Cibie) – dipped beam pattern (Sec 35)**

1   *Concentrated area of light*
2   *Beam 'kink' aiming point*
3   *Beam 'cut-off' ie light/dark boundary*
H   *Horizontal line 4 in (102 mm) below headlamp centres*
*Tolerance of kink aim point: from vertical line on screen to 6 in (152 mm) left only at 25 ft (7.5 mm). Tolerance to right not permitted (1° = 5 in (127 mm) at 25 ft (7.5 m)*

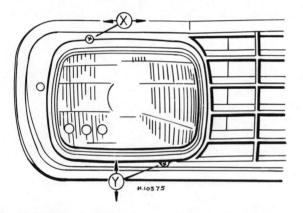

**Fig. 10.28 Rectangular headlamp – adjustment screws (Sec 35)**

X   *Horizontal adjustment*        Y   *Vertical adjustment*

## 35  Rectangular headlamp system – beam adjustment

1   Carry out the initial operations as described in the previous section, and, with reference to Fig. 10.27 make the appropriate marks on the wall.
2   Switch the headlamps to main beam. Adjust the screws in accordance with Fig. 10.28 to give the correct light pattern. Change over the mask, and adjust the remaining lamp.

## 36  Rear lamps and bulbs (up to Series 6 inclusive) – removal and refitting

1   On the saloon car, the rear lamp unit comprises stop/tail lamp, flasher lamp, reflector and (where fitted) reversing lamp. Bulb types and wattage are given in the Specifications.
2   To remove or renew a bulb in any section of the lamp unit, remove the protective hardboard covers and plastic retainers from inside the boot and pull out the bulb holder.
3   To remove the unit, remove the attachment parts, the earth connections, and the three U-straps.
4   Remove the unit, taking care not to tear the seal.
5   Detach the lens by removing the rubber seal, removing the lens securing screws, and easing the lens off.
6   Refit all parts in reverse sequence.
7   On the estate, remove a bulb by detaching the outer lens, unscrewing the retaining screws, and twisting the bulb out of its

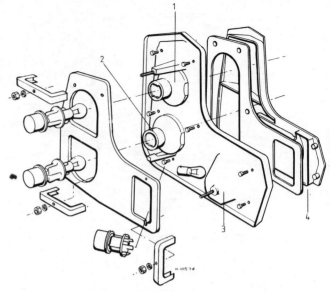

**Fig. 10.29 Rear lamp cluster (up to Series 6) – exploded view (Sec 36)**

1   *Flasher lamp position*        3   *Reversing position*
2   *Stop/tail lamp position*      4   *Lens*

holder. Remove the lamp body by unscrewing the retaining screws, withdrawing the unit, and disconnecting the leads.

## 37  Rear lamps and bulbs (Series 7) – removal and refitting

1   The rear lamps contain a foglamp bulb in addition to the lamp bulbs. A single lens covers the complete cluster. To renew bulbs, remove the six star-headed lens securing screws, withdraw the lens, and extract the bulbs.
2   To remove the lamp cluster, unscrew the two retaining nuts in the luggage compartment. Support the packing piece between the outer end of the unit and body, and withdraw the assembly. Separate the multi-pin plug and socket.
3   Refitting is a reversal of the removal procedure.

## 38  Flasher circuit – removing and refitting components, and correction of faults

1   To remove a front flasher lamp (early models) disconnect the battery earth lead, disconnect the snap connector in the lamp lead, remove the two nuts and withdraw the lamp.
2   Refit in reverse order.
3   To renew a bulb, remove the two lens securing screws and thus the lens. Remove the bulb. Renew the bulb and refit the lens.
4   To remove a front flasher lamp (Series 7 models on) remove the headlamp as described in Section 33 (do not disconnect the harness), and undo the green connection to the flasher lamp. Remove the cup nuts, followed by the lamp.
5   Refit in reverse order. To renew a bulb, proceed as in paragraph 3.
6   The rear flasher bulbs should be renewed as directed in Sections 36 or 37.
7   To remove the flasher unit, lower the steering column cowl as described in Section 44. Remove the flasher connections and thus the flasher unit.
8   Refit in reverse order.
9   If the flasher fails to operate or works very slowly, examine the front and rear bulbs for broken filaments. If these are satisfactory, check the facia warning bulb and renew if necessary. Check the flasher circuit connections against the appropriate circuit diagram at the end of this Chapter. Check fuse cartridge number 1 (Fig. 10.40 and 10.41). Switch on the ignition and check that current is reaching the flasher unit by connecting a voltmeter between the unit + terminal and earth. If this is the case, but the flashers are still inoperative, connect the two

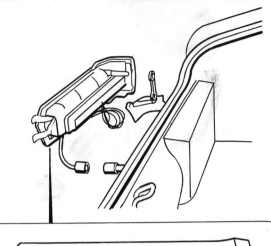

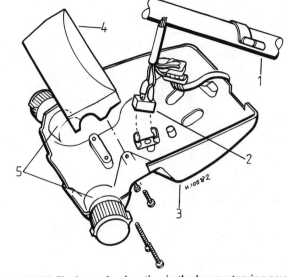

**Fig. 10.31 Flasher unit – location in the lower steering cowl
(Sec 38)**

| | |
|---|---|
| 1  Steering column | 4  Upper cowl |
| 2  Flasher unit | 5  Light switch and wiper |
| 3  Lower cowl | switch |

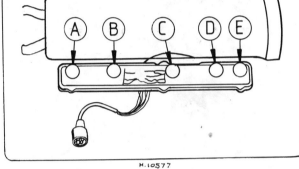

**Fig. 10.30 Rear lamp cluster (Series 7 on) (Sec 37)**

| | |
|---|---|
| A  Reversing lamp bulb | D  Stop lamp bulb |
| B  Fog lamp bulb | E  Indicator bulb |
| C  Tail lamp bulb | |

*(handwritten notes: Same as ⊥  12V 21W  P-25-1  12V 5W R19/5)*

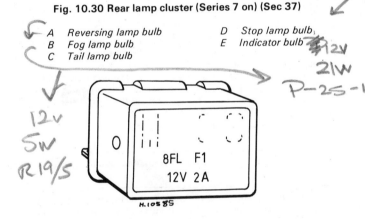

**Fig. 10.32 Flasher unit (Sec 38)**

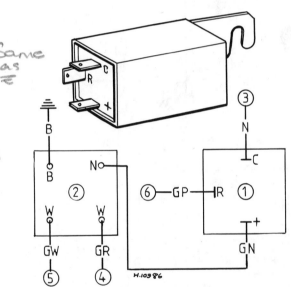

**Fig. 10.33 Combined indicator and hazard warning flasher
(Series 7 on) (Sec 38)**

| | | Colour code: | |
|---|---|---|---|
| 1 | Flasher unit | B | Black |
| 2 | Hazard warning switch | N | Brown |
| 3 | Electrical supply | R | Red |
| 4 | LH indicator lamps | G | Green |
| 5 | RH indicator lamps | P | Purple |
| 6 | Indicator warning light | W | White |
| | lead | | |

terminals together and operate the flasher switch. If the flasher warning light comes on, then the unit is faulty and must be renewed.

## 39 Hazard warning system – description and correction of faults

1   Models prior to Series 7 may be fitted with a flasher/hazard warning system incorporating two independent flasher units, one for the normal operation of the direction indicators, and the other for hazard warning operation. Each unit is rated to the electrical load it will have to carry and is also protected by independent fuses, the hazard unit fuse being in-line.

2   When in use, the hazard switch disconnects the normal flasher unit and completes the circuit through the hazard unit and all direction indicator lights. Note that there are a number of current ratings applicable to the hazard flasher unit, and it is imperative that the correct unit is fitted.

3   Should either flasher unit be inoperative, check the relative fuse for continuity. Clean the terminals if they are corroded.

4   Check each direction indicator bulb for broken filaments, and that

the bulb holders are earthed satisfactorily.

5   With a 12 volt test lamp and leads ensure that current is reaching each flasher unit (the ignition will have to be switched on to check the direction indicator unit). Referring to Fig. 10.35 check that the direction indicator flasher unit supply lead is routed through the hazard warning switch, which must be checked with the test lamp with the switch rocker in both positions. To do this, prise the multi-pin connector away from the switch enough to expose the terminals and to allow the test lamp probes to be inserted onto each terminal. Trace the current to the steering column indicator switch and then direct to the direction indicator bulbs at the front and rear of the car.

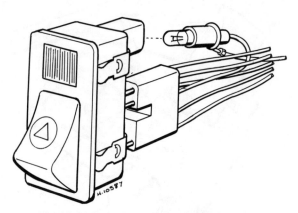

Fig. 10.34 Hazard warning switch (Sec 39)

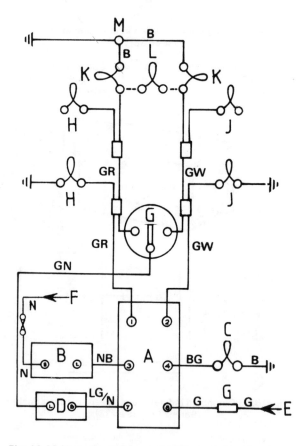

Fig. 10.35 Hazard warning system (up to Series 6) – circuit
diagram (Sec 39)

| A | Hazard warning switch | Colour code: | |
|---|---|---|---|
| B | Hazard warning flasher unit | N | Brown |
| C | Warning light | G | Green |
| D | Direction indicator flasher unit | W | White |
| E | Supply from number 1 fuse | LG | Light green |
| F | Supply wire from lighting switch | R | Red |
| G | Direction indicator switch | B | Black |
| H | LH indicator lamps | | |
| J | RH indicator lamps | | |
| K | Warning lights | | |
| L | Alternative warning light | | |
| M | Earth connection, plug and socket | | |

6   Models commencing at Series 7 are fitted with a combined
direction indicator and hazard warning unit, which is not fuse

Fig. 10.36 Side marker lamp assembly – exploded view (Sec 40)

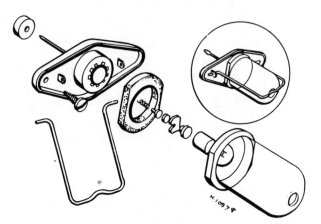

Fig. 10.37 Rear number plate lamp assembly – exploded view
(Sec 41)

protected. Refer to the wiring diagram in this Chapter to trace any
faults using the method previously described, but make sure that the
correct wires are fitted to their respective terminals as it is possible to
'burn out' the combined flasher unit if they are fitted incorrectly.
7   To renew the hazard warning switch or bulb, prise out the switch
and withdraw the bulb and holder. Renew the bulb if necessary. To
renew the switch, remove the harness plug.
8   Refit in reverse, taking care not to disturb the spring clips.

## 40 Side marker lamps (where fitted) and bulbs – removal and refitting

1   These lamps are fitted to North American Cricket versions. The
lamp mounted on the side of the front wing has an amber lens, and
that on the rear a red lens. They are illuminated in conjunction with the
side (parking) and tail lights. Prise the lens from its rubber surround to
renew a bulb.
2   To remove the front nut, disconnect the battery. Disconnect the
red cable to the lamp at the double connector behind the appropriate
headlamp. Remove the three nuts and washers inside the wing, and
withdraw the lamp. The rear unit is similarly removed.
3   Refitting is a reversal of removal.

## 41 Rear number plate lamp and bulb – removal and refitting

1   On early models, renew the bulb by springing off the clip and
removing the domed lens. Remove the lamp by disconnecting the
battery earth lead, disconnecting the snap connector behind the fuel
tank, and tying string or wire to the lamp lead. Remove the lamp,
leaving the string in place of the lamp cable. Refit in the reverse
sequence. Note that two lamps may be fitted to certain models.
2   On later models, renew the bulb as described in paragraph 1. To
remove the lamp, remove the two bolts from the rear bumper bracket,
and the two crosshead screws holding the lamp to the body panel.
Remove the rear right-hand lamp cluster (Section 37) and part the
relevant double bullet connectors. Refit in the reverse order.

## 42 Interior light, glovebox light and switch – removal and refitting

1 To remove the interior light, disconnect the battery earth lead, remove the securing screw at one end of the lamp, and disengage the lamp from the aperture. Refit in the reverse order.
2 To remove the glovebox light, disconnect the battery earth lead and detach the light from the glovebox slot. If a new light is fitted, cut the feed wire, and join using a connector. To remove the switch, disconnect the battery earth lead and remove the switch from the slotted glovebox. Refit in the reverse order.

## 43 Lighting switch – description, removal and refitting

1 The light switch is a rotary three-position type, and is located on the steering column cowling. A panel brightness control is fitted to certain models.
2 To remove the switch, lower the steering cowl as described in Section 44, disconnect the switch connections, and use a probe to release the switch knob heating peg. Remove the knob. Employing special tool RG 534, remove the switch securing nut and withdraw the switch. Refit in the reverse order.

## 44 Steering column switch (early cars) – removal and refitting

1 The switch operates the indicators, the headlamp beam, the headlamp flasher, and the horns.
2 To remove the switch, disconnect the battery earth lead, remove the two screws through the lower cowl and withdraw the upper cowl.
3 Remove the four screws retaining the lower cowl, and lower the cowl.
4 Disconnect the wiring connector, remove one saddle screw and slacken the other. Remove the switch.
5 Refit in reverse order.

## 45 Steering column switch (commencing Series 7) – removal and refitting

1 The switch controls lighting, horn and wash/wipe operations, and includes a self-cancelling device for the direction indicators.
2 To remove the switch, disconnect the battery earth lead and disengage the steering column lock.
3 Release the lower shroud by undoing seven cross-head screws, and remove the steering wheel as described in Chapter 11.
4 Remove the two $\frac{1}{2}$ in AF bolts and washers from the upper column bracket outside ends, and the two $\frac{1}{2}$ in AF nuts and washers from the lower bracket.
5 Lower the column, remove the two cross-head screws, and remove the upper shroud.
6 Remove the three cross-head screws and withdraw the column switch. Separate the multi-pin plugs and the two in-line connectors and lift the assembly over the end of the column.
7 Refitting is a reversal of the removal procedure. Ensure that the multi-pin plugs are fitted correctly and check the operation of the switch controls before fitting the lower shroud and steering wheel.

## 46 Reversing lamp switch – description and adjustment

1 The reversing lamp switch fitted to manual gearboxes is illustrated in Fig. 10.39. With automatic transmissions, a combined reversing lamp and starter solenoid inhibitor switch with four Lucar connections is fitted.
2 Removal or renewal of the manual gearbox type switch involves fitting shims so that with reverse gear selected, the ignition switched on and a test bulb connected in series with the switch, the bulb will light when the switch is tightened.
3 With the automatic transmission switch, select D and switch on the ignition.
4 Connect a test bulb in series with the reversing lamp switch (angled Lucar terminals) and, having loosened the switch locknut, screw in the switch until the bulb just lights.
5 Taking care not to rotate the switch, transfer the test bulb and

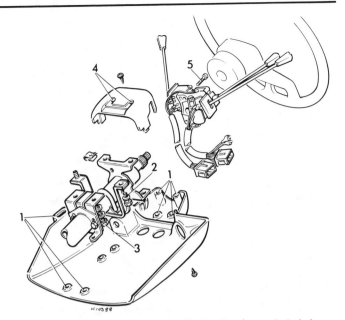

**Fig. 10.38 Steering column switch (Series 7 on) – exploded view (Sec 45)**

1 Lower support shroud securing screw locations
2 Upper support bracket bolts
3 Lower support bracket nuts
4 Upper shroud screw location
5 Switch assembly securing screws

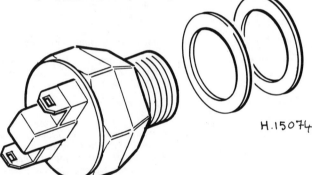

**Fig. 10.39 Reversing lamp switch and adjustment shims (manual gearbox) (Sec 46)**

leads to the solenoid inhibitor switch (straight Lucar terminals) and note the exact number of turns required to screw the switch in to make the test bulb light.
6 Halve this number of turns and unscrew the switch by this calculated number of rotations.
7 Tighten the locknut without moving the switch.

## 47 Stop lamp switch – description

The stop lamp switch is mounted on the brake pedal. Operation is automatic provided the correct brake pedal free movement is maintained as described in Chapter 9.

## 48 Fuse unit – description and servicing

1 On vehicles up to and including Series 3, a three-fuse unit is fitted. Wedge-shaped projections retain it to the bulkhead. Fuse applications are:

**Fuse No 1**      *Horn, reversing lamps, stop lamps, wiper motor, heater blower, fuel gauge, electric screen washer, direction in-*

dicators, water temperature gauge

Fuse No 2 — Interior lamp, cigar lighter, glovebox light

Fuse No 3 — Tail lamps

2   On vehicles from Series 4 to Series 7, an eight-fuse unit is fitted. Fuse applications are:

Fuse No 1 — Horn, reversing lamps, stop lamps, wiper motor, heater blower, electric screen washer, indicators, fuel gauge, water temperature gauge

Fuse No 2 — Interior lamp, cigar lighter, glovebox light

Fuse No 3 — RH side/tail lamps, panel lights, boot lamps

Fuse No 4 — LH side/tail lamps, number plate lamps

Fuse No 5 — RH headlamp main beam

Fuse No 6 — LH headlamp main beam

In addition, a separate in-line fuse for the heated rear window is fitted beneath the steering column, accessible through the hole in the lower shroud.

3   On vehicles from Series 8 onwards, a 12-fuse unit is fitted. Fuse applications are (as applicable):

Fuse No 1 — Heated rear window relay and element

Fuse No 2 — Horn(s)

Fuse No 3 — Heater blower motor and switch

Fuse No 4 — Interior lamps, clock, cigar lighter, luggage area lamp, brake warning lamp (PDWA)

Fuse No 5 — Direction indicators

Fuse No 6 — Reversing lamps, stop-lamps, heated rear window switch, brake pad indicator, windscreen wipers and washers, tailgate wiper and washer, oil level sensor system, automatic transmission gate illumination, headlamp wash/wipe motors and pump

Fuse No 7 — RH headlamp main beam

Fuse No 8 — RH headlamp dipped beam

Fuse No 9 — RH side/tail lamps, instrument illumination, heater control illumination, rear fog lamps and switch

Fuse No 10 — LH side/tail lamps, number plate lamps, clock illumination, switch panel illumination, under-bonnet lamp

Fuse No 11 — LH headlamp dipped beam, headlamp wash/wipe relay

Fuse No 12 — LH headlamp main beam

In-line fuse — Cooling fan motor and switch

4   Replacement fuses must be of the correct type and rating. If a replacement fuse burns out almost immediately, a fault must exist and should be rectified without delay. No maintenance is required other than ensuring that fuse connections are clean and tight.

## 49 Windscreen wiper assemblies (single and two speed, up to Series 6 inclusive) – description and testing

1   The windscreen wiper assembly (Fig. 10.42) is a link type

installation, mounted behind the facia panel. The motor is of unit construction and incorporates the gearing and self-parking mechanism. The single speed motor has a two brush assembly and the two speed motor a three brush assembly. The third stepped brush to which

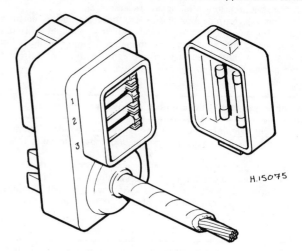

Fig. 10.40 Fuse unit – three fuse type (Sec 48)

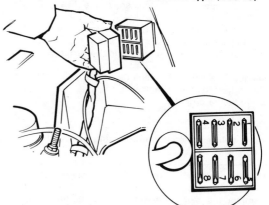

Fig. 10.41 Fuse unit – eight fuse type (Sec 48)

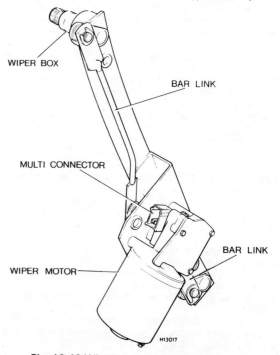

Fig. 10.42 Wiper motor assembly (Sec 49)

the positive supply is transferred is for high speed. No routine maintenance is required.

2　To check a faulty assembly remove the wiper arms from their splined shafts by depressing the retaining clip (Fig. 10.43) and pull the arms off.

3　Remove fuse number 1 from the fuse unit and connect an ammeter with a range of 0 to 10 amps in its place.

4　Switch on the ignition, check that the ammeter indicates zero, switch on the wiper motor and check that the running current and cycling of the driveshafts matches the figures given in the Specifications. Where low wiping speed is indicated then this may be due to binding of the linkage or a motor fault. Further examination calls for removal of the assembly.

### 50  Windscreen wiper assemblies (single and two speed, up to Series 6 inclusive) – removal and refitting

1　To remove the wiper assembly, disconnect the battery earth (negative) lead, detach the wiper arms and blades, and remove the instrument panel as described in Section 58 or 59.

2　Remove the radio escutcheon from the facia, and at the same time disconnect the cigarette lighter and blower switch. Remove the radio if fitted.

3　Use a probe in the removal hole to release the heater control knob retaining spring and withdraw each control knob.

4　Withdraw the facia air flow control panel from the facia vent duct.

5　Remove both heater control attachment screws and swing the control towards the scuttle and downwards.

6　Release the steering column side demister snout from the louvre by removing the packing pieces and gently pressing the fishtail to

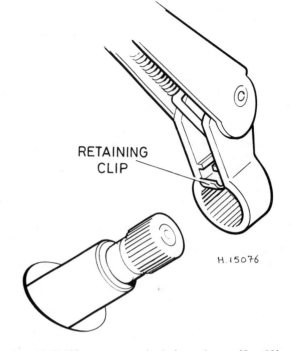

Fig. 10.43 Wiper arm – method of attachment (Sec 49)

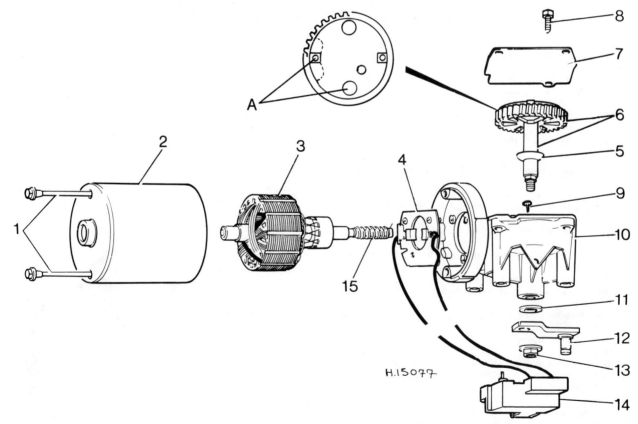

Fig. 10.44 Wiper motor – exploded view (Sec 49)

| | | | |
|---|---|---|---|
| 1　Yoke fixing bolts | 5　Dished washer | 9　Limit switch attachment screws | 12　Rotary link |
| 2　Yoke | 6　Shaft and gear | 10　Gearbox | 13　Link nut |
| 3　Armature | 7　Gearbox cover | 11　Flat washer | 14　Limit switch assembly |
| 4　Brush gear assembly | 8　Cover screws | | 15　Nylon thrust pad |

release the locating projections. Withdraw through the instrument panel aperture.

7    Withdraw the vent duct from the heater assembly by gently compressing the box section to release the locating projections.

8    Disconnect the wiper motor multi-connector plug and remove the screws from the wiper assembly attachment plate.

9    Ease the wiper assembly away from its location and withdraw through the instrument panel aperture and steering wheel spokes.

10   Refitting is a reversal of the removal procedure.

### 51  Windscreen wiper assemblies (single and two speed, up to Series 6 inclusive) – dismantling, servicing and reassembly

1    Refer to Fig. 10.44 and remove the snap ring assembly from the rotary link pivot.

2    Disengage the wiper motor by removing the drive bar attachment screws.

3    Remove the gearbox cover screws and cover and note the position of the rotary link relative to the zero mark on the shaft and gear (inset Fig. 10.44) to ensure exact refitting.

4    Keep the rotary link still, remove the nut, link and flat washer.

5    Remove the shaft and gear and dished washer from the gearbox. Should these components be separated note the relative positions of the zero mark and the gear cam.

6    Withdraw the yoke fixing bolts and disengage the yoke and armature from the gearbox.

7    Disengage the armature from the yoke and detach the brushgear and switch unit from the gearbox.

8    Check the condition of the brushes, and ensure that they move freely in their boxes. Clean the commutator with a petrol soaked rag and ensure that it is free from pitting or burning. Worn or damaged components should be renewed, but where windings are broken or armature insulation is faulty, then a factory replacement unit should be obtained.

9    Reassembly is a reversal of dismantling. Apply sparingly to the armature shaft bearings and bushes and soak the yoke and felt washer in oil. Apply grease to the gearwheel teeth, cam and worm gear. Set the armature endfloat by tightening the thrust screw until it just touches the end of the shaft, then unscrew $\frac{1}{4}$ turn and tighten the locknut. Operations for two speed wipers are similar to those described for single speed, but where two diametrically opposed main brushes are found to be worn, then the brushgear assembly must be renewed as a complete unit of three.

### 52  Windscreen wiper assembly (Series 7 on) – removal, refitting and servicing

1    Disconnect the battery negative terminal and detach the wiper arms and blades.

2    Remove the crash roll and instrument assembly as described in Section 57.

3    Detach the demister ducts from the heater unit, the face vent hoses and the centre duct.

4    Separate the multi-pin plug and socket at the wiper motor, remove the two securing bolts and screw, and withdraw the wiper motor assembly.

5    Refitting is a reversal of the removal procedure but, before fitting the wiper blades and arms, ensure that the wiper motor is in the parked position. Check the operation of all the instrument panel switches and gauges.

6    Servicing procedures remain basically as described for the single speed wiper motor, bearing in mind that on the two speed motor an extra brush is employed.

### 53  Tailgate wiper motor assembly (Series 7 on) – removal and refitting

1    Disconnect the battery negative terminal and detach the wiper arm and blade.

2    Release the locking bolt and remove the sleeve. Withdraw the nylon seal, unscrew the spindle nut, and extract the grommet.

3    Lift the tailgate and prise the trim away by inserting a thin screwdriver adjacent to each clip.

4    Note the location of the wiper motor supply leads, disconnect them from the wiper motor and release the harness from the retaining clip.

5    Withdraw the wiper motor from its bracket.

6    Refitting is a reversal of the removal procedure, but do not overtighten the spindle nut or the rear panel will deform. Before fitting the wiper arm and blade ensure that the wiper motor is in the parked position.

### 54  Headlamp wash/wipe system – description and adjustment

1    The system consists of a wiper motor assembly mounted to the rear of each headlamp, each assembly being 'handed' left and right. The armature spindles protrude through the grille, and are connected to cranked wiper arms. A single hole washer jet is mounted on the bumper in front of each headlamp, and is supplied with water from the windscreen washer reservoir. A two position switch, mounted below the facia panel, operates the system when the ignition is on and the switch depressed.

2    To adjust the blade sweep, first lift the wiper blade and arm away from the headlamp glass and steady it in the pivoted position.

3    With the ignition on and wash/wipe switch depressed, operate the wiper arm until it reaches its maximum upper travel, and switch the ignition off. One or two attempts may be necessary to position the spindle correctly.

4    Release the wiper arm and check that it lies on the top vertical face of the headlamp lens as shown in Fig. 10.45. If it is not properly placed, unscrew the wiper arm retaining nut and withdraw the wiper arm from the spindle splines. Reposition the wiper arm and tighten the retaining nut.

### 55  Headlamp wash/wipe system motor – removal and refitting

1    Disconnect the negative battery terminal.

2    Lift the wiper arm shroud and remove the retaining nut and washer. Withdraw the arm and blade from the spindle splines.

3    Refer to Chapter 12 and remove the grille retaining screws and spring clips. Tilt the grille forwards and lift it from the lower mounting sockets.

4    Remove the sleeve and seal from the end of the wiper spindle and unscrew and remove the wiper motor locknut and washer.

5    Withdraw the motor from the rear of the front panel, and retrieve the washer.

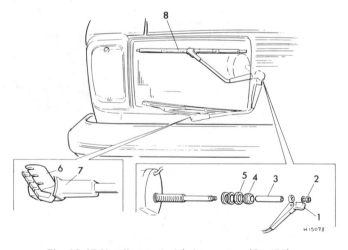

Fig. 10.45 Headlamp wash/wipe system (Sec 54)

1   Spindle nut cover
2   Wiper arm securing nut
3   Sleeve
4   Seal
5   Wiper mounting retaining locknut
6   Wiper arm spring-loaded head
7   Head bore
8   Sweep adjustment setting

6 Identify the three electrical leads and detach them.
7 Refit in the reverse order, adjusting the blade sweep as described in the previous Section. Ensure that the motor leads are fitted to the correct terminals; the red and black lead connects with the harness green lead, the red and white with the harness black and green, and the brown to the harness black.
8 Motors are non-serviceable. Defective wiper blades should be renewed.

## 56 Seat belt warning system – description and servicing

This system, fitted to North American Cricket and certain other vehicles, is designed to provide a visual and audible warning if an attempt is made to drive the vehicle without either the driver's or front passenger's seat belt having been fastened. The circuit comprises contact switches mounted in each front seat belt reel, an isolation switch mounted beneath the front passenger seat cushion, and a transmission-operated switch. On manually-operated gearboxes the transmission switch is screwed into the left-hand side of the gearbox housing, whereas on automatic transmission models an additional relay, mounted on the right-hand wing valance, is incorporated into the seat belt warning circuit, and is operated by the existing starter inhibitor and reversing light switches, which, in turn, are operated by the transmission selector lever. The principle of operation is that with the engine running and the gearlever in neutral ('N' or 'P' on automatic transmission) and the seat belts disconnected, no warning is given. Immediately the gearlever (or selector lever) is moved to engage a gear, the warning lamp illuminates and the buzzer sounds until the belts are fastened.

2 The seat switch is capable of adjustment by placing a weight (19 to 25 lbs/8.6 to 11.3 kg) on a piece of hardboard approximately 8 x 8 in (200 x 200 mm) square, towards the rear of the seat cushion.
3 Disconnect the wires from the seat switch and connect a test lamp and battery in series with it. With the weight on the seat the test lamp should illuminate. When it is removed it should extinguish.
4 Adjust the switch action if necessary by loosening the strap clamp bolt and increasing or reducing the effective length of the strap.
5 The switch fitted to the manual transmission is removed by taking off the connections, undoing the locknut, and unscrewing the switch.
6 To refit, select gearbox neutral, screw the switch in a short distance and place a test lamp and battery across the terminals. Screw the switch home until the lamp lights, screw out one full turn, and tighten the locknut.
7 Take away the test lamp and reconnect the leads. With the ignition on, gearlever in neutral and seatbelts unfastened, the illuminated sign and warning buzzer should not operate. Reset the switch by a small amount if necessary to achieve this condition.
8 The switch fitted to the automatic transmission is dealt with in Chapter 6. The 6RA relay employed is located on the right-hand wing valance, and is removed by disconnecting the wires and removing the securing screws.
9 To test, remove the wires, earth terminals W1 and C3, and connect C2 via a test bulb and battery to earth. The lamp should light, and if not it should be renewed. If the relay is serviceable but will not function when installed, check the feed and earth wiring (Figs. 10.46 and 10.47).

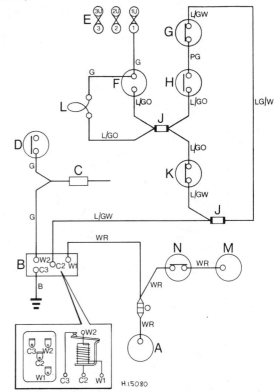

Fig. 10.47 Seat belt warning system (automatic transmission) – circuit diagram (Sec 56)

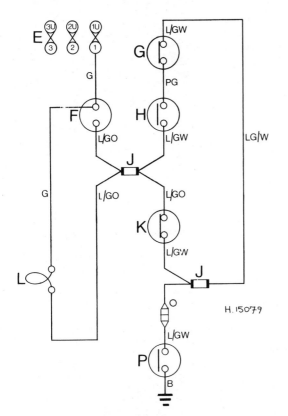

Fig. 10.46 Seat belt warning system (manual transmission) – circuit diagram (Sec 56)

| | | | |
|---|---|---|---|
| E | Fuse box | **Colour code:** | |
| F | Reminder buzzer | B | Black |
| G | RH reel switch | G | Green |
| H | RH seat switch | L/GO | Light green/orange |
| J | In-line connector | L/GW | Light green/white |
| K | LH reel switch | O | Orange |
| L | Warning lamp unit | PG | Purple/green |
| P | Transmission switch | | |

| | | | |
|---|---|---|---|
| A | Ignition switch | **Colour code:** | |
| B | Relay | B | Black |
| C | Snap connector | G | Green |
| D | Reversing lamp switch | L/G | Light green |
| E | Fuse box | O | Orange |
| F | Reminder buzzer | P | Purple |
| G | RH reel switch | R | Red |
| H | RH seat switch | W | White |
| J | In-line connector | | |
| K | LH reel switch | | |
| L | Warning lamp unit | | |
| M | Starter solenoid | | |
| N | Inhibitor switch | | |

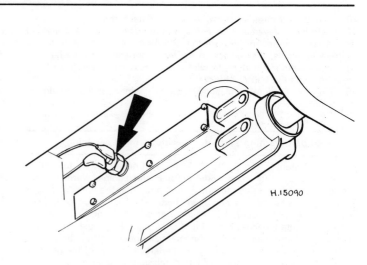

Fig. 10.49 Seat belt warning system (manual transmission) –
position of transmission switch (Sec 56)

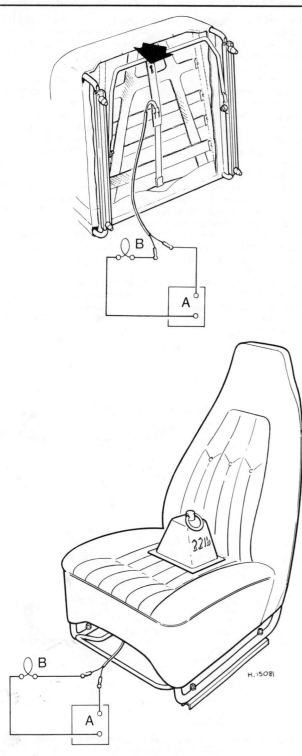

Fig. 10.48 Seat belt warning system – adjustment (Sec 56)

A – Test battery                    B – Test lamp

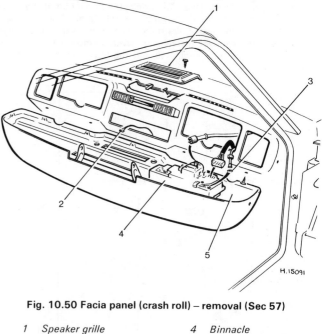

Fig. 10.50 Facia panel (crash roll) – removal (Sec 57)

| | | |
|---|---|---|
| 1 | *Speaker grille* | |
| 2 | *Cigarette lighter* | 4 *Binnacle* |
| 3 | *Leather washer* | 5 *Facia (crash roll)* |

### 57 Facia panel (crash roll) – removal and refitting

1    On early models, lower the steering column cowl by removing the
securing screws shown in Fig. 10.31. Where a radio is fitted, remove
the control knobs, spindle nuts and escutcheon.

2    Remove the attachment screws located along the underside and
ends of the facia (crash roll) (Fig. 10.50), remove the two speaker
attachment screws and detach the grille from the clips.

3    Remove the two screws located through the brackets adjacent to
the speaker aperture. (On cars with circular instrumentation, locating
pegs are used).

4    Pull the facia sufficiently far out to uncouple the speedometer, oil
gauge, multi-connector and switches and remove towards the left-
hand side. Refitting is a reversal of removal.

5    On models Series 7 onwards, disconnect the battery negative
terminal.

6    Remove the six screws securing the bottom half of the steering
column cowl and lower the cowl with the choke control.

7    Unscrew and remove the four nuts securing the upper and lower
column support brackets, and lower the column and steering wheel
onto the driver's seat.

10  The illuminated sign is removed by undoing the two screws and
disconnecting the wires. Remove the bulb by pressing down the catch
on the side of the cover and removing it. Pressing the catch again will
release the bulb holder. Turn the holder a quarter turn, and pull out the
bulb. Refit in the reverse order.

11  The reminder buzzer is secured to the main wiring harness to the
left of the glove compartment, inside the bulkhead.

8   Disconnect the cable from the speedometer head.

9   Withdraw the switches located beneath the instrument panel after identifying and removing their supply leads. Remove the cigar lighter and radio when fitted.

10  On estate models remove the backlight wash/wipe switch.

11  Withdraw the centre console panel by removing the four retaining screws, two upper and two lower, and disconnecting the rear wires and heater control bulbholder. Note the location of each wire.

12  Unbolt the heater control bracket and remove the left and right-hand face vent air ducts.

13  Refer to Fig. 10.56 and remove the facia panel (crash roll) screws.

14  Ease the panel away from the bulkhead and separate the two multi-pin plugs from each side of the instrument panel printed circuit.

15  The panel assembly can now be removed through the passenger door aperture.

16  Refitting is a reversal of the removal procedure, but ensure that the hazard warning switch leads are fitted to their correct terminals, as this component is not protected by a fuse and it is possible to short circuit the internal wiring. Connect the battery negative terminal and check the operation of all switches and instruments.

## 58 Instrument panel and binnacle (circular style) – removal and refitting

1   The circular style instrument panel takes the form of a moulded binnacle which houses the instruments and indicators and a printed circuit on its rear face (Fig. 10 51 and 10.52).

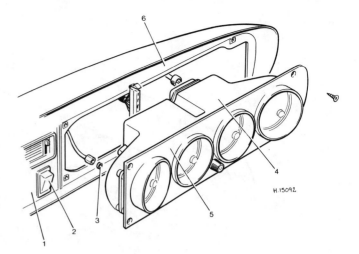

Fig. 10.51 Instrument panel (circular instruments) – removal (Sec 58)

| | |
|---|---|
| 1 Radio escutcheon | 4 Binnacle |
| 2 Heater blower motor switch | 5 Instrument panel |
| 3 Leather washer | 6 Facia (crash roll) |

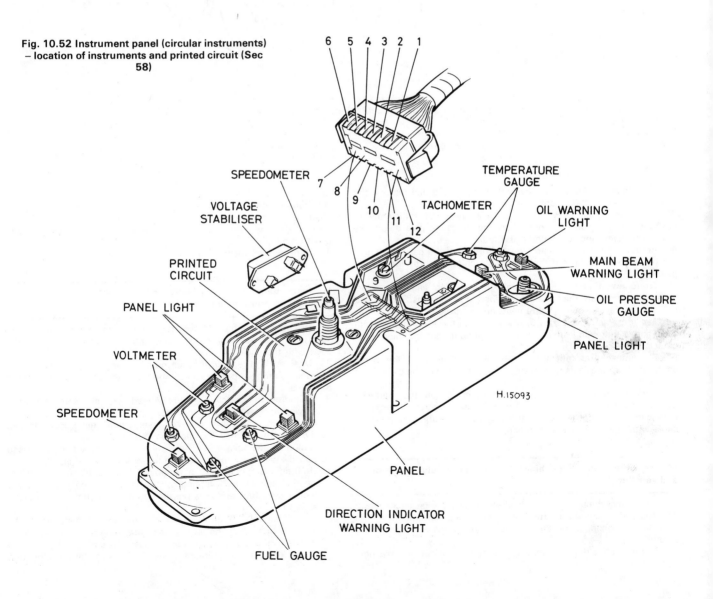

Fig. 10.52 Instrument panel (circular instruments) – location of instruments and printed circuit (Sec 58)

SPEEDOMETER

VOLTAGE STABILISER

PRINTED CIRCUIT

PANEL LIGHT

VOLTMETER

SPEEDOMETER

TEMPERATURE GAUGE

OIL WARNING LIGHT

TACHOMETER

MAIN BEAM WARNING LIGHT

OIL PRESSURE GAUGE

PANEL LIGHT

PANEL

DIRECTION INDICATOR WARNING LIGHT

FUEL GAUGE

H.15093

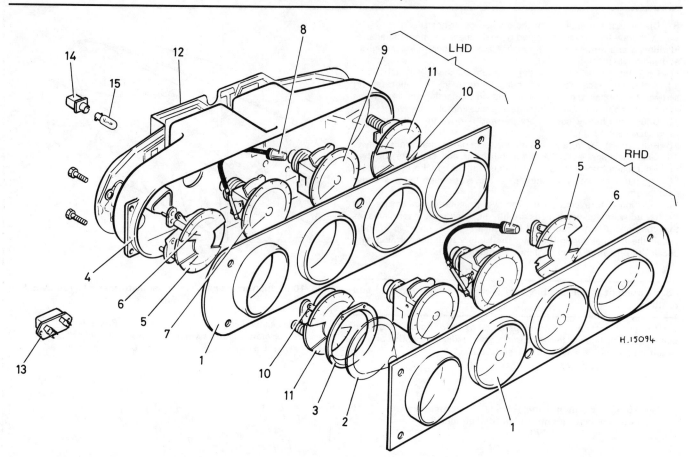

**Fig. 10.53 Instrument panel (circular instruments) – exploded view (Sec 58)**

| | | | |
|---|---|---|---|
| 1  Facia | 5  Battery condition indicator | 9  Tachometer | 13  Regulator |
| 2  Face | 6  Fuel gauge | 10  Water temperature gauge | 14  Bulb holder |
| 3  Mask | 7  Speedometer | 11  Oil gauge | 15  Bulb |
| 4  Case | 8  Trip reset | 12  Printed circuit | |

2   To dismantle, disconnect the battery earth lead and remove the instrument panel attachment screws.

3   Ease the panel away from the facia crash roll sufficiently to unscrew the speedometer connection, the oil gauge pipe union, the multi-connector, and rev counter (if fitted).

4   Remove the panel towards the centre line of the car and detach the binnacle by taking out the screws attaching it to the instrument panel.

5   To renew a panel bulb or voltage stabiliser, ease the panel assembly away from the facia as described in paragraphs 2 and 3 and pull out the item involved. Instruments are removed by dismantling as detailed in paragraphs 2 and 3, disconnecting the electrical connections and withdrawing the gauge. Do not bend or damage the printed circuit.

6   To remove and refit the speedometer cable, ease the panel assembly from the facia (paragraph 2), and disconnect the cable from the instrument.

7   Underneath the vehicle, disconnect the cable from the gearbox.

8   To refit, reverse the removal procedure, engaging the inner cable ends carefully before tightening the knurled nuts. Lubricate the inner cable with light grease before fitting.

## 59 Instrument panel and binnacle (rectangular style) – removal and refitting

1   Disconnect the battery earth lead and remove the facia (crash roll) as described in Section 57. Removal of bulbs and instruments is then possible by disconnecting the electrical connections and attachment screws.

2   To remove the binnacle, remove the attachment nuts and washers

and withdraw it from the studs.

3   Remove instruments from the binnacle by either disconnecting the electrical connections or removing the attachment screws, as appropriate, and withdrawing the item. Treat the printed circuit gently to avoid damage.

4   Refitting is a reversal of removal.

## 60 Instrument panel and instruments (Series 7 on) – removal, dismantling and refitting

1   Disconnect the battery negative terminal, remove the six screws securing the bottom half of the steering column cowl, and lower the cowl with the choke control.

2   Unscrew and remove the four nuts securing the upper and lower steering column support brackets, and lower the column and wheel to the driver's seat.

3   Withdraw the switches located beneath the instrument panel after identifying and removing their leads.

4   Disconnect the cable from the speedometer head. Refer to Fig. 10.57 and remove the instrument panel screws.

5   Pull the panel forward to allow the two multi-socket connectors to be prised away from the printed circuit. Withdraw the panel.

7   Refitting is the reverse of removal. Take particular care when connecting the hazard warning switch leads, as the circuit is not protected by a fuse and it is possible to short circuit the unit if the wires are incorrectly fitted.

8   To dismantle the unit remove the instrument panel from the binnacle by prising off the six clips and removing the panel.

9   The majority of instruments are removed by undoing the securing nuts and lifting the instrument away. To remove the speedometer,

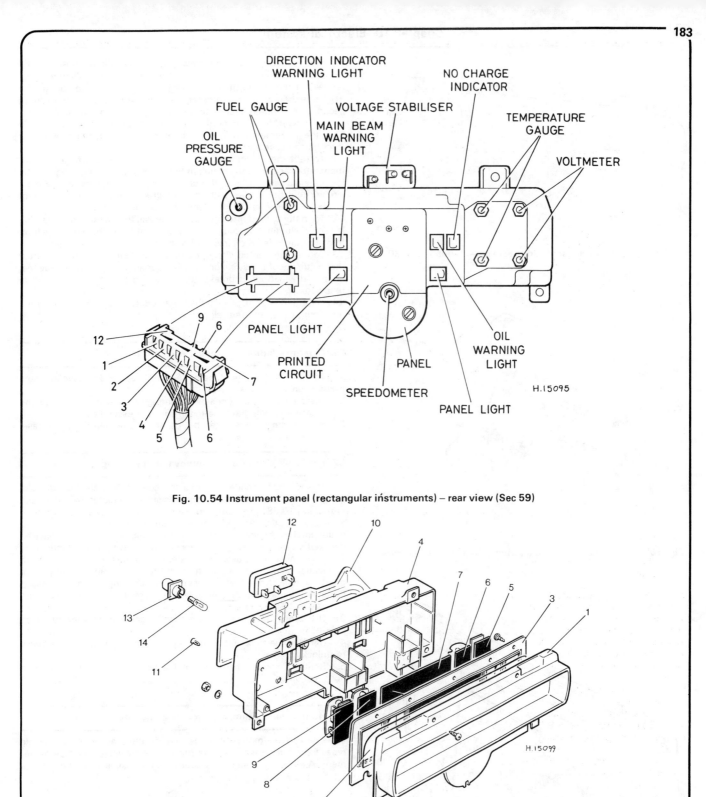

**Fig. 10.54 Instrument panel (rectangular instruments) – rear view (Sec 59)**

**Fig. 10.55 Instrument panel (rectangular instruments) – exploded view (Sec 59)**

| | | | | | | | |
|---|---|---|---|---|---|---|---|
| 1 | Front moulding | 5 | Oil pressure gauge | 9 | Voltmeter | 12 | Voltage stabiliser |
| 2 | Window | 6 | Fuel gauge | 10 | Printed circuit | 13 | Lamp holder |
| 3 | Mask | 7 | Speedometer | 11 | Rivet | 14 | Bulb |
| 4 | Case | 8 | Temperature gauge | | | | |

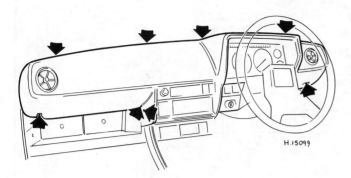

Fig. 10.56 Facia panel securing screws – Series 7 (Sec 60)

remove the two securing screws, withdraw the instrument, and retrieve the reset gear which will remain on the spindle. When refitting, enure that the slot in the gear engages the spindle drive spring.

10  To withdraw the tachometer, remove the tape and three screws securing the printed circuits to the instrument, lift off the tachometer printed circuit, followed by the extension of the main printed circuit. Take the instrument out from the front, feeding the tachometer circuit through the case slot.

11  To refit the tachometer, slide the circuit back and fit the instrument into place. Fold the main printed circuit onto the stubs behind the instrument case, and fold the tachometer circuit on top of the main circuit. Refit the screws with the correct size washer. Stick pieces of insulating tape $\frac{1}{2}$ in (12 mm) square over the screws.

12  To remove the printed circuit, remove all the instruments, warning lamp and illumination bulb, push out the four lower locating pegs from front to rear, prise the circuit from the other locations and remove it.

13  To test the printed circuit, clean it with methylated spirit and test the continuity of the strips on the circuit board using a low voltage test lamp and a battery. If breaks are found, the circuit board should be renewed.

14  To refit the board, push in the lower locating pegs, place it over the remaining pegs, and refit all parts.

## 61  Cigarette lighter – removal and refitting

1  To remove, disconnect the battery earth lead and remove the radio escutcheon securing screws.

2  Disconnect lighter connections, noting colour coding, unscrew the outer case and withdraw the inner from the escutcheon.

3  Refit in the reverse order, but do not overtighten the outer case.

## 62  Fuel tank sender unit – removal and refitting

1  The fuel tank sender controls the current flow through the fuel gauge, and is essentially a variable resistance actuated by a float and arm (Fig. 10.59). The fuel and temperature gauges rely for their accuracy on the applied voltage remaining constant, this being maintained by the voltage stabiliser. This component should always be checked when the instruments appear to be giving faulty readings.

2  To remove or renew a transmitter, remove the battery earth connection and drain the fuel from the tank by removing the plug at the tank rear (Note that on estate cars draining is not necessary. Remove the rear carpet, remove tank unit cover plate, and remove the unit).

3  Disconnect the tank unit electrical connection and the fuel feed pipe.

4  Remove the tank unit by turning the retaining ring anti-clockwise to unlock.

5  Refit in reverse, ensuring that the unit rubber sealing ring is in good condition.

## 63  Horn – description, maintenance and adjustment

1  One or two (matched) horns may be fitted according to vehicle type. Each horn has a self-interrupting electro-magnetic type movement. A vibrating armature is coupled to a flexible diaphragm and a

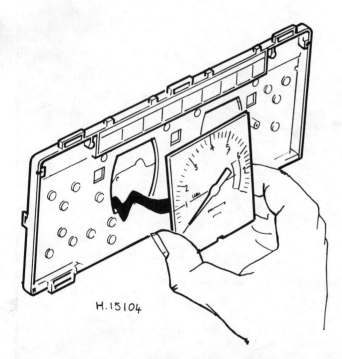

Fig. 10.57 Instrument panel and switch panel securing screws – Series 7 (Sec 60)

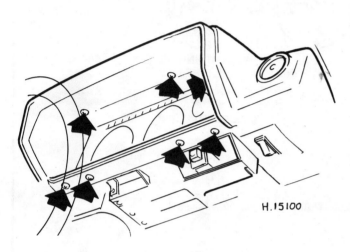

Fig. 10.58 Tachometer and tachometer printed circuit – Series 7 – removal (Sec 60)

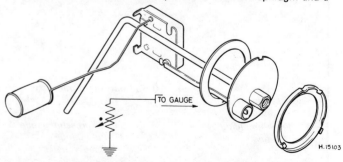

Fig. 10.59 Transmitter unit – fuel tank (Sec 62)

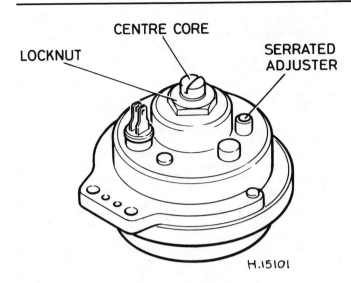

LOCKNUT   CENTRE CORE   SERRATED ADJUSTER

H.15101

**Fig. 10.60 Horn – general details (Sec 63)**

rigid tone disc. When the horn is energised the diaphragm vibrates and the impact of the armature on the core face vibrates the tone disc at a higher frequency than the diaphragm. These two sets of vibrations, together with their overtones, combine to give the horn its note.

2   Maintenance consists of checking the security of the mounting bolts and checking the electrical connections.

3   Adjustment of the contact breaker may occasionally be required to compensate for wear. It will not alter the horn note pitch. Where two are fitted, disconnect the horn not being adjusted, and, to guard against fuses blowing during adjustment, connect a shorting link across fuse No 1. Energise the horn and turn the screw on the serrated adjuster (Fig. 10.60) anti-clockwise until the horn just fails to sound, then immediately turn the screw a quarter of a turn clockwise. Do not disturb the centre core or locknut during breaker adjustment, and if the horn does not sound immediately after making the adjustment, de-energise the horn promptly.

4   Remove the shorting link and remake the connections.

## 64  Courtesy light switch – removal and refitting

The early type courtesy light switch is threaded, and screws into the door pillar. Unscrew with a spanner to remove. The later type switch is secured by a self-tapping screw. Neither switch can be dismantled for service.

## 65  Radios and tape players – installation

A radio or tape player is expensive, and will only give its best performance if fitted properly. Do not expect concert hall performance from a unit that is badly installed. There are in-car entertainment specialists who can do the fitting for you, if you wish. Ensure that the unit purchased is of the same polarity as the vehicle, and that units with adjustable polarity are correctly set before installation. Final positioning of the radio/tape player, speakers and aerial is a matter of personal preference. However, the following paragraphs give guidelines, relevant to all installations.

### Radios

Most radios are a standard 7 inches wide by 2 inches deep – this ensures that they will fit into the radio aperture provided in most cars. If your car does not have such an aperture, fit the radio in a suitable position either in, or beneath, the dashpanel. Alternatively, a console can be purchased which will fit between the dashpanel and the floor, or on the transmission tunnel. These consoles can also be used for additional switches and instrumentation. Where no aperture is provided, the following points should be borne in mind before deciding where to fit the unit.

(a)   The unit must be within easy reach of the driver wearing a seat belt

(b)   The unit must not be mounted close to an electric tachometer, the ignition switch and its wiring, or the flasher unit and associated wiring

(c)   The unit must be mounted within reach of the aerial lead, and in such a place that the aerial lead will not have to be routed near the components detailed in paragraph 'b'

(d)   The unit should not be positioned where it might cause injury to the car occupants in an accident; for instance, under the dashpanel above the driver's or passenger's legs

(e)   The unit must be fitted securely

Some radios will have mounting brackets provided together with instructions; others will need to be fitted using drilled and slotted metal strips, bent to form mounting brackets, and available from most accessory stores. The unit must be properly earthed, by a separate earth lead between the casing of the radio and the vehicle frame.

Use the radio manufacturer's instructions when wiring into the vehicle's electrical system. If no instructions are available refer to the relevant wiring diagram to find the location of the radio 'feed' connection in the vehicle's wiring circuit. A 1-2 amp 'in-line' fuse must be fitted in the 'feed' wire, and a choke may also be necessary (see next Section).

The type of aerial used and its position is a matter of personal preference. In general the taller the aerial, the better the reception. It is best to fit a fully retractable aerial, especially, if a car-wash is used or if you live where cars tend to be vandalised. In this respect electric aerials which are raised and lowered automatically when switching the radio on or off are convenient, but are more likely to give trouble than the manual type.

When choosing a site for the aerial the following points should be considered:

(a)   The aerial lead should be as short as possible – this means that the aerial should be mounted at the front of the vehicle

(b)   The aerial must be mounted as far away from the distributor and HT leads as possible

(c)   The part of the aerial which protrudes beneath the mounting point must not foul the roadwheels, or anything else

(d)   If possible the aerial should be positioned so that the coaxial lead does not have to be routed through the engine compartment

(e)   The plane of the panel on which the aerial is mounted should not be so steeply angled that the aerial cannot be mounted vertically (in relation to the 'end-on' aspect of the vehicle). Most aerials have a small amount of adjustment available

Having decided on a mounting position, a hole will have to be made in the panel. The size of the hole will depend upon the aerial being fitted, although, generally, the hole required is of $\frac{3}{4}$ inch diameter. A 'tank-cutter' of the relevant diameter is the best tool for making the hole. This tool needs a small diameter pilot hole drilled through the panel, through which the tool clamping bolt is inserted. When the hole has been made the raw edges should be de-burred with a file and then painted, to prevent corrosion.

Fit the aerial according to the manufacturer's instructions. If the aerial is very tall, or if it protrudes beneath the mounting panel for a considerable distance, it is a good idea to fit a stay between the aerial and the vehicle frame. This can be manufactured from the slotted and drilled metal strips previously mentioned. The stay should be securely screwed or bolted in place. For best reception it is advisable to fit an earth lead between the aerial body and the vehicle frame.

It will probably be necessary to drill one, or two, holes through bodywork panels in order to feed the aerial lead into the interior of the car. Ensure that the holes are fitted with rubber grommets to protect the cable, and to prevent the entry of water.

Positioning and fitting of the speaker depends mainly on the type. Generally, the speaker is designed to fit into the aperture provided in the car (usually in the shelf behind the rear seats, or in the top of the dashpanel). Where this is the case, fitting is just a matter of removing the protective grille from the aperture and securing the speaker. Take care not to damage the speaker diaphragm whilst doing this. It is a good idea to fit a 'gasket' between the speaker frame and the mounting panel to prevent vibration. Some speakers will already have such a gasket fitted.

If a 'pod' type speaker was supplied with the radio, the best acoustic results will normally be obtained by mounting it on the shelf behind the rear seat. The pod can be secured to the panel with self-tapping screws.

When connecting a rear mounted speaker to the radio, the wires should be routed through the vehicle beneath the carpets or floot mats – preferably through the middle, or along the side of the floorpan, where they will not be trodden on. There will now be several yards of additional wiring in the car. Use PVC tape to secure this out of the way. Do not leave electrical leads dangling. Ensure that new connections are properly made (wires twisted together will not do), and secure.

The radio should now be working, but it will be necessary to 'trim' the radio to the aerial. Follow the manufacturer's instructions in this respect.

### Tape players

Fitting instructions for both cartridge and cassette stereo tape players are the same and in general the same rules apply as when fitting a radio. Tape players are not prone to electrical interference like radio – although it can occur – so positioning is not so critical. If possible the player should be mounted on an 'even keel'. Also, it must be possible for a driver wearing a seat belt to reach the unit to change, or turn over, tapes.

For the best results from speakers recessed into a panel, mount them so that the back of the speaker protrudes into an enclosed chamber within the vehicle (eg door interiors or the boot cavity).

To fit recessed type speakers in the front doors check that there is room to mount the speaker in each door without it fouling the latch or window winding mechanism. Hold the speaker against the skin of the door, and draw a line around the periphery. With the speaker removed draw a second 'cutting' line, within the first, to allow enough room for entry of the speaker back, but providing a broad seat for the speaker flange. When you are sure that the 'cutting-line' is correct, drill a series of holes around its periphery. Pass a hacksaw blade through one of the holes and cut through the metal between the holes until the centre section of the panel falls out.

De-burr the edges of the hole and paint the raw metal to prevent corrosion. Cut a corresponding hole in the door trim panel – ensuring that it will be completely covered by the speaker grille. Now drill a hole in the door edge and a corresponding hole in the door surround. These holes are to feed the speaker leads through – so fit grommets. Pass the speaker leads through the door trim, door skin and out through the holes in the side of the door and surround. Refit the trim panel and then secure the speaker to the door using self-tapping screws. Note that if the speaker is fitted with a shield to prevent water dripping on it, ensure that this shield is at the top.

'Pod' type speakers can be fastened to the shelf behind the rear seat, or anywhere else offering a corresponding mounting point on each side of the car. If they are mounted on each side of the shelf, it is a good idea to drill several large diameter holes through to the boot cavity beneath each speaker – this will improve the sound reproduction. 'Pod' speakers sometimes offer a better reproduction quality if they face the rear window – which then acts as a reflector. It is worth experimenting before finally fixing them.

### 66  Radios and tape players – suppression of interference (general)

To eliminate buzzes, and other unwanted noises, costs very little and is not as difficult as sometimes thought. With common sense and patience and following the instructions in the following paragraphs, interference can be virtually eliminated.

The first cause for concern is the generator. The noise this makes over the radio is like an electric mixer and speeds up when you rev up the engine (if you wish to prove the point, remove the drivebelt and try it). The remedy is simple; connect a 1.0 mf-3.0 mf capacitor between earth, probably the bolt that holds down the generator base, and the *large* terminal on the alternator or dynamo. This is most important, for if you connect it to the small terminal, you will probably damage the generator permanently (see Fig. 10.61).

A second common cause of electrical interference is the ignition system. On non-electronic systems a 1.0 mf capacitor must be connected between earth and the SW or + terminal on the coil (see Fig. 10.62). This may stop the tick-tick-tick sound that comes over the speaker. Next comes the spark itself.

There are several ways of curing interference from the ignition HT system. One is the use of carbon-cored HT leads as original equipment. Where copper cable is employed, use resistive spark plug caps (see Fig. 10.63) of about 10 000 ohm to 15 000 ohm resistance. If, due to lack of room, these cannot be used, an alternative is to use 'in-line' suppressors – if the interference is not too bad, you may get away with only one suppressor in the coil to distributor line. If the interference does continue (a 'clacking' noise) then modify all HT leads.

At this stage it is advisable to check that the radio and aerial are well earthed, that the aerial plug is pushed well into the set and that the radio is properly trimmed (see preceding Section). Check that the wire which supplies the power to the set is as short as possible and does not wander all over the car. Check that the fuse is of the correct rating. For most sets this will be about 1 to 2 amps.

At this point the more usual causes of interference have been suppressed. If the problem still exists, a look at the causes of interference may help to pinpoint the component generating the stray electrical discharges.

The radio picks up electromagnetic waves in the air; some made by regular broadcasters, and some, which we do not want, made by the car itself. The home made signals are produced by stray electrical discharges floating around in the car. Common producers of these signals are electric motors, ie the windscreen wipers, electric screen washers, electric window winders, heater fan or an electric aerial and instruments. The remedy for these cases is shown in Fig. 10.64 for an electric motor whose interference is not too bad and Fig. 10.65 for instrument suppression. Turn signals are not normally suppressed. In recent years, radio manufacturers have included in the line (live) of the radio, in addition to the fuse, an 'in-line' choke. If your circuit lacks one of these, put one in as shown in Fig.10.66.

All the foregoing components are available from radio or accessory stores. If an electric clock is fitted, this should be suppressed by connecting a 0.5 mf capacitor across it as show for a motor in Fig. 10.64.

If after all this, you are still experiencing radio interference, first assess how bad it is, for the human ear can filter out unobtrusive unwanted noises quite easily. But if you are still adamant about eradicating the noise, then continue.

As a first step, a few 'experts' seem to favour a screen between the radio and the engine. However, the whole set is screened and if interference can get past that then a small piece of aluminium is not going to stop it.

A more sensible way of screening is to discover if interference is coming down the wires. First, take the live lead; interference can get between the set and the choke (hence the reason for keeping the wires short). One remedy here is to screen the wire and this is done by buying screened wire and fitting that. The loudspeaker lead could be screened also to prevent 'pick-up' getting back to the radio – although this is unlikely.

Without doubt, the worst source of radio interference comes from the ignition HT leads, even if they have been suppressed. The ideal way of suppressing these is to slide screening tubes over the leads themselves. As this is impractical, we can place an aluminium shield over the majority of the lead areas. In a vee- or twin-cam engine, this is relatively easy but for a straight engine the results are not particularly good.

Now for the really impossible cases, here are a few tips to try out. Where metal comes into contact with metal, an electrical disturbance is caused which is why good clean connections are essential. To remove interference due to overlapping or butting panels you must bridge the join with a wide braided earth strap (like that from the frame to the engine/transmission). The most common moving parts that could create noise and should be strapped are, in order of importance:

(a)  Silencer to frame
(b)  Exhaust pipe to engine block and frame
(c)  Air cleaner to frame
(d)  Front and rear bumpers to frame
(e)  Steering column to frame
(f)  Bonnet and boot lids to frame

These faults are most pronounced when (1) the engine is idling, (2) labouring under load. Although the moving parts are already connected with nuts, bolts etc, these do corrode, thus creating a high resistance interference source.

If you have a 'ragged' sounding pulse when mobile, this could be

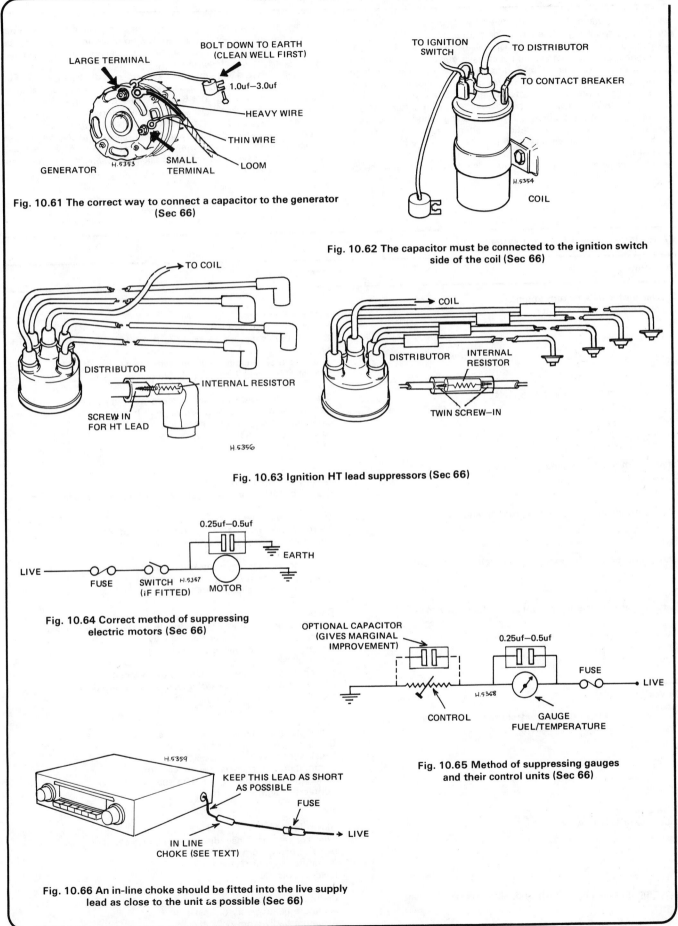

LARGE TERMINAL

BOLT DOWN TO EARTH
(CLEAN WELL FIRST)

1.0uf–3.0uf

HEAVY WIRE

THIN WIRE

GENERATOR      H.5353      SMALL      LOOM
                        TERMINAL

Fig. 10.61 The correct way to connect a capacitor to the generator
(Sec 66)

TO IGNITION
SWITCH

TO DISTRIBUTOR

TO CONTACT BREAKER

H.5354

COIL

Fig. 10.62 The capacitor must be connected to the ignition switch
side of the coil (Sec 66)

TO COIL

DISTRIBUTOR

INTERNAL RESISTOR

SCREW IN
FOR HT LEAD

H.5356

COIL

DISTRIBUTOR      INTERNAL
                RESISTOR

TWIN SCREW–IN

Fig. 10.63 Ignition HT lead suppressors (Sec 66)

0.25uf–0.5uf

EARTH

LIVE

FUSE      SWITCH      H.5367      MOTOR
          (IF FITTED)

Fig. 10.64 Correct method of suppressing
electric motors (Sec 66)

OPTIONAL CAPACITOR
(GIVES MARGINAL
IMPROVEMENT)

0.25uf–0.5uf

FUSE

LIVE

H.5368

CONTROL

GAUGE
FUEL/TEMPERATURE

Fig. 10.65 Method of suppressing gauges
and their control units (Sec 66)

H.5359

KEEP THIS LEAD AS SHORT
AS POSSIBLE

FUSE

LIVE

IN LINE
CHOKE (SEE TEXT)

Fig. 10.66 An in-line choke should be fitted into the live supply
lead as close to the unit as possible (Sec 66)

wheel or tyre static. This can be cured by buying some anti-static powder and sprinkling it liberally inside the tyres.

If the interference takes the shape of a high pitched screeching noise that changes its note when the car is in motion and only comes now and then, this could be related to the aerial, especially if it is of the telescopic or whip type. This source can be cured quite simply by pushing a small rubber ball on top of the aerial as this breaks the electric field before it can form; but it would be much better to buy a new aerial of a reputable brand. If a loud rushing sound occurs every time you brake, this is brake static. This effect is most prominent on hot dry days and is cured only by fitting a special kit, which is quite expensive.

In conclusion, it is pointed out that it is relatively easy and cheap, to eliminate 95 per cent of all noise, but to eliminate the final 5 per cent is time and money consuming. It is up to the individual to decide if it is worth it. Remember also that one cannot have concert hall performance from a cheap radio.

Finally, players and eight track players are not usually affected by car noise but, in a very bad case, the best remedies are the first three suggestions plus using a 3-5 amp choke in the 'live' line, and in incurable cases screen the live and speaker wires.

**Note**: *If your car is fitted with electronic ignition, it is not recommended that either the spark plug resistors or the ignition coil capacitor be fitted as these may damage the system. Most electronic ignition units have built-in suppression and should, therefore, not cause interference.*

---

## 67 Fault diagnosis – electrical system

| Symptom | Reason(s) |
| --- | --- |
| **Starter motor fails to turn engine** | |
| No electricity at starter motor | Battery discharged |
| | Battery defective internally |
| | Battery terminal leads loose or earth lead not securely attached to body |
| | Loose or broken connections in starter motor circuit |
| | Starter motor switch or solenoid faulty |
| Electricity at starter motor: faulty motor | Starter motor pinion jammed in mesh with ring gear |
| | Starter brushes badly worn, sticking, or brush wires loose |
| | Commutator dirty, worn, or burnt |
| | Starter motor armature faulty |
| | Field coils earthed |
| **Starter motor turns engine very slowly** | |
| Electrical defects | Battery in discharged condition |
| | Starter brushes badly worn, sticking, or brush wires loose |
| **Starter motor operates without turning engine** | Dirt or oil on drive gear |
| | Starter motor pinion sticking on the screwed sleeve |
| | Pinion or ring gear teeth broken or worn |
| **Starter motor noisy or excessively rough engagement** | Pinion or ring gear teeth broken or worn |
| | Starter drive main spring broken (inertia type) |
| | Starter motor retaining bolts loose |
| **Battery will not hold charge for more than a few days** | Battery defective internally |
| | Electrolyte level too low or electrolyte too weak due to leakage |
| | Plate separators no longer fully effective |
| | Battery plates severely sulphated |
| | Drivebelt slipping |
| | Battery terminal connections loose or corroded |
| | Short in lighting circuit causing continual battery drain |
| | Regulator unit not working correctly |
| **Ignition light fails to go out, battery runs flat in a few days** | |
| Dynamo or alternator not charging | Drivebelt loose and slipping, or broken |
| | Brushes worn, sticking, broken or dirty |
| | Brush springs weak or broken |
| | Commutator dirty, greasy, worn, or burnt |
| | Armature badly worn or armature shaft bent |
| | Contacts in light switch faulty |
| **Wipers faulty** | |
| Wiper motor fails to work | Blown fuse |
| | Wire connections loose, disconnected, or broken |
| | Brushes badly worn |
| | Armature worn or faulty |
| | Field coils faulty |
| Wiper motor works very slowly and takes excessive current | Commutator dirty, greasy, or burnt |
| | Armature bearings dry or unaligned |
| | Armature badly worn or faulty |

| Symptom | Reason(s) |
| --- | --- |
| Wiper motor works slowly and takes little current | Brushes badly worn<br>Commutator dirty, greasy or burnt<br>Armature badly worn or faulty |
| Wiper motor works but wiper blades remain static | Wiper motor gearbox parts badly worn |
| **Horn faulty**<br>Horn operates all the time | Horn push either earthed or stuck down<br>Horn cable to horn push earthed |
| Horn fails to operate | Cable or cable connection loose broken or disconnected<br>Horn has an internal fault<br>Blown fuse |
| Horn emits intermittent or unsatisfactory noise | Cable connections loose |
| **Lights faulty**<br>Lights do not come on | If engine not running, battery discharged<br>Wire connections loose, disconnected or broken<br>Light switch shorting or otherwise faulty |
| Lights come on but fade out | If engine not running, battery discharged<br>Wire connections loose<br>Light switch shorting or otherwise faulty |
| Lights work erratically – flashing on and off, especially over bumps | Battery terminals or earth connections loose<br>Lights not earthing properly<br>Contacts in light switch faulty |

**Key to wiring diagrams – owing to the numerous model variants, it is only possible to include a typical selection**

1  Battery
2  Starter motor
3  Starter motor – inertia engaged
4  Starter motor – pre-engaged
5  Starter motor solenoid
6  Earth
7  Fuse(s)
8  Fuse unit
9  Ignition switch
10  Alternative ignition switch
11  Ignition warning lamp
12  Ignition coil
13  Distributor
14  Spark plug
15  Column switch
16  Alternator
17  Generator
18  Control box
19  Voltage regulator
20  Light switch
21  Light switch and panel lamp rheostat
22  Headlamp main beam(s)
23  Headlamp main beam RH
24  Headlamp main beam LH
25  Main beam warning lamp
26  Headlamp dip beam(s)
27  Headlamp dip beam RH
28  Headlamp dip beam LH
29  Dip switch – foot type
30  Sidelamp RH
31  Sidelamp LH
32  Side marker lamp front
33  Side marker lamp rear
34  Tail lamp RH
35  Tail lamp LH
36  Stop lamp
37  Stop lamp switch
38  Reversing lamp
39  Reversing lamp switch
40  Fog lamp(s) front
41  Fog lamp(s) rear
42  Fog lamp switch front
43  Fog lamp switch rear
44  Fog lamp relay
45  Number plate lamp(s)
46  Horn push, headlamp flash and indicator switch
47  Direction indicator unit
48  Direction indicator front RH
49  Direction indicator front LH
50  Direction indicator rear RH
51  Direction indicator rear LH
52  Direction indicator warning lamp
53  Hazard warning lamp
54  Hazard warning switch
55  Hazard warning unit
56  Binnacle
57  Printed circuit
58  No charge indicator
59  Oil warning lamp
60  Voltage stabilizer
61  Oil temperature gauge

62  Water temperature gauge
63  Fuel gauge
64  Voltmeter
65  Ammeter
66  Tachometer
67  Clock
68  PDWA switch
69  Brake failure warning lamp
70  Brake failure warning switch
71  Handbrake switch
72  Battery condition indicator
73  Panel lamp(s)
74  Panel lamp(s) switch
75  Oil temperature gauge illumination
76  Water temperature illumination
77  Fuel gauge illumination
78  Ammeter illumination
79  Tachometer illumination
80  Speedometer illumination
81  Clock illumination
82  Switch illumination
83  BW illumination
84  Heater illumination
85  Cable connector
86  Overdrive connection
87  Radiator fan switch
88  Radiator fan relay
89  Radiator fan motor
90  Oil warning lamp switch
91  Oil temperature gauge sender unit
92  Oil pressure gauge sender unit
93  Water temperature gauge sender unit
94  Fuel gauge sender unit
95  Wiper motor
96  Wiper motor switch
97  Tailgate wiper motor
98  Tailgate wiper motor switch
99  Washer pump
100  Washer pump rear
101  Demister element
102  Demister element switch
103  Demister element indicator lamp
104  Demister element relay
105  Blower motor
106  Blower motor switch
107  Horn(s)
108  Door pillar switch
109  Door pillar switch RH
110  Door pillar switch LH
111  Interior lamp and switch
112  Interior lamp and switch rear
113  Boot lamp
114  Boot lamp switch
115  Glovebox lamp
116  Glovebox lamp switch
117  Ignition key audible warning device
118  Ignition key audible warning device switch
119  Cigar lighter
120  Radio pick-up
121  Panel illumination rheostat

**Colour code**

| | | |
|---|---|---|
| B | – | Black |
| G | – | Green |
| K | – | Pink |
| L/G | – | Light Green |
| N | – | Brown |
| O | – | Orange |
| P | – | Purple |
| R | – | Red |
| S | – | Slate |
| U | – | Blue |
| W | – | White |
| Y | – | Yellow |

SYMBOLS

| | | |
|---|---|---|
| Snap connector | • | ⎓ |
| Plug and socket connector | • | ⎓ |
| Moulded cable connection (inseparable - integral with loom) | • | ⎓ |
| In-line connector | • | ⎓ |
| Earth through cable | • | ⎓ |
| Earth through unit | • | • |
| When fitted | • | * |

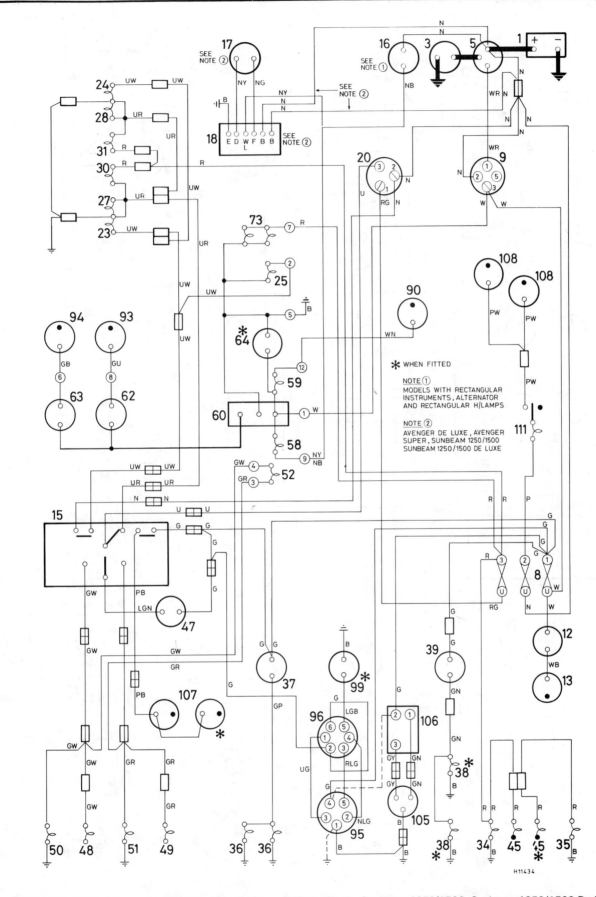

Fig. 10.67 Wiring diagram — early model Avenger De Luxe, Avenger Super, Sunbeam 1250/1500, Sunbeam 1250/1500 De Luxe, and models with rectangular instruments, alternator and rectangular headlamps

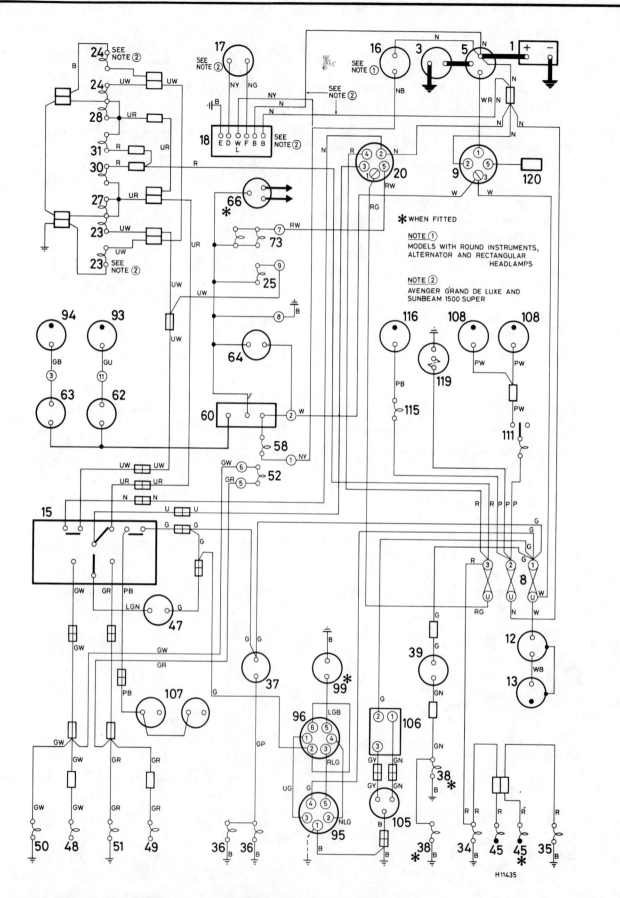

Fig. 10.68 Wiring diagram – early model Avenger Grande De Luxe, Sunbeam 1500 Super, and models with round instruments, alternator and rectangular headlamps

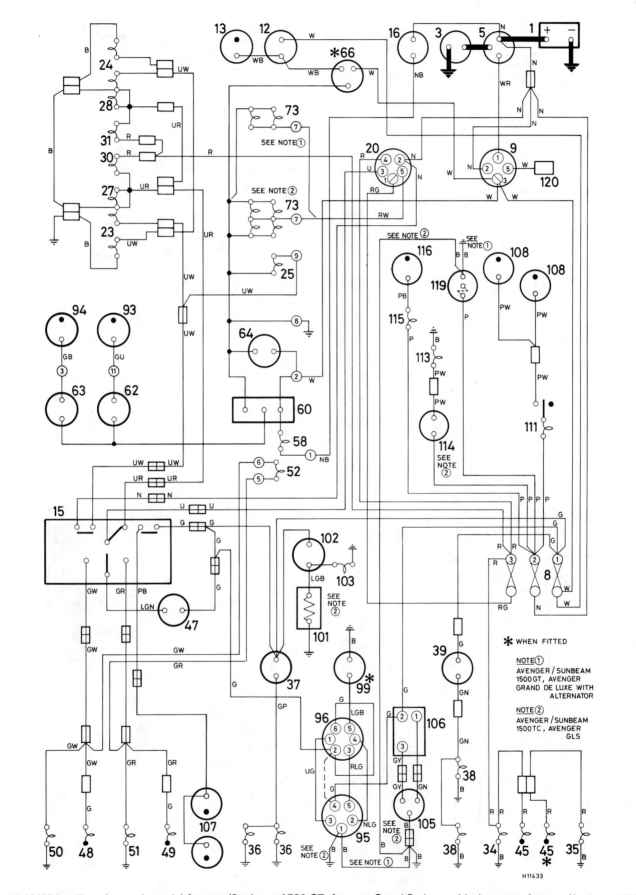

Fig. 10.69 Wiring diagram – early model Avenger/Sunbeam 1500 GT, Avenger Grand De Luxe with alternator, Avenger/Sunbeam 1500 TC and Avenger GLS

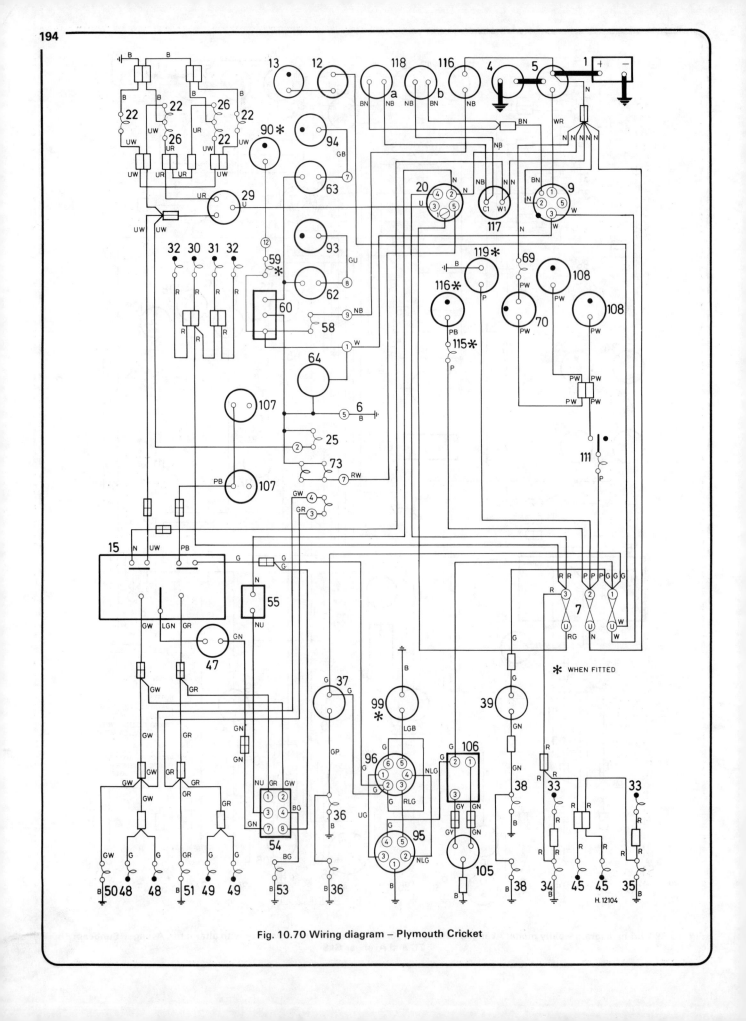

**Fig. 10.70 Wiring diagram – Plymouth Cricket**

H. 12104

* WHEN FITTED

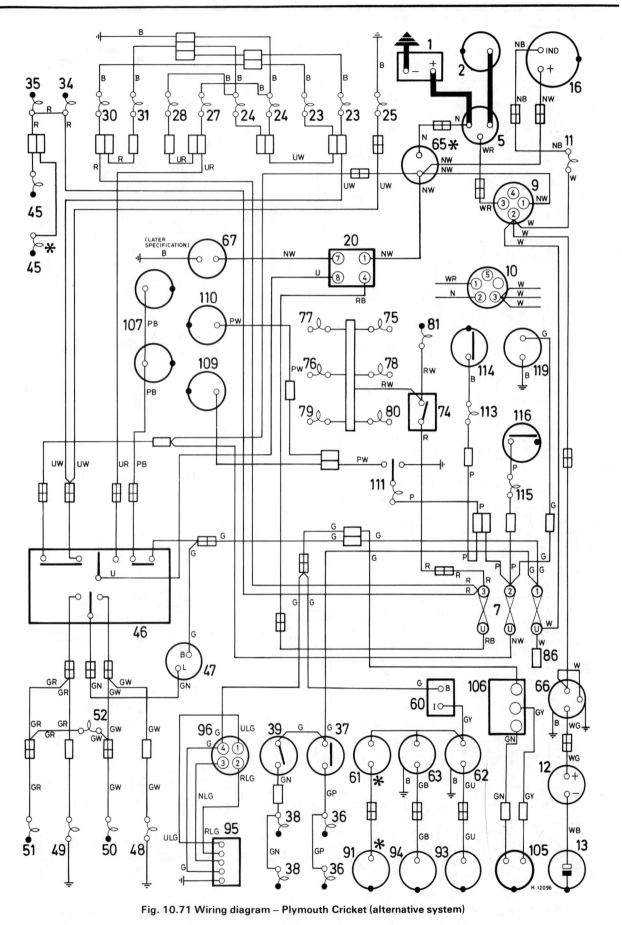

Fig. 10.71 Wiring diagram – Plymouth Cricket (alternative system)

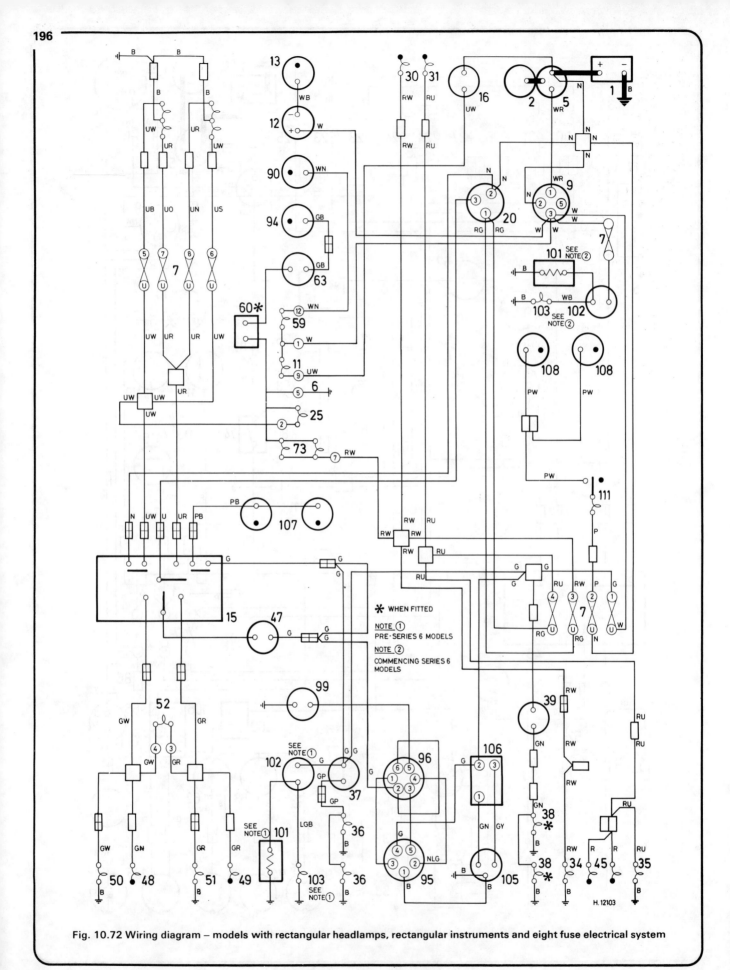

Fig. 10.72 Wiring diagram – models with rectangular headlamps, rectangular instruments and eight fuse electrical system

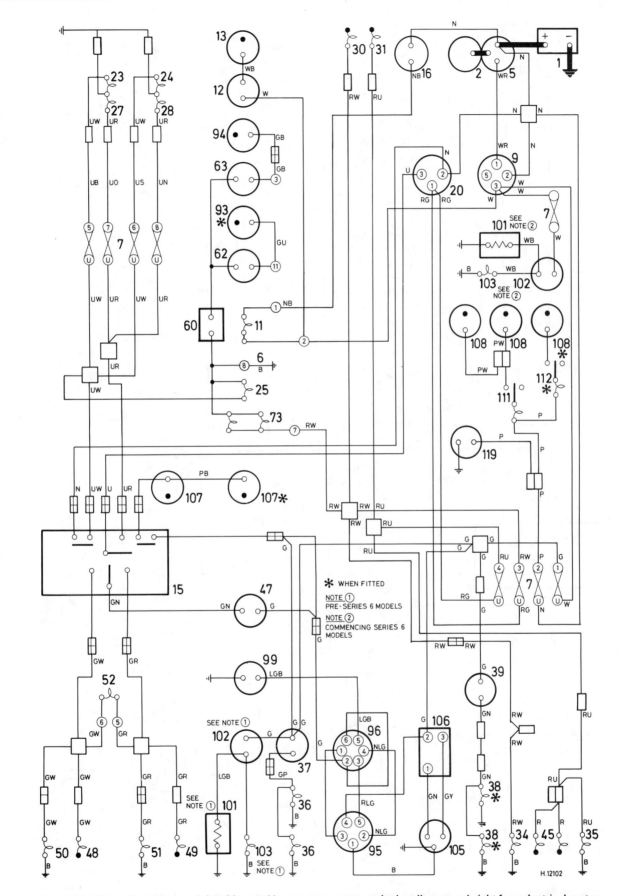

Fig. 10.73 Wiring diagram – models with round instruments, rectangular headlamps and eight fuse electrical system

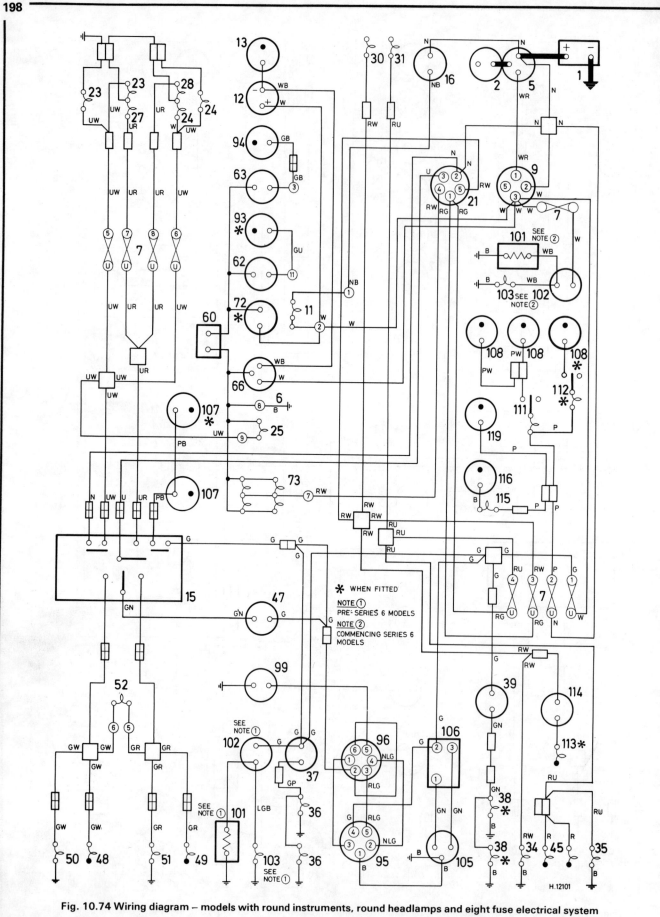

**Fig. 10.74 Wiring diagram – models with round instruments, round headlamps and eight fuse electrical system**

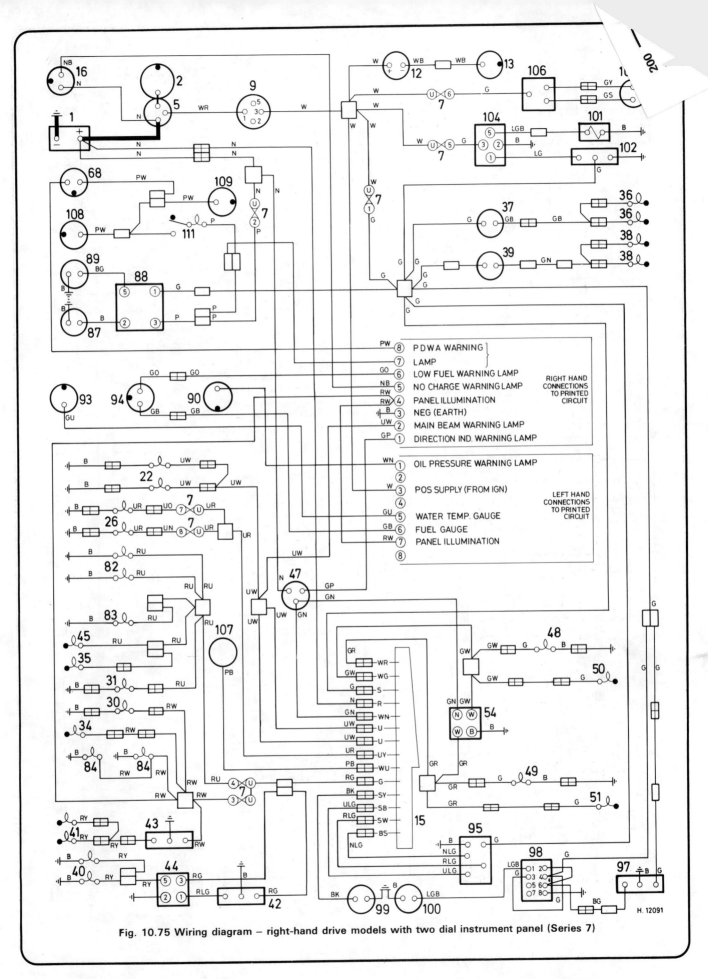

**Fig. 10.75 Wiring diagram – right-hand drive models with two dial instrument panel (Series 7)**

PW ⑧ P D W A WARNING
⑦ LAMP
GO ⑥ LOW FUEL WARNING LAMP
NB ⑤ NO CHARGE WARNING LAMP
RW ④ PANEL ILLUMINATION
B ③ NEG (EARTH)
UW ② MAIN BEAM WARNING LAMP
GP ① DIRECTION IND. WARNING LAMP

RIGHT HAND CONNECTIONS TO PRINTED CIRCUIT

WN ① OIL PRESSURE WARNING LAMP
②
W ③ POS SUPPLY (FROM IGN)
④
GU ⑤ WATER TEMP. GAUGE
GB ⑥ FUEL GAUGE
RW ⑦ PANEL ILLUMINATION
⑧

LEFT HAND CONNECTIONS TO PRINTED CIRCUIT

H. 12091

200

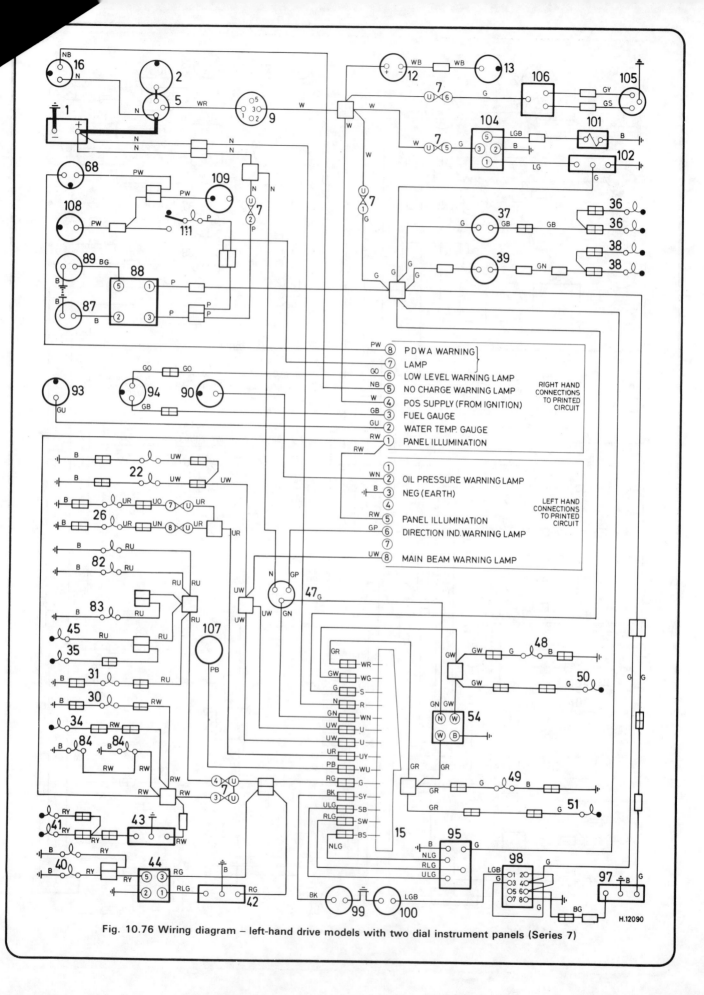

Fig. 10.76 Wiring diagram – left-hand drive models with two dial instrument panels (Series 7)

H.12090

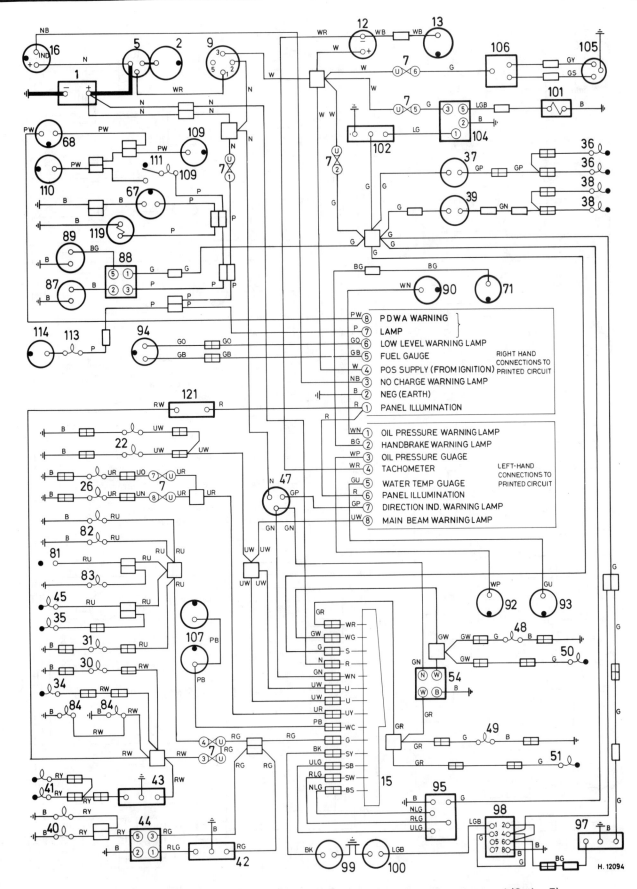

Fig. 10.77 Wiring diagram – right-hand drive models with six dial instrument panel (Series 7)

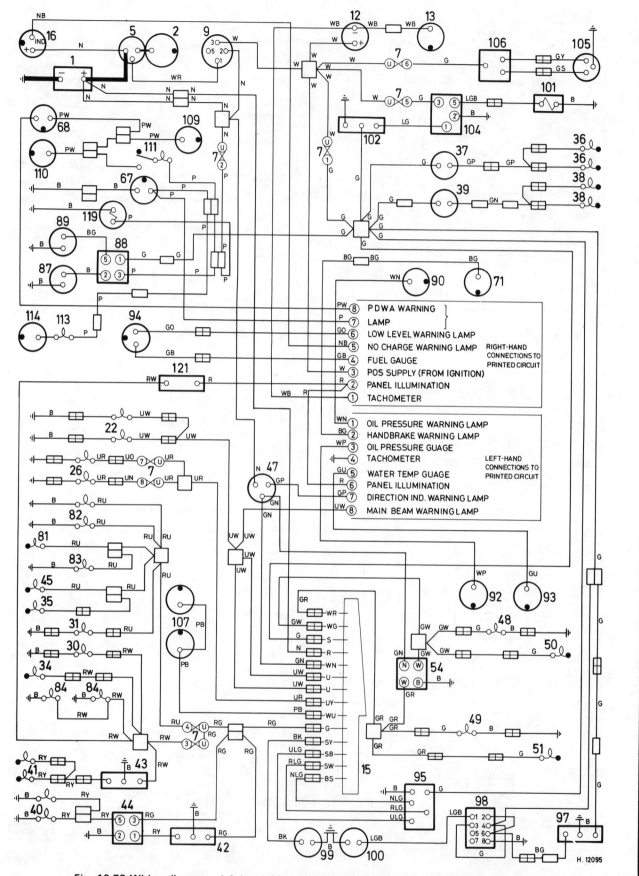

Fig. 10.78 Wiring diagram – left-hand drive models with six dial instrument panel (Series 7)

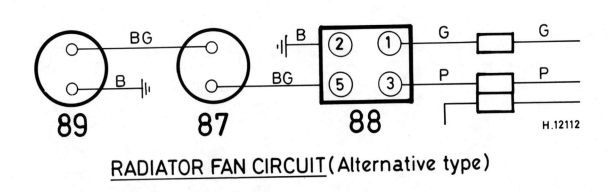

## RADIATOR FAN CIRCUIT (Alternative type)

Fig. 10.79 Additional wiring details as applicable to Figs. 10.75, 10.76, 10.77 and 10.78

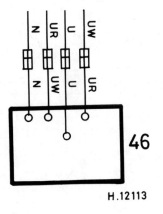

H.12113

Fig. 10.80 Additional wiring details of headlamp flash/dip switch as applicable to Figs. 10.67 to 10.74 inclusive

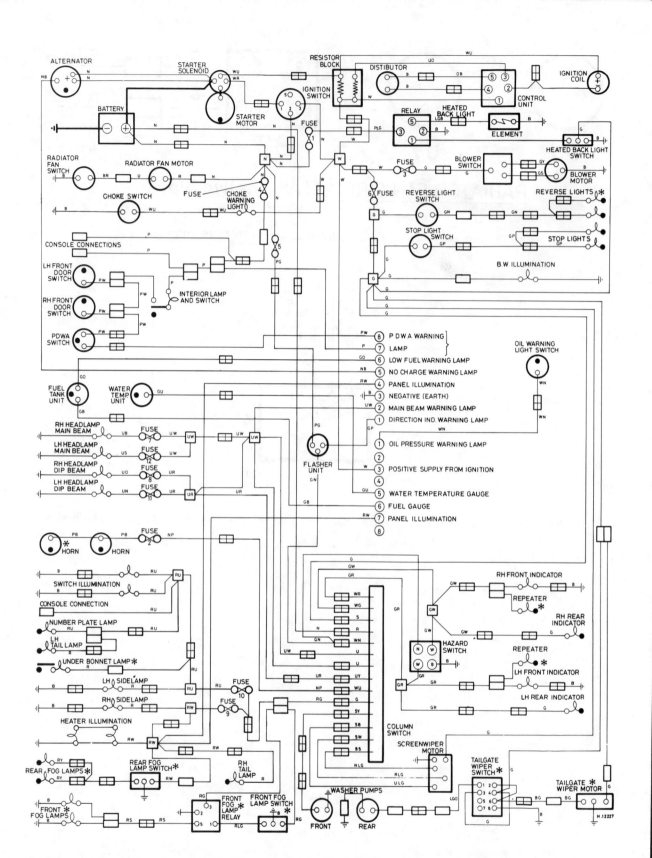

Fig. 10.81 Wiring diagram – right-hand drive models with two dial instrument panel (Series 8)

205

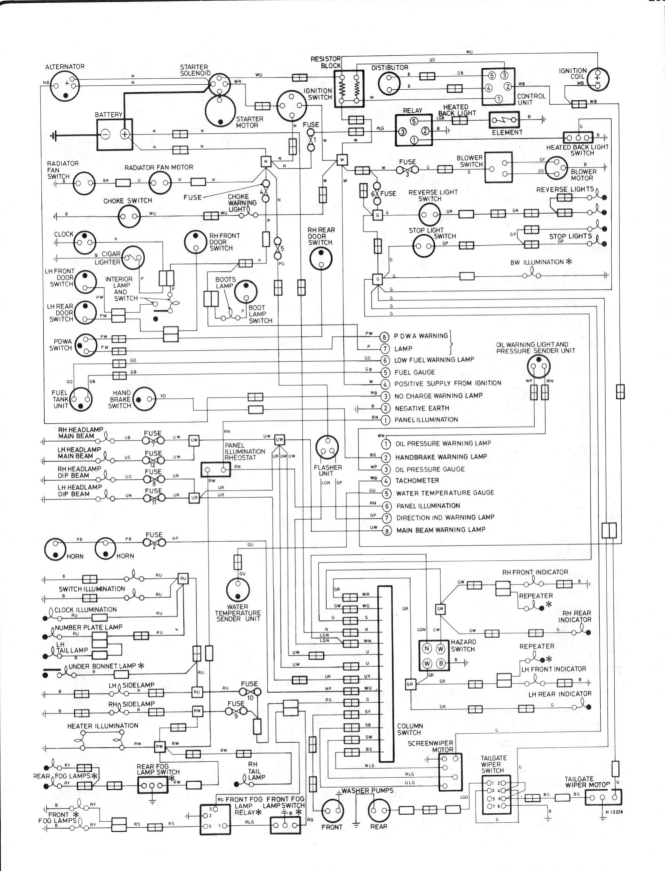

Fig. 10.82 Wiring diagram – right-hand drive models with six dial instrument panel (Series 8)

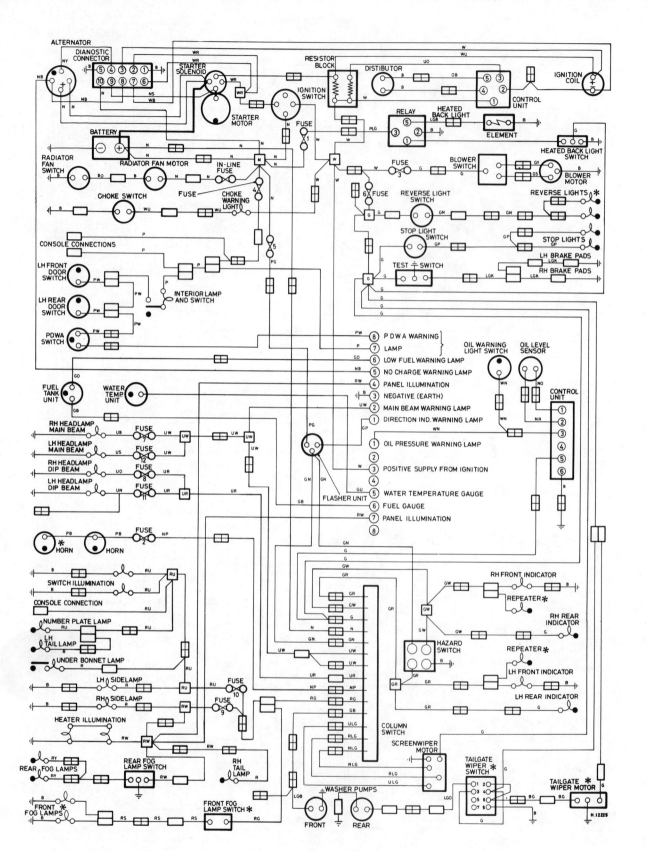

**Fig. 10.83 Wiring diagram – right-hand drive models with two dial instrument panel (commencing Series 9)**

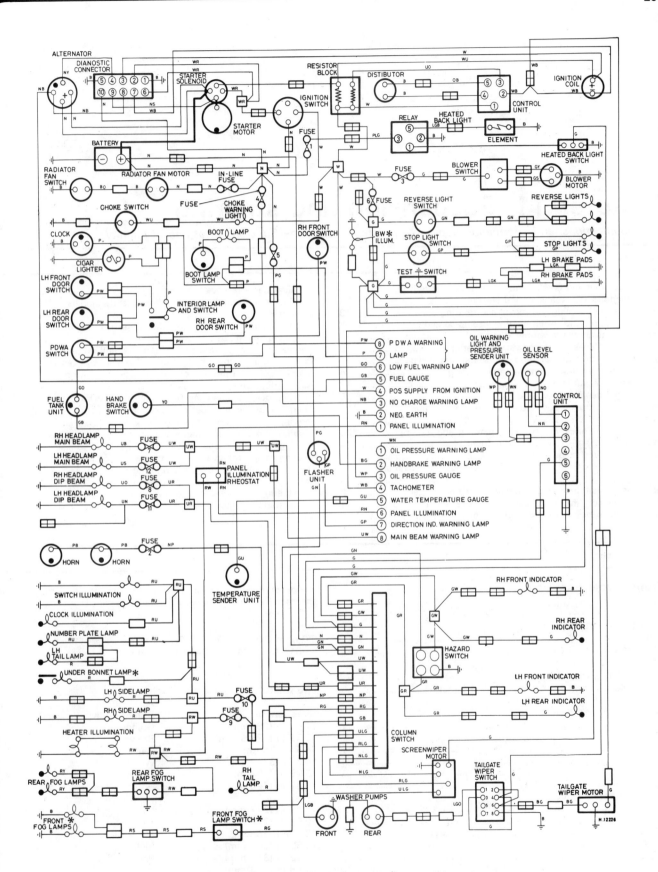

Fig. 10.84 Wiring diagram – right-hand drive models with six dial instrument panel (commencing Series 9)

# Chapter 11 Suspension and steering

*For modifications, and information applicable to later models, see Supplement at end of manual*

## Contents

## Specifications

### Front suspension type .........................................................

Independent; Macpherson struts, integral telescopic dampers (shock absorbers) and coil springs, with stabiliser bar

### Front hub endfloat
Early models ........................................................................
Later models ........................................................................

0.002 to 0.004 in (0.05 to 0.10 mm)
0.0015 to 0.004 in (0.04 to 0.10 mm)

### Front coil springs
Spring identification (up to and including Series 7) ....................

Two paint stripes of the stated colour

| *Free length | Colour code |
|---|---|
| 11.76 in (299 mm) | Orange |
| 11.79 in (299.5 mm) | Brown |
| 14.4 in (366 mm) | White |
| 14.6 in (371 mm) | White |
| 13.29 in (338 mm) | Green |
| 13.37 in (340 mm) | Green |
| | |
| 10.89 in (277 mm) | Yellow |
| 10.97 in (279 mm) | Yellow |
| 13.3 in (338 mm) | Blue |
| 13.53 in (344 mm) | Blue |
| 12.32 in (314 mm) | Pink |
| 12.46 in (316 mm) | Pink |

Right-hand Spring type:
A ............................................................................
B ............................................................................
C ............................................................................
D ............................................................................
E ............................................................................
F ............................................................................
Left-hand Spring type:
A ............................................................................
B ............................................................................
C ............................................................................
D ............................................................................
E ............................................................................
F ............................................................................

* *Removed from vehicle*

### Rear suspension type .........................................................

Two coil springs, four links, telescopic direct-acting dampers (shock absorbers). Panhard rod fitted on estate car

## Rear coil springs

Rear spring identification (up to and including Series 7) ...................... One paint stripe of the stated colour

Spring type:

| | *Free length | Colour code |
|---|---|---|
| A ................................................................................................ | 11.56 in (294 mm) | Green |
| B ................................................................................................ | 11.18 in (284 mm) | Blue |
| C ................................................................................................ | 11.51 in (292 mm) | Orange |
| D ................................................................................................ | 11.72 in (298 mm) | White |
| E ................................................................................................ | 11.13 in (282 mm) | Yellow |
| F ................................................................................................ | 11.72 in (298 mm) | None |

*Removed from vehicle*

Rear spring identification (Series 8) ............................................... Colour coded

Spring type:

| | **Free length** | **Colour code** |
|---|---|---|
| A ................................................................................................ | 11.70 in (297 mm) | None |
| B ................................................................................................ | 11.30 in (287 mm) | Blue |
| C ................................................................................................ | 10.70 in (272 mm) | Yellow |

## Steering

| | |
|---|---|
| Type ....................................................................................................... | Rack and pinion |
| Ratio ...................................................................................................... | 17.65 : 1 |
| Steering wheel diameter: | |
| Pre-Series 7 ...................................................................................... | 15.75 in (400 mm) |
| Series 7 on ....................................................................................... | 15.0 in (383 mm) |
| No of turns lock-to-lock ......................................................................... | 3.66 |
| Turning circle ........................................................................................ | 31 ft 9 in (9.7 m) |
| Rack shim availability: | |
| Cam Gears ......................................................................................... | 0.005, 0.0075, 0.010, 0.015, 0.020 in (0.13, 0.19, 0.25, 0.38, 0.50 mm) |
| Burman ............................................................................................. | 0.002, 0.005, 0.010 in (0.05, 0.13, 0.25 mm) |
| Pinion bearing preload shims: | |
| Cam Gears ......................................................................................... | 0.005, 0.0075, 0.010 in (0.13, 0.19, 0.25 mm) |
| Burman ............................................................................................. | 0.002, 0.005, 0.010 in (0.05, 0.13, 0.25 mm) |
| Front wheel toe-in ................................................................................. | $\frac{1}{32}$ to $\frac{1}{8}$ in (1 to 3 mm) |

## Wheels and tyres

| | |
|---|---|
| Wheel type ............................................................................................ | Safety ledge dish, pressed steel |
| Rim size: | |
| Avenger ............................................................................................ | $4\frac{1}{2}$J or 5J x 13 |
| Cricket .............................................................................................. | 5J x 13 |
| Tyres: | |
| Cross ply ........................................................................................... | 5.60 x 13 |
| Radial ply .......................................................................................... | 155 x 13 |
| Tyre pressures (with up to four occupants): | |
| Front ................................................................................................ | 24 lbf/in$^2$ (1.7 kgf/cm$^2$) |
| Rear ................................................................................................. | 24 lbf/in$^2$ (1.7 kgf/cm$^2$) |
| Tyre pressures (with four occupants plus luggage): | |
| Front ................................................................................................ | 24 lbf/in$^2$ (1.7 kgf/cm$^2$) |
| Rear ................................................................................................. | 30 lbf/in$^2$ (2.1 kgf/cm$^2$) |

*Note: On estate versions fitted with load carrying suspension, increase the rear pressure by 6 lbf/in$^2$ (0.4 kgf/cm$^2$) when fully laden*

## Torque wrench settings

*Up to and including Series 6*

| | lbf ft | Nm |
|---|---|---|
| Strut upper thrust bearing ................................................................... | 15 | 20 |
| Strut to upper swivel bearing (using tool P5026) ................................... | 31 | 42 |
| Steering arm to lower strut .................................................................. | 58 | 79 |
| Lower swivel balljoint to steering arm ................................................... | 44 | 60 |
| Strut gland nut .................................................................................... | 48 | 65 |
| Torsional rubber top mounting nut ........................................................ | 35 | 47 |
| Track control arm to crossmember ........................................................ | 28 | 38 |
| Crossmember to body .......................................................................... | 54 | 73 |
| Drag strut bracket to body ................................................................... | 28 | 38 |
| Drag strut to bracket ........................................................................... | 40 | 54 |
| Drag strut to track control arm ............................................................. | 36 | 49 |
| Stabiliser bar bracket to body .............................................................. | 28 | 38 |
| Suspension link pivot nuts and bolts (rear suspension) .......................... | 44 | 60 |
| Shock absorber spindle to top bracket (rear suspension) ....................... | 13 | 18 |
| Top bracket to body (rear suspension) .................................................. | 10 | 14 |
| Shock absorber lower fitting (rear suspension) ...................................... | 12 | 16 |
| Track rod end to steering arm .............................................................. | 32 | 43 |
| Track rod locknut ................................................................................ | 30 | 41 |
| Steering rack to crossmember .............................................................. | 18 | 24 |
| Steering wheel to column ..................................................................... | 32 | 43 |
| Intermediate shaft to column ............................................................... | 15 | 20 |
| Flexible coupling to intermediate shaft ................................................. | 15 | 20 |
| Flexible coupling to pinion flange ......................................................... | 15 | 20 |
| Pinion flange pinch bolt ....................................................................... | 10 to 15 | 14 to 20 |

| | lbf ft | Nm |
|---|---|---|
| Yoke cover bolts | 6 to 8 | 8 to 11 |
| Pinion cover plate bolts: | | |
|     Burman | 6 to 8 | 8 to 11 |
|     Cam Gears | 12 to 15 | 16 to 20 |
| Panhard rod to bodyframe | 44 | 60 |
| Panhard rod to rear axle | 32 | 43 |
| Wheel nuts: | | |
|     Steel wheels | 55 | 76 |
|     Alloy wheels | 60 | 83 |

*Series 7 on* (settings as above except for the following variations)

| | lbf ft | Nm |
|---|---|---|
| Track rod end to steering arm | 28 | 38 |
| Intermediate shaft to column | 18 | 24 |
| Stirrup bracket to facia (upper mounting) | 29.5 | 40 |
| Column U-bolt to stirrup bracket | 3.5 | 5 |
| Column support to pedal mounting bracket | 17 | 23 |
| Column to support bracket | 17 | 23 |
| Yoke cover bolts | 3 to 8 | 4 to 11 |
| Pinion cover plate bolts | 3 to 8 | 4 to 11 |

## 1 General description

The front suspension is of the MacPherson strut type. Each strut is secured at its top end to rubber mounted thrust bearings, while the lower end is secured to a swivel joint integral with the track control arm. The strut mounting points are non-adjustable. These are set in production and determine the castor, camber and steering axis angles. Each strut contains an integral direct-acting hydraulic shock absorber. Coil springs are mounted externally on the struts, and rebound from them is controlled by an in-built stop. At the lower end of each strut a stub axle carries the hub and brake assembly. The left and right-hand struts are not interchangeable. Suspension movement is controlled during vehicle motion by drag links and a stabiliser bar.

The rear suspension comprises two coil springs, a four link and two hydraulic shock absorber system. The links are rubber bushed and attached at the rear ends to mounting points on the rear axle casing. The coil springs are located at their top ends in a rubber lined seating pan and at their lower end in a depression formed in their lower links. The estate car has an additional link in the form of a Panhard rod, from the body to the rear axle.

The steering unit is of the rack and pinion type. Track rods which operate the swivel arms are attached to each end of the steering rack by balljoints protected with rubber bellows. The steering wheel transmits movement through the steering column, an intermediate shaft and a flexible coupling to a pinion which is in a mesh with the steering rack. The steering gear assembly may be one of two different makes and although they can be interchanged as a complete assembly, individual components cannot.

## 2 Maintenance and inspection

1 Inspect the condition of all rubber gaiters, balljoint covers and rubber protectors at each end of the steering gear for deterioration.
2 Check the security of the locknuts on the outer track rod ends, and of the ball-pin nuts.
3 Check the security of the front strut securing nuts. Examine the condition of the drag strut and stabiliser bar rubber bushes, and renew if necessary.
4 Secure the front hubs and check the front wheel alignment at the recommended intervals.
5 No maintenance is required for the rear suspension other than periodically checking the security of the link and shock absorber mounting bolts and nuts in accordance with the torque wrench settings given in the specifications.
6 Wear in the steering gear and linkage is indicated when there is excessive movement in the steering wheel without corresponding movement at the roadwheels, and when there is a tendancy for the vehicle to wander. The latter fault may be due to other factors as well as steering gear or linkage wear, such as incorrect steering geometry, incorrect front hub adjustment or buckled front wheels.
7 To check the steering, jack up the car under the front crossmember so that both front wheels hang free. With an assistant gripping one front wheel move the opposite one in the direction of steering left and right lock, at the same time observing any movement due to wear in the balljoints. Refer to Fig 11.1 and shake the track control arm to ensure that there is no wear in the bottom suspension leg swivel joint. Do not consider the steering gear at this stage. Any sign of wear in the swivel or balljoints will necessitate renewal.
8 Having established that the steering linkage is in good order, then any wear or lost motion must be in the steering gear itself. This may be eliminated by adjustment, or alternatively by fitting new parts.

## 3 Springs and shock absorbers – inspection

1 Vehicle safety is very dependent upon the steering and suspension, and the compulsory vehicle tests pay considerable attention to this aspect.
2 Check the front suspension by jacking the car up so that the wheel is clear of the ground. Place another jack under the track control arm near the outer end. When the arm is raised by the jack any movement in the suspension strut ball-stud will be apparent, as will any wear in the inner track control arm bush. The balljoint endfloat should not exceed 0.060 inch (1.5 mm). However, it is not possible to gauge this movement accurately without removing the joint, and it should therefore be dismantled. There should be no play in the track control arm bush.
3 The top end of the suspension unit should have no discernible movement. To check it grip the strut at the lower spring seat and and try pushing it from side to side. There should be no detectable movement either between the outer cylinder and the inner piston rod or at the top of the piston rod near the upper mounting.
4 The top and bottom anchor points of the rear shock absorbers should be firm. Signs of oil on the outside of the lower cylinder section indicate that the seals are faulty, and that the unit requires renewal. The shock absorber may also have failed internally and this is more difficult to detect. It is usually indicated by excessive bounce at the rear end and axle patter or 'tramp' on uneven surfaces. When this occurs remove the shock absorber in order to check its damping power in both directions.

## 4 Front suspension unit – removal and refitting

1 The strut assembly may be removed complete with hub, coil roadspring and top thrust bearing unit. Removal for left and right-hand assemblies is identical.
2 Apply the handbrake and jack up the front of the car, supporting adequately under the body sidemembers.
3 Remove the roadwheel from the the side to be dismantled.
4 Unbolt and remove the brake caliper unit, disengage the hydraulic fluid line from its bracket, and tie the caliper to the stabiliser bar.
5 Remove the two nuts which secure the steering arm to the foot of the strut and withdraw the arm, but allow it still to be connected to the track rod and track control arm.
6 Remove the lower nut, rubber bushes and washers from the stabiliser bar drop link, through the track control arm.
7 Support the strut at its base and remove the three nuts and

washers which secure the upper end of the strut assembly to the inner wing valance. Do not remove the thrust bearing securing nut which is visible through the hole in the wing valance.

8    Lift the strut assembly away. A new coil spring or other components may be fitted at a garage having the necessary equipment. If you are able to borrow the necessary tools (special tool nos P5045, RG549 and P5026) and make up a piece of wood, then the procedure given for this operation in Section 5 should be followed.

9    Refitting is the reverse of removal. Check the steering alignment on completion.

### 5  Front coil spring and thrust bearing – removal and refitting

1    Remove the strut assembly as described in Section 4, mount it complete on a roadwheel, and place on a bench using a wooden steadying wedge between the strut and tyre.

2    Using a suitable coil spring compressor, compress the coil spring. A tough encircling safety strap should be used round the compressor after fixing it to the spring (Fig. 11.3).

3    With tool RG549 remove the nut which secures the thrust bearing unit to the strut.

4    Remove the locating washer and bearing unit, push the damper rod into the strut, and either gently release the spring compressor (evenly) or remove the coil spring complete with compressor for subsequent detachment.

5    Refitting of a coil spring is a reversal of removal, but note that the right-hand spring is longer than the left and has, in consequence, wider spaced spring abutment platforms.

6    Check the conditions of the thrust bearing and strut dust cover. To adjust the bearing, employ tool RG549 to turn the nut while rotating the bearing to the specified torque. Do not exceed this figure otherwise stiff steering will result. Always check steering angles after steering or suspension dismantling.

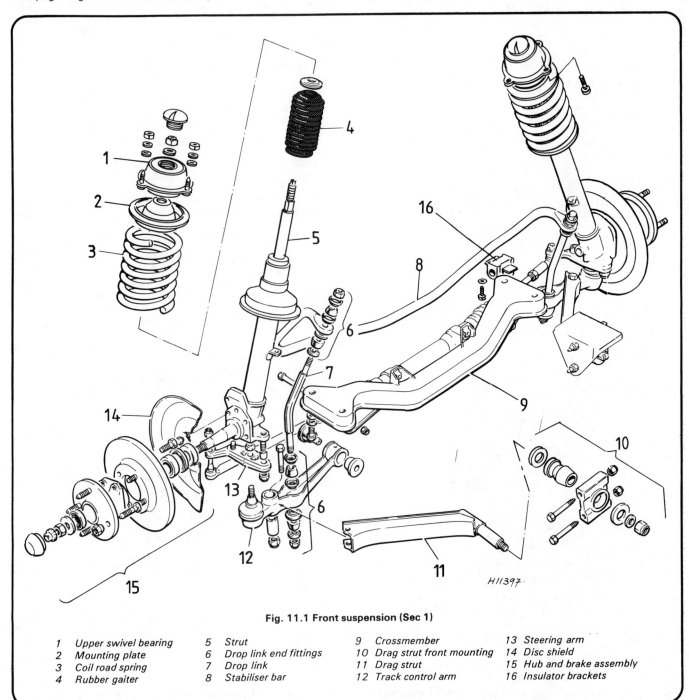

**Fig. 11.1 Front suspension (Sec 1)**

| | | | | | |
|---|---|---|---|---|---|
| 1 | Upper swivel bearing | 5 | Strut | 9 | Crossmember |
| 2 | Mounting plate | 6 | Drop link end fittings | 10 | Drag strut front mounting |
| 3 | Coil road spring | 7 | Drop link | 11 | Drag strut |
| 4 | Rubber gaiter | 8 | Stabiliser bar | 12 | Track control arm |

| | |
|---|---|
| 13 | Steering arm |
| 14 | Disc shield |
| 15 | Hub and brake assembly |
| 16 | Insulator brackets |

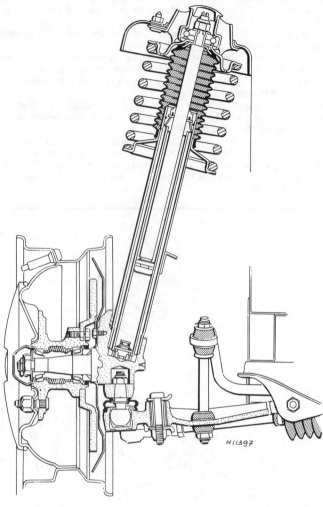

Fig. 11.2 Front suspension – section through one side (Sec 4)

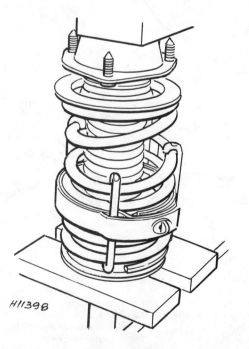

Fig. 11.3 Coil spring removal, showing compressor and safety
straps in place (Sec 5)

## 6   Front suspension strut – renewal or overhaul

1   When suspension struts become in need of renewal, it is recommended that they should be renewed as complete units. The
exchange unit will not include the coil spring on other ancillary items,
and these should be removed from the old unit as described in the
relevant Section.

2   Suspension struts may be overhauled by employing replacement
damper cartridges. When employing these for early type dampers,
cartridges must be fitted to both sides of the vehicle.

3   Remove the suspension unit, the coil spring and the thrust
bearing, as described in Sections 4 and 5. Remove the gaiter, push the
damper rod into the strut, ease back the staking locking the nut to the
strut, taking great care not to damage the threads, and remove the nut
and discard it (tool CS0014).

4   Remove the O-ring from inside the top edge of the strut (if fitted).
Pull the damper rod to dislodge the bush and seal from the top of the
strut. Withdraw the unit from the strut. Pour out the remaining oil.

5   Thoroughly clean the strut, and check the operation of the
replacement cartridge by operating it through a few strokes before
fitting. Insert the cartridge, pour in 50cc of engine oil, fit a new
retaining nut and tighten with tool CS0014. Secure the nut by staking
the top edge of the strut into the slot. Fit a new convoluted gaiter,
ensuring that it is correctly located on the damper rod and is not
twisted. Refit the coil spring and upper bearing assembly.

## 7   Front suspension top mounting – torsional rubber type

1   Certain models are fitted with an alternative front suspension strut
top mounting of torsional rubber construction instead of the ball-type
thrust bearing. The rubber type can be identified by noting the location
of the securing nut which is not fitted with a dust cover.

2   Removal of the mounting is identical to the thrust bearing type.
When refitting, care should be taken to ensure that the rubber is under
no torsional stress when the roadwheels are in the 'straight-ahead'
position.

3   Before releasing the coil spring onto the mounting, position one of
the three securing studs in line with the stub axle, and position the
rebound plate, located beneath the top securing nut, so that it points
towards the engine. Hold each item in position and run the securing
nut down to a full nut depth.

4   Release the coil spring and refit the suspension unit.

5   Refit the roadwheel and lower the car to the ground before finally
tightening the top securing nut to the specified torque setting. Hold
the rebound plate with a spanner when tightening the nut to prevent
stresses building up in the rubber mounting, and make sure that the
front wheels are set in the 'straight-ahead' position.

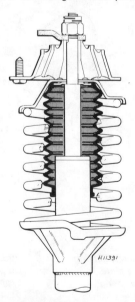

Fig. 11.4 Front suspension top mounting – torsional rubber type
(Sec 7)

## 8   Stabiliser bar – removal and refitting

1   Do not jack up the front of the car, but allow the weight of the car to remain on the wheels.
2   Refer to Fig 11.1 and remove the nuts, washers and rubber bushes which secure the lower ends of the drop links to the track control arms.
3   Remove the rubber insulated brackets which hold the stabiliser bar to the body side members. The stabiliser bar can now be withdrawn complete with drop links.
4   Renew any rubber bushes which have deteriorated.
5   Refitting is largely a reversal of the removal procedure, but be sure that the rubber bushes are compressed into the insulated brackets to facilitate the entry of their retaining bolts, and that the drop links are fitted with the shorter leg, from the bend, downwards.
6   Ensure that bushes, nuts and washers are fitted in the sequence shown in Fig 11.1. Tighten each nut until the rubber bush has sufficiently compressed to provide a measurement of between $\frac{9}{16}$ and $\frac{5}{8}$ inch (14.3 and 15.9 mm) from the nut-facing side of the washer to the tip of the drop link threads.

## 9   Front suspension crossmember – removal and refitting

1   Support the weight of the engine, either by using an engine hoist or by adequately supporting the engine sump.
2   Remove the lower bolts from the engine support mountings.
3   Remove the bolts from the steering clamps to crossmember.
4   Remove the nuts, washers and rubber bushes from the drop link lower mountings as described in Section 8.

5   Remove the drag strut front end mounting brackets as described in Section 30.
6   Remove the track control arm inner pivot nuts and bolts and prise the arms out of the crossmember (Fig 11.1).
7   Remove the setscrews which retain the crossmember to the body underframe and lift it away.
8   Refit in reverse order, employing new self-locking nuts. Tighten to the specified torque. Check the steering alignment.

## 10   Rear springs, shock absorbers and bump pads – removal and refitting

1   Rear spring removal procedure is described in Chapter 8.
2   The shock absorbers are completely sealed, and if they become faulty must be renewed complete. However, kits of parts are available to provide for servicing of the end mounting points of the unit, should these become worn.
3   Remove the shock absorber by detaching the upper securing nut and the lower bolt. (On early estate cars, two bolts will be found at the top). Disconnect the rear shock absorbers with the rear axle supported on stands, and the car standing on level ground. It should be noted that certain models may have washers below the upper fixing bracket nuts on the right-hand side. If so, these must always be refitted.
4   Before fitting replacement units, prime them by operating them in and out for two or three full length strokes, with them mounted vertically.
5   Refit in reverse order to removal, referring to Fig. 11.5 for the correct order of assembly of the two end components.
6   To remove the bump pads, support the rear of the vehicle, remove

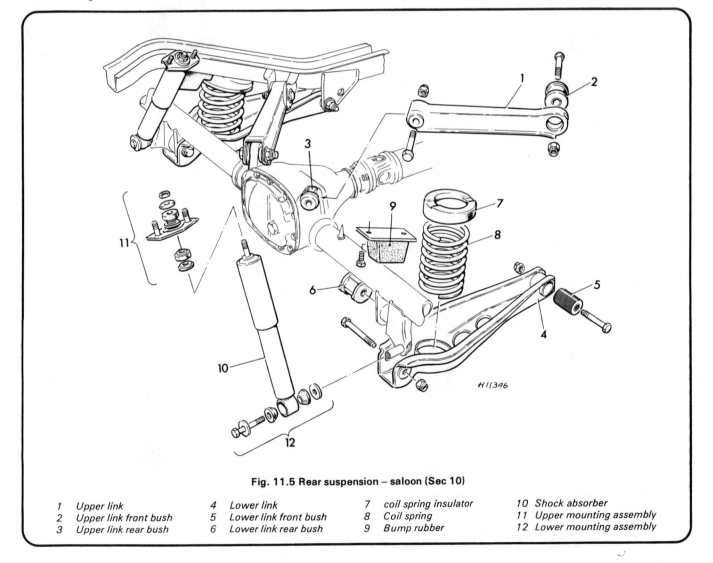

**Fig. 11.5 Rear suspension – saloon (Sec 10)**

|   |   |   |   |   |   |   |   |
|---|---|---|---|---|---|---|---|
| 1 | Upper link | 4 | Lower link | 7 | coil spring insulator | 10 | Shock absorber |
| 2 | Upper link front bush | 5 | Lower link front bush | 8 | Coil spring | 11 | Upper mounting assembly |
| 3 | Upper link rear bush | 6 | Lower link rear bush | 9 | Bump rubber | 12 | Lower mounting assembly |

the rear wheels as necessary, and lever away the bracket tabs. Remove the pad. To refit, soap the pad and bracket edges, feed the pad into the bracket, and knock up the tabs.

7    Note that when jacking under the rear axle a serious oil leak can occur if the jack platform is allowed to bear upon the rear cover.

## 11   Rear suspension links and bushes – removal and refitting

*Note: for estate cars refer to Section 12*

1    If it is necessary to remove all the links, the rear axle must first be removed as described in Chapter 8. If, however, only one link at a time need be removed, this may be carried out without removing the axle. Simply withdraw the pivot bolts, and remove the link, but remove the coil spring, when removing the lower link. To refit, refit the pivot bolts, lightly tighten the nuts, and bounce the vehicle to settle the bushes. Tighten the nuts to the specified torque figure.

2    A service tool, no RG551/1-10, is available for bush servicing work, but a screwed bolt with suitable distance piece and plates will be an adequate substitute. Lubricate the new bushes with brake fluid

or soft soap before fitting.

3    It is important that the bushes are withdrawn or inserted from the sides indicated in Figs. 11.6 to 11.13. The method of extraction or insertion using the tool illustrated is evident from the figures. Note that the lower link rear bushes (Fig. 11.9) must have their 'ears' horizontally located when assembled.

## 12   Rear suspension, including Panhard rod (estate) – general

1    Although similar in general design to the Saloon suspension, the upper links are parallel to the lower links and, in consequence, a Panhard rod is fitted to provide lateral stability.

2    When refitting the Panhard rod, tighten the securing bolts with the vehicle standing (unladen) on the ground.

3    The bushes of the upper suspension links cannot be renewed and, if worn, the complete link must be renewed as an assembly.

4    The rear bolts of the upper suspension links must always be fitted so that their nuts are towards the centre of the vehicle.

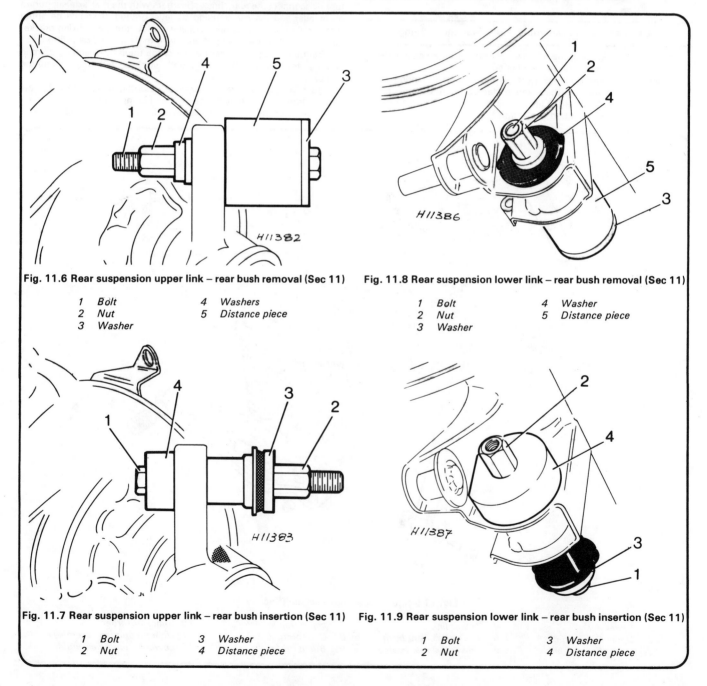

**Fig. 11.6 Rear suspension upper link – rear bush removal (Sec 11)**

| 1 Bolt | 4 Washers |
|--------|-----------|
| 2 Nut | 5 Distance piece |
| 3 Washer | |

**Fig. 11.8 Rear suspension lower link – rear bush removal (Sec 11)**

| 1 Bolt | 4 Washer |
|--------|-----------|
| 2 Nut | 5 Distance piece |
| 3 Washer | |

**Fig. 11.7 Rear suspension upper link – rear bush insertion (Sec 11)**

| 1 Bolt | 3 Washer |
|--------|-----------|
| 2 Nut | 4 Distance piece |

**Fig. 11.9 Rear suspension lower link – rear bush insertion (Sec 11)**

| 1 Bolt | 3 Washer |
|--------|-----------|
| 2 Nut | 4 Distance piece |

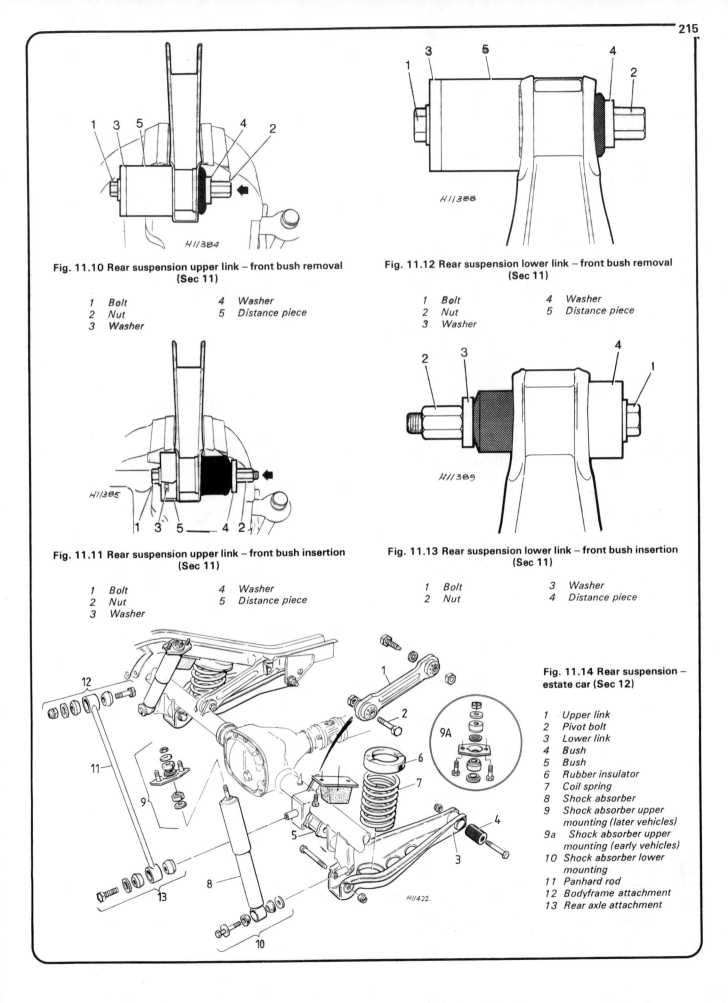

**Fig. 11.10 Rear suspension upper link – front bush removal (Sec 11)**

1 Bolt
2 Nut
3 Washer
4 Washer
5 Distance piece

**Fig. 11.12 Rear suspension lower link – front bush removal (Sec 11)**

1 Bolt
2 Nut
3 Washer
4 Washer
5 Distance piece

**Fig. 11.11 Rear suspension upper link – front bush insertion (Sec 11)**

1 Bolt
2 Nut
3 Washer
4 Washer
5 Distance piece

**Fig. 11.13 Rear suspension lower link – front bush insertion (Sec 11)**

1 Bolt
2 Nut
3 Washer
4 Distance piece

**Fig. 11.14 Rear suspension – estate car (Sec 12)**

1 Upper link
2 Pivot bolt
3 Lower link
4 Bush
5 Bush
6 Rubber insulator
7 Coil spring
8 Shock absorber
9 Shock absorber upper mounting (later vehicles)
9a Shock absorber upper mounting (early vehicles)
10 Shock absorber lower mounting
11 Panhard rod
12 Bodyframe attachment
13 Rear axle attachment

## 13 Front wheel alignment

1   Before front wheel alignment is checked, ensure that the tyres are correctly inflated, that the front wheels are not buckled, the hub bearings not worn or incorrectly adjusted and that the steering linkage is in good order.

2   Wheel alignment consists of four factors:

*Camber;* the angle at which the front wheels are set from the vertical when viewed from the front of the car. Positive camber is the amount (in degrees) that the wheels are tilted outwards at the top from the vertical.

*Castor;* the angle between the steering axis and a vertical line when viewed from each side of the car. Positive castor is when the steering axis is inclined rearward.

*Steering axis inclination;* the angle, when viewed from the front of the car, between the vertical and an imaginary line drawn between the upper and lower suspension leg pivots.

*Toe-in;* the amount by which the distance between the front inside edges of the roadwheels (measured at hub height) is less than the diametrically opposite distance measured between the rear inside edges of the front roadwheels.

3   Due to the need for special gap gauges and correct weighting of the car suspension, it is not within the scope of the home mechanic to check steering angles, ie camber, castor and steering axis inclination.

4   Toe-in may be checked and adjusted if a suitable gauge is available, and the vehicle should first be placed on level ground with the wheels in the straight-ahead position. The toe-in should then be checked as instructed by the manufacturer of the gauge and the result compared with the Specifications. If the reading is incorrect, slacken the track rod end locking nuts, slacken the screws on the clamps on the convoluted covers at the track rod inner ends, and ensure that the covers are not stuck to the rods. Rotate both track rods an equal amount, until the toe-in is correct. Tighten the locknuts, centralise the balljoints, straighten up the convoluted covers, and tighten up the cover clips. If oil is lost from the rack, the unit should be drained and refitted as described in Sections 33 and 34.

## 14 Steering linkage – centralisation

To ensure the correct wheel angle on turns, and to ensure the proper steering linkage setting, the vehicle must be properly prepared as for a full steering geometry check. This necessitates the use of certain special items of equipment, and the following of a lengthy setting procedure. It is therefore advised that the vehicle be entrusted to a main dealer for this work.

## 15 Front wheel bearings – adjustment

1   Correct front hub endfloat is essential. To adjust this, raise the front of the vehicle, and remove the wheels, and brake pads (where fitted).

2   Prise off the hub dust cap by tapping the rounded part of the cap in an outward direction. Withdraw the split pin and remove the castellated lock cap.

3   Using a torque wrench set at 15 to 20 lb ft (20 to 27 Nm) on the hub nut, tighten to the indicated torque at the same time rotating the hub. Back-off the nut 1 to 1½ flats and check the endfloat by using either a dial gauge or feelers between the hub nut and the thrust washer. The correct amount is given in the Specifications.

4   Fit a new split pin to the castellated lock cap, and do not fill the dust cap with grease. Refit the cap.

5   Replace the brake pads and wheels and pump the pedal to restore brake efficiency.

## 16 Front wheel bearings and hub – removal and refitting

1   Raise the front of the vehicle, remove the roadwheel, and remove the brake caliper assembly as described in Chapter 9.

2   Remove the hub dust cap, the split pin, the castellated lock cap, hub nut and thrust washer. Withdraw the hub, keeping it level and catching the outer bearing as it is pulled off the stub axle.

3   Prise out the grease seal before lifting out the inner bearing. Note

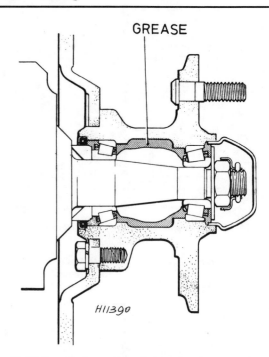

GREASE

H11390

**Fig. 11.15 Front hub – sectional view showing correct grease packing (Sec 16)**

the special distance piece positioned on the stub axle which impinges on the wiping edge of the grease seal. This may adhere to the seal when the hub assembly is withdrawn.

4   Where new bearings are to be fitted, drift out the outer bearing tracks using a brass or copper drift. Never use a new bearing with an old track.

5   Reassembly is essentially a reversal of dismantling. Press in the new bearing tracks, and fit the inner bearing followed by a new grease seal. Pack the hub with grease as shown in Fig. 11.15. Locate the new distance piece (supplied with the grease seal) on the stub axle. Reassemble the hub to the stub axle, keeping it level and without forcing to avoid damage to the grease seal. Locate the outer bearing, fit the plain thrust washer and the hub nut. Adjust the endfloat, as described in Section 15. Fit the castellated lock cap, new split pin, the dust cap, brake caliper unit and roadwheel, and lower the jack.

## 17 Wheel studs – removal and refitting

1   If stud breakage or thread damage occurs, the wheel securing studs must not be drifted out. They are an interference fit and removal other than by a balljoint remover or similar tool will cause bearing damage or hub distortion.

2   Refit a stud by using a forked-end clamp or using a wheel nut and distance piece to draw it into position.

## 18 Steering wheel – removal and refitting

1   Prise away the central motif. Note that some export vehicles have a centre pad, which should be turned anti-clockwise to remove.

2   Slacken the inner column top nut, *but do not remove.* Pull the wheel up to break the taper, remove the nut, and mark both wheel end and inner column to ensure correct refitting. Withdraw the wheel.

3   If difficulty in removal is experienced, pull the wheel upwards and give the inner column a sharp tap with a soft drift and a hammer. *Do not use heavy blows.*

4   Refit in reverse order, ensuring alignment of the marks previously made, and tighten the nut to the correct torque figure.

## 19 Steering column (pre-Series 7) – removal and refitting

1   Disconnect the battery earth lead.

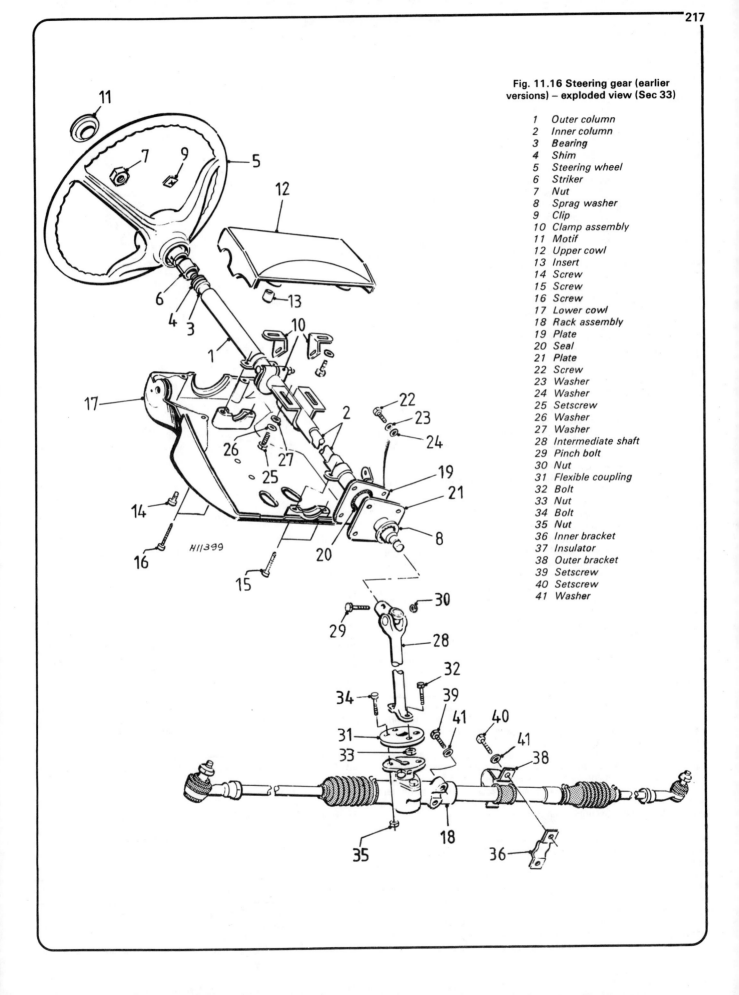

Fig. 11.16 Steering gear (earlier versions) – exploded view (Sec 33)

1　Outer column
2　Inner column
3　Bearing
4　Shim
5　Steering wheel
6　Striker
7　Nut
8　Sprag washer
9　Clip
10　Clamp assembly
11　Motif
12　Upper cowl
13　Insert
14　Screw
15　Screw
16　Screw
17　Lower cowl
18　Rack assembly
19　Plate
20　Seal
21　Plate
22　Screw
23　Washer
24　Washer
25　Setscrew
26　Washer
27　Washer
28　Intermediate shaft
29　Pinch bolt
30　Nut
31　Flexible coupling
32　Bolt
33　Nut
34　Bolt
35　Nut
36　Inner bracket
37　Insulator
38　Outer bracket
39　Setscrew
40　Setscrew
41　Washer

H11399

2    Turn the steering column key to the unlocked position.
3    Remove the six steering column cowl securing screws and with-draw the cowl.
4    Remove the indicator switch from the column by removing the screws.
5    Remove the four floor aperture plate screws.
6    Unscrew the two bolts, with spacers, from the steering column support bracket, noting the earth connection.
7    Slacken the large through-bolt on the upper clamp.
8    Mark the inner column in relation to its connection with the intermediate shaft for exact refitting.
9    Remove the pinch bolt at this connection and remove the steering column complete with wheel from inside the car.
10    Extract the inner column from the lower end of the outer, allowing the steering lock boss to push out the bottom bush.
11    Refitting of the steering column is a reversal of removal. Lubricate the inner column spline, observe all mating marks and grease the steering column top bearing. Tighten the intermediate shaft pinch bolt and the steering wheel nut to the correct torque settings.

## 20  Steering column (Series 7 onwards) – removal and refitting

1    Disconnect the battery.
2    Raise the front of the vehicle, place the wheels in the straight-ahead position and engage the steering lock.
3    Pull back the floor covering from the base of the steering column. Unhook the throttle return spring from the column lower mounting bracket (Series 7).
4    Remove the steering wheel (see Section 18).
5    Remove the upper and lower shrouds and remove the steering column switch assembly (see Chapter 10).
6    Unscrew and remove the two column retaining bolts from the upper support bracket, together with the shakeproof and plain wash-ers.
7    Unscrew and remove the two column retaining nuts from the lower column support bracket, together with the shakeproof and plain washers.
8    From within the engine compartment unscrew and remove the four nuts from the column base and floor aperture plate.
9    Mark the inner column in relation to its connection with the intermediate shaft for exact positioning when refitting, and disconnect the column from the intermediate shaft after removing the pinch bolt.
10    The steering column can now be withdrawn from inside the car.
11    Refitting is a reversal of the removal procedure, but lubricate the inner column spline and observe all mating marks. The steering column lock should be engaged before offering the column into location to ensure that the column assumes its exact original position. Apply sealing compound to the floor aperture plate and tighten all nuts and bolts to the correct specified torque settings.

## 21  Steering column endfloat and stiffness (early models) – adjustment

1    Withdraw the intermediate shaft, as detailed in Section 24.
2    Make a shim from 0.008 to 0.010 in (0.20 to 0.25 mm) material to the dimensions shown in Fig. 11.17 and engage the shim between the bottom bush and the sprag washer.
3    With an assistant applying light, downward pressure to the steering wheel, tap the sprag washer upwards using a mallet and tube of $1\frac{3}{8}$ in (35 mm) outside diameter. Withdraw the shim and check the column rotation for stiffness. Should any be apparent then gently tap the inner column upwards until the stiffness disappears. Where the sprag washer lacks security, then it should be renewed.

## 22  Steering column endfloat and stiffness (Series 7 vehicles on) – adjustment

1    The adjustment may be made with the steering column on or off the vehicle. Check that the sprag washer is in good order and is not tilted. Renew if defective.
2    To check the endfloat with the column in the vehicle, release the steering lock and disconnect the battery. Have a helper push down on the steering wheel, and measure the gap above the sprag washer.

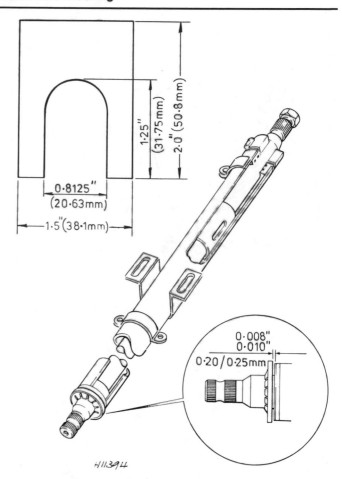

H11394

**Fig. 11.17 Steering column endfloat – test shim details (Sec 21)**

3    If the endfloat is less than 0.005 to 0.010 in (0.14 to 0.25 mm), spring the sprag washer down the column shaft by passing a long drift (about 30 in long by $\frac{1}{2}$ in dia) from below the radiator and over the crossmember to bear upon the intermediate shaft top yoke, (not upon the joint complete). Tap the yoke, to spring the washer down the column. Recheck the gap.
4    If the endfloat is greater than the specified maximum, move the spring washer squarely up the column by using a 21 mm open-ended spanner with its jaws over the end of the column shaft, between the sprag washer and the intermediate shaft yoke. Place gauge plate (Fig. 11.17) between the sprag washer and the thin washer. Gently lever the sprag washer up with the spanner as an assistant rotates the wheel to ensure even movement.
5    With the steering column off the vehicle, support the column top on a wooden block on the floor. Place the gauge plate between the plain and spring washers. Employ the tubular drift (see Section 26) to just nip the sprag washer up to the gauge. Remove the plate.

## 23  Flexible flange coupling – removal and refitting

1    Release the steering lock, raise the front of the vehicle, and support on stands.
2    Release the nuts and bolts securing the coupling, remove the bolts, and remove the coupling.
3    Refit in the reverse order, tightening the nuts to the specified torque figures.

## 24  Intermediate shaft – removal and refitting

1    Raise the front of the vehicle as necessary. Disconnect the battery.
2    Set the roadwheels to the straight-ahead position, and make alignment marks at each end of the intermediate shaft.
3    Remove the universal joint pinch bolt, and the bolts securing the

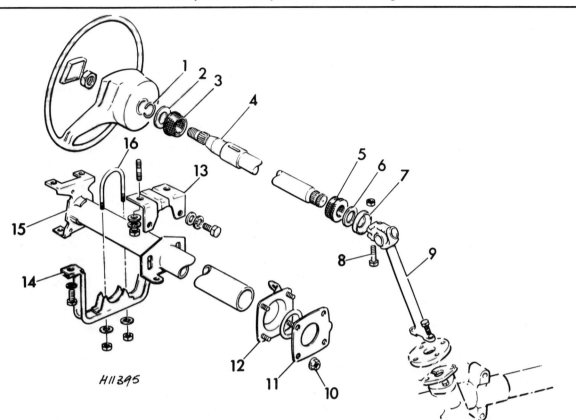

**Fig. 11.18 Steering column (Series 7 on) – exploded view (Sec 26)**

| | | | | | |
|---|---|---|---|---|---|
| 1 | Circlip | 5 | Bottom bush | 9 | Intermediate shaft | 13 | Lower mounting bracket |
| 2 | Washer | 6 | Washer | 10 | Baseplate nuts | 14 | Upper mounting bracket |
| 3 | Top bush | 7 | Sprag washer | 11 | Baseplate | 15 | Outer column (tube) |
| 4 | Inner column | 8 | Pinch bolt | 12 | Lower plate assembly | 16 | U-bolt |

bottom yoke to the coupling. Pull the intermediate shaft clear.
4    Refit in reverse order, greasing the column splines with an anti-corrosive grease, and observing the alignment marks made when dismantling. Hold the steering column down as the intermediate shaft is pushed on to the splines. Tighten the bolts to the specified torque figures, and if a new shaft has been fitted check the wheel alignment.

### 25 Steering column upper bush (Series 7 onwards) – renewal

1    The steering column upper bush can be removed with the steering column in position in the car.
2    Disconnect the battery. Turn the ignition key to the 'park' position to disengage the steering column lock.
3    Remove the steering wheel as detailed in Section 18.
4    Remove the seven screws retaining the lower surround.
5    Remove the combination switch retaining screws. Lift it away to expose the column upper bush retaining circlip.
6    Prise the circlip out together with the washer. Lever the bush from its location.
7    Refitting is a reversal of removal. Check the steering column assembly for endfloat or stiffness, and adjust the sprag washer as described in Section 22.

### 26 Inner column (Series 7 onwards) – removal and refitting

1    Remove the steering column assembly, as described in Section 20. Remove the circlip (1) and the washer (2), shown in Fig. 11.18.
2    Disengage the steering column lock. Pull the intermediate shaft to remove the inner column, thereby dislodging the bottom bush. Mark the inner column shaft and the intermediate shaft, before removing the pinch bolt and separating the items. Remove the sprag washer, plain washer and bottom bush.
3    To refit, check the lower end of the shaft for burrs and carefully

remove any present. Place the bottom bush and washer on the shaft. Carefully drift the sprag washer onto the shaft, employing a tubular drift $1\frac{3}{8}$ in (34.9 mm) outside diameter by $1\frac{1}{8}$ in (28.6 mm) inside diameter, until it is approximately $\frac{1}{8}$ in (3 mm) from the end.
4    Disengage the lock, feed the inner tube into position, locate the bottom bush, and fit the top bush, washer and clip.
5    Adjust the column endfloat as described in Section 22 and refit the intermediate shaft to the marks previously made. Refit the steering column assembly as described in Section 20.

### 27 Steering lock (early models) – removal and refitting

1    The unit is a combined lock and ignition switch secured by a special clamp with shear-head bolts. A key-operated peg engages in a slot in the inner steering column.
2    To remove the unit, disconnect the battery and remove the steering column cowl.
3    Disconnect the ignition switch cables.
4    Centre punch each of the centres of the shear-head bolts (Fig. 11.19). Do not remove the countersunk screws.

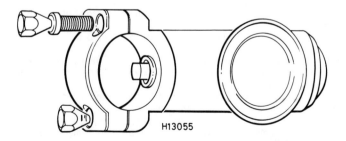

**Fig. 11.19 Steering column lock and ignition switch (Sec 27)**

5   Drill out the centres of the shear-bolt heads $\frac{1}{8}$ inch (3 mm) in depth using a 11/32 inch (9 mm) drill.
6   Release the countersunk screws and remove the two halves of the unit.
7   Refitting is carried out by first setting the lock to the 'park' position so that the locking peg is disengaged.
8   Fit the new lock so that its locating tag engages correctly in the steering column hole and insert the shear-head bolts and countersunk screws finger tight at this stage.
9   Check the operation of the lock for smoothness and engagement by inserting the key and if necessary, giving the lock unit a slight twist in either direction. When satisfied that the unit is correctly positioned, fully tighten the countersunk screws and tighten the shear-head bolts sufficiently to shear their heads.
10   Reconnect the ignition cable, the battery earth lead and refit the steering column cowl.

## 28 Steering lock (commencing Series 7) – removal and refitting

1   Disconnect the battery negative terminal.
2   Unscrew and remove the seven steering column lower surround retaining screws and withdraw the surround.
3   Disconnect the cables from the ignition switch and turn the ignition key to the locked position.
4   Remove the steering lock retaining bolts by using a centre punch on the outer edges of the shear head. If the shear bolts are seized it will be necessary to lower the end of the steering column in order to drill the bolt heads. Use a 11/32 in (9 mm) diameter drill in the centre of each bolt head in turn, drilling to a depth of $\frac{1}{8}$ in (3 mm). The bolt heads will become detached from the shanks if the drill has been correctly centralised.
5   Withdraw the lock from the steering column and remove the remaining bolt shanks from the body of the unit.
6   Refitting is carried out by first setting the lock to the 'park' position so that the locking peg is disengaged.
7   Offer the main lock body to its location on the steering column, ensuring that the spigot enters squarely into the location hole. Fit the clamp and retaining shear bolts, tightening them with the fingers only at this stage.
8   Check the operation of the lock and if satisfactory, tighten the bolts until the shear heads are detached.
9   Connect the supply cables to the ignition switch and refit the steering column lower surround.
10   Connect the battery negative terminal and check the operation of the ignition switch.

## 29 Track control arm and balljoint, drag strut, track rod end, and steering arm – removal and refitting

1   Jack the car and support on stands under the body frame.
2   Disconnect the track rod from the steering arm. First remove the retaining nut and then use an extractor or suitable wedges. Two club hammers of equal weight may be used to jar the ball-pin taper from its locating eye. They should be used to strike opposite edges of the eye simultaneously, when the pin will drop out.
3   Remove the nuts which secure the steering arm to the suspension strut.
4   Remove the lower nut, washers and rubber bushes from the stabiliser bar drop link.
5   Remove the drag strut by detaching the two nuts and bolts from the mounting bracket on the body underframe.
6   Remove the nut and bolt which secures the drag strut to the track control arm.
7   Pull the front mounting forward and downward to withdraw the drag strut.
8   Withdraw the pivot nut and bolt which locate the track control arm to the crossmember. This will necessitate full steering lock, to obtain access to the nut.
9   Prise out the track control arm from the crossmember and remove the rubber bushes from the inner pivot point.
10   Remove the nut which secures the steering arm to the track control rod balljoint and, using a suitable extractor (balljoint remover) (Fig. 11.20), separate the components.
11   Remove the track rod end by slackening the locknut adjacent to

Fig. 11.20 Steering arm – removal from a track control arm joint (Sec 29)

the track rod end. If not already done, remove the nut securing the track rod end to the steering arm, and detach it from the arm as described in paragraph 2. Unscrew the end, noting the number of turns required to free it. Refit in reverse, screwing the track rod on by the previously noted number of turns.
12   Refitting of the track control arm and its balljoint is made as a complete assembly and is largely a reversal of removal. Always use the new nut supplied with the new track control arm and tighten it to the specified torque given in the Specifications. Engage the locating dowels and fit the steering arm squarely to the bottom of the suspension strut.
13   Reassemble the track control arm to crossmember pivot bolts with their heads to the rear. If reversed, the nuts will damage the steering gear convolute rubber covers.
14   Adjust the drop link nuts as described in Section 8 and tighten all nuts to the torque given in the Specifications.

## 30 Drag strut mounting bracket bush – removal and refitting

1   Remove the drag strut as described in Section 29, remove the front nut and withdraw the bracket. Remove the bush by levering at the flanged end of the bush, whilst pressing through from the other end with a suitable bar.
2   Hold the bracket in a soft-jawed vice. Lubricate the bracket bore with rubber lubricant, place the new bush into the bracket, thin flange first, and ease it right through using a blunt screwdriver. Reassemble to the drag strut.
3   Note that, if the bush is assembled to the bracket with the thin flange to the casting number side, then that side faces rearwards with the casting number towards the outside of the car. However, if the bush is fitted with the thick flange to the casting number side, then that side faces forward with the casting number facing inwards.
4   Refit the drag strut, as described in Section 29.

## 31 Steering rack (Burman type) – adjustment

1   Remove the steering rack and place it in a vice with the pinion (Fig. 11.21) in the horizontal position.
2   Remove the yoke cover securing screws and withdraw the cover joint, shim, spring and yoke (slipper).
3   Remove the flange from the pinion.
4   Prise the pinion dust seal clip off the pinion shaft and remove the seal.
5   Withdraw the pinion bearing preload cover plate screws followed by the cover, shim pack and joint.
6   Refit the pinion cover and insert the retaining screws finger tight without any shims or gaskets.
7   Tighten the cover retaining screws evenly until the cover just contacts the pinion bearing. Measure the gap between the cover and the steering rack casing mating surfaces with feeler gauges. Take these measurements at various points to ensure that the cover is seated evenly.
8   Assemble a shim pack to include a gasket each side of the shims which is 0.002 to 0.004 in (0.05 to 0.10 mm) less in thickness than the gap previously measured. This will give the required bearing preload.
9   Reassemble the shim and gasket pack, cover and securing screws, using thread sealer. Tighten to the torque shown in the Specifications.
10   The rack damper adjustment is set by assembling the yoke (slipper) to the rear of the rack and pushing it fully home.
11   Refit the cover plate and measure the gap between its face and the mating face of the rack casing.
12   Assemble a shim pack to include one gasket each side of the

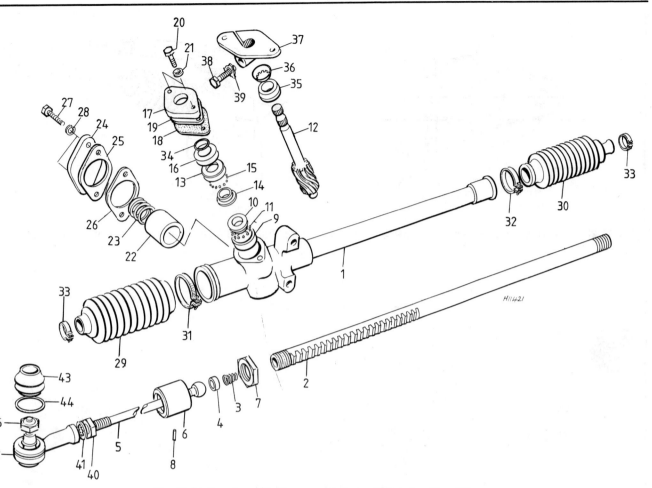

**Fig. 11.21 Steering rack (Burman type) – exploded view (Sec 31)**

| | | | |
|---|---|---|---|
| 1 Housing | 13 Adjuster | 24 Yoke cover | 35 Seal |
| 2 Rack | 14 Adjuster | 25 Joint | 36 Clip |
| 3 Spring | 15 Bearings | 26 Shim | 37 Flange |
| 4 Ball seat | 16 Spacer | 27 Setscrew | 38 Bolt |
| 5 Track rod | 17 Pinion bearing preload | 28 Washer | 39 Washer |
| 6 Housing | cover plate | 29 Bellows | 40 Locknut |
| 7 Locknut | 18 Joint | 30 Bellows | 41 Washer |
| 8 Pin | 19 Shim | 31 Clip | 42 Balljoint |
| 9 Adjuster | 20 Setscrew | 32 Clip | 43 Boot |
| 10 Adjuster | 21 Washer | 33 Clip | 44 Clip |
| 11 Bearings | 22 Yoke (slipper) | 34 Seal | 45 Locknut |
| 12 Pinion | 23 Spring | | |

shims having a total thickness 0.004 to 0.006 in (0.101 to 0.152 mm) greater than the gap determined in paragraph 11.

13 Fit the spring cover and shim pack using thread sealer on the securing bolts. Tighten to the torque given in the Specifications.

14 Fit the pinion dust seal and retaining clip and lubricate the pinion splines with grease.

15 Fit the coupling flange to the pinion so that it is parallel with the centre line of the rack with the rack centralised as shown in Fig. 11.22. Fit a new tab washer and tighten the pinch bolt to the specified torque.

16 A check for correct adjustment may be carried out by fitting the flexible flange coupling and using a spring balance. The required force to commence pinion rotation should be between 7 and 12 lbf (3.2 to 5.3 kgf) (Fig. 11.23).

## 32 Steering rack (Cam Gears type) – adjustment

1 Adjustments are similar to those for the Burman type but certain detail differences apply. Refer to Fig. 11.24 and carry out operations

1 to 7, Section 31, observing the detail differences in individual components.

2 To set the pinion preload refit the cover and securing bolts finger tight using additional shims. Tighten the cover plate setscrews evenly.

3 Measure the cover to casing gap with feelers.

4 Remove the cover and reduce the shim pack until, with the cover refitted, the gap measurement is between 0.001 and 0.003 in (0.03 and 0.07 mm).

5 Reassemble the cover, shim pack and gasket in correct sequence using thread sealer on the securing bolts. Tighten to the torque given in the Specifications.

6 Set the rack damper adjustment by assembling the yoke (slipper) and pushing it fully home.

7 Measure the distance between the machined face to which the yoke cover is attached and the bottom of the deeper recess in the yoke (slipper).

8 To this dimension add a gasket and shim pack between 0.002 and 0.005 in (0.050 and 0.127 mm).

9 Fit the spring into the yoke (slipper) recess and position the shim pack so that the gasket is next to the cover.

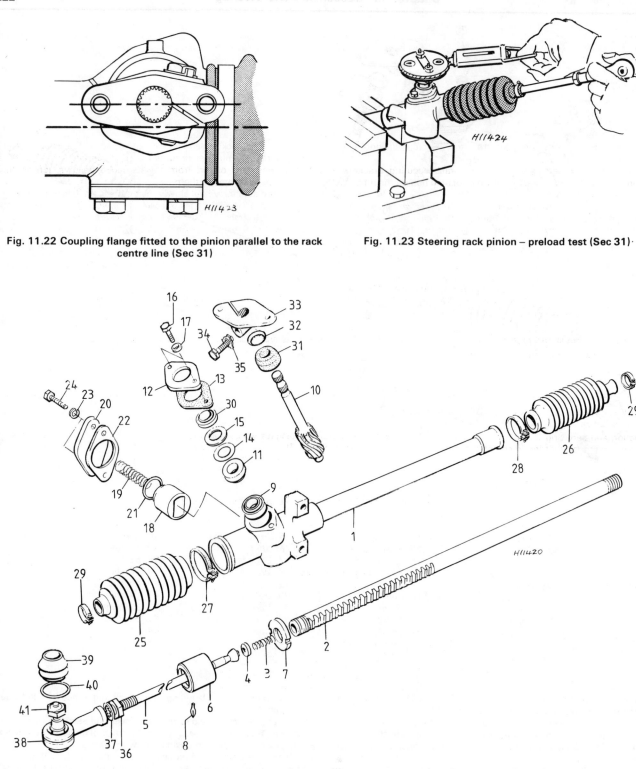

**Fig. 11.22 Coupling flange fitted to the pinion parallel to the rack centre line (Sec 31)**

**Fig. 11.23 Steering rack pinion – preload test (Sec 31)**

**Fig. 11.24 Steering rack (Cam Gears type) – exploded view (Sec 32)**

| | | | |
|---|---|---|---|
| 1 Casing | 10 Pinion | 18 Yoke (slipper) | 26 Bellows | 34 Bolt |
| 2 Rack | 11 Bearing | 19 Spring | 27 Clip | 35 Washer |
| 3 Spring | 12 Pinion cover | 20 Yoke cover | 28 Clip | 36 Locknut |
| 4 Ball seat | 13 Joint | 21 Seal | 29 Clips | 37 Washer |
| 5 Track-rod | 14 Shim | 22 Joint | 30 Seal | 38 Balljoint |
| 6 Housing | 15 Spacer | 23 Washer | 31 Seal | 39 Boot |
| 7 Locknut | 16 Setscrew | 24 Setscrew | 32 Clip | 40 Clip |
| 8 Pin | 17 Washer | 25 Bellows | 33 Flange | 41 Locknut |
| 9 Bearing | | | | |

10  Fit the cover and securing bolts, using thread sealer. Tighten to the correct torque.
11  Carry out operations 14, 15 and 16 described in Section 31.

### 33 Steering rack – removal and refitting

1  Jack up the front of the car and secure on stands.
2  Remove the front roadwheels.
3  Disconnect the track rod end balljoints.
4  Disconnect the intermediate shaft from the flexible coupling (Fig. 11.16).
5  Remove the two setscrews from each rack securing bracket, particularly noting the inner bracket which is located behind the rubber insulator. Remove the rack.
6  Note that if a replacement rack is being fitted, the small amount of storage preservative should be drained off. Refill the complete assembly with the correct amount of oil, by first placing it in a soft jawed vice, rack uppermost, at 45° to the vertical. Leave the top bellows outer clip released, and move the rack fully to the top of the tube. Using a pressure oil can containing 250 ml (0.45 pints) of SAE 90EP oil, insert it into the upper end of the bellows and inject some of the oil. Remove the can and move the rack from end to end to circulate the oil. Repeat the filling operation as necessary. Locate the bellows in the track rod groove, and tighten the clip.

7  Refit the rack in reverse order, but before fitting the intermediate shaft turn the roadwheels and the steering wheel to the straight-ahead position, and engage the steering lock. Reconnect the intermediate shaft. Secure all fixings to the torque figures specified.

### 34 Steering rack bellows – renewal

1  Release the appropriate track rod end balljoint from its steering arm as described in Section 29.
2  Unscrew the track rod end locknut and unscrew the track rod end, carefully noting the number of turns for exact refitting.
3  Clean any mud or dirt from the damaged bellows, loosen the securing clips and remove them.
4  Move the steering wheel slowly to compress the opposite bellows and allow the oil to drain. This is easier if the vehicle is jacked up on the side remote from the bellows being renewed.
5  Fit new bellows and clips, but before tightening them insert a fine nozzle-type pressure oil gun under one end of the bellows neck and insert $\frac{1}{4}$ pint (140 cc) of SAE 90EP oil. It is essential that the total capacity of the steering unit is not exceeded and therefore care should be taken to drain completely as described in the preceding paragraph. Refer to the general refitting procedure outlined in Section 33.
6  Reassembly is the reverse of removal. Check the toe-in after completion.

### 35 Fault diagnosis – suspension and steering

| Symptom | Reason(s) |
|---|---|
| **Steering feels vague, car wanders and floats at speed** | |
| General wear or damage | Tyre pressures uneven |
| | Shock absorbers worn |
| | Steering gear balljoints badly worn |
| | Suspension geometry incorrect |
| | Steering mechanism free play excessive |
| | Front suspension and rear suspension pickup points out of alignment or badly worn |
| | Steering or suspension lacking lubrication |
| **Stiff and heavy steering** | |
| Lack of maintenance or accident damage | Tyre pressures too low |
| | No oil in steering rack |
| | Worn steering balljoints |
| | Front wheel toe-in incorrect |
| | Suspension geometry incorrect |
| | Steering gear incorrectly adjusted too tightly |
| | Steering column badly misaligned |
| **Wheel wobble and vibration** | |
| General wear or damage | Wheel nuts loose |
| | Front wheels and tyres out of balance |
| | Steering balljoints badly worn |
| | Hub bearings badly worn |
| | Steering gear worn |

# Chapter 12 Bodywork and fittings

## Contents

## 1  General description

The combined body and underframe is of welded all-steel construction. The front wings are of bolt-on detachable design, to facilitate easy renewal. All normal fittings will be found on the vehicle, including a through-floor ventilation and heating system.

## 2  Maintenance – bodywork and underframe

1   The general condition of a car's bodywork is the thing that significantly affects it value. Maintenance is easy but needs to be regular. Neglect, particularly after minor damage, can lead quickly to further deterioration and costly repair bills. It is important also to keep watch on those parts of the car not immediately visible, for instance the underside, inside all the wheel arches and the lower part of the engine compartment.

2   The basic maintenance routine for the bodywork is washing – preferably with a lot of water, from a hose. This will remove all the loose solids which may have stuck to the car. It is important to flush these off in such a way as to prevent grit from scratching the finish. The wheel arches and underframe need washing in the same way to remove any accumulated mud which will retain moisture and tend to encourage rust. Paradoxically enough, the best time to clean the underframe and wheel arches is in wet weather when the mud is thoroughly wet and soft. In very wet weather the underframe is usually cleaned of large accumulations automatically and this is a good time for inspection.

3   Periodically, it is a good idea to have the whole of the underframe of the car steamed cleaned, engine compartment included, so that a thorough inspection can be carried out to see what minor repairs and renovations are necessary. Steam cleaning is available at many garages and is necessary for removal of the accumulation of oily grime which sometimes is allowed to become thick in certain areas. If steam cleaning facilities are not available, there are one or two excellent grease solvents available which can be brush applied. The dirt can then be simply hosed off.

4   After washing paintwork, wipe off with a chamois leather to give an unspotted clear finish. A coat of clear protective wax polish will give added protection against chemical pollutants in the air. If the paintwork sheen has dulled or oxidised, use a cleaner/polisher combination to restore the brilliance of the shine. This requires a little effort, but such dulling is usually caused because regular washing has been neglected. Always check that the door and ventilator opening drain holes and pipes are completely clear so that water can be drained out. Bright work should be treated in the same way as paintwork. Windscreens and windows can be kept clear of the smeary film which often appears, by adding a little ammonia to the water. If they are scratched, a good rub with a proprietary metal polish will often clear them. Never use any form of wax or other body or chromium polish on glass.

## 3  Maintenance – upholstery and carpets

1   Mats and carpets should be brushed or vacuum cleaned regularly to keep them free of grit. If they are badly stained remove them from the car for scrubbing or sponging and make quite sure they are dry before refitting. Seats and interior trim panels can be kept clean by a wipe over with a damp cloth. If they do become stained (which can be more apparent on light coloured upholstery) use a little liquid detergent and a soft nail brush to scour the grime out of the grain of the material. Do not forget to keep the head lining clean in the same way as the upholstery. When using liquid cleaners inside the car do not over-wet the surfaces being cleaned. Excessive damp could get into the seams and padded interior causing stains, offensive odours or even rot. If the inside of the car gets wet accidentally it is worthwhile taking some trouble to dry it out properly, particularly where carpets are involved. *Do not leave oil or electric heaters inside the car for this purpose.*

**4   Minor body damage – repair**

*The photographic sequences on pages 226 and 227 illustrate the operations detailed in the following sub-sections.*

### Repair of minor scratches in the car's bodywork

If the scratch is very superficial, and does not penetrate to the metal of the bodywork, repair is very simple. Lightly rub the area of the scratch with a paintwork renovator, or a very fine cutting paste, to remove loose paint from the scratch and to clear the surrounding bodywork of wax polish. Rinse the area with clean water.

Apply touch-up paint to the scratch using a thin paint brush; continue to apply thin layers of paint until the surface of the paint in the scratch is level with the surrounding paintwork. Allow the new paint at least two weeks to harden: then blend it into the surrounding paintwork by rubbing the paintwork, in the scratch area, with a paintwork renovator or a very fine cutting paste. Finally, apply wax polish.

Where the scratch has penetrated right through to the metal of the bodywork, causing the metal to rust, a different repair technique is required. Remove any loose rust from the bottom of the scratch with a penknife, then apply rust inhibiting paint to prevent the formation of rust in the future. Using a rubber or nylon applicator fill the scratch with bodystopper paste. If required, this paste can be mixed with cellulose thinners to provide a very thin paste which is ideal for filling narrow scratches. Before the stopper-paste in the scratch hardens, wrap a piece of smooth cotton rag around the top of a finger. Dip the finger in cellulose thinners and then quickly sweep it across the surface of the stopper-paste in the scratch; this will ensure that the surface of the stopper-paste is slightly hollowed. The scratch can now be painted over as described earlier in this Section.

### Repair of dents in the car's bodywork

When deep denting of the vehicle's bodywork has taken place, the first task is to pull the dent out, until the affected bodywork almost attains its original shape. There is little point in trying to restore the original shape completely, as the metal in the damaged area will have stretched on impact and cannot be reshaped fully to its original contour. It is better to bring the level of the dent up to a point which is about $\frac{1}{8}$ in (3 mm) below the level of the surrounding bodywork. In cases where the dent is very shallow anyway, it is not worth trying to pull it out at all. If the underside of the dent is accessible, it can be hammered out gently from behind, using a mallet with a wooden or plastic head. Whilst doing this, hold a suitable block of wood firmly against the outside of the panel to absorb the impact from the hammer blows and thus prevent a large area of the bodywork from being 'belled-out'.

Should the dent be in a section of the bodywork which has double skin or some other factor making it inaccessible from behind, a different technique is called for. Drill several small holes through the metal inside the area – particularly in the deeper section. Then screw long self-tapping screws into the holes just sufficiently for them to gain a good purchase in the metal. Now the dent can be pulled out by pulling on the protruding heads of the screws with a pair of pliers.

The next stage of the repair is the removal of the paint from the damaged area, and from an inch or so of the surrounding 'sound' bodywork. This is accomplished most easily by using a wire brush or abrasive pad on a power drill, although it can be done just as effectively by hand using sheets of abrasive paper. To complete the preparation for filling, score the surface of the bare metal with a screwdriver or the tang of a file, or alternatively, drill small holes in the affected area. This will provide a really good 'key' for the filler paste.

To complete the repair see the Section on filling and re-spraying.

### Repair of rust hole or gashes in the car's bodywork

Remove all paint from the affected area and from an inch or so of the surrounding 'sound' bodywork, using an abrasive pad or a wire brush on a power drill. If these are not available a few sheets of abrasive paper will do the job just as effectively. With the paint removed you will be able to gauge the severity of the corrosion and therefore decide whether to renew the whole panel (if this is possible) or to repair the affected area. New body panels are not as expensive as most people think and it is often quicker and more satisfactory to fit a new panel than to attempt to repair large areas of corrosion.

Remove all fittings from the affected area except those which will act as a guide to the original shape of the damaged bodywork (eg headlamp shells etc). Then, using tin snips or a hacksaw blade, remove all loose metal and any other metal badly affected by corrosion. Hammer the edges of the hole inwards in order to create a slight depression for the filler paste.

Wire brush the affected area to remove the powdery rust from the surface of the remaining metal. Paint the affected area with rust inhibiting paint; if the back of the rusted area is accessible treat this also.

Before filling can take place it will be necessary to block the hole in some way. This can be achieved by the use of Zinc gauze or Aluminium tape.

Zinc gauze is probably the best material to use for a large hole. Cut a piece to the approximate size and shape of the hole to be filled, then position it in the hole so that its edges are below the level of the surrounding bodywork. It can be retained in position by several blobs of filler paste around its periphery.

Aluminium tape should be used for small or very narrow holes. Pull a piece off the roll and trim it to the approximate size and shape required, then pull off the backing paper (if used) and stick the tape over the hole; it can be overlapped if the thickness of one piece is insufficient. Burnish down the edges of the tape with the handle of a screwdriver or similar, to ensure that the tape is securely attached to the metal underneath.

### Bodywork repairs – filling and re-spraying

Before using this Section, see the Sections on dent, deep scratch, rust holes and gash repairs.

Many types of bodyfiller are available, but generally speaking those proprietary kits which contain a tin of filler paste and a tube of resin hardener are best for this type of repair. A wide, flexible plastic or nylon applicator will be found invaluable for imparting a smooth and well contoured finish to the surface of the filler.

Mix up a little filler on a clean piece of card or board – measure the hardener carefully (follow the maker's instructions on the pack) otherwise the filler will set too rapidly or too slowly.

Using the applicator apply the filler paste to the prepared area; draw the applicator across the surface of the filler to achieve the correct contour and to level the filler surface. As soon as a contour that approximates the correct one is achieved, stop working the paste – if you carry on too long the paste will become sticky and begin to 'pick up' on the applicator. Continue to add thin layers of filler paste at twenty-minute intervals until the level of the filler is just proud of the surrounding bodywork.

Once the filler has hardened, excess can be removed using a metal plane or file. From then on, progressively finer grades of sandpaper should be used, starting with a 40 grade production paper and finishing with 400 grade wet-and-dry paper. Always wrap the abrasive paper around a flat rubber, cork, or wooden block – otherwise the surface of the filler will not be completely flat. During the smoothing of the filler surface the wet-and-dry paper should be periodically rinsed in water. This will ensure that a very smooth finish is imparted to the filler at the final stage.

At this stage the 'repair area' should be surrounded by a ring of bare metal, which in turn should be encircled by the finely 'feathered' edge of the good paintwork. Rinse the repair area with clean water, until all of the dust produced by the rubbing-down operation has gone.

Spray the whole repair area with a light coat of primer – this will show up any imperfections in the surface of the filler. Repair these imperfections with fresh filler paste or bodystopper, and once more smooth the surface with abrasive paper. If bodystopper is used, it can be mixed with cellulose thinners to form a really thin paste which is ideal for filling small holes. Repeat this spray and repair procedure until you are satisfied that the surface of the filler, and the feathered edge of the paintwork are perfect. Clean the repair area with clean water and allow to dry fully.

The repair area is now ready for final spraying. Paint spraying must be carried out in warm, dry, windless and dust free atmosphere. This condition can be created artificially if you have access to a large indoor working area, but if you are forced to work in the open, you will have to pick your day very carefully. If you are working indoors, dousing the floor in the work area with water will help to settle the dust which would otherwise be in the atmosphere. If the repair area is confined to one body panel, mask off the surrounding panels; this will help to minimise the effects of a slight mis-match in paint colours. Bodywork fittings (eg chrome strips, door handles etc) will also need to be

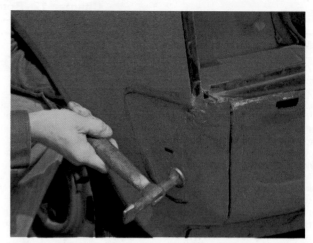

This sequence of photographs deals with the repair of the dent and paintwork damage shown in this photo. The procedure will be similar for the repair of a hole. It should be noted that the procedures given here are simplified — more explicit instructions will be found in the text

In the case of a dent the first job — after removing surrounding trim — is to hammer out the dent where access is possible. This will minimise filling. Here, the large dent having been hammered out, the damaged area is being made slightly concave

Now all paint must be removed from the damaged area, by rubbing with coarse abrasive paper. Alternatively, a wire brush or abrasive pad can be used in a power drill. Where the repair area meets good paintwork, the edge of the paintwork should be 'feathered', using a finer grade of abrasive paper

In the case of a hole caused by rusting, all damaged sheet-metal should be cut away before proceeding to this stage. Here, the damaged area is being treated with rust remover and inhibitor before being filled

Mix the body filler according to its manufacturer's instructions. In the case of corrosion damage, it will be necessary to block off any large holes before filling — this can be done with aluminium or plastic mesh, or aluminium tape. Make sure the area is absolutely clean before ...

... applying the filler. Filler should be applied with a flexible applicator, as shown, for best results; the wooden spatula being used for confined areas. Apply thin layers of filler at 20-minute intervals, until the surface of the filler is slightly proud of the surrounding bodywork

Initial shaping can be done with a Surform plane or Dreadnought file. Then, using progressively finer grades of wet-and-dry paper, wrapped around a sanding block, and copious amounts of clean water, rub down the filler until really smooth and flat. Again, feather the edges of adjoining paintwork

The whole repair area can now be sprayed or brush-painted with primer. If spraying, ensure adjoining areas are protected from over-spray. Note that at least one inch of the surrounding sound paintwork should be coated with primer. Primer has a 'thick' consistency, so will find small imperfections

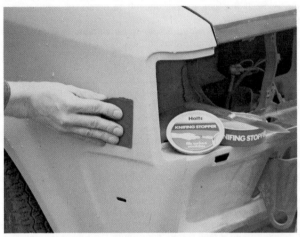

Again, using plenty of water, rub down the primer with a fine grade wet-and-dry paper (400 grade is probably best) until it is really smooth and well blended into the surrounding paintwork. Any remaining imperfections can now be filled by carefully applied knifing stopper paste

When the stopper has hardened, rub down the repair area again before applying the final coat of primer. Before rubbing down this last coat of primer, ensure the repair area is blemish-free — use more stopper if necessary. To ensure that the surface of the primer is really smooth use some finishing compound

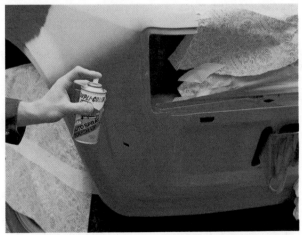

The top coat can now be applied. When working out of doors, pick a dry, warm and wind-free day. Ensure surrounding areas are protected from over-spray. Agitate the aerosol thoroughly, then spray the centre of the repair area, working outwards with a circular motion. Apply the paint as several thin coats

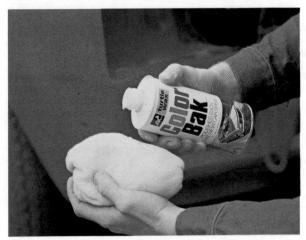

After a period of about two weeks, which the paint needs to harden fully, the surface of the repaired area can be 'cut' with a mild cutting compound prior to wax polishing. When carrying out bodywork repairs, remember that the quality of the finished job is proportional to the time and effort expended

masked off. Use genuine masking tape and several thicknesses of newspaper for the masking operations.

Before commencing to spray, agitate the aerosol can thoroughly, then spray a test area (an old tin, or similar) until the technique is mastered. Cover the repair area with a thick coat of primer; the thickness should be built up using several thin layers of paint rather than one thick one. Using 400 grade wet-and-dry paper, rub down the surface of the primer until it is really smooth. While doing this, the work area should be thoroughly doused with water, and the wet-and-dry paper periodically rinsed in water. Allow to dry before spraying on more paint.

Spray on the top coat, again building up the thickness by using several thin layers of paint. Start spraying in the centre of the repair area and then, using a circular motion, work outwards until the whole repair area and about 2 inches of the surrounding original paintwork is covered. Remove all masking material 10 to 15 minutes after spraying on the final coat of paint.

Allow the new paint at least two weeks to harden, then, using a paintwork renovator or a very fine cutting paste, blend the edges of the paint into the existing paintwork. Finally, apply wax polish.

## 5  Major body damage – repair

Where serious damage has occurred or large areas need renewal due to neglect, it means that completely new sections or panels will need welding in, and this is best left to professionals. If the damage is due to impact it will also be necessary to completely check the alignment of the bodyshell structure. Due to the principle of construction the strength and shape of the whole car can be affected by damage to one part. In such instances the services of a workshop with specialist checking jigs are essential. If a body is left misaligned it is first of all dangerous, as the car will not handle properly, and secondly uneven stresses will be imposed on the steering, engine and transmission, causing abnormal wear or complete failure. Tyre wear may also be excessive.

## 6  Maintenance – hinges and locks

1   Oil the hinges on the bonnet, boot lid and doors with a drop or two of light oil. A good time is after the car has been washed.
2   Oil the bonnet release catch pivot pin and the safety catch pivot pin periodically.
3   Do not over lubricate door latches and strikers. Normally a little oil on the rotary cam spindle alone is sufficient.

## 7  Doors – rattles and their rectification

1   Check that the door is not loose at the hinges and that the latch is holding the door firmly in position. Check also that the door lines up with the aperture in the body.
2   If the hinges are loose or the door is out of alignment it will be necessary to reset the hinge positions, as described in Sections 15 and 16.
3   If the latch is holding the door properly, it should hold the door tightly when fully latched and the door should line up with the body. If it is out of alignment it needs adjustment as described in Sections 15 and 16. If loose, some part of the lock mechanism must be worn out and requires renewal.
4   Other rattles from the door can be caused by wear or looseness in the window winder, the glass channels and sill strips, or the door buttons and interior latch release mechanism. All these are dealt with in Sections 21 and 22.

## 8  Front wing – removal and refitting

1   Remove the headlamp unit as described in Chapter 10, the flasher indicator, front grille, bumper and chrome sill finisher (if fitted).
2   Jack up the front of the car and secure with blocks or stands under the bodyframe. Remove the roadwheel.
3   Remove the bonnet height adjuster and bonnet lid anti-rattle rubber from their locations.

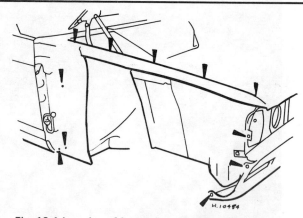

Fig. 12.1 Location of front wing securing bolts (Sec 8)

4   Remove the row of spire bolts from the top seam and the other six securing bolts and self-tapping screws as indicated in Fig. 12.1. Note that a grommet conceals the rear lower screw.
5   Break the joints, to separate the sealant originally used. Lift away the wing. If the joint proves difficult to break, an application of very gentle heat may help.
6   Refit in reverse order, employing a suitable sealant between the joints. Apply underbody protection to any areas where this has become disturbed.

## 9  Windscreen glass (standard type) – removal and refitting

1   It is not unknown for difficulties to arise in work connected with the fitting of replacement screens, and the owner is advised to place such work with one of the numerous specialists in the field. However, the following procedure is given for the owner who wishes to attempt the work himself.
2   When renewing a shattered windscreen, first cover the facia air vents. Adhesive sheet, stuck to the outside of the glass, will be helpful when removing large areas of crystallised glass.
3   Where the screen is to be removed intact, an assistant will be required. First release the rubber surround from the bodywork by running a blunt, small screwdriver under the rubber weatherstrip both inside and outside the car, to break the adhesion of the sealer originally used. Take care not to damage the paintwork or cut the rubber surround.
4   Have the assistant push the inner lip of the rubber surround off the flange of the windscreen body aperture. The screen may then be forced gently outwards by careful hand pressure. The second person should support and remove the screen complete with rubber surround and metal beading.
5   Remove the beading from the rubber surround (Fig. 12.2).
6   Before fitting a windscreen, ensure that the rubber surround is completely free from old sealant and glass fragments, and that it has not hardened or cracked. Fit the rubber surround to the glass and apply a bead of a recommended sealer between the glass outer edge and the rubber.

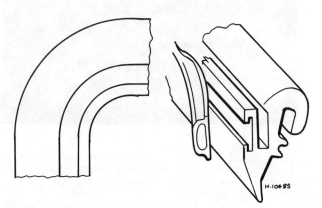

Fig. 12.2 Screen weatherseal – compound sealed type (Sec 9)

7    Refit the bright moulding and joining caps to the rubber surround. Employ special tool RG535 and adaptor 18G468B.

8    Cut a piece of strong cord, greater in length than the periphery of the glass, and insert it into the body flange locating channel of the rubber surround. Apply a coating sealer to the body mating face of the rubber surround.

9    Offer the windscreen up to the body aperture and pass the ends of the cord (at the bottom centre as shown in Fig. 12.3) into the car. Press the windscreen into place, at the same time pulling on the ends of the cords simultaneously to engage the rubber surround lip over the body flange.

10   Carefully clean off any excess sealer to avoid contamination of the windscreen wiper blades and main area of glass.

## 10   Windscreen glass (dry-glazed type used on certain Series 7 on cars) – removal and refitting

1    Note that on the dry-glazed arrangement the plastic beading is positioned centrally.

2    The removal and refitting procedure is basically as that described in Section 9, but the following points should be noted.

3    No sealant is required except where a vinyl roof covering is fitted, and then only where the vinyl meets the weatherstrip.

4    The plastic beading must only be removed or inserted with the weatherstrip and windscreen fitted in the body aperture. Remove the beading *before* removing the windscreen and insert it *after* refitting the windscreen; immerse the beading in hot water at hand temperature to facilitate refitting.

5    Two types of glass are used – toughened and laminated: special care should be exercised when handling the laminated type. Each type is identified in one corner of the glass.

6    Soft soap applied to the beading channel before the screen is fitted will assist in the fitting of the bead.

## 11   Backlight glass – removal and refitting

1    The method employed is basically as described for the equivalent type of windscreen glass, noting that either standard or dry-glazed type of glass may be encountered.

2    Where relevant, disconnect the battery and detach the connections from the backlight heater element.

3    Employ a little silicone lubricant on the headlining material where it adheres to the body flange.

4    When inserted into the body aperture, use a wedge to spread the beading channel in the weatherstrip and insert a soft soap lubricant.

## 12   Windscreen, tailgate window and rear side windows (estate car up to Series 7)

Proceed as described for the corresponding saloon car.

## 13   Windscreen, tailgate window and rear side windows (estate car commencing Series 7)

1    Proceed, for the windscreen, as described for the corresponding saloon car.

2    Proceed, for the tailgate window and rear side windows as described for saloon cars with standard type windscreen.

## 14   Rear quarterlight (commencing Series 7) – removal and refitting

1    This type of window is fitted to the two-door models only.

2    Removal of the window is effected by unscrewing the three toggle catch retaining screws with the window in the closed position.

3    Swing the window open, and unhook the hinges from the rubber supports. Carefully lift the window away from the body aperture.

4    Refitting is a reversal of the removal procedure, but smear the two hinges with soft soap to facilitate entry into the rubber supports.

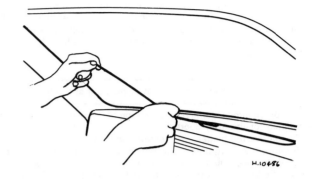

Fig. 12.3 Windscreen fitment – use of cord (Sec 9)

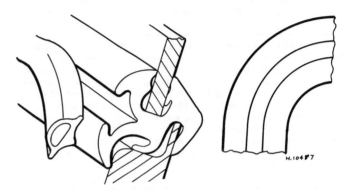

Fig. 12.4 Screen weatherseal – dry glazed type (Sec 10)

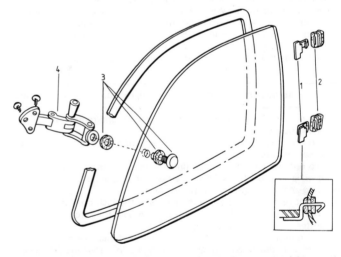

Fig 12.5 Rear quarterlight (two-door Series 7 on models) (Sec 14)

| | | | |
|---|---|---|---|
| 1 | *Hinge* | 3 | *Mounting* |
| 2 | *Buffer hinge support* | 4 | *Toggle catch assembly* |

## 15   Front doors and hinges – removal, refitting and adjustment

1    To remove a front door, remove the six screws securing the hinges to the door shut face. The hinges need not be disturbed. To refit the door, refit the screws.

2    To remove the front door hinges on the driver's side, first remove the door. Remove the two screws which secure the front wing to the front face of the door pillar and the single screw securing it to the body sill. Pull the wing away from the door pillar. Remove the scuttle kick pad by prising out the plastic retaining plugs. Pack some cloth into the base of the door pillar to prevent loss of the hinge nuts, then remove the nuts. The hinges on the front passenger side are similarly removed, except that the glovebox must first be removed. Refit in the reverse order.

3    Adjustment of the front face of the door in relation to the wing is obtained by either using packing washers under the hinge, or by moving the wing about in its slotted fixing holes before retightening the bolts. The oversize holes in the door pillar provide front to rear and up and down adjustment.

## 16 Rear doors and hinges – removal, refitting and adjustment

1    The procedure for removal and refitting of the rear doors is exactly as outlined for the front doors.
2    To remove the hinges, first remove the door.
3    Remove the draught excluder from the door pillar, peel off the trim to reveal the hinge nuts, remove the nuts and thus the hinges.
4    To refit, loosely secure the hinges to the door pillar. Refit the door to the hinges and fully tighten the screws. Adjust the door in the body and secure the hinge nuts. Refit the trim and the draught excluder.
5    Door adjustment, provided for by the oversize holes in the door pillar, is carried out as described in the preceding paragraphs.

## 17 Bonnet and bonnet hinges – removal, refitting and adjustment

1    To remove the bonnet, place cloth pads under the lower corners to prevent damage to paintwork. Either obtain assistance, or place wooden blocks under the bottom corners of the bonnet. Mark the position of the hinges with a pencil then remove the four screws which secure the bonnet to the hinges, and lift it clear.
2    Refit in reverse order, adjusting as necessary.
3    To remove the hinges, first remove the bonnet.
4    Remove the screws holding the hinges to the wing valances, and remove the hinges.
5    Refit in reverse sequence.
6    The front-to-rear adjustment of the bonnet is obtained by loosening the bonnet-to-hinge bolts, and moving the bonnet as necessary. One method of adjustment is to lightly secure the bolts, close the bonnet, and tap it into the correct position with the hand. Carefully open the bonnet, and fully tighten the screws. The height adjustment is given by the slotted holes in the hinges where they are screwed to the wing valances, and a similar method of adjustment may be employed as has been described for front to rear positioning.

## 18 Bonnet lock and striker pin – removal, refitting and adjustment

1    To remove the striker pin, open the bonnet and remove the three retaining screws.
2    To refit the pin, refit the screws, adjusting from side to side as necessary before tightening.
3    To remove the bonnet lock (internal release system), remove the front grille (see Section 25) and release the operating cable inner by undoing the securing nut and pulling clear.
4    Remove the three bolts and disengage the lock from the panel.
5    Refit in reverse order adjusting as necessary from front to rear on to slotted holes in the platform.
6    To remove and refit the bonnet lock (external release system) proceed as in the preceding paragraphs 3 to 5 inclusive, except for the remarks concerning the control cable. When in proper adjustment the bonnet should have a minimum of $\frac{1}{32}$ in (1 mm) up-and-down movement in the locked position.

## 19 Boot lid, hinges and lock – removal, refitting and adjustment

1    To remove the boot lid and hinges, unclip the torsion bars, remove the bolts securing the hinges to the vehicle, and those securing the hinges to the boot lid.
2    Remove the hinges complete with torsion bars. Remove the boot lid.
3    Refit in reverse order.
4    To adjust the boot lid for height, slacken the bolts securing the hinges to the body, reposition as necessary and tighten. To adjust in the horizontal plane, loosen the bolts securing the boot lid to the hinges, reposition and tighten.
5    To remove and refit the boot lid lock, remove the three securing bolts (Fig. 12.7), and remove the lock.

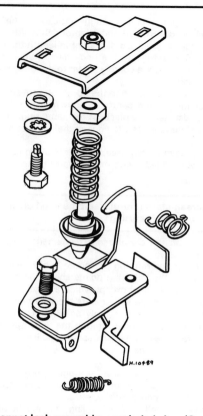

**Fig. 12.6 Bonnet lock assembly – exploded view (Sec 18)**

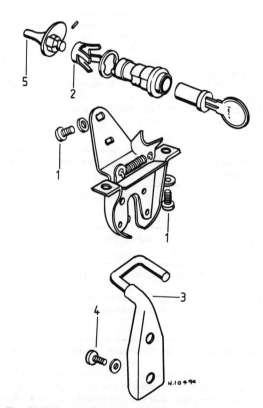

**Fig. 12.7 Boot lid lock – exploded view (Sec 19)**

| | | |
|---|---|---|
| 1 | Lock securing bolts | 4    Striker plate bolts |
| 2 | Spring clip | 5    Cam pivot |
| 3 | Striker plate | |

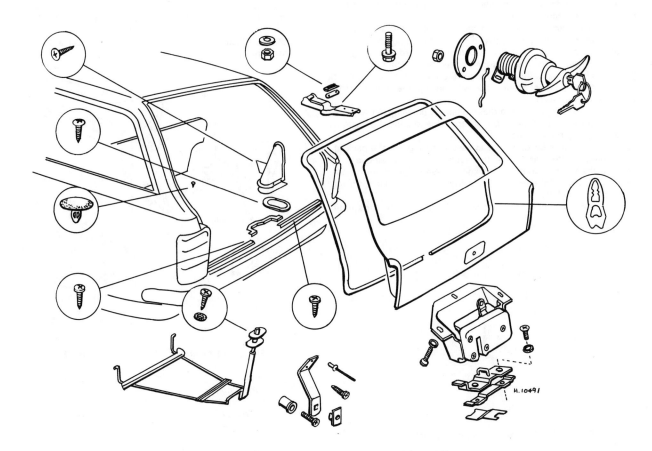

**Fig. 12.8 Tailgate and fittings (estate car) (Sec 20)**

6   Compress the spring clip legs and withdraw the lock barrel.
7   Remove the striker plate bolts and remove the striker plate.
8   Refit in reverse sequence.

### 20 Tailgate door and lock (estate car) – removal, refitting and adjustment

1   To remove the tailgate, disconnect the battery, open the tailgate, remove the rear roof lamp and disconnect the leads. Remove the screws and cover which conceal the torsion rods.
2   Support the tailgate in the fully open position by using a piece of wood as a prop.
3   Release the electrical leads from the tailgate hinge link straps and, if a wipe/wash system is installed, lever the lower trim pad away.
4   Detach the washer tube, identify and disconnect the wiper motor supply leads, and pull away the retaining adhesive tape.
5   Disconnect the heated rear window supply leads, and detach them from their retaining clip.
6   Withdraw the electrical leads through the grommet hole in the upper right-hand corner of the tailgate.
7   Slacken evenly the bolts which secure the torsion bar levers to the tailgate and remove the levers.
8   Remove the hinge securing nuts and lift off the tailgate, noting the thickness and position of the spacers between the hinge plates and the body.
9   Refitting is a reversal of removal, but before finally tightening the hinge bolts, centralise the tailgate within the body-frame.
10  Check the closing action of the tailgate and adjust the striker plate if necessary.
11  If the tailgate lock needs removing, withdraw the screws which secure the lock mechanism to the tailgate, and then compress the spring legs located around the lock panel to release the assembly.

### 21 Front door and window mechanisms – dismantling and reassembly

1   To remove the regulator handle on early models, prise out the plastic insert, remove the cross-head screw thus revealed, and lift off the handle and packing washer.
2   On later models, prise the handle and the escutcheon apart with a flat blade to expose the spring clip, and pull out the clip with a hooked piece of wire or screwdriver. Remove the handle.

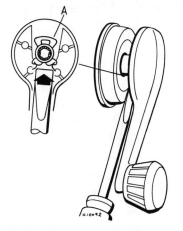

**Fig. 12.9 Window regulator handle (later models) – removal (Sec 21)**

*A    Spring clip*

3   To remove the interior door handle, pull it to reveal the cross-head screw. Remove the screw, and thence the handle.

4   To remove the arm rest, take out the two concealed screws.

5   To remove the trim pad, carry out the foregoing operations; remove the two door pocket screws which are revealed by sliding the plastic screw covers outwards, and then prise the trim pad clips from their locations by sliding a flat blade under the edge of the pad until it meets a clip. A careful twist of the blade will dislodge the clips, and the pad can then be removed.

6   Remove the door pocket from the trim pad by pressing in the sides of the pocket, disengaging the two rear tags, disengaging the bottom tags, and removing both sections.

7   To remove the interior door handle escutcheon, press the back of the escutcheon together and pass it through the trim to remove it.

8   Remove the interior door locking knob assembly from the metal surround on the back of the trim by squeezing it until it is released from the two protruding clips.

9   Remove the escutcheon by squeezing the four plastic lugs until

the metal surround can be lifted off.

10   To refit, put the escutcheon in place and locate two of the lugs over the metal surround. Push fully home whilst supporting the escutcheon. Place the locking knob assembly under a protruding clip, and snap into position.

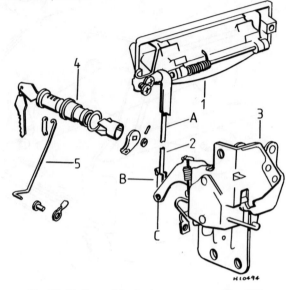

**Fig. 12.11 Front door lock components (Sec 21)**

| | | | |
|---|---|---|---|
| 1 | Handle | 5 | Connecting rod |
| 2 | Connecting rod | A | Thread |
| 3 | Lock | B | Clip |
| 4 | Lock barrel | C | Hole |

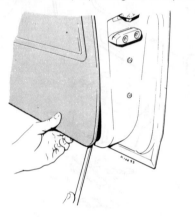

**Fig. 12.10 Door trim – removal (Sec 21)**

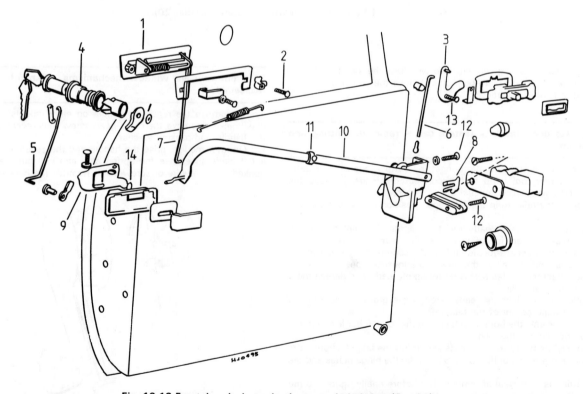

**Fig. 12.12 Front door lock mechanism – exploded view (Sec 21)**

| | | | |
|---|---|---|---|
| 1 | Exterior handle | 9 | Control mechanism |
| 2 | Handle screws | 10 | Remote control rod |
| 3 | Internal locking lever | 11 | Anti-rattle guides |
| 4 | Lock barrel | 12 | Door lock screws |
| 5 | Rod | 13 | Interior handle screws |
| 6 | Connecting rod | 14 | Locking lever screw |
| 7 | Connecting rod | | |
| 8 | Clip | | |

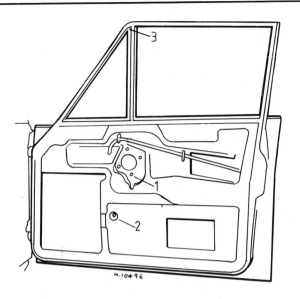

Fig. 12.13 Front door glass – fastening locations (Sec 21)

1  Screws – securing regulator
2  Screw – securing glass run channel
3  Pop rivets – securing glass run channel

11 To remove the window and the fixed light, refit the winder handle and wind to the fully closed position. Insert wedges to prevent the glass falling.
12 Remove the four regulator securing screws, remove the arm from the channel on the glass, and withdraw the unit.
13 Lower the glass to the bottom of the door. Referring to Fig. 12.13, remove the screw (2) from the bottom of the glass run channel, and drill out the two pop rivets (3) securing the upper end.
14 Lift out the rubber weatherstrip from the glass aperture.
15 Pull out the fixed light with sealing rubber from the door channel.
16 Remove the glass run channel through the lower door apertures.
17 Refit in reverse sequence.
18 To remove the exterior door handle, remove the window regulator handle, the interior door handle, the arm rest, plastic covers and screws from the door pocket, and the trim pad.
19 Take out the plug on the door shut face, and unscrew the screw thus exposed by three or four turns.
20 Remove the front screw and plate from the door handle, accessible through the inner panel. Unclip the rod from the handle to the lock, at the lower end.
21 Slide the handle forward, and remove it from the door panel.
22 Refit in reverse order.
23 To remove the lock (Fig. 12.11), disconnect rod (5) at its lower end.

24 Compress the legs on the spring clips surrounding the lock and push the lock out through the door panel hole complete with the connecting rod.
25 To refit, enter the lock through the hole and snap it home. Check for correct operation.
26 To remove the door lock (Fig. 12.12) disconnect the rod (5) at the lower end.
27 Disconnect rod (7) at its lower end. Remove the screw from the lever (3) and release the lever.
28 Remove the clip (8) and disengage the control rod (10).
29 Take out the screws securing the rear lower glass run channel from the door shut face. Remove the channel through the door aperture.
30 Remove the three screws (12) securing the lock to the door shut face, and remove the lock complete with the internal locking lever connecting rod.
31 Refit in reverse order, and check operation. The rotary wheel must turn freely when the handle is in the open position, and this is adjusted by disconnecting the operating rod from the clip at (B) and from locating hole (C) (Fig. 12.11). Adjust by means of the thread at (A) until the rod engages hole (C) with the operating lever at rest and unloaded. Refit the clip and check operation. Check the private lock operation.
32 The striker unit is adjusted if necessary by slackening the fixing screws. The unit can then be moved and the screws tightened.

## 22 Rear door and window mechanisms – dismantling and reassembly

1  To remove and refit the following items, proceed as instructed for the front doors in Section 21:

*Window regulator handle*
*Interior door handle*
*Arm rest*
*Interior door handle escutcheon*
*Interior door lock escutcheon*
*Private lock*
*Striker unit*

2  To remove the trim pad, proceed as for the front door, but note that no door pocket is fitted.
3  To remove the exterior door handle, proceed as for the front door, but note that no plastic plug is fitted in the hole adjacent to the door shut face.
4  To remove the window, the fixed light, and the regulator, proceed as for the front door, but note that no door pocket is fitted, and that only one pop rivet is used at the upper end of the glass run channel.
5  To remove the rear door lock, remove the window regulator handle, the interior door handle, arm rest and trim pad.
6  Wind the window to the fully closed position.
7  Referring to Fig. 12.14, disconnect the clip at the lower end of connecting rod (3), take out two screws securing the interior door handle mechanism to the inside door panel, and disconnect the spring (8).

Fig. 12.14 Rear door lock mechanism – exploded view (Sec 22)

1  Exterior door handle
2  Door lock
3  Exterior door handle-to-door lock connecting rod
4  Door lock screws
5  Anti-rattle guides
6  Internal locking lever-to-door lock connecting rod
7  Remote control rod
8  Return spring

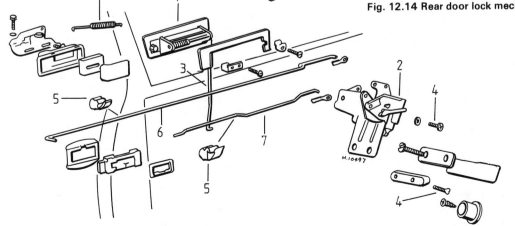

8   Disconnect the clip securing the remote control rod (7) to the door lock, and remove the rod from the guide (5).
9   Disconnect the clip securing the internal locking lever to the connecting rod (6), and detach the rod from the guides (5).
10  Remove four screws (4) securing the lock (2) to the door shut face, and remove the lock through the door aperture.
11  Refit in reverse order, and check the operation of all parts.

## 23  Front and rear seats – removal and refitting

1   To remove the front seat, remove the four nuts and washers retaining the seat runners. These are visible underneath the car. Lift out the seat. Do not lose the spacers. Refit in reverse sequence.
2   To remove the rear seat cushion on saloon cars, lift the plastic flap at the end of each sill finisher. Remove the screws thus exposed, and lift out the cushion. Refit in reverse order.
3   To remove the rear seat squab on saloon cars, first remove the cushion. Bend the metal tabs up to free the squab, and lift it to disengage the retaining clips below the shelf. Remove the squab. Refit in reverse order.
4   To remove the reat seat cushion on estate cars, hinge the seat forward and drive out the hinge pins, taking care to avoid distortion of the pillars. Lift out the seat. Refit in reverse sequence.
5   To remove the rear seat squab on estate cars, release the retaining catches and swing it forward. Remove the screws securing the hinge plates to the squab, and remove squab. Remove the hinge plates, noting that they are left- and right-handed. To refit, place the hinge plates on their respective pins, put the squab in position cushion side down, and fit the plate securing screws.

## 24  Internal trim and accessories – removal and refitting

1   To remove the centre console, release the gear lever gaiter by pushing inside the console, and remove the rear compartment ashtray. Remove the screws securing the console to the body, slide forward and up to clear the gear lever and handbrake, and lift clear. Refit in reverse order. On later models, remove the gear lever knob. Remove the two screws in the console tray, one from the inner end of the parcel tray, and two at the rear of the console. Spring the console over the two clips and lift out. Refit in reverse order.
2   To remove the glovebox, lower the lid, remove the bulb and holder (if fitted), remove the screw from the centre of the lock, and lift off the catch. Push out the seven rivet pins from inside the glovebox, and remove the rivets. Lift and turn the glovebox, and lower it to the floor behind the facia. Refit in reverse order, ensuring that the spring on the hinge locates in the lower hole at the left-hand edge of the glovebox.
3   To remove the glovebox lid, remove the three screws along the lower edge of the lid, and lift out the lid complete with the hinge. To refit the lid, refit the screws, align the lid, and tighten the screws securely.
4   To remove the rear parcel tray, remove the rear seat cushion and squab. Pull out the two plastic retainer plugs next to the quarterlight panels, and pull the tray clear. Reverse the sequence to refit.
5   To remove the front panel shelf (where fitted), remove the draught seal from the door aperture adjacent to the shelf. With a thin blade inserted between the post and kick panel, prise out the retaining clip. Remove the five securing screws, and lift out the tray. Reverse the sequence to refit.
6   To remove the rear quarter trim pads (estate cars), remove the carpet securing strips and bring the carpet forward. Ease out the clips which secure the trim pad, using a wide blade. Slide the trim pad down and out of the metal lip.
7   Removal of the roof lining is a complicated operation, and in the unlikely event of it being necessary to renew it, the owner is advised to consult a specialist in this field.

## 25  External trim – removal and refitting

1   Remove the front grille (early versions) by removing the screws indicated on the appropriate diagram in Fig. 12.15. On later versions Fig. 12.16 applies, and in this case remove the three screws arrowed at the top, tilt the grille forward, and extract from the lower lug sockets. Note that if the lamps are fitted with a wash/wipe system, the

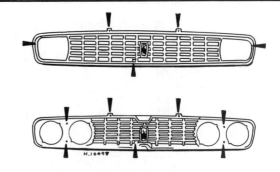

Fig. 12.15 Front grille screw locations – early models (Sec 25)

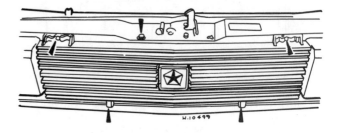

Fig. 12.16 Front grille screw location – later models (Sec 25)

arms and blades must be detached before the screws are removed. To refit, position the bottom lugs in their sockets and lightly tighten the screw at the top centre. Centralise the grille in the aperture, tighten the centre screw, and refit the two remaining screws and spring clips. Refit the wiper arms and blades, if applicable.
2   To remove a sill moulding, remove the nut and washers securing the moulding to the front wing, and pull it away from the clips on the sill panel. Remove the other moulding by prising up gently at each end, and then gently pull it away from the remaining clips. To refit, press the mouldings on to their locations. Refit nuts and washers, if applicable.
3   To remove the bumper bars and rubbing strips on later models, proceed as follows. For the front bumper bar, remove the two cross-headed screws from under the wings, at each end of the bumper. Note the disposition of spacers and washers. Remove the nuts and bolts securing the bumper to the chassis brackets, and remove the bar. Refit in reverse order. To remove the rear bumper bar, remove the bolts and nuts securing the bar to the chassis brackets, and take away the bar. When refitting, note that the brackets have two sets of holes, the lower for saloons and the upper for estates. Refit the bar to the appropriate holes, realign as necessary, and tighten the fixings. To remove the bumper rubbing strip, remove the eleven nuts from inside the bumper and take off the strip. When refitting, lightly secure the strip with the nuts and align as necessary. Tighten the nuts from the centre outwards, keeping the strip flat and avoiding overtightening.
4   The rear embellisher (later models only) is secured to the body by three clips, and is removed by using a broad-bladed hooked lever under the lower rim of the embellisher to disengage it from the clips. Remove the clips by compressing the ends, thereby disengaging the tongues from the body panel. Refit the clips by compressing the ends and entering the tongues into the body holes. To refit the embellisher, centralise it, hook the upper edge over the clips and press the lower edge to snap it into place.
5   To remove the rear wing end capping (later models only), remove the three securing nuts inside the boot and withdraw the capping. Clean the sealant from the nuts. To refit, fill each nut with a non-setting plastic sealant, refit the capping and secure with the nuts. Before finally tightening, ensure correct alignment of the body and the capping, which should be just below the continuing lines of the bodywork.

## 26  Seat belts – general description

1   Various seat belt arrangements may be encountered. No alteration should be made to the fixing point positions as the original anchorages

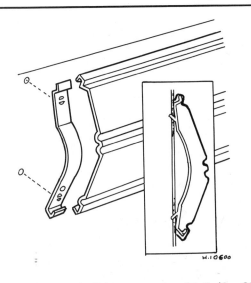

Fig. 12.17 Rear embellisher – mounting details (Sec 25)

are especially strengthened.

2    The belts, which are made from synthetic fibre, should be cleaned in a warm detergent solution only.

3    Periodically inspect the belts for wear or chafing and renew if necessary. The belts should also be renewed when they have been subjected to accident impact shock of severe proportions.

4    When fitting new belts, ensure that the fixing point attachment bolt assemblies are correctly made.

5    The shoulders and lap belts of the reminder system may remain connected once adjusted to suit a particular wearer. Details of the electrical circuitry are given in Chapter 10.

## 27 Spare wheel carrier – removal and refitting

1    On saloon models, lift the boot floor trim, unscrew the centre securing bolt, unhook the catch and take out the spare wheel.

2    Refit in reverse order.

3    On estate car models, lower the spare wheel by turning the bolt head on the boot floor anti-clockwise, unhook the carrier, and remove the spare wheel. Remove the split pin and washer from the left-hand pivot, and spring the pivot from the frame. Turn the carrier and withdraw the right-hand pivot from the frame.

4    Refit in reverse order. Periodic greasing of the screw thread on the spare wheel carrier is advised.

## 28 Water leaks – rectification

1    Water entering the interior of the car or the luggage boot can usually be overcome by proper attention to the windscreen seal and the rubber sealing of doors or boot lid. A suitable sealant may be squeezed between the glass of the screen and the rubber surround and between the rubber and the body. The windscreen may be left in position during the operation, and should the bright moulding become detached, it can be refitted with the use of a small screwdriver. Where a pressure gun is not available the small tubes available from most shops can have the nozzles pressed into a flattened spout to facilitate entry behind the rubber screen seal. Paraffin or white spirit, generously applied, will clean off surplus sealant and impart a smooth finish to the seal.

2    Inspection of rubber grommets used in floor holes, and to seal cables and controls entering from the engine compartment, should be regularly carried out and renewal implemented where necessary.

3    A persistent source of water leakage into the interior can be rectified by adequately sealing the V-shaped welded seam on the rear engine bulkhead. Water leaks in the luggage boot very often originate at the lower ends of the rear (back) window. Peel back the rubber seal carefully and apply sealant as required.

## 29 Heating and ventilation system – general description

The heater system delivers fresh air to the windscreen, for demisting purposes, and to the car interior. The flow to each may be varied in respect of volume and temperature by the two facia-mounted controls. A through-flow fresh air ventilation system is fitted, with extractor vents at the rear of the rear side windows to exhaust stale air. Two face level controllable ducts, independent of the heater system, can provide unheated air at ambient temperature.

The heater assembly comprises a matrix heated by water from the engine cooling system, and a booster fan controlled by a two-position switch located on the facia panel. During normal forward motion of the car, air is forced through the air intake just forward of the windscreen and passes through the heater matrix absorbing heat and carrying it to the car interior. When the car is stationary or travelling at low speed then the booster fan may be actuated.

## 30 Heater (early models) – removal and refitting

1    Disconnect the battery negative terminal.

2    Disconnect each heater hose at its bulkhead connection. If the heater hoses are now moved upwards together and the radiator cap is left in position, the cooling system need not be drained.

3    Remove the facia panel according to style as described in Chapter 10. Remove the underscuttle apron from below the facia by removing the screws shown in Fig. 12.19.

4    Remove the heater control knobs by depressing their spring retainers. Withdraw the fresh air face vents and remove the heater control (Fig. 12.18) retaining screws.

5    Refer to Fig. 12.23 and remove the demist ducts.

6    Ease the heater control forward and downward clear of the facia support rail and then remove the face vent duct.

7    Remove the two upper mounting screws from the heater assembly and ease the assembly, complete with controls, away and to the left so that the heater water pipes clear the bulkhead aperture. Withdraw towards the passenger side.

8    Refitting is a reversal of removal, but ensure that the heater unit front flange engages its support ledge properly before pushing the unit upwards and engaging the securing screws.

9    Run the engine until warm with the heater control fully on and test for leaks. Check the coolant level in the radiator.

## 31 Heater – inspection and servicing

1    Malfunction of the heater may be due to one or more factors. These include a blockage in the heater hoses or matrix, incorrectly adjusted or connected controls, faulty booster motor, air in the heater system or a faulty thermostat.

2    Reference should be made to Sections 32 and 33 and a process of elimination carried out until the fault is found. In the event of the heater matrix being blocked, it should be inverted and reverse flushed

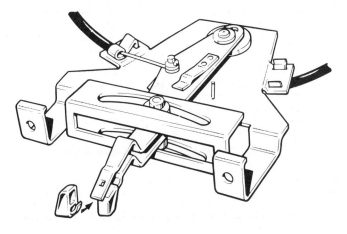

Fig. 12.18 Heater control (Sec 30)

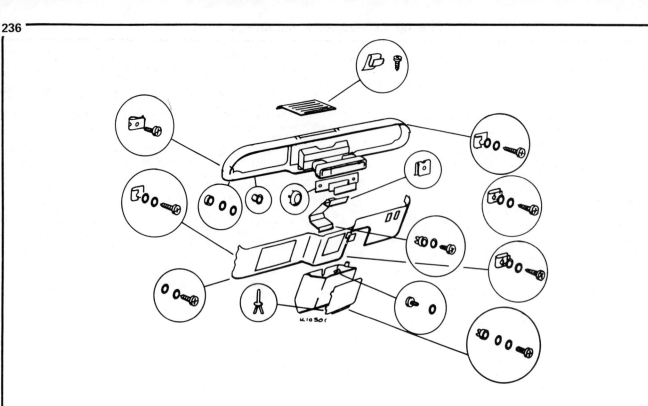

Fig. 12.19 Facia underscuttle apron securing screws – circular instrument version (Sec 30)

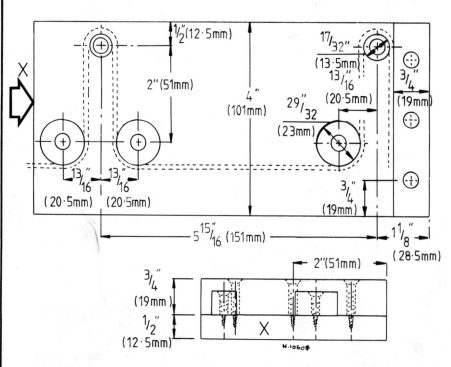

Fig. 12.20 Heater capillary tube shaping former (not to scale) (Sec 32)

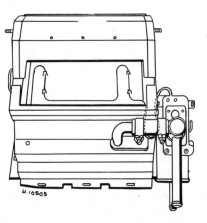

Fig. 12.21 Water valve, showing correctly shaped capillary (Sec 32)

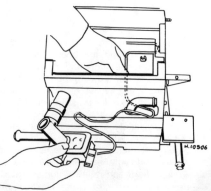

Fig. 12.22 Water valve and capillary – removal (Sec 32)

with a cold water hose. Where this procedure does not clear it an exchange unit should be obtained. Do not use chemical cleaners in the heater matrix or the fine cooling tubes will clog or become perforated.

## 32 Heater – dismantling and reassembly

1   Refer to Fig. 12.23 and release the blower harness plastic socket.
2   Release the eight plastic clips which retain the heater top cover assembly and lift it off.
3   Remove the seven self-tapping screws from the deflector plate and withdraw it.
4   Note the position of each flap valve bearing (the wider slot accommodates the deflector plate), and having set the flap valve to its mid position, prise out the bearings and withdraw the flap valve assembly.
5   Carefully release the capillary tube from the four clips and then release the water valve-to-heater block inlet pipe hose clip and remove

the bulkhead seal (Fig. 12.22).
6   Release the water valve, which is retained by four screws, and withdraw valve and capillary assembly as far as possible.
7   Turn the heater casing over and withdraw the heater block. The water valve and capillary may now be removed.
8   Carefully prise off the fan securing clip and detach the fan.
9   Disconnect the motor cables, detach the motor securing clips and withdraw the motor.
10  Reassembly is a reversal of dismantling, but carefully observe the following points. The three fan motor cables should be connected in the correct positions: green/yellow adjacent to the endplate groove, black in the centre and green/brown in the remaining location.
11  Where a replacement water valve and capillary assembly is being fitted, then the capillary tube must conform to the shape of the original and must be refitted as shown in Fig. 12.21. If the original capillary tube was distorted during removal, then a template may be made up similar to the one shown in Fig. 12.20 using a piece of wooden board and small sections of dowel to form an elementary type of tube bender.

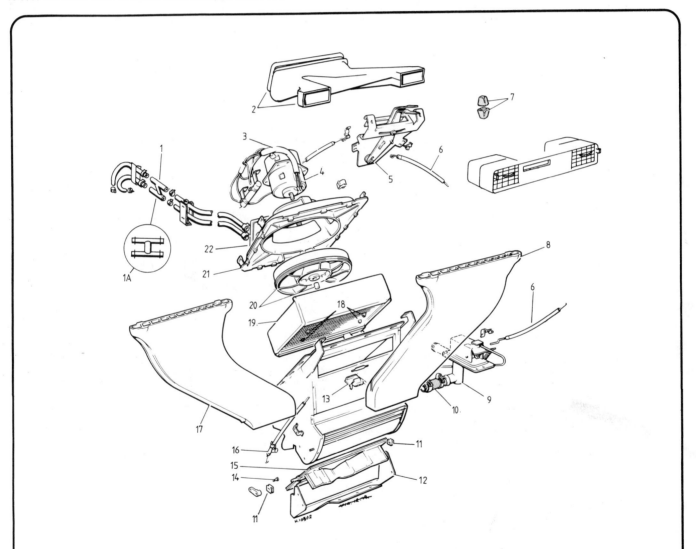

**Fig. 12.23 Heating and ventilation system – exploded view (Sec 30)**

| | | |
|---|---|---|
| 1 or 1A Alternative types of bypass connectors | 6 Thermostatic valve cable | 12 Deflector plate | 18 Capillary tube clips |
| 2 Face vent duct and seal | 7 Control lever knob | 13 Blower motor harness socket | 19 Matrix and seals |
| 3 Blower motor harness | 8 Right-hand demister duct | 14 Cable trunnion | 20 Fanblade assembly |
| 4 Blower motor | 9 Valve and capillary assembly | 15 Flap valve | 21 Top cover assembly |
| 5 Heater control | 10 Hose and clips | 16 Flap valve cable | 22 Bulkhead seal |
| | 11 Flap valve bearing | 17 Left-hand demister duct | |

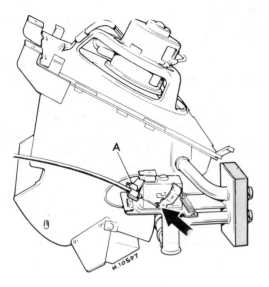

Fig. 12.24 Water valve – cable adjustment
(See text) (Sec 33)

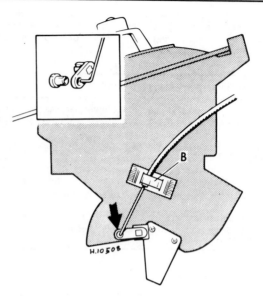

Fig. 12.25 Flap valve – cable adjustment
(see text) (Sec 33)

## 33  Heater – adjustments

1    The heat control and the air distribution flap valve control do not normally require alteration or adjustment unless the clips A or B (Figs. 12.24 and 12.25) have been disturbed or the heater unit removed or dismantled.

2    Where necessary, release clip A and set the heater facia control to the cold position (extreme left).

3    Set the lever on the heater unit fully clockwise as shown by the arrow in Fig. 12.24 and refit the clip A to the outer cable and snap it closed while holding the lever in its previously set position.

4    To adjust the air distribution flap valve, release clip B (Fig. 12.25) and set the upper facia control to the off position, marked 'O'.

5    Set the heater unit lever anti-clockwise as indicated by the arrow in Fig. 12.25 and secure clip B to the outer cable.

## 34  Heater (commencing Series 7) – removal and refitting

1    Disconnect the battery negative terminal.

2    Drain the cooling system and disconnect the heater hoses at the bulkhead.

3    Remove the facia and instrument panel assembly, as described in Chapter 10.

4    Remove the gear lever knob and withdraw the centre console after removing the retaining screws.

5    Separate the connector on the handbrake warning switch lead, and disconnect the multi-plug to the heater motor.

6    Withdraw the demister ducts, disconnect the face vent hoses, and remove the centre duct from the heater unit.

7    Remove the two securing screws and withdraw the heater unit, lifting it clear of the support bracket, and removing it through the passenger's door aperture.

8    Refitting is a reversal of the removal procedure, but make sure that the heater front flange engages with the support bracket before fitting the securing screws. Refill the cooling system as described in Chapter 2.

## 35  Heater (Ipra type) – removal, refitting, dismantling and reassembly

1    Removal and refitting of the Ipra heater is as described for the heater discussed in Section 30. Dismantling details are as given in the following paragraphs.

2    Remove the water control valve cable by extracting the retaining pin and clip and unhooking the inner cable from the valve.

3    Withdraw the fan motor/cover assembly by prising the eight retaining lugs through their slots in the main heater body. Release the supply lead from the heater body by removing the adjacent spring clip, and separating the two halves sufficiently to remove the lead.

4    Disconnect the heater bypass hose and remove the water valve by unscrewing the two retaining screws.

5    Remove the remaining clips retaining the two halves of the heater, and carefully pull the casing apart to expose the heater matrix.

6    Extract the two matrix retaining bars, lift the capillary tubing clear, and then withdraw the matrix from the heater casing, at the same time easing the water inlet tube and grommet through the casing aperture.

7    Reassembly of the heater is a reversal of the dismantling procedure, but take particular care to ensure that the locating pegs and lugs are correctly positioned before fitting the spring clips.

# Chapter 13 Supplement:
# Revisions and information on later models

## Contents

## 1  Introduction

This Chapter covers changes which appeared on later Avenger models. The Sections in this Chapter follow the same order as the first twelve Chapters of the book. The Specifications are grouped together for convenience, but they too are arranged in Chapter order.

It is suggested that before undertaking a particular job, reference is first made to this Supplement, then to the appropriate Chapter earlier in the book. In this way any revisions can be noted before the job begins.

## 2  Specifications

*The specifications listed here are supplementary to those given in the preceding Chapters*

### Fuel system
### Zenith/Stromberg 150CD3 carburettor

| 8 and 9 Series models | Slow running rpm | Needle | Piston spring | Fast idle gap |
|---|---|---|---|---|
| 1300 HC ........................... | 770/830 | B5DU | Blue | 0.025 to 0.035 in (0.64 to 0.89 mm) |
| 1300 LC ........................... | 770/830 | B5DK | Blue | 0.025 to 0.035 in (0.64 to 0.89 mm) |
| 1600 HC ........................... | 770/830 (auto in 'N') | B5EE | Blue | 0.025 to 0.035 in (0.64 to 0.89 mm) |
| 1600 LC ........................... | 770/830 (auto in 'N') | B5DK | Blue | 0.025 to 0.035 in (0.64 to 0.89 mm) |
| **A Series models** | | | | |
| 1300 HC ........................... | 770/830 (auto in 'N') | B5DU | Blue | 0.025 to 0.035 in (0.64 to 0.89 mm) |
| 1300 HC* ........................... | 770/830 (auto in 'N') | B5DV | Blue | 0.025 to 0.035 in (0.64 to 0.89 mm) |
| 1300 LC ........................... | 770/830 (auto in 'N') | B5DK | Blue | 0.025 to 0.035 in (0.64 to 0.89 mm) |
| 1600 HC ........................... | 770/830 (auto in 'N') | B5EE | Blue | 0.025 to 0.035 in (0.64 to 0.89 mm) |
| 1600 HC* ........................... | 770/830 (auto in 'N') | B5DU | Blue | 0.025 to 0.035 in (0.64 to 0.89 mm) |
| 1600 LC ........................... | 770/830 (auto in 'N') | B5DK | Blue | 0.025 to 0.035 in (0.64 to 0.89 mm) |
| **B Series models** | | | | |
| 1300 HC ........................... | 770/830 (auto in 'N') | B5DV | Blue | 0.025 to 0.035 in (0.64 to 0.89 mm) |
| 1300 LC ........................... | 770/830 (auto in 'N') | B5DK | Blue | 0.025 to 0.035 in (0.64 to 0.89 mm) |
| 1600 HC ........................... | 770/830 (auto in 'N') | B5DU | Blue | 0.025 to 0.035 in (0.64 to 0.89 mm) |
| 1600 LC ........................... | 770/830 (auto in 'N') | B5DK | Blue | 0.025 to 0.035 in (0.64 to 0.89 mm) |

*\* Engines with repositioned spark plugs. Identified by orange paint on the thermostat housing*

### Zenith/Stromberg 175CD3 carburettor

| 8 and 9 Series models | Slow running rpm | Needle | Piston spring | Fast idle gap |
|---|---|---|---|---|
| 1300 HC ........................... | 870/930 | B1EB | None | 0.025 to 0.035 in (0.64 to 0.89 mm) |
| 1600 HC ........................... | 870/930 (auto in 'N') | B1EC | None | 0.025 to 0.035 in (0.64 to 0.89 mm) |
| **A Series models** | | | | |
| 1300 HC ........................... | 870/930 (auto in 'N') | B1EB | None | 0.025 to 0.035 in (0.64 to 0.89 mm) |
| 1600 HC ........................... | 870/930 (auto in 'N') | B1EC | None | 0.025 to 0.035 in (0.64 to 0.89 mm) |
| **B Series models** | | | | |
| 1300 HC ........................... | 870/930 (auto in 'N') | B1EB | None | 0.025 to 0.035 in (0.64 to 0.89 mm) |
| 1600 HC ........................... | 870/930 (auto in 'N') | B1EC | None | 0.025 to 0.035 in (0.64 to 0.89 mm) |

*Note: LC – low compression; HC – high compression*

*Transmission*
## Speedometer drive pinion

| Axle ratio (commencing 8 Series) | Number of teeth | Colour |
|---|---|---|
| 3.545:1 ..................................... | 16 | Blue |
| 3.700:1 ..................................... | 16 | Blue |
| 3.889:1 ..................................... | 17 | White |
| 4.111:1 ..................................... | 18 | Red |

*Suspension*
## Front coil spring

Spring identification (commencing
8 Series) ........................................... Two paint stripes of the stated
colour

| Right-hand spring type: | Free length | Colour code |
|---|---|---|
| A ..................................... | 16.9 in (429 mm) | White |
| B ..................................... | 15.5 in (394 mm) | Red |
| C ..................................... | 11.8 in (300 mm) | Brown |
| Left-hand spring type: | | |
| A ..................................... | 16.8 in (427 mm) | Blue |
| B ..................................... | 15.0 in (381 mm) | Red |
| C ..................................... | 10.6 in (269 mm) | Yellow |

\* *Removed from car*

---

### 3    Cooling system

*No-loss system*
1    Some models are fitted with a no-loss cooling system. This incorporates an expansion tank which is mounted on the left-hand wing valance and is connected to the radiator header tank.
2    The coolant level should be kept up to the level mark on the expansion tank. Topping-up should only be done when the engine is cold, as a hot engine can give a false reading. Remove the expansion tank pressure cap and top up with the correct coolant mixture. It is not necessary to remove the radiator header cap when topping-up.

**Draining**
3    Remove the expansion tank pressure cap. If the engine is still hot, cover the cap with a cloth to prevent scalding, and turn the cap to its stop to vent the pressure first. Remove the radiator header cap after the expansion tank pressure cap.
4    Set the heater control to HOT.
5    Position suitable containers beneath the radiator and sump, and unscrew the radiator and cylinder block drain taps to drain the coolant.

**Refilling**
6    With the heater control still set at HOT, close the radiator and cylinder block drain taps.
7    Refill the radiator completely, using a suitable coolant mixture containing antifreeze – see Chapter 2.
8    Check the expansion tank level, then refit both caps. Run the engine to its normal operating temperature.
9    Allow the engine to cool and check that the coolant is up to the top of the radiator filler neck and also to the level mark on the expansion tank; top up if necessary and refit both caps.

---

### 4    Electrical system

*Windscreen/tailgate washer reservoir and pump*
1    The combined windscreen/tailgate/headlamp washer reservoir is located under the left-hand front wing valance on most models. (On some Series 8 vehicles the reservoir is located in the engine compartment at the left-hand side). Up to three electric pumps are located at the front of the reservoir – one for each function; The left-hand pump (green/black supply wire) feeds the windscreen washers, the centre pump (green/orange supply wire) feeds the tailgate washer, and the right-hand pump (green/white supply wire) feeds the headlamp washers.
2    A non-return valve is fitted to the tailgate washer tube at the rear corner of the vehicle. On some early models, non-return valves are fitted in the windscreen and headlamp washer tubes at the T-connectors. These are not present on later models.

3    To remove the reservoir and pump(s), proceed as follows. Remove the washer reservoir filler cap, then undo the screws securing the filler neck flange to the reservoir and remove the filler neck. Slacken the left-hand roadwheel nuts, then jack up the front of the car, support it securely on axle stands and remove the left-hand roadwheel.
4    Support the washer reservoir and undo the screws securing the retaining clips. Unhook the clips and partially withdraw the reservoir to gain access to the washer pump. Remove the pump boot(s), if fitted, then identify the tubes and wires to the pump(s) and disconnect them. Remove the reservoir.
5    Insert a long screwdriver through the filler aperture and locate the blade in one of the slots in the plastic nut inside the reservoir. Unscrew the pump.
6    To refit, wind soft wire around the nut and hold it in position inside the reservoir. Screw the pump into the nut, preventing the nut from turning by using the same method used at removal. Finally position the pump with the outlet towards the right (towards the engine compartment).
7    Refitting the washer reservoir is a reversal of the removal sequence, but be sure to reconnect the wires and hoses correctly. Smear the filler neck O-ring with silicone grease or detergent before refitting.
8    Check the operation of the washer system(s).

*Diagnostic connector and timing probe*
9    A special 10-pin connector for diagnostic equipment is mounted on the right-hand wing valance. This can only be used in conjunction with commercial testing equipment not normally available to the home mechanic.
10   Part of the diagnostic equipment incorporates a timing probe which provides the facility for checking the ignition timing electromagnetically. Commencing Series 9 models, two slots are formed on the crankshaft pulley at 20° after TDC for cylinders 1 and 4, and 2 and 3.
11   A bracket is mounted on the timing cover, and this is used to locate the timing probe during use.

*Electronic engine oil level indicator*
12   Every time the engine is started, the electronic oil level indicator system is actuated to warn the driver if the engine oil level is low. This is indicated by a flashing oil warning light; steady illumination indicates low oil pressure, as usual.
13   The oil level sensor operates at start-up, being switched off about two seconds after the ignition is turned on. The system only works accurately with the vehicle situated on level ground.
14   Fault diagnosis in the event of malfunction of the system is somewhat complex, and is considered beyond the scope of the average home mechanic. In such a case, fault diagnosis should be entrusted to a qualified auto-electrician.

# General repair procedures

Whenever servicing, repair or overhaul work is carried out on the car or its components, it is necessary to observe the following procedures and instructions. This will assist in carrying out the operation efficiently and to a professional standard of workmanship.

## Joint mating faces and gaskets

Where a gasket is used between the mating faces of two components, ensure that it is renewed on reassembly, and fit it dry unless otherwise stated in the repair procedure. Make sure that the mating faces are clean and dry with all traces of old gasket removed. When cleaning a joint face, use a tool which is not likely to score or damage the face, and remove any burrs or nicks with an oilstone or fine file.

Make sure that tapped holes are cleaned with a pipe cleaner, and keep them free of jointing compound if this is being used unless specifically instructed otherwise.

Ensure that all orifices, channels or pipes are clear and blow through them, preferably using compressed air.

## Oil seals

Whenever an oil seal is removed from its working location, either individually or as part of an assembly, it should be renewed.

The very fine sealing lip of the seal is easily damaged and will not seal if the surface it contacts is not completely clean and free from scratches, nicks or grooves. If the original sealing surface of the component cannot be restored, the component should be renewed.

Protect the lips of the seal from any surface which may damage them in the course of fitting. Use tape or a conical sleeve where possible. Lubricate the seal lips with oil before fitting and, on dual lipped seals, fill the space between the lips with grease.

Unless otherwise stated, oil seals must be fitted with their sealing lips toward the lubricant to be sealed.

Use a tubular drift or block of wood of the appropriate size to install the seal and, if the seal housing is shouldered, drive the seal down to the shoulder. If the seal housing is unshouldered, the seal should be fitted with its face flush with the housing top face.

## Screw threads and fastenings

Always ensure that a blind tapped hole is completely free from oil, grease, water or other fluid before installing the bolt or stud. Failure to do this could cause the housing to crack due to the hydraulic action of the bolt or stud as it is screwed in.

When tightening a castellated nut to accept a split pin, tighten the nut to the specified torque, where applicable, and then tighten further to the next split pin hole. Never slacken the nut to align a split pin hole unless stated in the repair procedure.

When checking or retightening a nut or bolt to a specified torque setting, slacken the nut or bolt by a quarter of a turn, and then retighten to the specified setting.

## Locknuts, locktabs and washers

Any fastening which will rotate against a component or housing in the course of tightening should always have a washer between it and the relevant component or housing.

Spring or split washers should always be renewed when they are used to lock a critical component such as a big-end bearing retaining nut or bolt.

Locktabs which are folded over to retain a nut or bolt should always be renewed.

Self-locking nuts can be reused in non-critical areas, providing resistance can be felt when the locking portion passes over the bolt or stud thread.

Split pins must always be replaced with new ones of the correct size for the hole.

## Special tools

Some repair procedures in this manual entail the use of special tools such as a press, two or three-legged pullers, spring compressors etc. Wherever possible, suitable readily available alternatives to the manufacturer's special tools are described, and are shown in use. In some instances, where no alternative is possible, it has been necessary to resort to the use of a manufacturer's tool and this has been done for reasons of safety as well as the efficient completion of the repair operation. Unless you are highly skilled and have a thorough understanding of the procedure described, never attempt to bypass the use of any special tool when the procedure described specifies its use. Not only is there a very great risk of personal injury, but expensive damage could be caused to the components involved.

# Conversion factors

## Length (distance)

| | | | | | |
|---|---|---|---|---|---|
| Inches (in) | X | 25.4 | = Millimetres (mm) | X 0.0394 | = Inches (in) |
| Feet (ft) | X | 0.305 | = Metres (m) | X 3.281 | = Feet (ft) |
| Miles | X | 1.609 | = Kilometres (km) | X 0.621 | = Miles |

## Volume (capacity)

| | | | | | |
|---|---|---|---|---|---|
| Cubic inches (cu in; in$^3$) | X | 16.387 | = Cubic centimetres (cc; cm$^3$) | X 0.061 | = Cubic inches (cu in; in$^3$) |
| Imperial pints (Imp pt) | X | 0.568 | = Litres (l) | X 1.76 | = Imperial pints (Imp pt) |
| Imperial quarts (Imp qt) | X | 1.137 | = Litres (l) | X 0.88 | = Imperial quarts (Imp qt) |
| Imperial quarts (Imp qt) | X | 1.201 | = US quarts (US qt) | X 0.833 | = Imperial quarts (Imp qt) |
| US quarts (US qt) | X | 0.946 | = Litres (l) | X 1.057 | = US quarts (US qt) |
| Imperial gallons (Imp gal) | X | 4.546 | = Litres (l) | X 0.22 | = Imperial gallons (Imp gal) |
| Imperial gallons (Imp gal) | X | 1.201 | = US gallons (US gal) | X 0.833 | = Imperial gallons (Imp gal) |
| US gallons (US gal) | X | 3.785 | = Litres (l) | X 0.264 | = US gallons (US gal) |

## Mass (weight)

| | | | | | |
|---|---|---|---|---|---|
| Ounces (oz) | X | 28.35 | = Grams (g) | X 0.035 | = Ounces (oz) |
| Pounds (lb) | X | 0.454 | = Kilograms (kg) | X 2.205 | = Pounds (lb) |

## Force

| | | | | | |
|---|---|---|---|---|---|
| Ounces-force (ozf; oz) | X | 0.278 | = Newtons (N) | X 3.6 | = Ounces-force (ozf; oz) |
| Pounds-force (lbf; lb) | X | 4.448 | = Newtons (N) | X 0.225 | = Pounds-force (lbf; lb) |
| Newtons (N) | X | 0.1 | = Kilograms-force (kgf; kg) | X 9.81 | = Newtons (N) |

## Pressure

| | | | | | |
|---|---|---|---|---|---|
| Pounds-force per square inch (psi; lbf/in$^2$; lb/in$^2$) | X | 0.070 | = Kilograms-force per square centimetre (kgf/cm$^2$; kg/cm$^2$) | X 14.223 | = Pounds-force per square inch (psi; lbf/in$^2$; lb/in$^2$) |
| Pounds-force per square inch (psi; lbf/in$^2$; lb/in$^2$) | X | 0.068 | = Atmospheres (atm) | X 14.696 | = Pounds-force per square inch (psi; lbf/in$^2$; lb/in$^2$) |
| Pounds-force per square inch (psi; lbf/in$^2$; lb/in$^2$) | X | 0.069 | = Bars | X 14.5 | = Pounds-force per square inch (psi; lbf/in$^2$; lb/in$^2$) |
| Pounds-force per square inch (psi; lbf/in$^2$; lb/in$^2$) | X | 6.895 | = Kilopascals (kPa) | X 0.145 | = Pounds-force per square inch (psi; lbf/in$^2$; lb/in$^2$) |
| Kilopascals (kPa) | X | 0.01 | = Kilograms-force per square centimetre (kgf/cm$^2$; kg/cm$^2$) | X 98.1 | = Kilopascals (kPa) |

## Torque (moment of force)

| | | | | | |
|---|---|---|---|---|---|
| Pounds-force inches (lbf in; lb in) | X | 1.152 | = Kilograms-force centimetre (kgf cm; kg cm) | X 0.868 | = Pounds-force inches (lbf in; lb in) |
| Pounds-force inches (lbf in; lb in) | X | 0.113 | = Newton metres (Nm) | X 8.85 | = Pounds-force inches (lbf in; lb in) |
| Pounds-force inches (lbf in; lb in) | X | 0.083 | = Pounds-force feet (lbf ft; lb ft) | X 12 | = Pounds-force inches (lbf in; lb in) |
| Pounds-force feet (lbf ft; lb ft) | X | 0.138 | = Kilograms-force metres (kgf m; kg m) | X 7.233 | = Pounds-force feet (lbf ft; lb ft) |
| Pounds-force feet (lbf ft; lb ft) | X | 1.356 | = Newton metres (Nm) | X 0.738 | = Pounds-force feet (lbf ft; lb ft) |
| Newton metres (Nm) | X | 0.102 | = Kilograms-force metres (kgf m; kg m) | X 9.804 | = Newton metres (Nm) |

## Power

| | | | | | |
|---|---|---|---|---|---|
| Horsepower (hp) | X | 745.7 | = Watts (W) | X 0.0013 | = Horsepower (hp) |

## Velocity (speed)

| | | | | | |
|---|---|---|---|---|---|
| Miles per hour (miles/hr; mph) | X | 1.609 | = Kilometres per hour (km/hr; kph) | X 0.621 | = Miles per hour (miles/hr; mph) |

## Fuel consumption*

| | | | | | |
|---|---|---|---|---|---|
| Miles per gallon, Imperial (mpg) | X | 0.354 | = Kilometres per litre (km/l) | X 2.825 | = Miles per gallon, Imperial (mpg) |
| Miles per gallon, US (mpg) | X | 0.425 | = Kilometres per litre (km/l) | X 2.352 | = Miles per gallon, US (mpg) |

## Temperature

Degrees Fahrenheit = (°C x 1.8) + 32

Degrees Celsius (Degrees Centigrade; °C) = (°F - 32) x 0.56

*It is common practice to convert from miles per gallon (mpg) to litres/100 kilometres (l/100km), where mpg (Imperial) x l/100 km = 282 and mpg (US) x l/100 km = 235

# Index

Printed by
Haynes Publishing Group
Sparkford Yeovil Somerset
England